Focus on GRAMMAR 2

FOURTH EDITION

Irene E. Schoenberg

ALWAYS LEARNING PEARSON

Focus on Grammar 2: An Integrated Skills Approach, Fourth Edition

Pearson Education, 10 Bank Street, White Plains, NY 10606

Staff credits: The people who made up the ***Focus on Grammar 2, Fourth Edition*** team, representing editorial, production, design, and manufacturing, are Elizabeth Carlson, Tracey Cataldo, Aerin Csigay, Dave Dickey, Christine Edmonds, Nancy Flagmann, Ann France, Lise Minovitz, Barbara Perez, Robert Ruvo, Debbie Sistino, and Kim Steiner.

Cover image: Shutterstock.com
Text composition: ElectraGraphics, Inc.
Text font: New Aster

Library of Congress Cataloging-in-Publication Data

Schoenberg, Irene, 1946–
Focus on grammar. 1: an integrated skills approach / Irene E. Schoenberg, Jay Maurer. — 3rd ed.
p. cm.
Includes index.
ISBN 0-13-245591-9 — ISBN 0-13-254647-7 — ISBN 0-13-254648-5 — ISBN 0-13-254649-3 — ISBN 0-13-254650-7 1. English language—Textbooks for foreign speakers. 2. English language—Grammar—Problems, exercises, etc. I. Maurer, Jay. II. Title.
PE1128.S3456824 2011
428.2'4—dc22

2011014126

Printed in the United States of America

ISBN 10: 0-13-254647-7
ISBN 13: 978-0-13-254647-8

5 6 7 8 9 10—V082—16 15 14 13

ISBN 10: 0-13-211443-7 (with MyLab)
ISBN 13: 978-0-13-211443-1 (with MyLab)

3 4 5 6 7 8 9 10—V082—16 15 14 13

Contents

WELCOME TO *FOCUS ON GRAMMAR*

Now in a new edition, the popular five-level ***Focus on Grammar*** course continues to provide an integrated-skills approach to help students understand and practice English grammar. Centered on thematic instruction, ***Focus on Grammar*** combines controlled and communicative practice with critical thinking skills and ongoing assessment. Students gain the confidence they need to speak and write English accurately and fluently.

NEW for the FOURTH EDITION

VOCABULARY

Key vocabulary is highlighted, practiced, and recycled throughout the unit.

PRONUNCIATION

Now, in every unit, pronunciation points and activities help students improve spoken accuracy and fluency.

LISTENING

Expanded listening tasks allow students to develop a range of listening skills.

UPDATED CHARTS and NOTES

Target structures are presented in a clear, easy-to-read format.

NEW READINGS

High-interest readings, updated or completely new, in a variety of genres integrate grammar and vocabulary in natural contexts.

NEW UNIT REVIEWS

Students can check their understanding and monitor their progress after completing each unit.

MyFocusOnGrammarLab

An easy-to-use online learning and assessment program offers online homework and individualized instruction anywhere, anytime.

Teacher's Resource Pack

One compact resource includes:

THE TEACHER'S MANUAL: General Teaching Notes, Unit Teaching Notes, the Student Book Audioscript, and the Student Book Answer Key.

TEACHER'S RESOURCE DISC: Bound into the Resource Pack, this CD-ROM contains reproducible Placement, Part, and Unit Tests, as well as customizable Test-Generating Software. It also includes reproducible Internet Activities and PowerPoint® Grammar Presentations.

THE *FOCUS ON GRAMMAR* APPROACH

The new edition follows the same successful four-step approach of previous editions. The books provide an abundance of both controlled and communicative exercises so that students can bridge the gap between identifying grammatical structures and using them. The many communicative activities in each Student Book provide opportunities for critical thinking while enabling students to personalize what they have learned.

- **STEP 1: GRAMMAR IN CONTEXT** highlights the target structures in realistic contexts, such as conversations, magazine articles, and blog posts.
- **STEP 2: GRAMMAR PRESENTATION** presents the structures in clear and accessible grammar charts and notes with multiple examples of form and usage.
- **STEP 3: FOCUSED PRACTICE** provides numerous and varied controlled exercises for both the form and meaning of the new structures.
- **STEP 4: COMMUNICATION PRACTICE** includes listening and pronunciation and allows students to use the new structures freely and creatively in motivating, open-ended speaking and writing activities.

Recycling

Underpinning the scope and sequence of the ***Focus on Grammar*** series is the belief that students need to use target structures and vocabulary many times, in different contexts. New grammar and vocabulary are recycled throughout the book. Students have maximum exposure and become confident using the language in speech and in writing.

Assessment

Extensive testing informs instruction and allows teachers and students to measure progress.

- **Unit Reviews** at the end of every Student Book unit assess students' understanding of the grammar and allow students to monitor their own progress.
- Easy to administer and score, **Part and Unit Tests** provide teachers with a valid and reliable means to determine how well students know the material they are about to study and to assess students' mastery after they complete the material. These tests can be found on MyFocusOnGrammarLab, where they include immediate feedback and remediation, and as reproducible tests on the Teacher's Resource Disc.
- **Test-Generating Software** on the Teacher's Resource Disc includes a bank of *additional* test items teachers can use to create customized tests.
- A reproducible **Placement Test** on the Teacher's Resource Disc is designed to help teachers place students into one of the five levels of the ***Focus on Grammar*** course.

COMPONENTS

In addition to the Student Books, Teacher's Resource Packs, and MyLabs, the complete ***Focus on Grammar*** course includes:

Workbooks Contain additional contextualized exercises appropriate for self-study.

Audio Program Includes all of the listening and pronunciation exercises and opening passages from the Student Book. Some Student Books are packaged with the complete audio program (mp3 files). Alternatively, the audio program is available on a classroom set of CDs and on the MyLab.

The *Focus on Grammar* Unit

Focus on Grammar introduces grammar structures in the context of unified themes. All units follow a **four-step approach**, taking learners from grammar in context to communicative practice.

STEP 1 GRAMMAR IN CONTEXT

This section presents the target structure(s) in a natural context. As students read the **high-interest texts**, they encounter the form, meaning, and use of the grammar. **Before You Read** activities create interest and elicit students' knowledge about the topic. **After You Read** activities build students' reading vocabulary and comprehension.

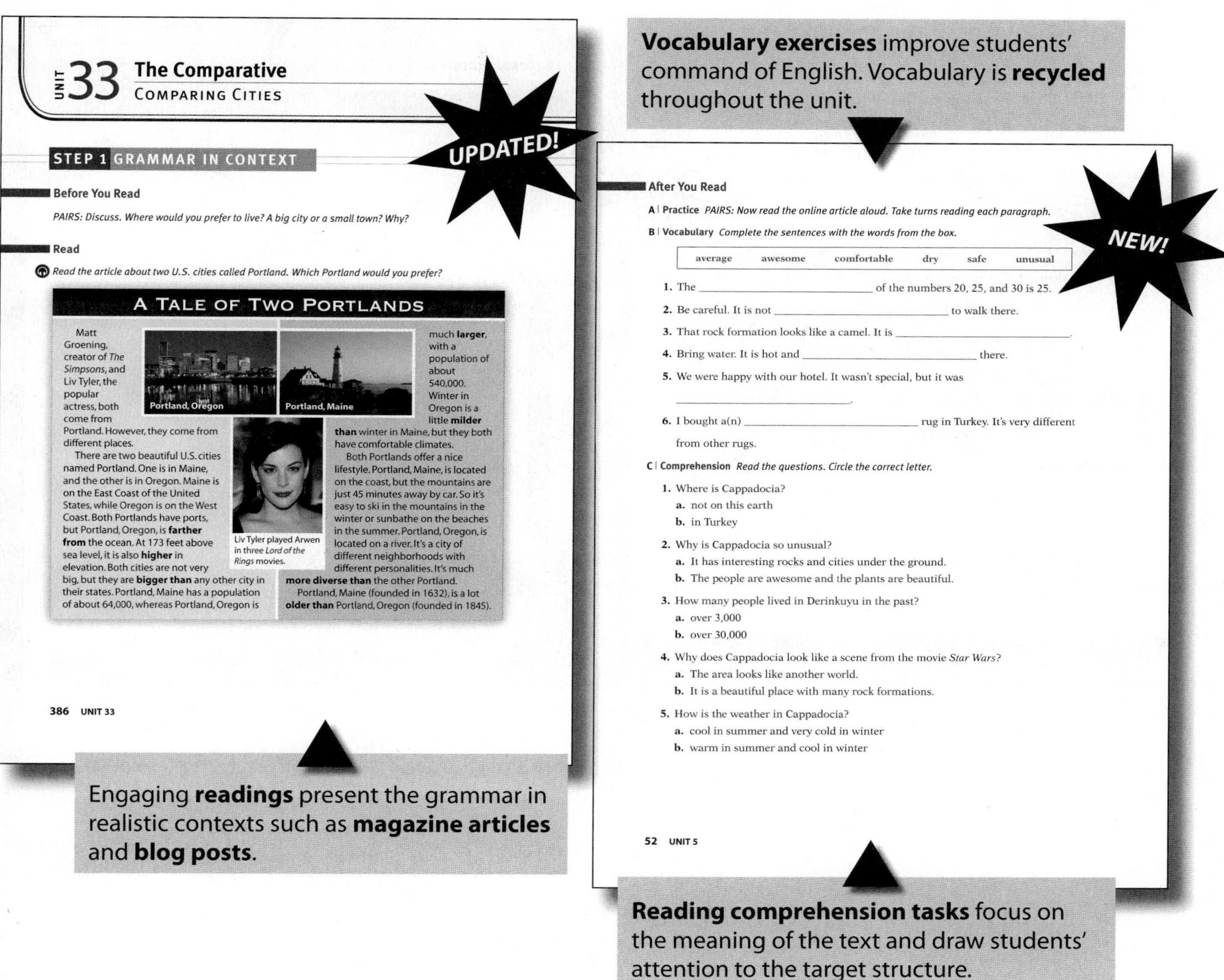

UNIT 33 **The Comparative**
COMPARING CITIES

UPDATED!

STEP 1 GRAMMAR IN CONTEXT

Before You Read

PAIRS: Discuss. Where would you prefer to live? A big city or a small town? Why?

Read

Read the article about two U.S. cities called Portland. Which Portland would you prefer?

A TALE OF TWO PORTLANDS

Portland, Oregon

Portland, Maine

Matt Groening, creator of *The Simpsons*, and Liv Tyler, the popular actress, both come from Portland. However, they come from different places.

There are two beautiful U.S. cities named Portland. One is in Maine, and the other is in Oregon. Maine is on the East Coast of the United States, while Oregon is on the West Coast. Both Portlands have ports, but Portland, Oregon, is **farther from** the ocean. At 173 feet above sea level, it is also **higher** in elevation. Both cities are not very big, but they are **bigger than** any other city in their states. Portland, Maine has a population of about 64,000, whereas Portland, Oregon is much **larger**, with a population of about 540,000. Winter in Oregon is a little **milder than** winter in Maine, but they both have comfortable climates.

Both Portlands offer a nice lifestyle. Portland, Maine, is located on the coast, but the mountains are just 45 minutes away by car. So it's easy to ski in the mountains in the winter or sunbathe on the beaches in the summer. Portland, Oregon, is located on a river. It's a city of different neighborhoods with different personalities. It's much **more diverse than** the other Portland.

Portland, Maine (founded in 1632), is a lot **older than** Portland, Oregon (founded in 1845).

Liv Tyler played Arwen in three *Lord of the Rings* movies.

386 UNIT 33

Engaging **readings** present the grammar in realistic contexts such as **magazine articles** and **blog posts**.

Vocabulary exercises improve students' command of English. Vocabulary is **recycled** throughout the unit.

NEW!

After You Read

A | Practice *PAIRS: Now read the online article aloud. Take turns reading each paragraph.*

B | Vocabulary *Complete the sentences with the words from the box.*

average	awesome	comfortable	dry	safe	unusual

1. The ______________ of the numbers 20, 25, and 30 is 25.
2. Be careful. It is not ______________ to walk there.
3. That rock formation looks like a camel. It is ______________.
4. Bring water. It is hot and ______________ there.
5. We were happy with our hotel. It wasn't special, but it was ______________.
6. I bought a(n) ______________ rug in Turkey. It's very different from other rugs.

C | Comprehension *Read the questions. Circle the correct letter.*

1. Where is Cappadocia?
   a. not on this earth
   b. in Turkey
2. Why is Cappadocia so unusual?
   a. It has interesting rocks and cities under the ground.
   b. The people are awesome and the plants are beautiful.
3. How many people lived in Derinkuyu in the past?
   a. over 3,000
   b. over 30,000
4. Why does Cappadocia look like a scene from the movie *Star Wars*?
   a. The area looks like another world.
   b. It is a beautiful place with many rock formations.
5. How is the weather in Cappadocia?
   a. cool in summer and very cold in winter
   b. warm in summer and cool in winter

52 UNIT 5

Reading comprehension tasks focus on the meaning of the text and draw students' attention to the target structure.

STEP 2 GRAMMAR PRESENTATION

This section gives students a comprehensive and explicit overview of the grammar with detailed **Grammar Charts** and **Grammar Notes** that present the form, meaning, and use of the structure(s).

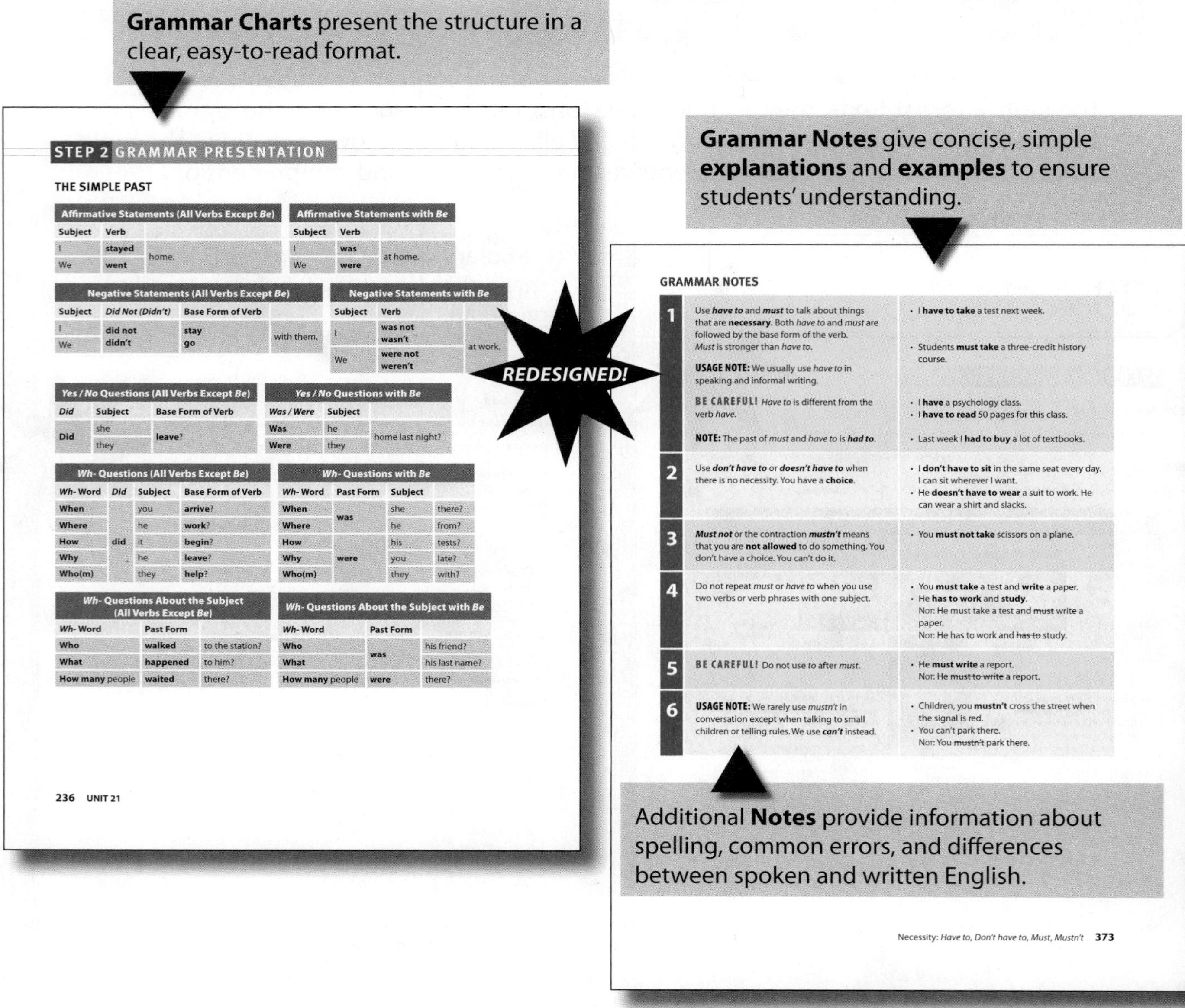
Grammar Charts present the structure in a clear, easy-to-read format.
Grammar Notes give concise, simple **explanations** and **examples** to ensure students' understanding.
REDESIGNED!
Additional **Notes** provide information about spelling, common errors, and differences between spoken and written English.

STEP 2 GRAMMAR PRESENTATION

THE SIMPLE PAST

Affirmative Statements (All Verbs Except *Be*)		
Subject	Verb	
I	stayed	home.
We	went	

Affirmative Statements with *Be*		
Subject	Verb	
I	was	at home.
We	were	

Negative Statements (All Verbs Except *Be*)			
Subject	*Did Not (Didn't)*	Base Form of Verb	
I We	did not didn't	stay go	with them.

Negative Statements with *Be*		
Subject	Verb	
I	was not wasn't	at work.
We	were not weren't	

Yes / No Questions (All Verbs Except *Be*)		
Did	Subject	Base Form of Verb
Did	she they	leave?

Yes / No Questions with *Be*		
Was / Were	Subject	
Was	he	home last night?
Were	they	

Wh- Questions (All Verbs Except *Be*)			
Wh- Word	*Did*	Subject	Base Form of Verb
When	did	you	arrive?
Where		he	work?
How		it	begin?
Why		he	leave?
Who(m)		they	help?

Wh- Questions with *Be*			
Wh- Word	Past Form	Subject	
When	was	she	there?
Where		he	from?
How	were	his	tests?
Why		you	late?
Who(m)		they	with?

Wh- Questions About the Subject (All Verbs Except *Be*)		
Wh- Word	Past Form	
Who	walked	to the station?
What	happened	to him?
How many people	waited	there?

Wh- Questions About the Subject with *Be*		
Wh- Word	Past Form	
Who	was	his friend?
What		his last name?
How many people	were	there?

236 UNIT 21

GRAMMAR NOTES

1	Use ***have to*** and ***must*** to talk about things that are **necessary**. Both *have to* and *must* are followed by the base form of the verb. *Must* is stronger than *have to*.	• I **have to take** a test next week. • Students **must take** a three-credit history course.
	USAGE NOTE: We usually use *have to* in speaking and informal writing.	
	BE CAREFUL! *Have to* is different from the verb *have*.	• I **have** a psychology class. • I **have to read** 50 pages for this class.
	NOTE: The past of *must* and *have to* is ***had to***.	• Last week I **had to buy** a lot of textbooks.
2	Use ***don't have to*** or ***doesn't have to*** when there is no necessity. You have a **choice**.	• I **don't have to sit** in the same seat every day. I can sit wherever I want. • He **doesn't have to wear** a suit to work. He can wear a shirt and slacks.
3	***Must not*** or the contraction ***mustn't*** means that you are **not allowed** to do something. You don't have a choice. You can't do it.	• You **must not take** scissors on a plane.
4	Do not repeat *must* or *have to* when you use two verbs or verb phrases with one subject.	• You **must take** a test and **write** a paper. • He **has to work** and **study**. Not: He must take a test and ~~must~~ write a paper. Not: He has to work and ~~has to~~ study.
5	**BE CAREFUL!** Do not use *to* after *must*.	• He **must write** a report. Not: He ~~must to write~~ a report.
6	**USAGE NOTE:** We rarely use *mustn't* in conversation except when talking to small children or telling rules. We use ***can't*** instead.	• Children, you **mustn't** cross the street when the signal is red. • You can't park there. Not: You ~~mustn't~~ park there.

Necessity: *Have to, Don't have to, Must, Mustn't* 373

STEP 3 FOCUSED PRACTICE

Controlled practice activities in this section lead students to master form, meaning, and use of the target grammar.

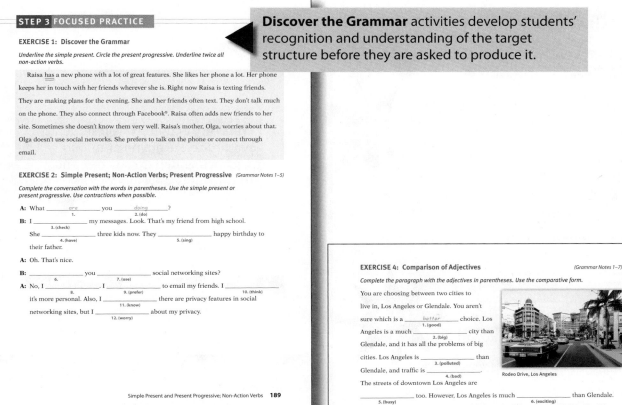

STEP 3 FOCUSED PRACTICE

EXERCISE 1: Discover the Grammar

Underline the simple present. Circle the present progressive. Underline twice all non-action verbs.

Raisa has a new phone with a lot of great features. She likes her phone a lot. Her phone keeps her in touch with her friends wherever she is. Right now Raisa is texting friends. They are making plans for the evening. She and her friends often text. They don't talk much on the phone. They also connect through Facebook®. Raisa often adds new friends to her site. Sometimes she doesn't know them very well. Raisa's mother, Olga, worries about that. Olga doesn't use social networks. She prefers to talk on the phone or connect through email.

EXERCISE 2: Simple Present; Non-Action Verbs; Present Progressive *(Grammar Notes 1–5)*

Complete the conversation with the words in parentheses. Use the simple present or present progressive. Use contractions when possible.

A: What ___are___ (1.) you ___doing___ (2. (do))?

B: I ________ (3. (check)) my messages. Look. That's my friend from high school. She ________ (4. (have)) three kids now. They ________ (5. (sing)) happy birthday to their father.

A: Oh. That's nice.

B: ________ (6.) you ________ (7. (use)) social networking sites?

A: No, I ________ (8.). I ________ (9. (prefer)) to email my friends. I ________ (10. (think)) it's more personal. Also, I ________ (11. (know)) there are privacy features in social networking sites, but I ________ (12. (worry)) about my privacy.

Discover the Grammar activities develop students' recognition and understanding of the target structure before they are asked to produce it.

A **variety of exercise types** engage students and guide them from recognition and understanding to accurate production of the grammar structures.

EXERCISE 4: Comparison of Adjectives *(Grammar Notes 1–7)*

Complete the paragraph with the adjectives in parentheses. Use the comparative form.

You are choosing between two cities to live in, Los Angeles or Glendale. You aren't sure which is a ___better___ (1. (good)) choice. Los Angeles is a much ________ (2. (big)) city than Glendale, and it has all the problems of big cities. Los Angeles is ________ (3. (polluted)) than Glendale, and traffic is ________ (4. (bad)). The streets of downtown Los Angeles are ________ (5. (busy)) too. However, Los Angeles is much ________ (6. (exciting)) than Glendale. Los Angeles has a great night life. Glendale is much ________ (7. (quiet)) at night. Both cities have the same great climate. It's hard to compare housing costs. Some parts of Los Angeles are ________ (8. (more / expensive)) than Glendale and other parts are ________ (9. (less / expensive)). Both cities are close, so if you make a mistake, you can always move.

Rodeo Drive, Los Angeles

Bicycle trail, Glendale, California

EXERCISE 5: Editing

Correct the sentences. There are seven mistakes. The first one is already corrected. Find and correct six more.

1. Our new apartment is ^more^ comfortable than our old one.
2. Florida is more hotter than Maine.
3. Oregon is far north than California.
4. A motorcycle is more fast than a bicycle.
5. Traffic at 8:00 A.M. is more heavy than traffic at 10:00 A.M.
6. The climate in Portland, Oregon, is mild than the climate in Anchorage, Alaska.
7. The location of Jake's apartment is more convenient than his sister.

An **Editing** exercise ends every Focused Practice section and teaches students to find and correct typical mistakes.

STEP 4 COMMUNICATION PRACTICE

This section provides practice with the structure in **listening** and **pronunciation** exercises as well as in communicative, open-ended **speaking** and **writing** activities that move students toward fluency.

Listening activities allow students to hear the grammar in natural contexts and to practice a range of listening skills.

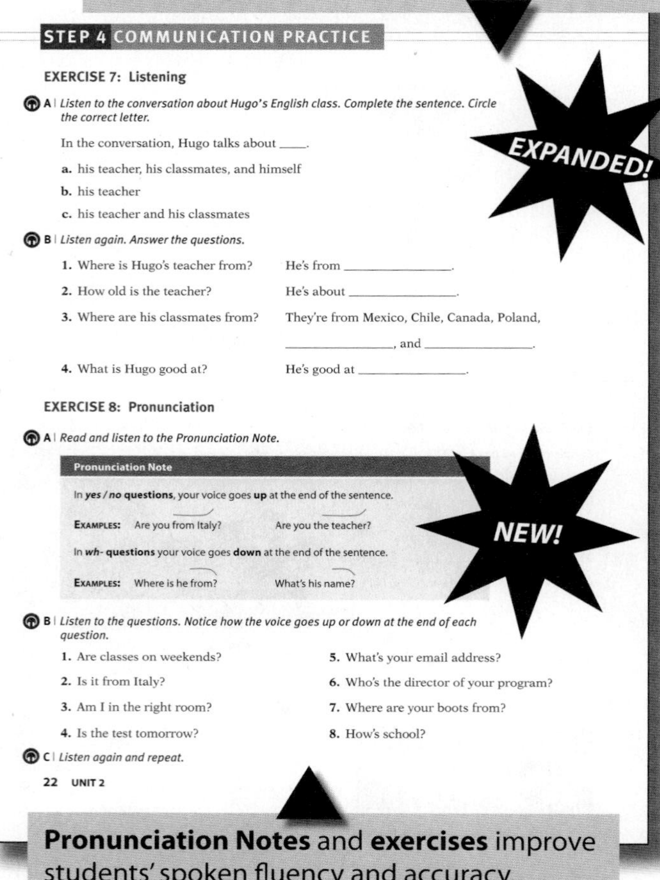
STEP 4 COMMUNICATION PRACTICE

EXERCISE 7: Listening

A | *Listen to the conversation about Hugo's English class. Complete the sentence. Circle the correct letter.*

In the conversation, Hugo talks about ____.

a. his teacher, his classmates, and himself
b. his teacher
c. his teacher and his classmates

B | *Listen again. Answer the questions.*

1. Where is Hugo's teacher from? He's from ____________.
2. How old is the teacher? He's about ____________.
3. Where are his classmates from? They're from Mexico, Chile, Canada, Poland, ____________, and ____________.
4. What is Hugo good at? He's good at ____________.

EXERCISE 8: Pronunciation

A | *Read and listen to the Pronunciation Note.*

Pronunciation Note

In ***yes / no* questions**, your voice goes **up** at the end of the sentence.

EXAMPLES: Are you from Italy? Are you the teacher?

In ***wh-* questions** your voice goes **down** at the end of the sentence.

EXAMPLES: Where is he from? What's his name?

B | *Listen to the questions. Notice how the voice goes up or down at the end of each question.*

1. Are classes on weekends?
2. Is it from Italy?
3. Am I in the right room?
4. Is the test tomorrow?
5. What's your email address?
6. Who's the director of your program?
7. Where are your boots from?
8. How's school?

C | *Listen again and repeat.*

22 UNIT 2

Pronunciation Notes and **exercises** improve students' spoken fluency and accuracy.

Speaking activities help students synthesize the grammar through discussions, debates, games, and problem-solving tasks, developing their fluency.

EXERCISE 8: Comparing Train Systems

PAIRS: Look at the information about the London Underground and the Moscow Metro. Together write as many comparative questions as you can. Ask other pairs your questions. Answer their questions. Then compare these subways to others you know.

EXAMPLE: A: Is the Underground faster than the Moscow Metro?
B: No, it isn't. It's slower.

	London Underground	Moscow Metro
Year opened	1863	1935
Length of tracks	250 miles (400 kilometers)	187.2 miles (301.2 kilometers)
Number of passengers each day	4 million	6.6 million
Hours of operation	5:30 A.M. to 1:15 A.M. (Fri. & Sat. closes at 2:00 A.M.)	5:30 A.M. to 1:00 A.M.
Cost of ride in euros	4 euros for shortest distance	26 rubles = .66 euro
Speed	20.5 mph (33 km / h)	25.82 mph (41.55 km / h)

EXERCISE 11: Writing

A | *Compare two ways of travel. Use at least three comparative adjectives.*

EXAMPLE: Most cities have busses and trains, but in San Francisco some people also travel by trolley, and in Venice people sometimes travel by gondola. Both the trolley and the gondola are more fun than the bus or the train. The gondola is more romantic than the trolley, but the trolley is more exciting, especially when you're traveling down one of San Francisco's steep streets.

B | *Check your work. Use the Editing Checklist.*

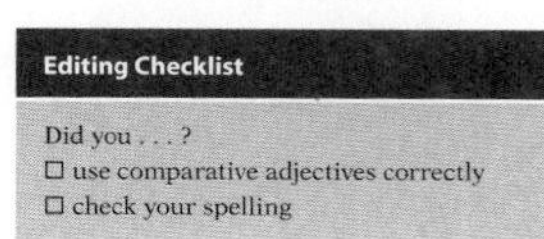
Editing Checklist

Did you . . . ?
☐ use comparative adjectives correctly
☐ check your spelling

Writing activities encourage students to produce meaningful writing that integrates the grammar structure.

An **Editing Checklist** teaches students to correct their mistakes and revise their work.

Unit Reviews give students the opportunity to check their understanding of the target structure. **Answers** at the back of the book allow students to monitor their own progress.

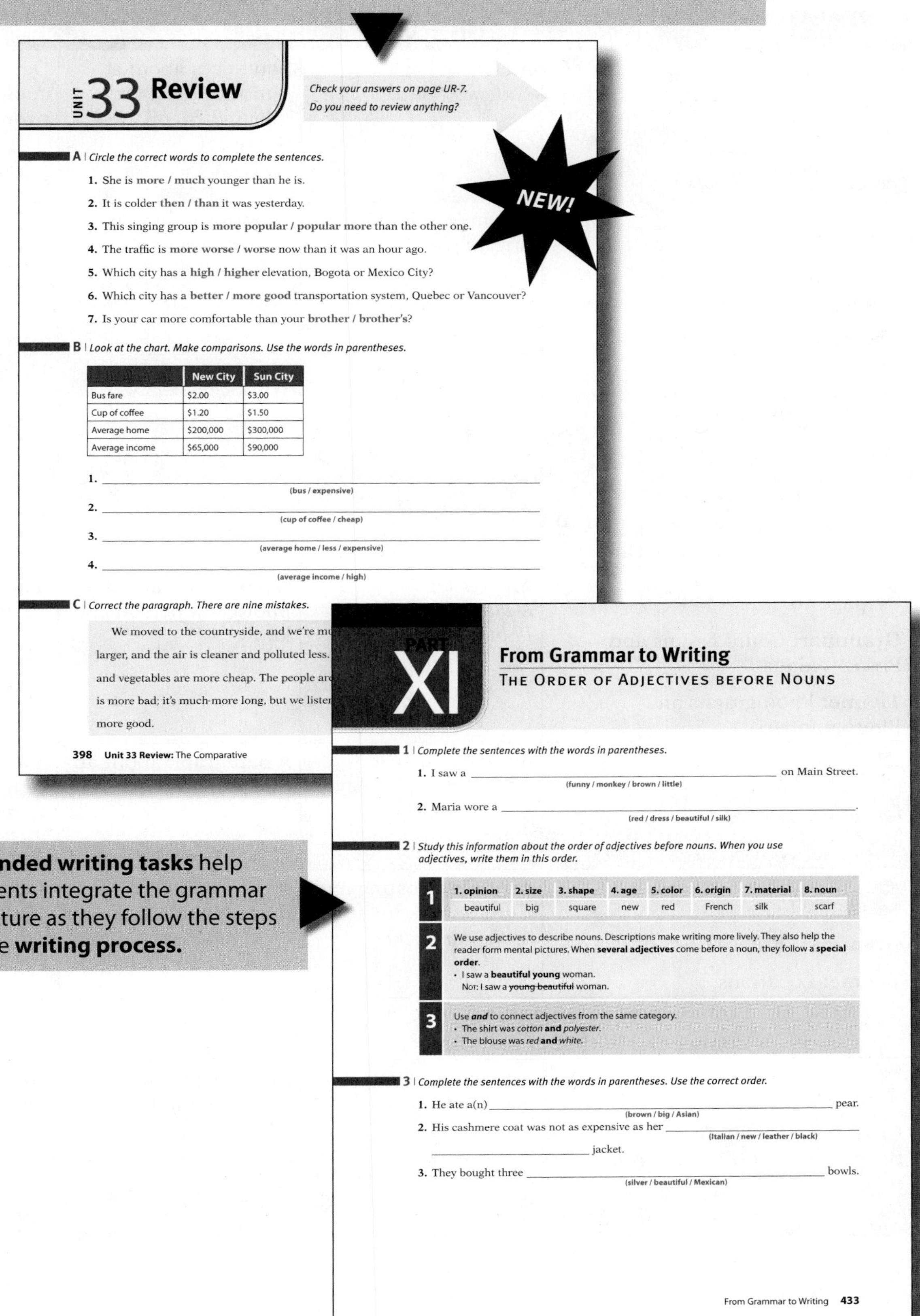

UNIT 33 **Review**

Check your answers on page UR-7.
Do you need to review anything?

NEW!

A | *Circle the correct words to complete the sentences.*

1. She is **more / much** younger than he is.
2. It is colder **then / than** it was yesterday.
3. This singing group is **more popular / popular more** than the other one.
4. The traffic is **more worse / worse** now than it was an hour ago.
5. Which city has a **high / higher** elevation, Bogota or Mexico City?
6. Which city has a **better / more good** transportation system, Quebec or Vancouver?
7. Is your car more comfortable than your **brother / brother's**?

B | *Look at the chart. Make comparisons. Use the words in parentheses.*

	New City	Sun City
Bus fare	$2.00	$3.00
Cup of coffee	$1.20	$1.50
Average home	$200,000	$300,000
Average income	$65,000	$90,000

1. ______________________________ (bus / expensive)
2. ______________________________ (cup of coffee / cheap)
3. ______________________________ (average home / less / expensive)
4. ______________________________ (average income / high)

C | *Correct the paragraph. There are nine mistakes.*

We moved to the countryside, and we're mu
larger, and the air is cleaner and polluted less.
and vegetables are more cheap. The people ar
is more bad; it's much more long, but we liste
more good.

398 **Unit 33 Review:** The Comparative

PART XI

From Grammar to Writing

THE ORDER OF ADJECTIVES BEFORE NOUNS

1 | *Complete the sentences with the words in parentheses.*

1. I saw a ______________________________ on Main Street. (funny / monkey / brown / little)
2. Maria wore a ______________________________. (red / dress / beautiful / silk)

2 | *Study this information about the order of adjectives before nouns. When you use adjectives, write them in this order.*

1

1. opinion	2. size	3. shape	4. age	5. color	6. origin	7. material	8. noun
beautiful	big	square	new	red	French	silk	scarf

2 We use adjectives to describe nouns. Descriptions make writing more lively. They also help the reader form mental pictures. When **several adjectives** come before a noun, they follow a **special order**.

- I saw a **beautiful young** woman.
  NOT: I saw a ~~young beautiful~~ woman.

3 Use ***and*** to connect adjectives from the same category.

- The shirt was *cotton* **and** *polyester*.
- The blouse was *red* **and** *white*.

3 | *Complete the sentences with the words in parentheses. Use the correct order.*

1. He ate a(n) ______________________________ pear. (brown / big / Asian)
2. His cashmere coat was not as expensive as her ______________________________ (Italian / new / leather / black) ______________________________ jacket.
3. They bought three ______________________________ bowls. (silver / beautiful / Mexican)

From Grammar to Writing **433**

Extended writing tasks help students integrate the grammar structure as they follow the steps of the **writing process.**

SCOPE AND SEQUENCE

SPEAKING	PRONUNCIATION	VOCABULARY	
Pair Discussion: Occupations *Class Discussion*: Talented People	Tips for *he, she, he's,* and *she's*	athlete busy exciting	famous husband talented
Pair Activity: Asking and Answering Questions *Role Play*: Meeting at a Party	Rising intonation in *yes / no* questions Falling intonation in *wh-* questions	by the way excuse me on time	right room
Guided Conversation: Describing the Weather *Group Discussion*: The First Day of School	Extra pronounced syllable in negative forms of *be* Clipped /t/ sound in *wasn't, weren't*	a big deal boring busy	make money still
Game: Describing Things *Game*: Comparing Choices	Sound of plurals: /s/, /z/, /ɪz/	all over almost be born	holiday special striking
Group Discussion: Asking Questions about a Place	Syllable stress	average awesome comfortable	dry safe unusual
Game: Guessing Countries *Game*: Describing Locations	Stressed words for emphasis	appointment be free cafeteria	flight rest room sculpture
Pair Activity: Making Suggestions for You and Another Person *Pair Activity*: Giving Advice *Pair Activity*: Giving Directions	Linking sound in *don't* + *you*	advice dead island	nap pray secret

UNIT	READING	WRITING	LISTENING
8 page 81 **Grammar:** Simple Present: Affirmative and Negative Statements **Theme:** Shopping	An online article: *Teen Trends*	A paragraph about the way you and a relative dress	A conversation about shopping
9 page 91 **Grammar:** Simple Present: *Yes / No* Questions and Short Answers **Theme:** Roommates	A questionnaire: *Roommate Questionnaire*	An email of introduction to a new roommate	A conversation about finding a compatible roommate
10 page 102 **Grammar:** Simple Present: *Wh-* Questions **Theme:** Dreams	A radio talk show interview: *Dreams*	A paragraph about a dream or daydream	A conversation about a dream and its interpretation
PART III **From Grammar to Writing,** page 114 **Time Word Connectors: *First, Next, After that, Then, Finally***			
11 page 116 **Grammar:** *There is / There are* **Theme:** Shopping Malls	An advertisement: West Edmonton Mall, Canada	A paragraph about a place where you like to shop	A conversation about directions
12 page 130 **Grammar:** Possessives: Nouns, Adjectives, Pronouns; Object Pronouns; Questions with *Whose* **Theme:** Possessions	A conversation: Student compositions	A paragraph about yourself and your family for a school newsletter	A conversation about possessions
13 page 143 **Grammar:** Ability: *Can* or *Could* **Theme:** Abilities of Animals	An online article: *A Genius Parrot*	A paragraph about an interesting pet or other animal	A conversation about dolphins' abilities
14 page 153 **Grammar:** Permission: *Can* or *May* **Theme:** Health and Diet	An online article: *The Right Diet*	Sentences about the requirements of a diet	A telephone conversation between a patient and a doctor
PART IV **From Grammar to Writing,** page 163 **Punctuation I: The Apostrophe, The Comma, The Period, The Question Mark**			

SPEAKING	PRONUNCIATION	VOCABULARY	
Pair Discussion: Likes and Dislikes *Group Discussion*: Clothing Customs of the World	Third person singular ending /s/, /z/, or /ɪz/	alone companies cute	middle school senior teenager
Pair Discussion: Comparing Habits and Personality *Game*: Find Someone Who . . . *Game*: What's in Your Backpack?	Linking sound in *does it* and *does he*	bother easygoing messy neat	outgoing private stay up wake up
Pair Survey: Sleeping Habits *Group Survey*: Sleeping Habits *Pair Activity*: Information Gap	Consonant clusters with /r/ and /l/	author guest nightmares	remember unfortunately
Pair Activity: Comparing Pictures of a Street *Game*: Tic Tac Toe	Homophones: *there, their,* and *they're*	amusement park attraction get away include	indoor international market one of a kind
Class Activity: Asking about Family Photos *Game*: Find Someone Who . . .	Ending sounds with possessives: /z/, /s/, /ɪz/	back composition grade	handwriting recognize
Game: Find Someone Who . . . *Game*: What Can Your Group Do?	Reduced vowel in *can* when followed by base form verb Stressed vowel in *can't*	be surprised genius intelligent	invent professor
Information Gap: Asking Questions about a Website	Vowel sounds /eɪ/ and /ɛ/	especially gain lose	overweight pound

UNIT	READING	WRITING	LISTENING
15 page 166 **Grammar:** Present Progressive: Affirmative and Negative Statements **Theme:** High School	An online article: High school schedules in the U.S. and East Asia	A description of two people and their activities	A telephone conversation between family members
16 page 174 **Grammar:** Present Progressive: *Yes / No* and *Wh-* Questions **Theme:** Movies	A conversation: *The Wizard of Oz*	A paragraph about your favorite movie	A conversation about shopping for electronics
17 page 185 **Grammar:** Simple Present and Present Progressive; Non-Action Verbs **Theme:** Smartphones	An online article: *Cell Phone Mania*	Sentences about doing many things at once	Phone messages from family and co-workers
PART V **From Grammar to Writing,** page 195 **Subjects and Verbs**			
18 page 198 **Grammar:** Simple Past: Affirmative and Negative Statements with Regular Verbs **Theme:** Travel	Online messages: A Trip	A postcard about an imaginary trip you took to a city you would like to visit	A conversation about a trip to Japan
19 page 209 **Grammar:** Simple Past: Affirmative and Negative Statements with Irregular Verbs **Theme:** You Never Know	A Chinese folktale: *You Never Know What Will Happen*	A paragraph telling your autobiography	A man's story about his grandfather
20 page 219 **Grammar:** Simple Past: *Yes / No* and *Wh-* Questions **Theme:** Interviews	A radio talk show interview: Shakespeare	Questions about famous people	A conversation about Shakespeare and movies
PART VI **From Grammar to Writing,** page 231 **Punctuation II: The Exclamation Point (!), The Hyphen (-), Quotation Marks (" . . .")**			

SPEAKING	PRONUNCIATION	VOCABULARY	
Game: Describing a Classroom Photo	Unstressed *-ing* ending in the present progressive	competition extracurricular give up	top tough wealthy
Role Play: Talking about Movies *Pair Activity*: Describing Pictures for a Partner to Draw	Stressed final syllable in abbreviations	catch a cold classic cough	favorite fever scene
Pair Discussion: Guessing About People *Group Activity*: Survey	Intonation to express emotions	connect constantly improving	minor waterproof
Pair Discussion: Talking About your Weekend *Game*: Truths or Lies	Final sound with simple past verbs: /d/, /t/, or /ɪd/	bumpy canceled freezing	landed picked up
Group Activity: A Memory Game *Group Discussion*: A Wonderful and Terrible Day	Vowel sounds /æ/ and /ɛ/	appeared border lucky	shout suddenly terrible
Pair Discussion: Describing a Performance or Event	/ʤ/ and /y/ sounds	author be out mystery	play poem

UNIT	READING	WRITING	LISTENING
21 page 234 **Grammar:** Simple Past Review **Theme:** Biographies	An article: *A Loyal Friend*	A short biography of a musician	A conversation about a TV show
22 page 248 **Grammar:** Gerunds and Infinitives **Theme:** Careers and Abilities	Comments by people about work they enjoy	A paragraph about your future career goals	A conversation between long lost friends
23 page 258 **Grammar:** Simple Present, Present Progressive, and Simple Past **Theme:** Creativity	An online article: Creativity	Sentences about an imaginary year in the future	A talk about the invention of X-rays
PART VII **From Grammar to Writing,** page 268 **Organization: Time Sequence Markers**			
24 page 270 **Grammar:** *Be going to* for the Future **Theme:** City and Campus Planning	An online school newspaper: *Letters to the Editor*	An email letter of opinion about a change to a school and city	A conversation about a new building
25 page 283 **Grammar:** *Will* for the Future; Future Time Markers **Theme:** The Future	An online article: *What's in Store for Us in 2050?*	A paragraph about how things will be different in the future	A conversation between a TV news reporter and two people
26 page 294 **Grammar:** *May* or *Might* for Possibility **Theme:** Weather	A conversation and TV weather report	A weather report	A conversation between two people traveling
PART VIII **From Grammar to Writing,** page 304 **Time Clauses with *When***			
27 page 308 **Grammar:** Count and Non-Count Nouns, Quantifiers, Articles **Theme:** Restaurants and Food	Online restaurant reviews: *Al Hambra and Topkapi*	A restaurant review	A conversation about party preparations

SPEAKING	PRONUNCIATION	VOCABULARY	
Group Activity: A Quiz Show *Pair Discussion*: What Were You Like as a Child? *Information Gap*: Guess the Musician	/ɝ/ and /ɔ/ and the consonant cluster /kt/	admire be based on illustrated	noticed statue
Pair Discussion: Preferences *Game*: What Do I Do? *Pair Activity*: Problem Solving	Unstressed sound /əv/ in *of* Linking of consonant with *of*	avoids can't stand competitive	dress clothes personality predictable
Information Gap: Inventions	Stress on first syllable in compound nouns	accepted came up with comes after	invented rejected
Pair Discussion: Changes in Your Life	Reduced pronunciation of *going to* "gonna"	against announced be worth it	in my opinion increased tuition
Group Activity: Survey *Class Survey*: In the Future *Class Activity*: Making Predictions	Linking between subject pronoun and *will*	common disappear meal	spend time vegetarian
Pair Discussion: Describing Plans	Stress on numbers ending in *-ty* and *-teen*	commute entire flooding highways	mild predicted storm
Class Activity: Cooking Class Presentation *Group Discussion*: Your Favorite Restaurant	Schwa sound /ə/ in the indefinite article	atmosphere delicious main course	menu reservation service

UNIT	READING	WRITING	LISTENING
28 page 321 **Grammar:** *How much / How many*, Quantifiers, *Enough*, Adverbs of Frequency **Theme:** Desserts, Cooking, and Baking	A conversation: Desserts	A paragraph describing desserts	A conversation about a recipe
29 page 334 **Grammar:** *Too much / Too many*, *Too* + Adjective **Theme:** The Right Place to Live	An online article: Three U.S. cities	An email of complaint to a newspaper about an aspect of city life	A conversation about apartment rentals
PART IX From Grammar to Writing, page 344 **A Business Letter**			
30 page 348 **Grammar:** Advice: *Should*, *Ought to*, *Had better* **Theme:** Dos and Don'ts of the Business World	An online article: Global Business	A paragraph of advice to a businessperson about a culture that you know well	A conversation about travels to Japan
31 page 360 **Grammar:** Requests, Desires, and Offers: *Would you*, *Could you*, *Can you . . . ?*, *I'd like . . .* **Theme:** Neighbors	A message board: Problems with neighbors	Two email requests to neighbors	A telephone conversation between neighbors
32 page 370 **Grammar:** Necessity: *Have to*, *Don't Have to*, *Must*, *Mustn't* **Theme:** Rules at School	A conversation: Requirements for a history class	A paragraph about an elementary school where you grew up	Advice from a college counselor to a student
PART X From Grammar to Writing, page 382 **Expressing and Supporting an Opinion**			
33 page 386 **Grammar:** The Comparative **Theme:** Comparing Cities	An article: *A Tale of Two Portlands*	A paragraph comparing two ways to travel	A conversation about city improvements

SPEAKING	PRONUNCIATION	VOCABULARY	
Class Survey: Eating Habits *Information Gap*: Recipes *Group Presentation*: Desserts	/aʊ/ sound	in season ingredients neighborhood	prepare pretty good taste
Role Play: Living Situations *Group Discussion*: Describing Your City	/t/, /θ/, and /ð/ sounds	climate crime free time	housing pollution unemployment
Pair Discussion: Gift Giving *Group Discussion*: Body Language	Reduction of /t/ sound after *shouldn't* before a verb	business receptions confusion consider	customs insult
Group Survey: Making Requests *Role Play*: Making Polite Requests *Pair Activity*: Offering Invitations *Role Play*: Offering Invitations and Making Requests	Vowel sound /ʊ/ in *would*; Reduced forms of *would you* /wʊdʒə/ and *could you* /kʊdʒə/	be hurt go away lend me a hand	post a message selfish
Class Discussion: School Rules *Class Survey*: Preventing Cheating	Stress and unstress in *have to* or *has to*	average due final hard copy	midterm outline pass percent
Pair Activity: Comparing Train Systems *Pair Discussion*: Making Comparisons *Class Discussion*: Comparing Cities	Unstressed vowel in *than*	be located coast diverse mild	personality port sea level ski

UNIT	READING	WRITING	LISTENING
34 page 399 **Grammar:** Adverbs of Manner **Theme:** Public Speaking	A blog: *Public Speaking*	A paragraph describing a sports event	Tips for giving a speech
35 page 408 **Grammar:** *Enough, Too / Very, As* + Adjective + *As, Same / Different* **Theme:** Proms and Parties	A conversation: High school prom dates	A paragraph comparing two friends or two events	A discussion between two managers
36 page 421 **Grammar:** The Superlative **Theme:** Penguins	An online article: *The Penguin*	A paragraph about animals in the zoo, literature, or movies	A quiz show
PART XI **From Grammar to Writing,** page 433 **The Order of Adjectives Before Nouns**			

SPEAKING	PRONUNCIATION	VOCABULARY	
Group Game: A Chain Story *Pair Discussion*: A Sports Event	Intonation to express emotions	applause appreciated audience facts	jokes polite seriously
Pair Activity: Describing Yourself *Class Survey*: Comparing Similarities	Unstressed vowel in *as . . . as*	I'm a loser I'm not going to make a fool of myself I'm not his type Making excuses No one can get a word in edgewise	
Group Survey: Animals	Unstressed *-est* syllable in superlatives	centimeter explorer extinct feathers	inch kilogram pound species

About the Author

Irene E. Schoenberg has taught ESL for more than two decades at Hunter College's International English Language Institute and at Columbia University's American Language Program. Ms. Schoenberg holds a master's degree in TESOL from Columbia University. She has trained ESL and EFL teachers at Columbia University's Teachers College and at the New School University. She has given workshops and academic presentations at conferences, English language schools, and universities in Brazil, Chile, Dubai, El Salvador, Guatemala, Japan, Mexico, Nicaragua, Peru, Taiwan, Thailand, Vietnam, and throughout the United States.

Ms. Schoenberg is the author of *Talk about Trivia*; *Talk about Values*; *Speaking of Values 1: Conversation and Listening*; *Topics from A to Z*, Books 1 and 2; and *Focus on Grammar 2: An Integrated Skills Approach*. She is the co-author with Jay Maurer of the *True Colors* series and *Focus on Grammar 1: An Integrated Skills Approach*. She is one of the authors of *Future 1: English for Results* and *Future 3: English for Results*.

Acknowledgments

I gratefully acknowledge the many reviewers for their suggestions and comments. There are many people at Pearson who have contributed to the development and production of this edition. I would like to thank them all, in particular:

- The people in production who helped carry the project through: **Rhea Banker** and especially **Robert Ruvo** for his indefatigable efforts.
- **Lise Minovitz**, the supervising editor, for her expert guidance and unflagging energy in keeping a very complex project on target.
- **Debbie Sistino**, the series director, who, in addition to managing the entire series, was always available to answer any of my questions.
- **Joanne Dresner** for her original vision and guidance of the *Focus on Grammar* series.
- My editors of the first three editions for helping to bring the books to fruition.
- **Ann France**, for her attractive new design, and **Aerin Csigay** and **Kim Steiner** for great photos that make the pages come alive.
- Above all, I'm most grateful to my editor **Kim Steiner**. Her dedication to the project, her brilliant solutions to problems, her creativity, her availability and her eye for detail, have made working on the revised edition a joy.
- Finally, I thank my family for their love and understanding: **Harris**, **Dan**, **Dahlia**, **Jonathan**, and **Olivia**.

Reviewers

We are grateful to the following reviewers for their many helpful comments:

Aida Aganagic, Seneca College, Toronto, Canada; **Aftab Ahmed**, American University of Sharjah, Sharjah, United Arab Emirates; **Todd Allen**, English Language Institute, Gainesville, FL; **Anthony Anderson**, University of Texas, Austin, TX; **Anna K. Andrade**, ASA Institute, New York, NY; **Bayda Asbridge**, Worcester State College, Worcester, MA; **Raquel Ashkenasi**, American Language Institute, La Jolla, CA; **James Bakker**, Mt. San Antonio College, Walnut, CA; **Kate Baldrige-Hale**, Harper College, Palatine, IL; **Leticia S. Banks**, ALCI-SDUSM, San Marcos, CA; **Aegina Barnes**, York College CUNY, Forest Hills, NY; **Sarah Barnhardt**, Community College of Baltimore County, Reisterstown, MD; **Kimberly Becker**, Nashville State Community College, Nashville, TN; **Holly Bell**, California State University, San Marcos, CA; **Anne Bliss**, University of Colorado, Boulder, CO; **Diana Booth**, Elgin Community College, Elgin, IL; **Barbara Boyer**, South Plainfield High School, South Plainfield, NJ; **Janna Brink**, Mt. San Antonio College, Walnut, CA; **AJ Brown**, Portland State University, Portland, OR; **Amanda Burgoyne**, Worcester State College, Worcester, MA; **Brenda Burlingame**, Independence High School, Charlotte, NC; **Sandra Byrd**, Shelby County High School and Kentucky State University, Shelbyville, KY; **Edward Carlstedt**, American University of Sharjah, Sharjah, United Arab Emirates; **Sean Cochran**, American Language Institute, Fullerton, CA; **Yanely Cordero**, Miami Dade College, Miami, FL; **Lin Cui**, William Rainey Harper College, Palatine, IL; **Sheila Detweiler**, College Lake County, Libertyville, IL; **Ann Duncan**, University of Texas, Austin, TX; **Debra Edell**, Merrill Middle School, Denver, CO; **Virginia Edwards**, Chandler-Gilbert Community College, Chandler, AZ; **Kenneth Fackler**, University of Tennessee, Martin, TN; **Jennifer Farnell**, American Language Program, Stamford, CT; **Allen P. Feiste**, Suwon University, Hwaseong, South Korea; **Mina Fowler**, Mt. San Antonio Community College, Rancho Cucamonga, CA; **Rosemary Franklin**, University of Cincinnati, Cincinnati, OH; **Christiane Galvani**, Texas Southern University, Sugar Land, TX; **Chester Gates**, Community College of Baltimore County, Baltimore, MD; **Luka Gavrilovic**, Quest Language Studies, Toronto, Canada; **Sally Gearhart**, Santa Rosa Community College, Santa Rosa, CA; **Shannon Gerrity**, James Lick Middle School, San Francisco, CA; **Jeanette Gerrity Gomez**, Prince George's Community College, Largo, MD; **Carlos Gonzalez**, Miami Dade College, Miami, FL; **Therese Gormley Hirmer**, University of Guelph, Guelph, Canada; **Sudeepa Gulati**, Long Beach City College, Long Beach, CA; **Anthony Halderman**, Cuesta College, San Luis Obispo, CA; **Ann A. Hall**, University of Texas, Austin, TX; **Cora Higgins**, Boston Academy of English, Boston, MA; **Michelle Hilton**, South Lane School District, Cottage Grove, OR; **Nicole Hines**, Troy University, Atlanta, GA; **Rosemary Hiruma**, American Language Institute, Long Beach, CA; **Harriet Hoffman**, University of Texas, Austin, TX; **Leah Holck**, Michigan State University, East Lansing, MI; **Christy Hunt**, English for Internationals, Roswell, GA; **Osmany Hurtado**, Miami Dade College, Miami, FL; **Isabel Innocenti**, Miami Dade College, Miami, FL; **Donna Janian**, Oxford Intensive School of English, Medford, MA; **Scott Jenison**, Antelope Valley College, Lancaster, CA; **Grace Kim**, Mt. San Antonio College, Diamond Bar, CA; **Brian King**, ELS Language Center, Chicago, IL; **Pam Kopitzke**, Modesto Junior College, Modesto, CA; **Elena Lattarulo**, American Language Institute, San Diego, CA; **Karen Lavaty**, Mt. San Antonio College, Glendora, CA; **JJ Lee-Gilbert**, Menlo-Atherton High School, Foster City, CA; **Ruth Luman**, Modesto Junior College, Modesto, CA; **Yvette Lyons**, Tarrant County College, Fort Worth, TX; **Janet Magnoni**, Diablo Valley College, Pleasant Hill, CA; **Meg Maher**, YWCA Princeton, Princeton, NJ; **Carmen Marquez-Rivera**, Curie Metropolitan High School, Chicago, IL; **Meredith Massey**, Prince George's Community College, Hyattsville, MD; **Linda Maynard**, Coastline Community College, Westminster, CA; **Eve Mazereeuw**, University of Guelph, Guelph, Canada; **Susanne McLaughlin**, Roosevelt University, Chicago, IL; **Madeline Medeiros**, Cuesta College, San Luis Obispo, CA; **Gioconda Melendez**, Miami Dade College, Miami, FL; **Marcia Menaker**, Passaic County Community College, Morris Plains, NJ; **Seabrook Mendoza**, Cal State San Marcos University, Wildomar, CA; **Anadalia Mendoza**, Felix Varela Senior High School, Miami, FL; **Charmaine Mergulhao**, Quest Language Studies, Toronto, Canada; **Dana Miho**, Mt. San Antonio College, San Jacinto, CA; **Sonia Nelson**, Centennial Middle School, Portland, OR; **Manuel Niebla**, Miami Dade College, Miami, FL; **Alice Nitta**, Leeward Community College, Pearl City, HI; **Gabriela Oliva**, Quest Language Studies, Toronto, Canada; **Sara Packer**, Portland State University, Portland, OR; **Lesley Painter**, New School, New York, NY; **Carlos Paz-Perez**, Miami Dade College, Miami, FL; **Ileana Perez**, Miami Dade College, Miami, FL; **Barbara Pogue**, Essex County College, Newark, NJ; **Phillips Potash**, University of Texas, Austin, TX; **Jada Pothina**, University of Texas, Austin, TX; **Ewa Pratt**, Des Moines Area Community College, Des Moines, IA; **Pedro Prentt**, Hudson County Community College, Jersey City, NJ; **Maida Purdy**, Miami Dade College, Miami, FL; **Dolores Quiles**, SUNY Ulster, Stone Ridge, NY; **Mark Rau**, American River College, Sacramento, CA; **Lynne Raxlen**, Seneca College, Toronto, Canada; **Lauren Rein**, English for Internationals, Sandy Springs, GA; **Diana Rivers**, NOCCCD, Cypress, CA; **Silvia Rodriguez**, Santa Ana College, Mission Viejo, CA; **Rolando Romero**, Miami Dade College, Miami, FL; **Pedro Rosabal**, Miami Dade College, Miami, FL; **Natalie Rublik**, University of Quebec, Chicoutimi, Quebec, Canada; **Matilde Sanchez**, Oxnard College, Oxnard, CA; **Therese Sarkis-Kruse**, Wilson Commencement, Rochester, NY; **Mike Sfiropoulos**, Palm Beach Community College, Boynton Beach, FL; **Amy Shearon**, Rice University, Houston, TX; **Sara Shore**, Modesto Junior College, Modesto, CA; **Patricia Silva**, Richard Daley College, Chicago, IL; **Stephanie Solomon**, Seattle Central Community College, Vashon, WA; **Roberta Steinberg**, Mount Ida College, Newton, MA; **Teresa Szymula**, Curie Metropolitan High School, Chicago, IL; **Hui-Lien Tang**, Jasper High School, Plano, TX; **Christine Tierney**, Houston Community College, Sugar Land, TX; **Ileana Torres**, Miami Dade College, Miami, FL; **Michelle Van Slyke**, Western Washington University, Bellingham, WA; **Melissa Villamil**, Houston Community College, Sugar Land, TX; **Elizabeth Wagenheim**, Prince George's Community College, Lago, MD; **Mark Wagner**, Worcester State College, Worcester, MA; **Angela Waigand**, American University of Sharjah, Sharjah, United Arab Emirates; **Merari Weber**, Metropolitan Skills Center, Los Angeles, CA; **Sonia Wei**, Seneca College, Toronto, Canada; and **Vicki Woodward**, Indiana University, Bloomington, IN.

PART I

BE: PRESENT AND PAST

UNIT	GRAMMAR FOCUS	THEME
1	Present of *Be*: Statements	Famous People
2	Present of *Be*: *Yes / No* Questions and *Wh-* Questions	First Day of School
3	Past of *Be*: Statements, *Yes / No* Questions, *Wh-* Questions	First Jobs

UNIT 1

Present of *Be*: Statements

FAMOUS PEOPLE

STEP 1 GRAMMAR IN CONTEXT

Before You Read

GROUPS: Name a young and famous person. Tell your group one thing about this person.

EXAMPLE: Lionel Messi. He is a great soccer player.

Read

Read the article about the people in the photos.

POP Culture News

Famous Couples

They'**re** young. They'**re** rich. They'**re** talented and famous. Who **are** they? Where **are** they from? What do they do?

The woman on the left **is** Carrie Underwood. She **is** from the United States. She'**s** from the state of Oklahoma. Carrie **is** an American country singer. She **isn't** just a singer. She'**s** also a pianist and a songwriter.

Carrie is married to Mike Fisher. He **is** also talented and famous. He **isn't** from the United States, and he **isn't** a singer. He'**s** an athlete from Ottawa, Canada. Now he'**s** an ice hockey player for the Nashville Predators. Carrie Underwood and Mike Fisher have homes in the United States and Canada.

Who **are** the people in the second photo? They'**re** Gisele Bündchen and Tom Brady. Gisele **is** a supermodel. She'**s** from Brazil, but she **is** famous all over the world. Her husband **is** Tom Brady. He **is** an American football player. He'**s** from California. He plays quarterback for the New England Patriots.

The lives of these famous people **are** exciting. Their lives **aren't** easy. They **are** always very busy.

It'**s** wonderful to be young and famous. Many young people want to be rich and famous. It takes talent, hard work, and good luck.

After You Read

A | Practice *PAIRS: Now read the article aloud. Take turns reading each paragraph.*

B | Vocabulary *Complete the sentences with the words from the box.*

athlete	busy	exciting	famous	husband	talented

1. Mike Fisher is Carrie Underwood's ________________.
2. Carrie Underwood plays piano, sings, and writes music. She is very ________________.
3. People know Gisele Bündchen all over the world. She is very ________________.
4. Tom Brady is a great ________________. He's a football player for the New England Patriots.
5. Brady works hard. He is ________________ all the time.
6. Bündchen goes to many parties and travels to many interesting places. She has a(n) ________________ life.

C | Comprehension *Complete the sentences. Circle the correct letter.*

1. Carrie Underwood is married to ______________________________.
   a. Tom Brady **b.** Mike Fisher
2. Underwood is a singer and ______________________________.
   a. an athlete **b.** a pianist
3. Underwood's husband is an ______________________________.
   a. ice hockey player **b.** actor
4. The New England Patriots are a ______________________________.
   a. football team **b.** talented player
5. Gisele Bündchen is a ______________________________.
   a. supermodel **b.** pianist
6. Bündchen is from ______________________________.
   a. Canada **b.** Brazil
7. Tom Brady is from ______________________________.
   a. New England **b.** California
8. To be rich and famous takes ______________________________.
   a. time and money **b.** hard work and good luck

STEP 2 GRAMMAR PRESENTATION

PRESENT OF *BE*: STATEMENTS

Affirmative Statements

Singular		
Subject	***Be***	
I	**am**	talented.
You	**are**	
Mike He	**is**	
Carrie She		
Hockey It		a sport

Plural		
Subject	***Be***	
Masami and I We	**are**	students.
You and Josh You		
Ivona and Juan They		
Seoul and London They		cities.

Contractions	
I am → **I'm**	we are → **we're**
you are → **you're**	you are → **you're**
he is → **he's**	they are → **they're**
she is → **she's**	
it is → **it's**	

Negative Statements

Singular	
Subject + *Be* / *Not*	
I **am not** I**'m not**	from California.
You **are not** You**'re not** You **aren't**	
He **is not** He**'s not** He **isn't**	
She **is not** She**'s not** She **isn't**	
It **is not** It**'s not** It **isn't**	new.

Plural	
Subject + *Be* / *Not*	
We **are not** We**'re not** We **aren't**	in Brazil.
You **are not** You**'re not** You **aren't**	
They **are not** They**'re not** They **aren't**	

GRAMMAR NOTES

1	The **present of *be*** has three forms: ***am*, *is*, *are***.	• I **am** a student. • He **is** from Brazil. • They **are** famous.
2	Use the correct form of ***be*** + ***not*** to make a **negative statement**.	• I **am not** from Turkey. • It **is not** from Canada. • We **are not** famous.
3	Use **contractions** (short forms) in speaking and informal writing. There are two **negative contractions** for *is not* and *are not*.	• **I'm** from Mexico. • **I'm not** from Ecuador. • Mr. Crane**'s** from Los Angeles. • It**'s not** difficult. OR It **isn't** difficult. • We**'re not** single. OR We **aren't** single.
4	All **sentences** have a **subject** and a **verb**. **BE CAREFUL!** You cannot make a sentence without a subject. You cannot make a sentence without a verb.	SUBJECT VERB • **Gisele is** from Brazil. NOT: ~~Is from Brazil~~. NOT: ~~Gisele from Brazil~~.
5	The **subject** is a noun or a pronoun. Subject pronouns (*I, you, he, she, it we, you, they*) replace subject nouns. **BE CAREFUL!** You cannot put a subject pronoun right after a subject noun.	SUBJECT NOUN • **Mike Fisher** is from Canada. SUBJECT PRONOUN • **He** is from Canada. NOT: ~~Fisher he~~ is from England.

STEP 3 FOCUSED PRACTICE

EXERCISE 1: Discover the Grammar

A | *Check (✓) the negative statements.*

__✓__ **1.** Carrie Underwood isn't single.

_____ **2.** Underwood is married to Mike Fisher.

_____ **3.** Fisher and Tom Brady are athletes.

_____ **4.** They aren't actors.

_____ **5.** I'm from Canada.

_____ **6.** I'm not from the United States.

B | *Look back at Part A. Underline the contractions.*

C | *Look back at sentences 1–3 in Part A. Change the subject nouns to subject pronouns.*

EXERCISE 2: Affirmative Statements

(Grammar Note 1)

Complete the sentences with **am, is,** *or* **are.**

1. Soccer ____*is*____ popular all over the world.
2. Football ________ popular in the United States.
3. Football and soccer ________ different sports.
4. Tom Brady ________ a great football player.
5. Lionel Messi ________ a great soccer player.
6. I ________ a football fan. I love football.
7. My cousins ________ soccer fans. They love soccer.

EXERCISE 3: Affirmative and Negative Statements

(Grammar Notes 1–2)

Complete the sentences with **am, is,** *or* **are,** *and the word in parentheses.*

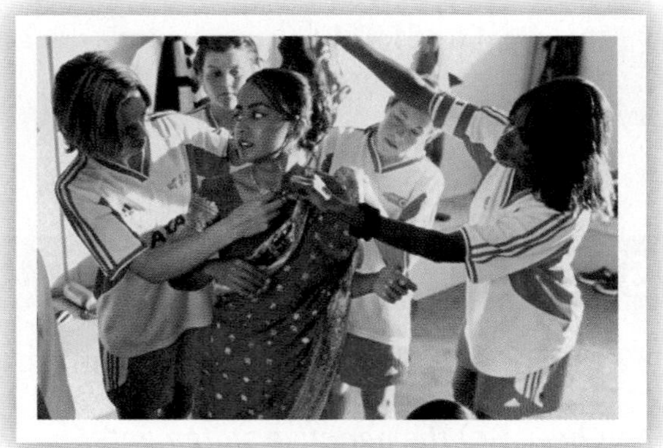

Parminder Nagra ____*is*____ (1.) a talented actor. She and Keira Knightley ________ (2.) the stars of the movie *Bend It Like Beckham*. It ________ (3.) a comedy. In the movie, Nagra ________ (4.) a young Indian girl in England. She ________ (5.) a good soccer player, and she loves soccer. But her parents ________ (6.) traditional. They ________ (7. (not)) happy. They do not want her to play soccer. They say, "Soccer ________ (8. (not)) for girls. Marriage ________ (9.) for girls. Look at your sister. Your sister ________ (10. (not)) a soccer player, and she ________ (11.) about to marry." Parminder says, "I ________ (12. (not)) my sister."

EXERCISE 4: Subject Pronouns and Contractions

(Grammar Notes 3, 5)

Change the underlined words. Change nouns to pronouns and write contractions of **be**.

1. Lionel Messi is from Argentina. ~~Messi is~~ *He's* a great soccer player.
2. Mr. Smith is a soccer fan. Mr. Smith is a football fan too.
3. My partner and I are on a soccer team. My partner and I are not on a football team.
4. Soccer is a great sport. Soccer is popular all over the world.
5. Parminder Nagra and Halle Berry are actors. Nagra and Berry are talented.
6. Ms. Brown is an English teacher. Ms. Brown is a supervisor too.
7. Tennis and ping-pong are great sports. Tennis and ping-pong are exciting games.

EXERCISE 5: Affirmative and Negative Contractions

(Grammar Notes 1–4)

Write true sentences with the words in parentheses. Use the affirmative or negative. Use contractions when possible.

1. Lionel Messi is a soccer player. (He / popular all over the world)

   He's popular all over the world.

2. Soccer is a great game. (It / popular in my country)

   ____

3. Rafael Nadal is a tennis player. (He / from Spain)

   ____

4. Cristiano Ronaldo and David Beckham are famous. (They / talented soccer players)

   ____

5. (I / a student)

   ____

6. (I / from London)

   ____

7. (My friends and I / soccer fans)

   ____

8. (Soccer / my favorite sport)

   ____

EXERCISE 6: Editing

Correct the paragraph. There are nine mistakes. The first mistake is already corrected. Find and correct eight more.

My family ^is^ in Mexico. I in Los Angeles. My father is a businessman, and my mother a math teacher. Alessandra is my sister. She an engineer. Marco is my brother. Is in the family business with my father. We all soccer fans. Our favorite team is the Club de Fútbol Monterrey. Our team on TV very often. I call my family, and we talk about the game on TV. They far away, but thanks to email and cell phones, we close.

STEP 4 COMMUNICATION PRACTICE

EXERCISE 7: Pronunciation

A | *Read and listen to the Pronunciation Note.*

Pronunciation Note

Some students confuse ***he*** and ***she***. To pronounce ***he*** and ***she*** correctly, follow these tips:

- **Smile** when you say ***he*** or ***he's***.
- **Relax** your lips to say ***she*** or ***she's***.

B | *Listen to the sentences. Check (✓) the correct box.*

	He's	She's
1.		✓
2.		
3.		
4.		
5.		
6.		

C | *Listen again and repeat.*

EXERCISE 8: Listening

A | *PAIRS: Look at the pictures. Do you know these talented people? Try to complete the chart with the words from the box. Follow the example answer.*

actor	Argentina	~~baseball player~~	England	ice skater	Korea	soccer player	Ukraine
actress	Barbados	Brazil	film director	~~Japan~~	singer	Taiwan	writer

Name	 Hideki Matsui	 Lionel Messi	 Rihanna	 Kim Yu-na
Occupation	*baseball player*			
Country of Origin	*Japan*			

Name	 Rob Pattinson	 Olga Kurylenko	 Paulo Coehlo	 Ang Lee
Occupation				
Country of Origin				

B | *Listen and write the correct occupation and country of origin for each person. Discuss your answers with your partner.*

EXAMPLE: **A:** Who is Hideki Matsui?
B: He's a soccer player from Japan.
A: He's from Japan, but he's not a soccer player. He's a baseball player.

C | *Listen again and check your answers.*

EXERCISE 9: Talking about Occupations

A | *PAIRS: Look at the occupations. Make a list of other occupations. Check (✓) your occupation and the occupations of your relatives and friends.*

______________________ ______________________

______________________ ______________________

______________________ ______________________

- ❑ a nurse
- ❑ a stay-at-home mom or dad 
- ❑ a doctor 
- ❑ an athlete 
- ❑ a plumber 
- ❑ a writer 
- ❑ an electrician 
- ❑ a detective 
- ❑ a lawyer 
- ❑ a carpenter 

B | *Talk about the occupations of your relatives and friends. Use the words from the box.*

boring	dangerous	difficult	exciting	interesting

Example: **A:** My cousin is a detective. His job is dangerous, but it's interesting.
B: My uncle is a businessman. His job is difficult.

EXERCISE 10: Talking about Talented People

A | *PAIRS: Look at the list of qualities. Add four more qualities to the list.*

successful   funny   smart   hardworking

________   ________   ________   ________

B | *Fill in the circles with information about a talented person you know. Then tell your partner.*

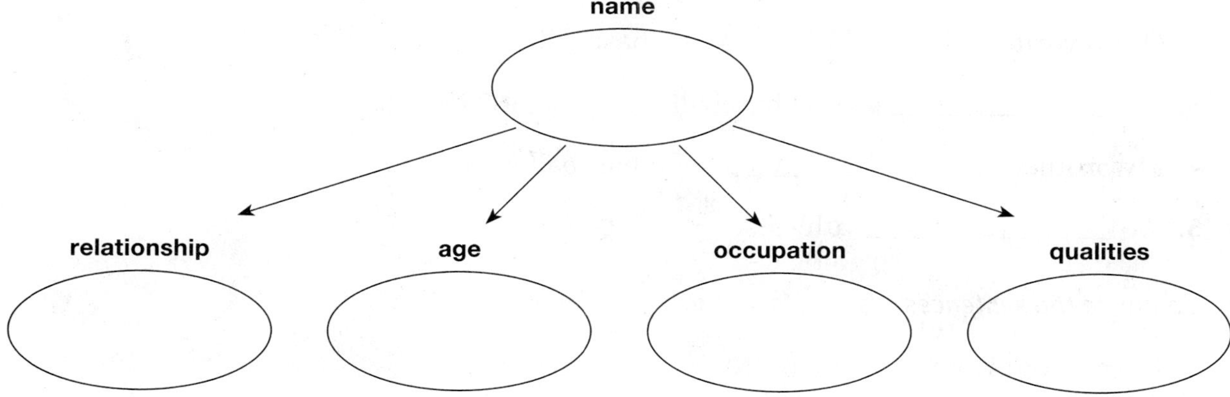

Example: Noah is my brother. He's 19 years old. He's a baseball player and a musician. He's talented and hardworking. His dream is to be a great musician. Noah is not famous now. But one day everyone will know him.

EXERCISE 11: Writing

A | *Write four sentences about a famous person from Exercise 8 or a talented friend or relative. Give the person's name, country, and qualities. Add any information you know about the person. Use the present form of* **be**.

Example: Hideki Matsui is a baseball player. He's from Japan. His nickname is "Godzilla." He's big and strong and talented.

B | *Check your work. Use the Editing Checklist.*

Editing Checklist

Did you . . . ?

☐ use the present form of ***be*** correctly
☐ use a subject and verb in each sentence
☐ check your spelling

UNIT 1 Review

Check your answers on page UR-1.
Do you need to review anything?

A | *Complete the sentences. Use* **am, is,** *or* **are.**

1. My brother and I ________________ baseball fans.
2. Our favorite sport ________________ baseball.
3. I ________________ a good baseball player.
4. My brother ________________ a good baseball player too.
5. We ________________ athletes.

B | *Complete the sentences. Use* **'m, 's,** *or* **'re.**

1. I ____ from Korea.
2. She ____ from Brazil.
3. We ____ in school in New York.
4. It ____ a good school.
5. We ____ happy to be here.

C | *Change the underlined words. Change nouns to pronouns and use contractions.*

1. <u>Lionel Messi is not</u> in Argentina now.
2. <u>Soccer and baseball are</u> exciting sports.
3. <u>My partner and I are not</u> baseball fans.
4. <u>Ms. Nagra is</u> the star of the movie *Bend It Like Beckham*.

D | *Correct the paragraph. There are six mistakes.*

My father and mother are from India, but they're in Canada now. My parents are doctors. My father a sports doctor, and my mother she is a foot doctor. My parents and I love sports. My father are a soccer fan, and my mother a baseball fan. I'm a soccer fan. My father and I am fans of Lionel Messi and Nuno Gomes. My sister no is good at sports. She's not a sports fan. She loves movies.

UNIT 2

Present of *Be*: *Yes / No* Questions and *Wh-* Questions

FIRST DAY OF SCHOOL

STEP 1 GRAMMAR IN CONTEXT

Before You Read

A | *Talk to four students. Write their names in the chart. Ask them the question, "Are you always on time for ________?" Write* **Yes** *or* **No** *for each response.*

Are you always on time for these things?				
Student's name	**School**	**Work**	**Dates**	**Parties**

EXAMPLE: **MARIA:** Juan, are you always on time for school?
JUAN: Yes, I am.

B | *Report to the class.*

EXAMPLE: **MARIA:** Juan is always on time for school. Sekura is always on time for dates.

Read

It's the first day of an English class. Read the conversation.

Arriving in Class

Lida Kozlov: Excuse me. **Where's room 2?**

Alex Brown: It's right here, next to the office.

Lida: Thanks. Uh . . . **are we late for class?**

Alex: No, we're right on time.

Lida: Whew! That's good. I hate to be late on the first day. **Is the teacher here?**

Alex: Yes, he is.

Lida: **How is he? Is he a good teacher?**

Alex: I think he's very good. My name is Alex, by the way. **What's your name?**

Lida: Lida.

Alex: Nice to meet you. **Are you new here?**

Lida: Yes, I am.

Alex: Nice jacket.

Lida: Thanks. It's from Italy.

Alex: Oh, **are you from Italy?**

Lida: No, I'm from Moscow. Hey, your English is so good! . . . **Where are you from?**

Alex: I'm from Michigan.

Lida: Michigan? But that's in the United States. **Are you in the right class?**

Alex: Yes, I am.

Lida: **Why are you here? Who are you?**

Alex: I'm not a new student. I'm a new teacher. I'm your new teacher.

Lida: Oh . . . !

After You Read

A | Practice *PAIRS: Read the conversation again aloud.*

B | Vocabulary *Complete the sentences with the words from the box. Remember to start sentences with a capital letter.*

by the way	excuse me	on time	right	room

1. ________________, where's the elevator?
2. Your class is in ________________ 102 next to the stairs.
3. Room 202 is ________________ over there, near the elevator.
4. We're ________________. We're not late or early.
5. Thanks for the coffee. ________________, is the computer lab nearby?

C | Comprehension *Read the questions. Circle the correct letter.*

1. Are Lida and Alex on time for class?

   a. Yes, they are. **b.** No, they're late. **c.** They're early for class.

2. Where is Lida from?

   a. Italy **b.** Michigan **c.** Russia

3. Where is Michigan?

   a. in the United States **b.** in Mexico **c.** in Italy

4. Are Lida and Alex students?

   a. He is, but she isn't. **b.** She is, but he isn't. **c.** Yes, they are.

5. What's the teacher's name?

   a. Lida Kozlov **b.** Alex Brown **c.** Alex Kozlov

6. What do you know is true? Alex is ___.

   a. not in the right class **b.** a good teacher **c.** Lida's teacher

STEP 2 GRAMMAR PRESENTATION

PRESENT OF *BE*: *YES / NO* QUESTIONS AND *WH-* QUESTIONS

Yes / No Questions

Singular		
Be	**Subject**	
Am	I	in room 2?
Are	you	
Is	he	
	she	
	it	

Plural		
Be	**Subject**	
Are	we	on time?
	you	
	they	

Short Answers

Singular			
Yes		***No***	
Yes,	you **are**.	**No,**	you**'re not**. you **aren't**.
	I **am**.		I**'m not**.
	he **is**.		he**'s not**. he **isn't**.
	she **is**.		she**'s not**. she **isn't**.
	it **is**.		it**'s not**. it **isn't**.

Plural			
Yes		***No***	
Yes,	you **are**.	**No,**	you**'re not**. you **aren't**.
	we **are**.		we**'re not**. we **aren't**.
	they **are**.		they**'re not**. they **aren't**.

Wh- Questions / Short Answers / Long Answers

***Wh-* Word**	***Be***	**Subject**		Short Answers	Long Answers
Where	**are**	you	from?	Michigan.	I'm from Michigan.
Why			here?	I'm the teacher.	I'm here because I'm the teacher.
What	**is**	your	name?	Alex.	My name is Alex.
How		he?		Good.	He's a good teacher.
Who		she?		A student.	She's a student.

GRAMMAR NOTES

1	***Yes / no* questions** usually have a *yes* or *no* answer. ***Wh-* questions** ask for information.	**A:** Is he a student? **B: Yes**, he is. OR **No**, he isn't. **A: Who** is he? **B:** He's the teacher.
2	Use ***am***, ***is***, or ***are*** before a subject in ***yes / no* questions**.	*BE* SUBJECT • **Am** I in English 2? • **Is** she a student? • **Are** we late?
3	We usually **answer *yes / no* questions** with short answers, but we can also give long answers. **BE CAREFUL!** Do not use contractions in short answers with *yes*.	**A:** Are you a new student? **B: Yes.** OR **Yes, I am.** OR **Yes, I am new.** NOT: Yes, ~~I'm~~.
4	***Wh-* questions** ask about the following: *Who* → people *What* → things *Where* → places *When* → time *How* → in what way *Why* asks for a reason. We can give short or long answers. In long answers, use *because* before the reason.	• **Who** are they? • **What** is in your bag? • **Where** is our classroom? • **When** is lunch? • **How** is school? **A: Why** are you late? **B:** My bus was late. OR I'm late **because** my bus was late.
5	Use a ***wh-* word** before *is* or *are* in *wh-* questions.	*WH-* WORD *BE* • **What** **is** your name? • **Where** **are** the books?
6	You can use **contractions** (short forms) with *wh-* words in speaking and informal writing. We usually don't write the contraction with *are*.	• **Where's** the library? • **When's** the class trip? SPOKEN ONLY: Where're the kids?
7	We usually give short answers to *wh-* questions. We can also give long answers.	**A:** Where are you from? **B: Mexico.** OR **I'm from Mexico.**
8	When we do not know the answer to a question, we say, "I don't know." When someone asks a *yes / no* question that we think is true, we say, "Yes, I think so." If we think it is not true, we can say, "No, I don't think so."	**A:** Is the men's room nearby? **B: I don't know.** **A:** Is she in the library? **B: Yes, I think so.** OR **No, I don't think so.**

STEP 3 FOCUSED PRACTICE

EXERCISE 1: Discover the Grammar

Look at the picture. Match the questions and answers.

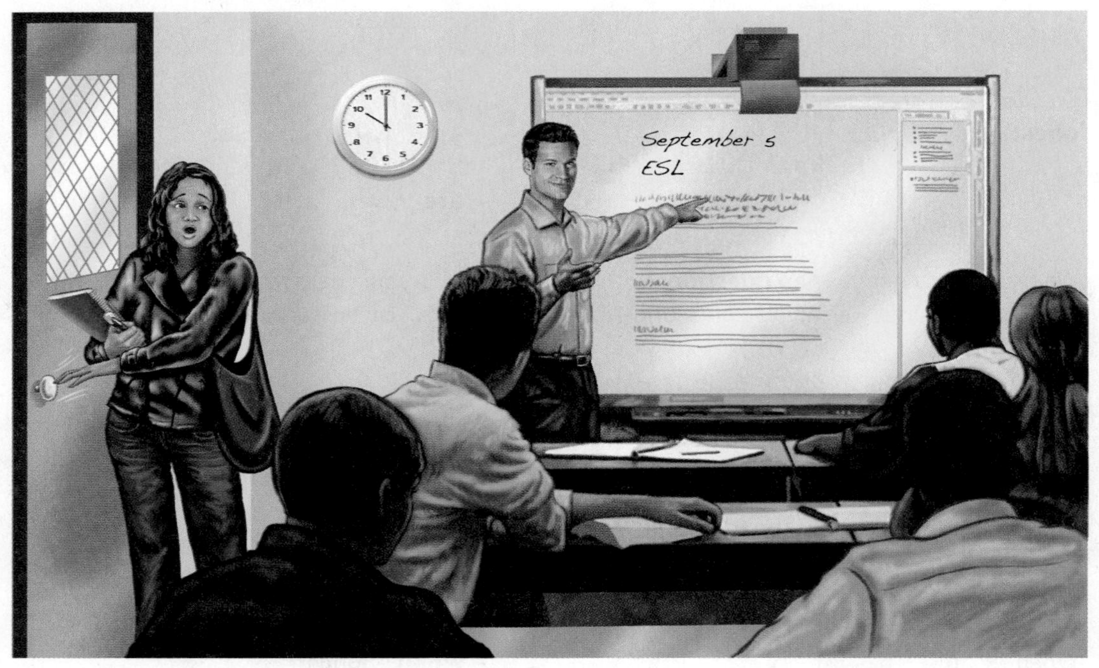

__e__ **1.** Is the door open?		**a.** Yes, he is.
____ **2.** What time is it?		**b.** I don't know.
____ **3.** Is the teacher a man?		**c.** It's ten o'clock.
____ **4.** Are the students hungry?		**d.** Near the blackboard.
____ **5.** Is the woman at the door early?		**e.** No, it's not.
____ **6.** Is the woman at the door unhappy?		**f.** No, she's late.
____ **7.** Where is the teacher?		**g.** September.
____ **8.** What month is it?		**h.** Yes, I think so.

EXERCISE 2: *Yes / No* Questions

(Grammar Note 2)

Write **yes / no** *questions about the statements in parentheses.*

1. (Today is Friday.) *Is today Friday?*
2. (We are in the right building.) ______________________
3. (You are a new student.) ______________________
4. (The teacher is from Canada.) ______________________
5. (It's ten o'clock.) ______________________

6. (They are new computers.) ____________________

7. (Two students are absent today.) ____________________

8. (I'm in the right room.) ____________________

EXERCISE 3: Word Order of *Yes / No* Questions

(Grammar Notes 1–3)

Write **yes / no** *questions with the words in parentheses. Then write true short answers. Use contractions when possible. Use* **yes / no, I don't know,** *or* **I think so / I don't think so.**

1. (you / Are / usually early)

   A: *Are you usually early?*

   B: *Yes, I am.* OR *No, I'm not.*

2. (your watch / fast / Is)

   A: ____________________

   B: ____________________

3. (from Italy / your jacket / Is)

   A: ____________________

   B: ____________________

4. (your birthday / in the spring / Is)

   A: ____________________

   B: ____________________

5. (your name / Is / easy to pronounce)

   A: ____________________

   B: ____________________

6. (different cities / Are / from / you and your classmates)

   A: ____________________

   B: ____________________

7. (busy / Are / your classmates / now)

   A: ____________________

   B: ____________________

EXERCISE 4: *Wh-* Questions

(Grammar Notes 1–4)

Read the answers. Then write **wh-** *questions with the words in parentheses.*

1. **A:** (Who) *Who's Alex Brown?*

   B: Alex Brown is the teacher.

2. **A:** (Where) ______________________

   B: The computers are in room 304.

3. **A:** (What) ______________________

   B: Today's date is September 3.

4. **A:** (Why) ______________________

   B: We're late because we were in the wrong classroom.

5. **A:** (Why) ______________________

   B: She's the teacher because Alex isn't here today.

6. **A:** (How) ______________________

   B: My computer class is great.

EXERCISE 5: *Yes / No* Questions and *Wh-* Questions

(Grammar Notes 1–8)

A | *Read Alejandra's question on SmartGirl's blog. Write questions with the words in parentheses. Then write short answers.*

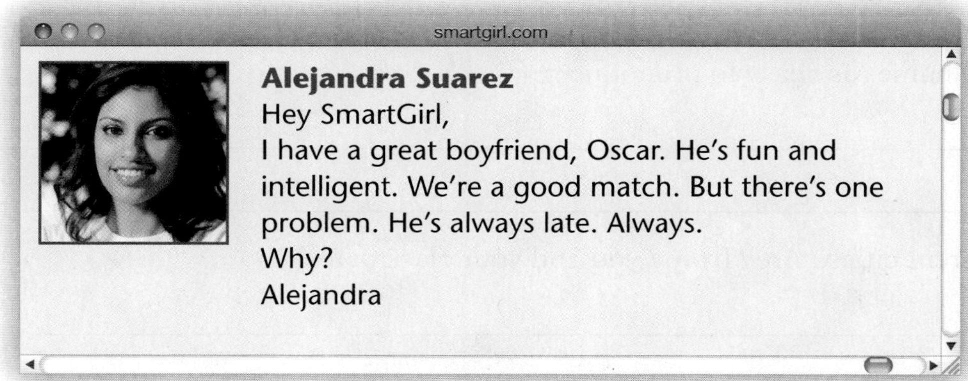

smartgirl.com
Alejandra Suarez
Hey SmartGirl,
I have a great boyfriend, Oscar. He's fun and intelligent. We're a good match. But there's one problem. He's always late. Always.
Why?
Alejandra

1. (Oscar / fun)

   A: *Is Oscar fun?*

   B: *Yes, he is.*

2. (Oscar / smart)

   A: ______________________

   B: ______________________

3. (Alejandra and Oscar / a good pair)

   A: ______________________

   B: ______________________

4. (Who / always late)

   A: ______________________

   B: ______________________

B | *Now read SmartGirl's answer. Write* **yes / no** *questions. Use the words in parentheses. Then answer the questions with* **Yes, I think so, No, I don't think so,** *or* **I don't know.**

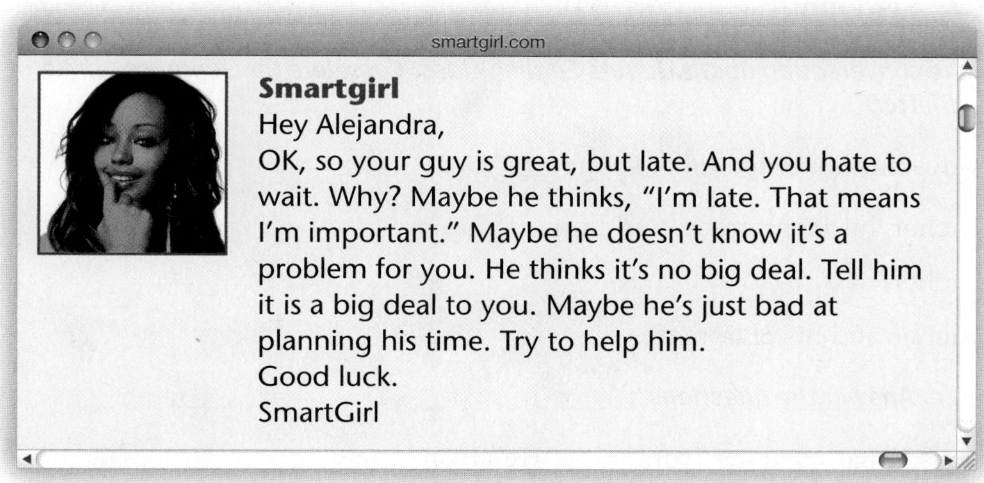

smartgirl.com
Smartgirl
Hey Alejandra,
OK, so your guy is great, but late. And you hate to wait. Why? Maybe he thinks, "I'm late. That means I'm important." Maybe he doesn't know it's a problem for you. He thinks it's no big deal. Tell him it is a big deal to you. Maybe he's just bad at planning his time. Try to help him.
Good luck.
SmartGirl

1. (Oscar / great)

A: Is Oscar great?

B: *I don't know.*

2. (Oscar / a bad boyfriend)

A: ______________________

B: ______________________

3. (Oscar / bad at planning time)

A: ______________________

B: ______________________

4. (Smartgirl's answer / good)

A: ______________________

B: ______________________

EXERCISE 6: Editing

Correct the conversations. There are nine mistakes. The first mistake is already corrected. Find and correct eight more.

1. A: Are you in the office?

B: Yes, ~~I'm~~ *I am*.

2. A: Is easy?

B: No, it's hard.

3. A: He Korean?

B: No, he's isn't.

4. A: Excuse me. Where's the office?

B: Yes, it's here.

5. A: Is this English 3?

B: Yes, I think.

6. A: Is they in room 102?

B: I don't know.

7. A: Where you from?

B: I'm from Peru.

8. A: How your class is?

B: It's very good.

9. A: What your nickname?

B: Susie.

STEP 4 COMMUNICATION PRACTICE

EXERCISE 7: Listening

A | *Listen to the conversation about Hugo's English class. Complete the sentence. Circle the correct letter.*

In the conversation, Hugo talks about ____.

a. his teacher, his classmates, and himself

b. his teacher

c. his teacher and his classmates

B | *Listen again. Answer the questions.*

1. Where is Hugo's teacher from?	He's from ________________.
2. How old is the teacher?	He's about ________________.
3. Where are his classmates from?	They're from Mexico, Chile, Canada, Poland, ________________, and ________________.
4. What is Hugo good at?	He's good at ________________.

EXERCISE 8: Pronunciation

A | *Read and listen to the Pronunciation Note.*

Pronunciation Note

In ***yes / no* questions**, your voice goes **up** at the end of the sentence.

EXAMPLES: Are you from Italy? Are you the teacher?

In ***wh-* questions**, your voice goes **down** at the end of the sentence.

EXAMPLES: Where is he from? What's his name?

B | *Listen to the questions. Notice how the voice goes up or down at the end of each question.*

1. Are classes on weekends?

2. Is it from Italy?

3. Am I in the right room?

4. Is the test tomorrow?

5. What's your email address?

6. Who's the director of your program?

7. Where are your boots from?

8. How's school?

C | *Listen again and repeat.*

EXERCISE 9: Asking and Answering Questions

PAIRS: Look at Exercise 2 on page 18. Take turns. Ask your partner the questions. Use **yes / no** *short answers or* **I don't know, I think so,** *or* **I don't think so.**

EXERCISE 10: Role Play: Meeting at a Party

PAIRS: Imagine you and your partner are at a party. Give yourself a new name, a new country, and a new occupation. Introduce yourself to your partner.

EXAMPLE: **A:** Hi, I'm Eun Young.
B: Nice to meet you. I'm Ana. Are you from around here?
A: No, I'm from Korea. I'm here on business. What about you?

EXERCISE 11: Writing

A | *PAIRS: Read the ad for University Language School. Together write five* **wh-** *questions and five* **yes / no** *questions. Read your questions to other pairs. They close their books and answer your questions.*

LEARN ENGLISH AT ULS!

Register now for English classes at University Language School

Placement Test: Sept. 1 in Room 203

Classes begin September 8

Director: Jim Reilly

phone: 989-870-3456
email : ULS@GreatSchools.com
University Language School 650 Elm Street, Long Beach, New York

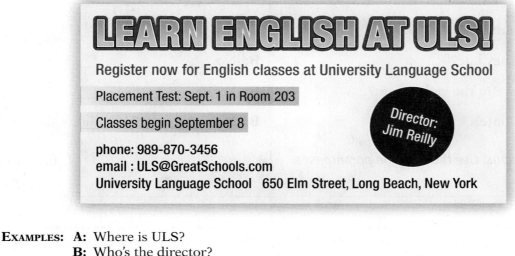

EXAMPLES: **A:** Where is ULS?
B: Who's the director?
A: Is ULS in Canada?

B | *Check your work. Use the Editing Checklist.*

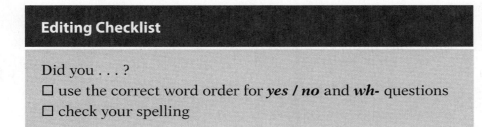

Editing Checklist

Did you . . . ?
☐ use the correct word order for ***yes / no*** and ***wh-*** questions
☐ check your spelling

UNIT 2 Review

Check your answers on page UR-1.
Do you need to review anything?

A | *Complete the questions. Circle the correct word or words.*

1. **A:** **Where's / What's** the library? **B:** In room 3.
2. **A:** **Who's / How's** your class? **B:** It's great.
3. **A:** **What's / How's** your name? **B:** Jin-Hee Lee.
4. **A:** **Is / Are** you from Seoul? **B:** Yes, I am.
5. **A:** **Is / Are** it cold in Seoul now? **B:** No, it isn't.

B | *Complete the short answers.*

1. **A:** Are you home? **B:** Yes, ________________.
2. **A:** Is your nickname JD? **B:** No, ________________.
3. **A:** Are they late? **B:** No, ________________.
4. **A:** Are we in the right room? **B:** Yes, ________________.
5. **A:** Am I late? **B:** No, ________________.

C | *Write questions. Use the words in parentheses.*

1. ____?
   (What / today's date)
2. ____?
   (Where / the men's room)
3. ____?
   (Why / he / absent)
4. ____?
   (When / your first class)
5. ____?
   (Who / your teacher)

D | *Correct the questions. There are five mistakes.*

1. She your teacher?
2. What your name?
3. Where your class?
4. Is Bob and Molly good friends?
5. Why you late?

UNIT 3

Past of *Be*: Statements, *Yes / No* Questions, *Wh-* Questions

FIRST JOBS

STEP 1 GRAMMAR IN CONTEXT

Before You Read

A | *Look at the pictures on this page and page 26. Guess the story.*

B | *PAIRS: Discuss the questions.*

1. What was your first job?
2. Was it easy? Was it hard?

Read

Read the story about Hugo Rubio's first job.

I **was** 16 years old. It **was** my first job. I **was** a lifeguard at a swimming pool for the summer. I **was** happy to have a job.

But I really wanted to be a hero. The weather **wasn't** hot, and the pool **wasn't** busy. Only five or six people **were** there every day. My days **were** long and boring. They **weren't** fun.

One day a woman slipped in the pool. I wanted to jump in to save her, but two guys **were** there before me.
!

They helped the woman, and they **were** the heroes.

(continued on next page)

Finally it **was** the last day of the season. The pool **was** crowded. More than 50 people **were** there.

A little boy fell in the pool. I jumped in and saved him.

It **wasn't** a big deal, but the little boy **was** the son of the mayor. The next day my picture **was** in the paper. I **was** a hero. It **was** exciting and fun.

Lifeguard Saves Mayor's Son

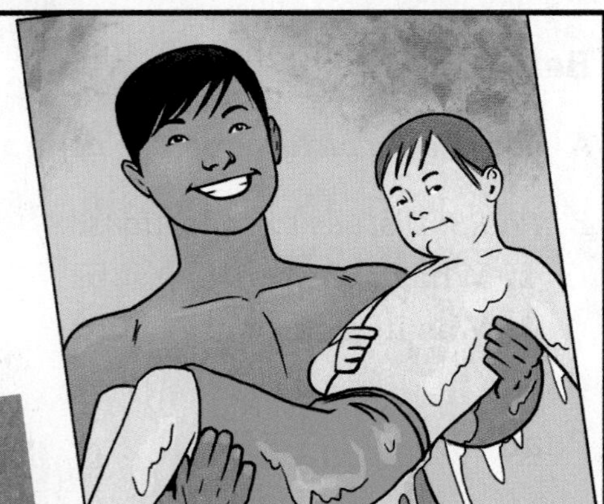

After You Read

A | Practice *PAIRS: Now read the story aloud. Take turns reading each paragraph.*

B | Vocabulary *Complete the sentences with the words from the box.*

a big deal	boring	busy	make money	still

1. I'm sorry. I don't have the report. I was very ________________ last week.
2. I can't study full time. I need to work and ________________.
3. I can work late today. It's not ________________.
4. It's 11:00 P.M. Is he ________________ at work?
5. Every day I do the same thing. My job is ________________.

C | Comprehension *Answer the questions.*

1. What was Hugo's first job? ________________________
2. How old was he? ________________________
3. Was he a hero? ________________________
4. Was the job fun? Why or why not? ________________________
5. Was Hugo happy to be in the news? ________________________

STEP 2 GRAMMAR PRESENTATION

PAST OF *BE*: AFFIRMATIVE STATEMENTS

Singular			
Subject	***Be***		**Time Marker**
I	**was**	a student	**last year**.
You	**were**		
He She	**was**		
It		busy	

Plural			
Subject	***Be***		**Time Marker**
We You They	**were**	in New York	**two weeks ago**.

PAST OF *BE*: NEGATIVE STATEMENTS

Singular			
Subject	***Be / Not***		**Time Marker**
I	**was not** **wasn't**	at school	**last night**.
You	**were not** **weren't**		
He She It	**was not** **wasn't**		

Plural			
Subject	***Be / Not***		**Time Marker**
We You They	**were not** **weren't**	at work	**last week**.

PAST OF *BE*: *YES / NO* QUESTIONS

Singular			
Be	**Subject**		**Time Marker**
Was	I	in the wrong room	**yesterday?**
Were	you		
Was	he she it		

Plural			
Be	**Subject**		**Time Marker**
Were	we you they	in the wrong building	**last week?**

SHORT ANSWERS

Singular					
Yes	**Subject**	***Be***	***No***	**Subject**	***Be***
Yes,	you	**were.**	**No,**	you	**weren't.**
	I	**was.**		I	**wasn't.**
	he she it			he she it	

Plural					
Yes	**Subject**	***Be***	***No***	**Subject**	***Be***
Yes,	you we they	**were.**	**No,**	you we they	**weren't.**

PAST OF *BE*: *WH-* QUESTIONS

Wh- word	*Be*	
What	was	your first job?
Where		the movie theater?
When		the last movie over last night?
How		the movie?
Why		it bad?
Who	were	the actors?

LONG ANSWERS

I was a ticket taker at a movie theater.
In Jacksonville, Florida.
The last movie was over at 1:00 A.M.
It was pretty bad.
The acting was bad.
I'm not sure.

GRAMMAR NOTES

1	The **past of *be*** has two forms: ***was*** and ***were***.	• She **was** at the airport. • They **were** late.
2	Use ***was*** or ***were* + *not*** to make **negative statements.**	• He **was not** at work. • They **were not** in class.
3	In informal writing and speaking, use the **contractions *wasn't*** and ***weren't*** in negative statements and negative short answers.	• He **wasn't** at an interview. • They **weren't** in class. • No, he **wasn't**. • No, they **weren't**.
4	To ask a ***yes / no* question**, put *was* or *were* before the subject.	BE SUBJECT • **Was** she at work? • **Were** you a server?
	Use a ***wh-* word** before *was* or *were* in ***wh-* questions**.	• **How** was your day?
5	**Time markers** (*yesterday, last week, two days ago,* etc.) are usually at the end of statements.	• We **were** in Toronto **yesterday**.
	Time markers are sometimes at the beginning of statements.	• **Yesterday** we **were** in Toronto.
	Time markers go at the end of a question.	• **Was** he in Toronto **yesterday**?

STEP 3 FOCUSED PRACTICE

EXERCISE 1: Discover the Grammar

Read about the first jobs of famous people. Then underline **was, wasn't, were,** *and* **weren't.**

A new job is exciting. A first job is very exciting. A first boss and a first paycheck are hard to forget. But a first job is not always the job of your dreams. Here are the first jobs of some famous people: Mick Jagger wasn't always a singer. As a teen he was an ice cream salesman. Ray Romano, the comedian, was a bank teller. Jennifer Aniston and Madonna weren't always stars. Before they were famous, they were servers in restaurants.

And Warren Beatty, the actor, was a rat catcher in a Virginia movie theater. So maybe you're not happy with your job today. Maybe it isn't the job you really want. Don't feel bad. Just keep looking.

EXERCISE 2: Questions and Answers

(Grammar Notes 1–4)

Complete the conversation. Use **was, wasn't, were,** *or* **weren't.**

A: ___Were___ you at work yesterday?

B: No, I ________ (1.). I ________ (2.) at a job interview.

A: Oh? How ________ (3.) the interview?

B: Good, I think.

A: ________ (4.) the questions hard?

B: Well, some ________ (5.) hard, but I ________ (6.) prepared.

A: Well, that sounds good. Good luck.

B: Thanks. It sounds like a good job. How ________ (7.) school?

A: It ________ (8.) fun. I really like my classmates.

B: ________ (9.) you on time?

A: Yes, but my teacher ________ (10.) there. She was away. We had a substitute.

EXERCISE 3: Affirmative and Negative Statements

(Grammar Notes 1–3)

Complete the sentences. Change the statements from the present to the past.

1. They are busy now. Last month ___they were busy___ too.
2. It's not sunny today. ___It wasn't sunny___ yesterday either.
3. My uncle, Jun, is in Seoul now. ______________________ last year too.
4. Today it's cold. Yesterday ______________________ too.
5. She's not in class this week. ______________________ last week.
6. He's at a job interview this morning. ______________________ yesterday morning too.
7. She's in the swimming pool now. She ______________________ last Wednesday too.
8. His phone is busy. It ______________________ yesterday evening too.

EXERCISE 4: Questions and Answers

(Grammar Notes 1–5)

Complete the conversation with the words in parentheses. Use the correct form of the past of **be**.

A: ___Was David at the party Friday night___?
(David / be / at the party / Friday night)

B: ______________________.
(No, he / not)

A: ______________________?
(Where / he)

B: ______________________.
(He / in Vancouver)

A: ______________________?
(Why / he / in Vancouver)

B: ______________________.
(He / there for work)

A: ______________________?
(How / the weather / in Vancouver)

B: ______________________.
(It / terrible)

A: ______________________?
(the airport / closed)

B: ______________________.
(No, but all the planes / late)

EXERCISE 5: Editing

Correct the email. There are five mistakes. The first mistake is already corrected. Find and correct four more.

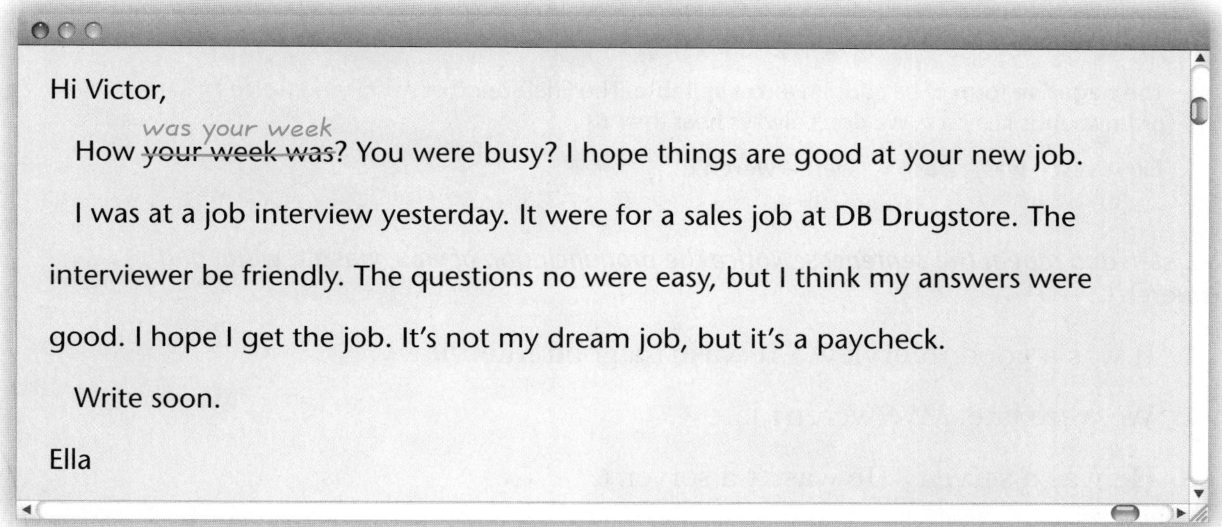

Hi Victor,

How ~~your week was~~ *was your week*? You were busy? I hope things are good at your new job.

I was at a job interview yesterday. It were for a sales job at DB Drugstore. The interviewer be friendly. The questions no were easy, but I think my answers were good. I hope I get the job. It's not my dream job, but it's a paycheck.

Write soon.

Ella

STEP 4 COMMUNICATION PRACTICE

EXERCISE 6: Listening

A | *Listen to the phone messages. Who is each message from? Check (✓) the correct column.*

	Friend	Family	Business
Message 1	✓		
Message 2			
Message 3			
Message 4			
Message 5			

B | *Listen again. Complete the quotes. Write the correct words or numbers.*

Message 1. "How was the *interview?*"

Message 2. "The __________ was great. We __________ so happy to __________ Jay."

Message 3. "The __________ in Ottawa __________."

Message 4. "Please call me at __________."

Message 5. "We were __________ with Mona."

EXERCISE 7: Pronunciation

A | *Read and listen to the Pronunciation Note.*

Pronunciation Note

The **negative** form of *be* adds an **extra syllable**. The final sound of *wasn't* and *weren't* often sounds like **/ n /**. We don't always hear the **/ t /**.

EXAMPLES: was – **wasn't** were – **weren't**

B | *Listen and repeat the sentences. Notice the pronunciation of* **was, wasn't, were,** *and* **weren't.**

1. It was a good interview. / It wasn't a good interview.
2. We were late. / We weren't late.
3. He was a server. / He wasn't a server.
4. I was an accountant. / I wasn't an accountant.

C | *Listen to the sentences. Which negative form do you hear? Check (✓) the correct box.*

	Was	Wasn't	Were	Weren't
1.		✓		
2.				
3.				
4.				
5.				

EXERCISE 8: Describing the Weather

A | *Study the words for weather.*

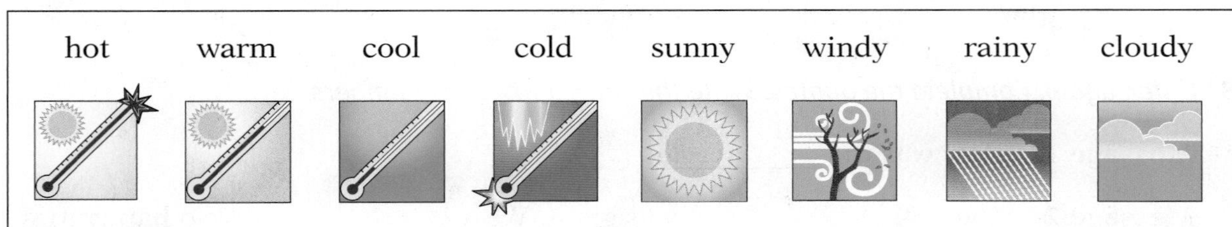

B | *PAIRS: Look at the chart below and choose a country. You are an airline flight attendant. A friend calls. Have a conversation about the weather in the country you are in. Take turns.*

A: Hello.

B: Maria? This is Bob. Where are you?

A: In ________________.

B: How's the weather?

A: Well, today it's ________________, but yesterday it was ________________.

City	Yesterday	Today
Bangkok	 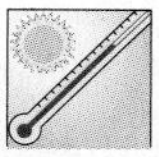	
Beijing	 	
Budapest		
Istanbul	 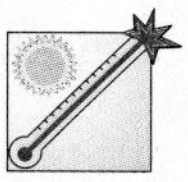	
Rio de Janeiro	 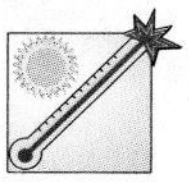	
Seoul		
Vancouver		

EXERCISE 9: Talking about the First Day of School

GROUPS: Each student says one true thing about the first day in school. Use **was, wasn't, were,** *or* **weren't** *in each sentence. Continue as long as you can.*

EXAMPLES: **A:** It was warm and sunny on the first day of class.
B: I wasn't nervous.
C: Our class was exciting.

EXERCISE 10: Writing

A | *Write an email message to a friend. Tell about last weekend. Use contractions and the past and present of* **be.**

EXAMPLE:

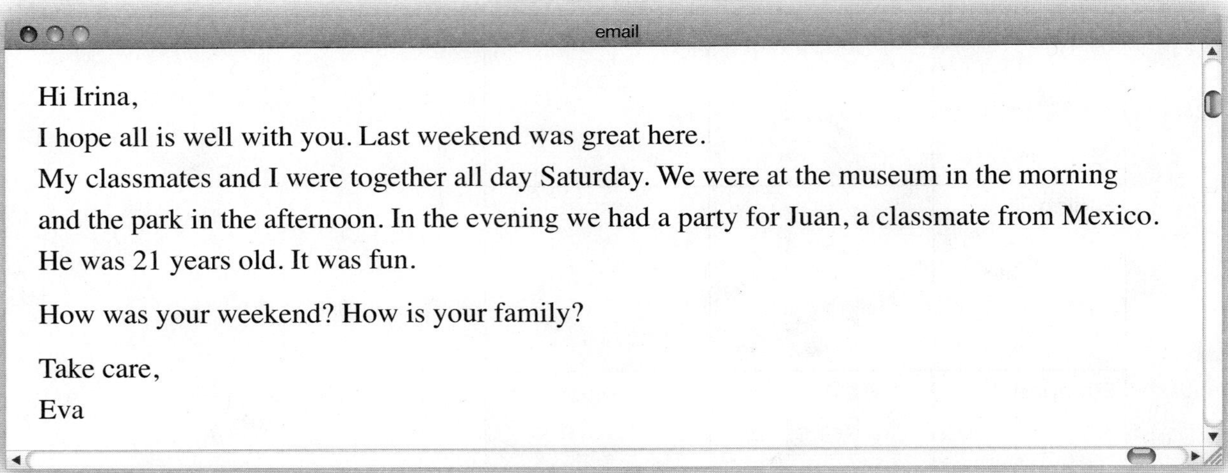

email
Hi Irina,
I hope all is well with you. Last weekend was great here.
My classmates and I were together all day Saturday. We were at the museum in the morning and the park in the afternoon. In the evening we had a party for Juan, a classmate from Mexico. He was 21 years old. It was fun.
How was your weekend? How is your family?
Take care,
Eva

B | *Check your work. Use the Editing Checklist.*

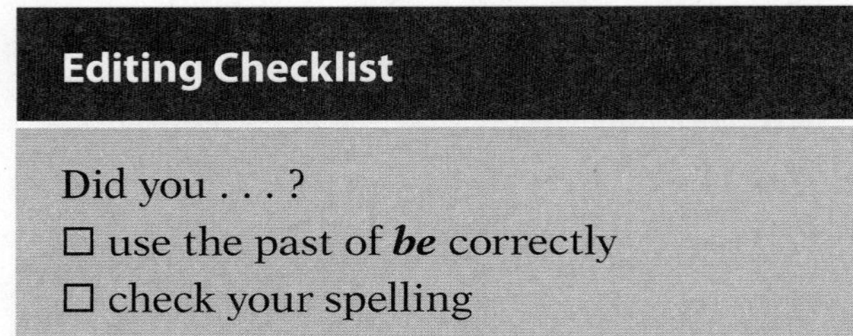

Editing Checklist
Did you . . . ?
☐ use the past of *be* correctly
☐ check your spelling

UNIT 3 Review

Check your answers on page UR-1.
Do you need to review anything?

A | *Complete the questions. Use* **was** *or* **were.**

1. When ________________ your interview?
2. Where ________________ your interview?
3. ________________ you nervous?
4. How ________________ the questions?
5. ________________ she at a job interview too?

B | *Match the questions and answers.*

____ 1. How was the weather?
____ 2. Who was there?
____ 3. Were they home all evening?
____ 4. Were you late last week?

a. No, I wasn't.
b. Jon and Sri.
c. Warm and sunny.
d. No, they weren't.

C | *Complete the conversation. Use the affirmative or negative form of* **was** *or* **were.**

A: How ________________ (1.) your weekend?

B: Great. I ________________ (2.) at the park all day Saturday.

A: ________________ (3.) you with Ali?

B: Yes, I ________________ (4.). We ________________ (5.) together all day Saturday and Sunday.

A: Ali ________________ (6.) in class this morning. Where ________________ (7.) he?

B: I don't know.

D | *Correct the paragraph. There are four mistakes.*

John is at a job interview yesterday. It were for a job at a bank. The questions no were easy, but John's answers were good. He was happy. It a good day for John.

From Grammar to Writing

CAPITALIZATION

1 | *Look at A and B. What's wrong with A?*

A	**B**
mr. john smith	Mr. John Smith
342 dryden road	342 Dryden Road
ithaca, new york	Ithaca, New York 14850

2 | *Study the information about capitalization.*

1	Use a **capital letter** for the first word in every sentence.	• **We** are new students.
2	Use capital letters for **titles**.	• This is **Mr.** Winston. • She is **Dr.** Jones.
3	Use capital letters for the names of **people** and **places** (proper nouns).	• **Lila Roberts** is from **Vancouver, Canada.**
4	Use capital letters for the names of **streets**, **cities**, **states**, **countries**, and **continents**.	• 5 **Elm Street** • **West Redding, Connecticut** • **USA** • **Africa**
5	Use a capital letter for the word ***I***.	• **I** am happy to be here.

3 | *Add capital letters.*

1. this is ms. herrera.
2. her address is 4 riverdale avenue.
3. i'm her good friend.
4. she was in bangkok and taiwan last year.

4 | *Correct the postcard from Ellen to Ruth. Add capital letters.*

Hi ruth,

john and i are in acapulco this week. it's beautiful here. the people are friendly, and the weather is great. it's sunny and warm.

last week we were in mexico city for two days. i was there on business. my meetings were long and difficult, but our evenings were fun. hope all is well with you.

Regards,

ellen

To:

ms. ruth holland

10 oldwick st.

ringwood, new jersey 07456

usa

5 | *Write a postcard to a friend. Remember to use capital letters.*

6 | *Exchange papers with a partner. Did your partner follow the directions? Correct any mistakes in grammar and spelling.*

7 | *Talk to your partner. Discuss the mistakes you made. Then rewrite your own paper and make any necessary changes.*

NOUNS, ADJECTIVES, PREPOSITIONS

UNIT	GRAMMAR FOCUS	THEME
4	Count Nouns and Proper Nouns	Photographs and Photographers
5	Descriptive Adjectives	Cave Homes
6	Prepositions of Place	Locations

UNIT 4

Count Nouns and Proper Nouns

PHOTOGRAPHS AND PHOTOGRAPHERS

STEP 1 GRAMMAR IN CONTEXT

Before You Read

PAIRS: Where do you keep your photos? Talk about a photo you have.

EXAMPLE: This is a photo of my sister. She's a nurse. She's 23 years old.

Read

Read the article about Henri Cartier-Bresson and one of his photographs.

A PHOTOGRAPHER AND A PHOTO

Henri Cartier-Bresson was **a photographer** and **an artist**. He was born in **France** in 1908. He died in 2004. At that time he was almost 96 **years** old. **Cartier-Bresson** traveled the **world**. He was in **West Africa**, the **United States**, **India**, **China**, **Egypt**, and **Russia**. His **photos** are from all over the **world**.

Cartier-Bresson is famous for "street" **photography**. Street **photographs** are about **people** in the **street** or other public **places** such as **parks** and **beaches**. They are sometimes about a special **moment** in **time**.

Look at this **photo** by **Cartier-Bresson**. Do you like it? It's **a photo** of **a woman** and **a man** on the **holiday** of **Easter**. They are both wearing fine **clothes**. The **woman** is wearing a big **hat** with many **flowers**. The man is wearing **a suit**. The **man** is looking at the **woman**. They are in **Harlem**, in **New York City**. It's 1947. **People** say **Cartier-Bresson's photos** are striking and beautiful. What do you think? Is it true for this **photo**?

After You Read

A | Practice *PAIRS: Now read the article aloud. Take turns reading each paragraph.*

B | Vocabulary *Circle the best meaning for the words in* **blue**.

1. Henri Cartier-Bresson **was born** in France.
   a. came into the world **b.** lived
2. He was **almost** 96 years old.
   a. less than **b.** more than
3. His photos are from **all over** the world.
   a. in some parts of **b.** everywhere in
4. It's a **holiday**.
   a. a day when you do not work **b.** a birthday or anniversary
5. His photos are **striking** and beautiful.
   a. very dangerous **b.** unusual and attractive
6. A holiday is a **special** time. It is exciting and different.
   a. not ordinary **b.** bad

C | Comprehension *Write* **T (True)** *or* **F (False)** *for each statement.*

_____ **1.** The place of Henri Cartier-Bresson's birth was Russia.
_____ **2.** Almost all of Cartier-Bresson's photos were of Europe.
_____ **3.** Cartier-Bresson was in many countries during his life.
_____ **4.** Cartier-Bresson is famous for "street" photography.
_____ **5.** Street photography shows people in places like parks or beaches.
_____ **6.** Harlem, New York, is not in the United States.

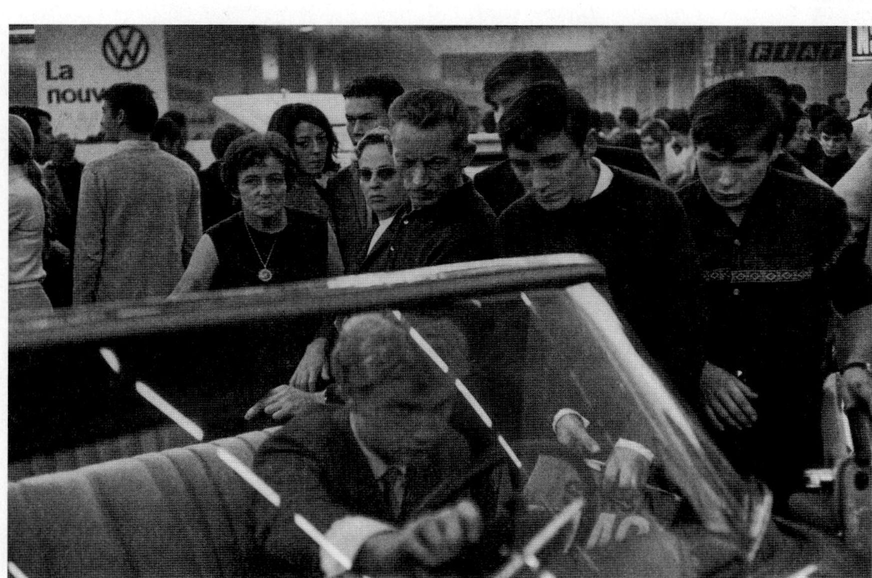

Cartier-Bresson,
Automobile Show, Paris. 1968

STEP 2 GRAMMAR PRESENTATION

SINGULAR AND PLURAL COUNT NOUNS; PROPER NOUNS

Singular Nouns	Plural Nouns
He is **a photographer**.	They are **photographers**.
He is **an artist**.	They are **artists**.

Irregular Plural Nouns	
Singular	**Plural**
man	men
woman	women
child	children
foot	feet
tooth	teeth
person	people

Proper Nouns
Harlem is in **New York City**.
The poet **Maya Angelou** has a home in **Harlem**.

GRAMMAR NOTES

1	**Nouns** are names of people, places, and things.	• a **student**, **Jung Eun** • a **country**, **Korea** • a **camera**, a **photograph**
2	**Count nouns** are easy to count. They have a singular and plural form.	• **one** photo, **two** photos, **three** photos
3	Use ***a*** before **singular count nouns** that begin with a **consonant sound** like **/ n /**, **/ b /**, **/ h /**.	• She's **a n**urse. • He's **a b**aker. • It's **a h**ouse.
	BE CAREFUL! Use ***a*** before a ***u*** that sounds like "*yew*."	• This is **a u**nit about nouns.
	Use ***an*** before singular count nouns that begin with a **vowel sound**.	• She's **an a**rtist. • He's **an e**ngineer. • It's **an u**mbrella.
	BE CAREFUL! Use ***an*** before an ***h*** that is silent.	• It's **an h**our too early. (*Hour* sounds like *our*.)

4	To form the **plural** of most **count nouns**, add *-s* or *-es*.	• one **friend** three **friends** • one **class** three **classes**
	Some nouns have irregular plural endings.	• one **man** two **men** • one **tooth** two **teeth**
	Some nouns such as *clothes, glasses, jeans, scissors* are always plural.	• My **jeans are** blue.
	Do not put *a* or *an* before plural nouns.	• They are **photos** of **friends**. NOT: They are ~~a~~ photos of ~~a~~ friends.
5	Names of specific people and places are **proper nouns**. Write these with a capital letter.	• **Paris** is in **France**. • **Harlem** is in **New York City**.
	Do not put *a* or *an* before proper nouns.	NOT: ~~A~~ Paris is in ~~a~~ France.

REFERENCE NOTES

For a discussion of **non-count nouns and *the*** (the definite article), see Unit 27 page 311.
For the **spelling and pronunciation** rules for **plural nouns**, see Appendix 5 on pages A-5–A-6.

STEP 3 FOCUSED PRACTICE

EXERCISE 1: Discover the Grammar

A | *Read the conversation.*

MIKE: Is that you in the photo?

DOUG: Yes, it is. It's a photo of me with friends from college.

MIKE: Where are they now?

DOUG: Well, the woman on the left, Jasmine, is in Brazil.

MIKE: Really?

DOUG: Uh-huh. She's a teacher there. And the guy on the right, Bob, is here in New York. He's an accountant.

MIKE: Who's the woman in the center?

DOUG: That's Amy. She's a street photographer. Her camera is always with her. What a life! She travels all over the world. Last month she was in India. Before that she was in Central America. Now her photos are in a show at the library here.

MIKE: I'd love to see them.

DOUG: Them? Or her?

B | *Look back at the conversation in Part A. Find these nouns and write them:*

1. One noun that begins with a vowel: ________________

2. Two singular nouns that begin with a consonant (not proper nouns):

________________, ________________

3. Two proper nouns: ________________, ________________

4. Two plural nouns: ________________, ________________

EXERCISE 2: *A* or *An*

(Grammar Note 3)

A | *Write* **a** *or* **an** *before each word.*

1. ____ man

2. ____ hand

3. ____ hat

4. ____ earring

5. ____ flower

6. ____ suit

7. ____ eye

8. ____ ear

9. ____ lip

10. ____ woman

B | *Look at the photo,* Harlem, 1947. *Label the parts of the photo with the words from Part A. Number them* **1–10.**

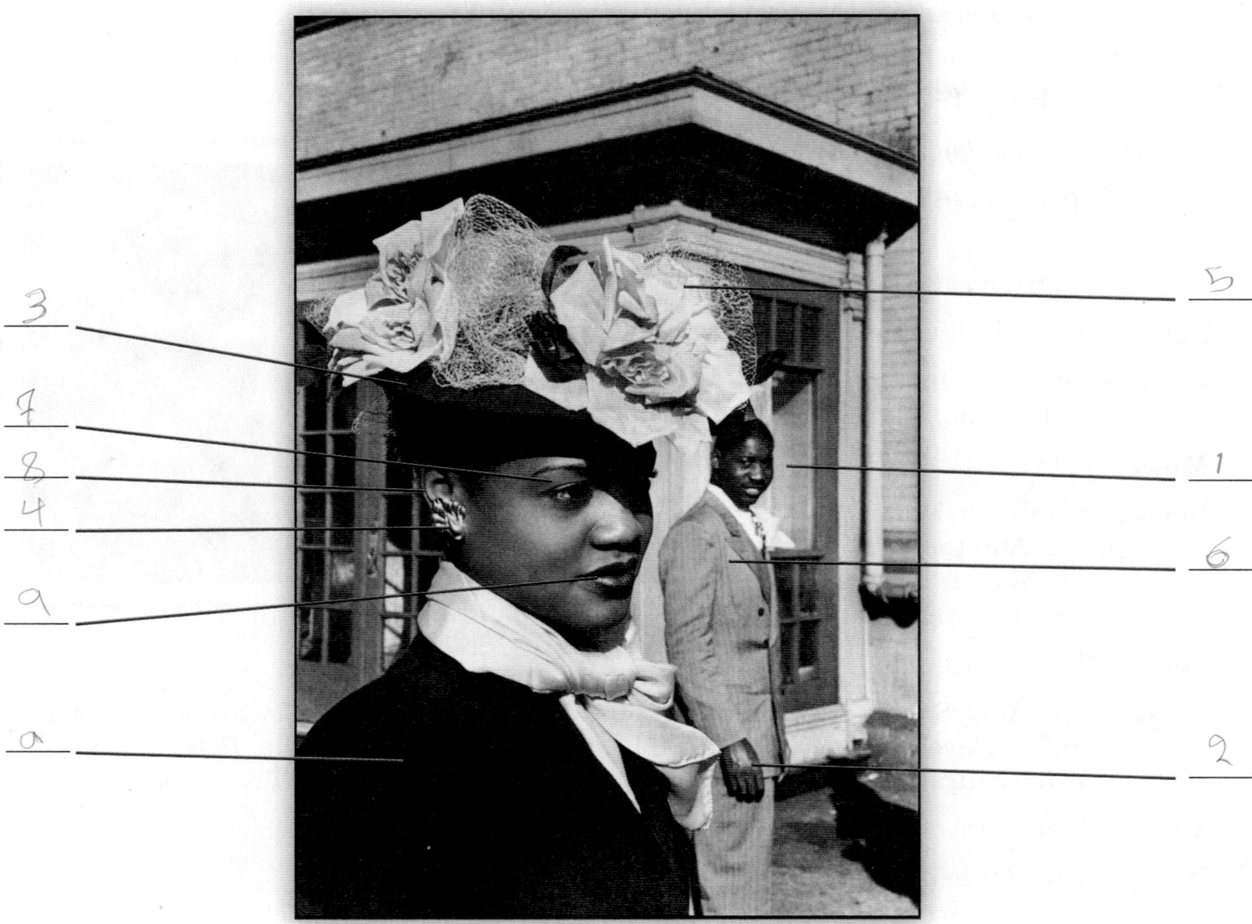

EXERCISE 3: *A* or *An*

(Grammar Notes 3–5)

Complete the sentences with **a** *or* **an**. *Write* **Ø** *if you don't need* **a** *or* **an**.

1. Henri Cartier-Bresson was __a__ photographer.
2. Cartier-Bresson and Ansel Adams were __Ø__ photographers.
3. Cartier-Bresson was __an__ artist too.
4. All good photographers are __Ø__ artists.
5. Adams was __a__ pianist before he was __a__ photographer.
6. Adams was born in __Ø__ San Francisco, California.
7. For Adams, photography began with __a__ trip to Yosemite National Park.
8. __Ø__ Cartier-Bresson was born in __Ø__ Normandy.
9. __Ø__ Normandy is in __Ø__ France.
10. Cartier-Bresson has __Ø__ photos in the Louvre Museum.

EXERCISE 4: Regular and Irregular Plural Nouns

(Grammar Note 4)

Complete the sentences with the nouns from the box. Use the correct form. Look at the spelling rules for plural nouns in Appendix 5 on page A-5 for help.

artist	class	country	fish	life	person
~~city~~	clothes	earrings	flower	museum	watch

1. San Francisco and Los Angeles are __cities__ in California.
2. Brazil and France are __Countries__.
3. The Louvre and the Prado are __musems__.
4. Seiko and Rolex are kinds of __watches__.
5. Your photos of __fish__ in the water are striking.
6. There are two __people__, a man and a woman, in the photo *Harlem, 1947*.
7. The woman in *Harlem, 1947* has a hat with __flowers__.
8. Her jewelry is beautiful, especially her __earrings__.
9. The man and woman in the photo *Harlem, 1947* are wearing fine __clothes__.
10. Many __artists__ and photographers live in New York City.
11. The __life__ of famous artists are interesting to read.
12. I like photography. I'm taking two photography __Classes__ at The New School in New York.

EXERCISE 5: Proper Nouns

(Grammar Note 5)

Change small letters to capital letters where necessary.

MIKE: Hi, are you ~~amy~~ *Amy* lan?

AMY: Yes, I am.

MIKE: I'm mike cho. I work with Doug.

AMY: Nice to meet you, mike.

MIKE: It's nice to meet you. Your photos are great.

AMY: Thanks. So, mike, are you from phoenix?

MIKE: No, I'm not. I'm from san francisco. I'm here for the Labor Day holiday.

AMY: Oh, san francisco is beautiful. I was there last year.

MIKE: Doug says you travel a lot.

AMY: Yes, I do. I was in india last year. And the year before that I was in almost every country in Central America.

MIKE: That's great.

AMY: Do you travel?

MIKE: When I can. I was in mexico last november during the thanksgiving vacation, and I was in canada with my family for a week last summer.

AMY: Any photos?

MIKE: No. My dad's brother sam is the photographer in our family.

EXERCISE 6: Editing

Correct the sentences. There are nine mistakes. The first mistake is already corrected. Find and correct eight more.

1. Henri Cartier-Bresson's photos are often of famous ~~person~~ *people*.
2. This is photo of Henri Matisse.
3. Henri Matisse was great artist.
4. Before Matisse was artist, he was lawyer.
5. Matisse's paintings are in museum all over the world.

Matisse and His Doves, 1944

6. In this photo Matisse is in the south of france.
7. We see four bird outside their cages.

STEP 4 COMMUNICATION PRACTICE

EXERCISE 7: Pronunciation

A | *Read and listen to the Pronunciation Note.*

Pronunciation Note

When **nouns are plural**, the **ending** can have one of three sounds: **/ s /**, **/ z /**, or **/ ɪz /**.

Examples: students / **s** /
teachers / **z** /
buses / **ɪz** /

B | *Listen and complete each sentence with the correct word from the box. Then listen again and check the ending of the sound that you hear.*

artists	books	boxes	classes	glasses	~~photos~~	scissors

	/ s /	/ z /	/ ɪz /
1. The photos are ready.	☐	☑	☐
2. Her art ________ are from 10:00 to 1:00.	☐	☐	☐
3. Be careful. The ________ are sharp.	☐	☐	☐
4. The ________ are full of old photos.	☐	☐	☐
5. The paintings are by different ________.	☐	☐	☐
6. I need my ________ to see the names of the artists.	☐	☐	☐
7. I have some interesting ________ about Africa in that bookcase.	☐	☐	☐

C | *Listen again and repeat.*

EXERCISE 8: Listening

A | *Listen to a conversation between Doug and Lily. What is Lily telling Doug about? Circle the correct letter.*

a. a birthday party

b. a holiday

c. a family photo

B | *Listen again. Then read the questions. Circle the correct letter.*

1. Who are the people in the photo?

   a. Lily's family and friends   **(b.)** Lily's family

2. What is the holiday?

   a. Easter   **b.** Thanksgiving

3. Who is the photographer?

   a. a cousin   **b.** an uncle

4. When is Lily's birthday?

   a. before Thanksgiving   **b.** after Thanksgiving

5. What is in the boxes?

   a. gifts   **b.** games

EXERCISE 9: Game: Describing Things

PAIRS: Look at these things. You have 15 minutes. Together list as many nouns as you can. The pair with the most correct nouns wins.

EXERCISE 10: Game: Comparing Choices

A | *PAIRS: Name the following people, places, and things.*

an artist or a photographer	
a music band	
three countries	
three things in your class	
three parts of the body	
two holidays	
three occupations	
two electronic items	

B | *Compare your choices with those of another pair. How many of the same choices do you have?*

EXERCISE 11: Writing

A | *Write a paragraph about a photo of a person you know. Tell about the person. Tell about the photo.*

Example: This is a photo of my grandmother. She was born in China in 1945. She lives in Los Angeles now. She was a dancer. In this photo she's in her garden. It was her birthday. My grandmother is old, but she is still a striking woman.

B | *Check your work. Use the Editing Checklist.*

Editing Checklist

Did you . . . ?

- ☐ use singular and plural count nouns and proper nouns correctly
- ☐ check your spelling

UNIT 4 Review

Check your answers on page UR-1.
Do you need to review anything?

A | *Complete the sentences. Use* **a, an,** *or Ø.*

1. This is ____ photo of my best friend.
2. He is ____ actor.
3. He is ____ talented.
4. His friends are ____ actors too.
5. They all are ____ hardworking.

B | *Complete the sentences with the words from the box. Use the plural form.*

city	clothes	fish	person	watch

1. My favorite ________________ are Venice and Rio de Janeiro.
2. The two ________________ in the photograph show midnight.
3. The ________________ in the photos are from the 1980s, so the photos are probably from that time.
4. We take photos of the ________________ in the sea with our underwater camera.
5. We see three ________________ in the photo: a man and two women.

C | *Add capital letters where necessary.*

Ali: Hi, are you the photographer?
Amy: Yes, I'm Amy lin.
Ali: Nice to meet you. I'm ali Mohammed.
Amy: Are you from london?
Ali: Yes, I am. I'm here for your thanksgiving Day holiday.

D | *Correct the paragraph. There are six mistakes.*

Melanie Einzig is artist and an photographer. She was born in Minnesota, but lives in New york. Einzig captures moments in time. Her photograph are striking. They are in museum in San francisco, Chicago, and Princeton.

UNIT 5

Descriptive Adjectives

Cave Homes

STEP 1 GRAMMAR IN CONTEXT

Before You Read

Look at the photographs on this page. What words describe them?

beautiful **boring** **exciting** **ordinary** **ugly** **unusual**

Read

Read the online article about an interesting place.

rock formations

underground caves

Cappadocia, a Place of Mystery

This place is like another world, but it is here on Earth. It's so **different**, it's **awesome**. What is this place? It's Cappadocia, in Turkey. Why is it so **different**? What's so **unusual** about it? **Beautiful** rock formations and **underground** cities make it a very **special** place.

Cappadocia has a **long** history. Many people lived in the **underground** cities to be **safe** from enemies.[1] These cities were **big**. One city, Derinkuyu, had room for more than 30,000 people.

Today only a few people live in these cave homes in **underground** cities. But many people from all over the world visit them. They are full of **interesting** things to see. From above, Cappadocia looks like another world, like a *Star Wars* movie.

The weather in Cappadocia is **comfortable** all year long. It has **warm**, **dry** summers and **cold**, **snowy** winters. There is a **big** difference between day and night temperatures. The **average** summer temperature is 73 degrees Fahrenheit, and the **average** winter temperature is 28 degrees Fahrenheit.

Awesome underground cities, **beautiful** rock formations, and an **interesting** history—these things make Cappadocia a place you won't forget.

[1] ***enemies:*** people who want to hurt you

After You Read

A | Practice *PAIRS: Now read the online article aloud. Take turns reading each paragraph.*

B | Vocabulary *Complete the sentences with the words from the box.*

average	awesome	comfortable	dry	safe	unusual

1. The ______________________ of the numbers 20, 25, and 30 is 25.
2. Be careful. It is not ______________________ to walk there.
3. That rock formation looks like a camel. It is ______________________.
4. Bring water. It is hot and ______________________ there.
5. We were happy with our hotel. It wasn't special, but it was ______________________.
6. I bought a(n) ______________________ rug in Turkey. It's very different from other rugs.

C | Comprehension *Read the questions. Circle the correct letter.*

1. Where is Cappadocia?
   a. not on this earth
   b. in Turkey
2. Why is Cappadocia so unusual?
   a. It has interesting rocks and cities under the ground.
   b. The people are awesome and the plants are beautiful.
3. How many people lived in Derinkuyu in the past?
   a. over 3,000
   b. over 30,000
4. Why does Cappadocia look like a scene from the movie *Star Wars*?
   a. The area looks like another world.
   b. It is a beautiful place with many rock formations.
5. How is the weather in Cappadocia?
   a. cool in summer and very cold in winter
   b. warm in summer and cold in winter

STEP 2 GRAMMAR PRESENTATION

DESCRIPTIVE ADJECTIVES

Noun	*Be*	Adjective
The room	is	**small.**
The rooms	are	

	Adjective	Noun
It is a	**small**	room.
They are		rooms.

GRAMMAR NOTES

1	**Adjectives** describe nouns.	• **Cappadocia** (NOUN) is **beautiful** (ADJECTIVE). • It's a **beautiful** (ADJECTIVE) **place** (NOUN).
2	Adjectives can come • after the verb ***be*** • before a noun	• The room is **big**. • It's a **big** room. NOT: It's a ~~room big.~~
3	**BE CAREFUL!** Do not add ***-s*** to adjectives.	• a **hot** summer, a **cold** winter • **hot** summers, **cold** winters NOT: ~~colds winters~~
4	For **adjective** + **noun**: Use ***a*** before the adjective if the adjective begins with a **consonant sound**. Use ***an*** before the adjective if the adjective begins with a **vowel sound**.	 • It's **a b**eautiful place. • It's **an u**nusual place.
5	Some adjectives end in ***-ing***, ***-ly***, or ***-ed***.	• It's **interesting**. • They're **friendly**. • We're **tired**.

EXERCISE 1: Discover the Grammar

Maria is visiting Turkey. Read her travel blog about her hotel in Cappadocia. Underline eleven more adjectives.

maria.blogspot.com

I'm at a cave hotel in Cappadocia. Gamirasu Cave Hotel is in a traditional village. In the past it was a cave home. Now it's a hotel. The hotel is in a small village in the center of Cappadocia. My cave room is fun. It's old but has a modern bathroom and Internet service! The rooms are not expensive. The price of the room includes a delicious breakfast and dinner. The food is good. The service is good too—the people are helpful and friendly. Also, it's easy to visit all of Cappadocia from the hotel. It was a great choice.

EXERCISE 2: Word Order

(Grammar Notes 1–5)

Complete the conversations with the words in parentheses. Remember to use a capital letter at the start of each sentence.

1. **A:** Where are we?

   B: *We are at an old market.*
   (market / at / we / are / old / an)

2. **A:** ______________________ Are they for sale?
   (awesome / carpets / the / are)

   B: Yes, they are.

3. **A:** How are the prices? Are they expensive?

   B: No, ______________________
   (the / prices / reasonable / are)

4. **A:** How's the weather?

   B: ______________________
   (warm / it / and / sunny / is)

5. **A:** How are you?

   B: ______________________
   (tired / happy / I'm / but)

EXERCISE 3: Sentences with Adjectives

(Grammar Notes 1–5)

Write sentences with the words in parentheses. Add the correct form of the verb **be**. *Add* **a** *if necessary.*

1. Ali Baba Kitchen is a good restaurant.
   (Ali Baba Kitchen / good restaurant)

2. ______________________________
   (the food / delicious)

3. ______________________________
   (the waiters / friendly and helpful)

4. ______________________________
   (the Bilton / comfortable hotel)

5. ______________________________
   (the rooms / not expensive)

6. ______________________________
   (the outdoor market / safe)

7. ______________________________
   (the carpets / expensive)

8. ______________________________
   (that / beautiful carpet)

9. ______________________________
   (the climate / mild)

10. ______________________________
   (the weather / comfortable all year round)

EXERCISE 4: Editing

Correct the conversation. There are five mistakes. The first mistake is already corrected. Find and correct four more.

A: Is that a ~~lamp new~~ new lamp?

B: Yes, it is. It's from Turkey.

A: The colors are beautifuls.

B: Thanks. I got it at old market in Cappadocia.

A: Were there many things interesting to buy?

B: Yes. These plates are from the market too.

A: The colors unusual. I like them a lot.

B: Here. This one is for you.

STEP 4 COMMUNICATION PRACTICE

EXERCISE 5: Listening

A | *Listen to the conversation. Sun Hi is talking to her friend Russ. What are they talking about? Circle the correct letter.*

a. Russ and Sun Hi's vacation

b. Sun Hi's visit to a national park

c. unusual places

B | *Listen again. Complete the sentences. Circle the correct letter.*

1. Sun Hi says Mesa Verde is ________________.

(**a.**) awesome **b.** awful

2. The homes in the mountains are very ________________.

a. cold **b.** old

3. The hotel is ________________.

a. clean **b.** nice

4. The weather is ________________.

a. warm **b.** cold

5. The park is ________________.

a. crowded **b.** not crowded

EXERCISE 6: Pronunciation

A | *Read and listen to the Pronunciation Note.*

Pronunciation Note

Words have one or more **syllables**.

Examples: hat happy

One syllable in a word is always **stressed**. Stressed syllables are long and loud.

Example: happy

B | *Listen and repeat each adjective.*

One syllable	Two syllables	Three syllables	Four syllables
cold	boring	usual beautiful expensive important	traditional

C | *Listen and mark the stressed syllable in each word.*

1. ugly
2. warm
3. unusual
4. friendly
5. modern
6. cheap
7. unimportant

D | *PAIRS: Take turns. Name an adjective from Parts B and C. Your partner names the opposite.*

EXAMPLE: **A:** Ugly.
B: Beautiful!

EXERCISE 7: Guided Conversation

GROUPS: Each student writes the name of a city or place he or she knows well. The group asks questions about the place. Use the adjectives in Exercise 6 and the rest of the unit.

EXAMPLE: **A:** Woodside, Queens, in New York City.
B: Are the homes in Woodside expensive?
C: Are the people friendly?
D: Is the weather mild?

EXERCISE 8: Writing

A | *Write a paragraph about an interesting place. Use* **be** *and adjectives.*

EXAMPLE: JeJu Island is in South Korea. It is a popular vacation place. Many Koreans go to this island on their honeymoon. The people are friendly, and the climate is mild. It's a good place for hiking and horseback riding. It's safe and the beaches are awesome.

B | *Check your work. Use the Editing Checklist.*

Editing Checklist

Did you . . . ?

☐ use the correct form of descriptive adjectives

☐ use the correct word order with descriptive adjectives

☐ check your spelling

UNIT 5 Review

Check your answers on page UR-1.
Do you need to review anything?

A | *Complete the sentences. Add* **a, an,** *or* **Ø**.

1. Mesa Verde has ____ long history.
2. We like to visit ____ big cities.
3. Miami has ____ hot, humid summers.
4. It is ____ interesting place.
5. The Grand Canyon has ____ beautiful rock formations.

B | *Complete the sentences. Circle the correct letter.*

1. We are at ____________________.
   - **a.** a hotel small
   - **b.** small hotel
   - **c.** a small hotel
2. The hotel has ____________________.
   - **a.** an interesting garden
   - **b.** an garden interesting
   - **c.** a garden interesting
3. Our room is ____________________.
   - **a.** a big and a comfortable
   - **b.** big and comfortable
   - **c.** a big and comfortable
4. The people here are ____________________.
   - **a.** kinds and helpful
   - **b.** kinds and helpfuls
   - **c.** kind and helpful
5. It was ____________________
   - **a.** a choice great
   - **b.** a great choice
   - **c.** great choice

C | *Write sentences with the words in parentheses.*

1. (museum / I'm / the / at / new) ______________________________
2. (full of / to see / things / interesting / It is) ______________________________
3. (bowls / unusual / from / It has / long ago) ______________________________
4. (has / It / carpets / beautiful / too) ______________________________
5. (place / is / to visit / The museum / a great) ______________________________

D | *Correct the paragraph. There are five mistakes.*

The Grand Canyon National Park in Arizona is a awesome place to visit. Almost five million people visit this park unusual each year. The weather is good in the late spring and summer, but it crowded is during those months. There are seven differents places to stay in the park. I like El Tovar. It is a old hotel with a great view.

UNIT 6

Prepositions of Place

LOCATIONS

STEP 1 GRAMMAR IN CONTEXT

Before You Read

PAIRS: Answer the questions. Look at the map to answer questions 1 and 2.

1. Where is the Chinese Garden? Where are the African Masks?
2. Where are the rest rooms?
3. Is there an art museum in your city? Where is it? What kind of art is there?
4. What kind of art do you like?

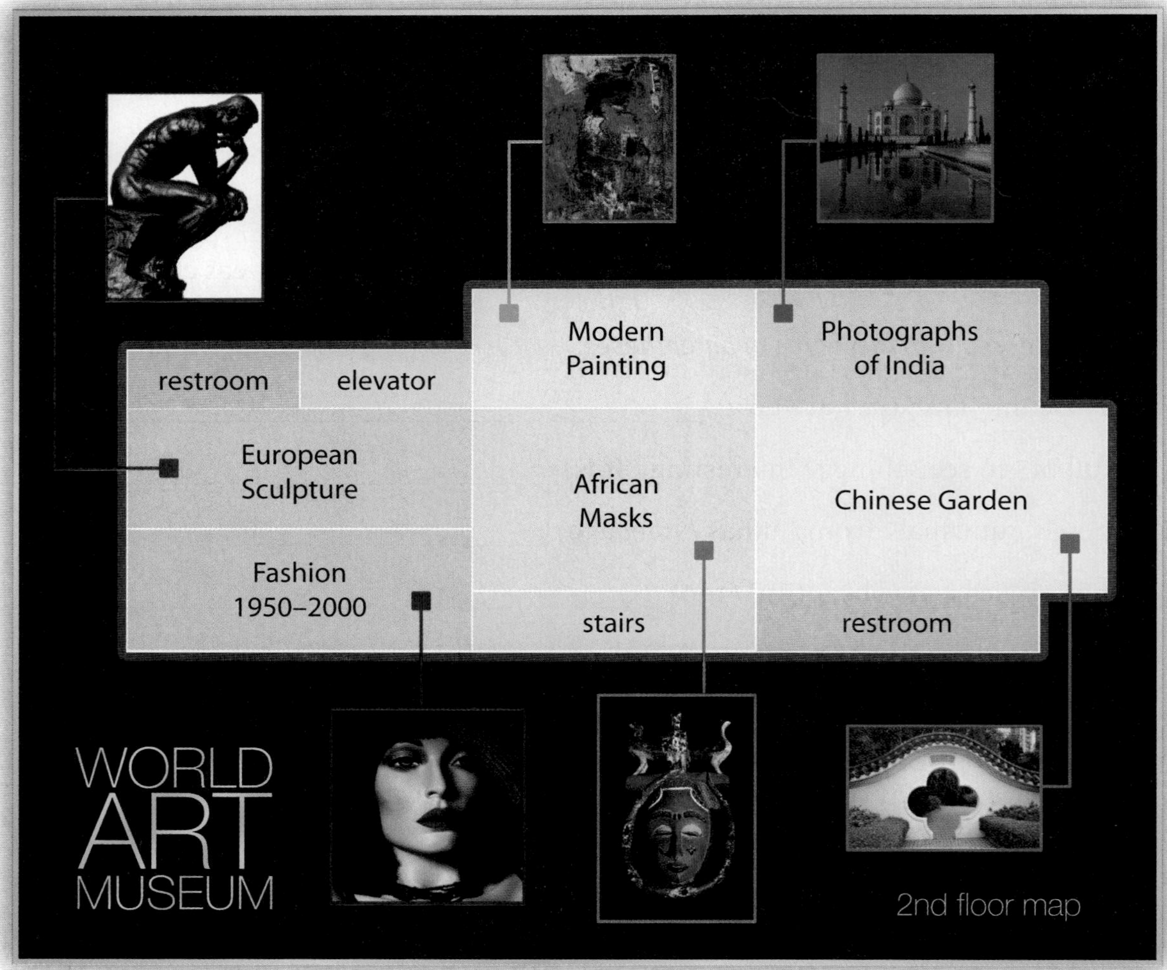

Read

 *Read Marina's posting and the conversation between Marina and a museum guard.*

Marina Olitskaya

WALL
FRIENDS
PHOTOS

Marina Olitskaya Hey everyone. I want new glasses, and I need an eye exam. Any suggestions?[1] What's the best place to go?
September 3 at 10:16am · Comment · Like

George Rami Try *Your Color Eyes*. It's **at** 7 East 89th Street, **between** Madison and Fifth Avenue. The doctor there is really good. His name is Dr. Green. And the glasses are a great deal.[2]
September 3 at 12:31pm · Like

Marina Olitskaya So that's **near** the World Art Museum? Great! I'll go to the museum after I see the doctor. I want to see their African masks. Are you free then?
September 3 at 1:15pm · Like

At the Museum

Marina: Excuse me, where are the African masks?

Guard: They're **on** the second floor. We're **on** the first floor.

Marina: OK.

Guard: So take the elevator or the stairs. The elevator is **on your left**, **behind** the gift shop. The stairs are **on your right**, **in back of** the information booth.[3] Then go up one flight.[4] The African Masks are just **up the stairs**. They're **between** the sculpture and the Chinese garden.

Marina: Great. Oh, I'm sorry, one more thing. Where's . . .

Guard: The restroom?

Marina: No, the cafeteria. I'm starving.[5]

---

[1] ***suggestions:*** ideas
[2] ***a great deal:*** not very expensive
[3] ***information booth:*** a place where people ask questions
[4] ***go up one flight:*** go one floor upstairs.
[5] ***I'm starving:*** I'm very hungry.

After You Read

A | Practice *PAIRS: Now read the posting and the conversation aloud. Take turns reading each part.*

B | Vocabulary *Complete the conversations with the words from the box. Use the correct form.*

appointment	be free	cafeteria	flight	restroom	sculpture

1. A: I'm hungry. Where's the ________________?

B: Downstairs.

2. A: What do you make in your ________________ class?

B: We make things from stone or metal.

3. A: Where is the garden with the unusual flowers?

B: It's one ________________ up, on the second floor.

4. A: Are you busy Thursday?

B: No, I ________________.

5. A: Where's Marina?

B: At the eye doctor, I think. Her ________________ is at 3:00.

6. A: Is the ________________ in the back of the cafeteria?

B: No, it's in the front, next to the elevator.

C | Comprehension *Write* **T (True)**, **F (False)**, *or* **? (it doesn't say)** *for each statement.*

_____ **1.** Dr. Green's office is on 98th Street.

_____ **2.** The glasses at *Your Color Eyes* are expensive.

_____ **3.** The African masks are on the second floor.

_____ **4.** The stairs are next to the elevator.

_____ **5.** At the museum, Marina is hungry.

_____ **6.** The cafeteria is closed.

STEP 2 GRAMMAR PRESENTATION

PREPOSITIONS OF PLACE

The glasses are **between** the book and the watch.

The glasses are **next to** the newspaper.

The glasses are **behind** the box.

The glasses are **under** the table.

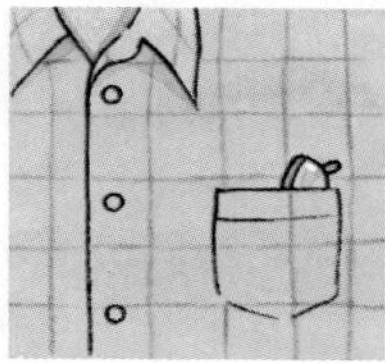

The glasses are **in** his pocket.

The glasses are **on** the table **near** the window.

The man is **in back of** the woman.

The man is **in front of** the woman.

GRAMMAR NOTES

1

Prepositions of place tell where something is.
Some common prepositions of place are:

in	*on your left*
in front of	*behind*
in back of	*between*
on	*near*
on your right	*next to*

- My bag is **under** my seat.
- Your umbrella is **near** the door.

(continued on next page)

2	For **prepositions in addresses**, use:	
	in before a country, a state, a province, a city, a room number	• He's **in** Canada. He's **in** British Columbia. • He's **in** Vancouver. He's **in** room 302.
	on before a street, an avenue, a road	• It's **on** Main Street. It's **on** 10th Avenue.
	at before a building number	• We're **at** 78 Main Street.
	on the before a floor	• We're **on the** second floor.
	on the corner of before a street or streets	• It's **on the corner of** Main Street.
	USAGE NOTE: In informal conversation, *street* or *avenue* is dropped.	• It's on the corner of **Main Street** and **Mott Avenue**. • It's on the corner of **Main** and **Mott**.
3	For **prepositions before places** use:	
	in school OR ***at*** school	• I'm **in** school from 9 to 11. • I'm **at** school now.
	at work	• She's **at** work right now.
	at home OR home	• No one is **at** home. OR No one is home.

REFERENCE NOTE

For lists of ordinal and cardinal numbers, see Appendix 3 on page A-3.

STEP 3 FOCUSED PRACTICE

EXERCISE 1: Discover the Grammar

Look at the eye chart. Then answer the questions to find the message. There are three words.

E

R T N

I L W O V

E G S L I P H

1. The first word has one letter. This letter is next to an *L*. It isn't a *W* or an *S*. What's the word? ______I______

2. The second word has four letters. The first letter is between the *S* and an *I*. The second letter is under the *N*. The third letter is a *V*. A *T* is under the last letter. What's the word? ________________

3. The third word has seven letters. A *T* is under the first letter. The second letter is an *N*. The third letter is between an *E* and the *S*. The fourth letter is an *L*. The fifth letter is an *I*. The sixth letter is between the *L* and the *G*. The last letter is an *H*. What's the word? ________________

4. What's the message? ___ ___ ___ ___ ___ ___ ___ ___ ___ ___ ___ ___ ___!

EXERCISE 2: Prepositions of Place

(Grammar Notes 1–2)

Look at the map. Complete the sentences with the words from the box.

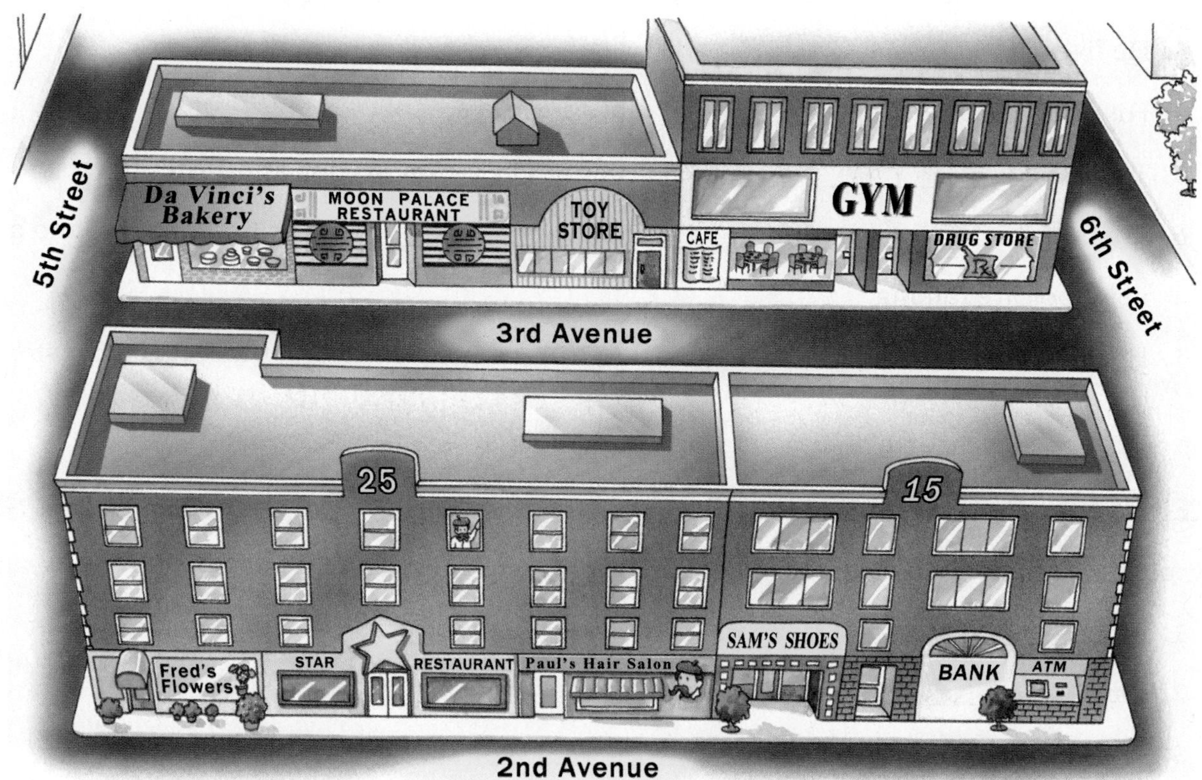

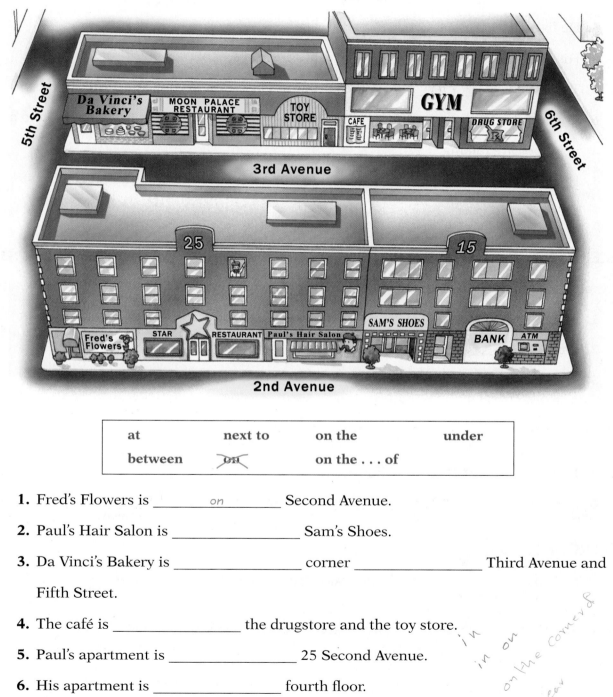

at	next to	on the	under
between	~~on~~	on the . . . of	

1. Fred's Flowers is ___*on*___ Second Avenue.

2. Paul's Hair Salon is ________________ Sam's Shoes.

3. Da Vinci's Bakery is ________________ corner ________________ Third Avenue and Fifth Street.

4. The café is ________________ the drugstore and the toy store.

5. Paul's apartment is ________________ 25 Second Avenue.

6. His apartment is ________________ fourth floor.

7. The café and drug store are ________________ a gym.

EXERCISE 3: Prepositions of Place

(Grammar Notes 1–3)

Complete the sentences. Choose from the words in the box. Use some words more than once.

at	between	in	of	on

1. My best friend lives in an apartment ___*in*___ Lakeville.
2. He lives ________ 435 East Water Street.
3. He lives ________ the third floor.
4. His apartment is ________ a library and a bank.
5. The bank is ________ the corner of Lexington Avenue and 77th Street.
6. My friend is now ________ front ________ his building. He and a neighbor are talking.
7. His neighbor's little boy is ________ school for the first time. It is a big step for him.

EXERCISE 4: Prepositions of Place

(Grammar Notes 1–3)

Complete the sentences. Write true sentences.

1. I am ___*in*___ school.
2. I am ________ room ________.
3. My classroom is ________________________________.
   (floor)
4. My school is ________________________________.
   (school address)
5. I am not ________ home. I'm not ________ work.
6. I am in ________________, in ________________
   (your city) **(your country)**

EXERCISE 5: Editing

Correct the conversations. There are six mistakes. The first mistake is already corrected. Find and correct five more.

1. **A:** I'm in school until 2:00, but I'm free after that. Let's go to the Modern Art Museum.

   B: OK. Where is it?

   A: It's ~~in~~ *on* Fifth Avenue between Eight and Ninth Streets.

2. **A:** Excuse me. Are the masks the third floor?

B: I don't know. Ask at the Information Booth.

A: Where is that?

B: It's in front the stairs, near to the gift shop.

And the sculptures are on the second floor, in back the paintings.

STEP 4 COMMUNICATION PRACTICE

EXERCISE 6: Pronunciation

A | *Read and listen to the Pronunciation Note.*

Pronunciation Note

Stressed words are longer and louder. Sometimes we stress words to make our meaning clear.

EXAMPLE: I'm not at school. I'm at the museum.

B | *Listen and mark a dot (•) over the stressed words.*

1. I'm on the first floor. I'm not on the fifth floor.
2. I'm on the first floor. He's on the fifth floor.
3. The museum is on Fifth Street. It's not on Fifth Avenue.
4. The museum is on Fifth Street. The library is on Fifth Avenue.
5. Your glasses are on the table. Your gloves are in the drawer.

C | *Listen and repeat each sentence.*

EXERCISE 7: Listening

A | *Look at the world map in Appendix 1 on pages A-0–A-1. Listen to the locations of countries. Find the countries on the map. Write the countries.*

1. __ __ __ __ __
2. __ __ __ __ __ __ __
3. __ __ __ __ __ __ __ __ __ __
4. __ __ __ __ __

B | *Listen again. Then compare your answers with a partner's.*

EXERCISE 8: Guessing Countries

A | *PAIRS: Write sentences about a country's location. Use the prepositions* **between, near, next to,** *and* **in.**

B | *Join another group. They guess the country. (See the map in Appendix 1, pages A-0—A-1.)*

EXAMPLE: This country is in Central America. It is between Costa Rica and Colombia. What country is it?

EXERCISE 9: Game: Describing Locations

GROUPS: Name a place everyone knows. Each student describes its location in a different way. The group with the most correct sentences wins.

EXAMPLE: **Central Park**
A: It's between Fifth Avenue and Central Park West.
B: It's in New York.
C: It's near our school.
D: It's between 59th Street and 110th Street.

EXERCISE 10: Writing

A | *Write an invitation to a party. Give the address and nearby places. Use prepositions with addresses and locations.*

EXAMPLE:

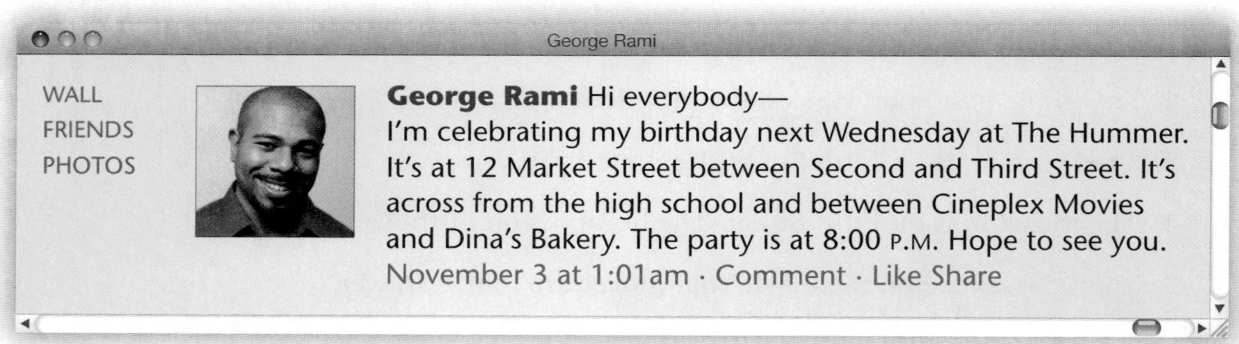

George Rami
WALL
FRIENDS
PHOTOS
George Rami Hi everybody—
I'm celebrating my birthday next Wednesday at The Hummer. It's at 12 Market Street between Second and Third Street. It's across from the high school and between Cineplex Movies and Dina's Bakery. The party is at 8:00 P.M. Hope to see you.
November 3 at 1:01am · Comment · Like Share

B | *Check your work. Use the Editing Checklist.*

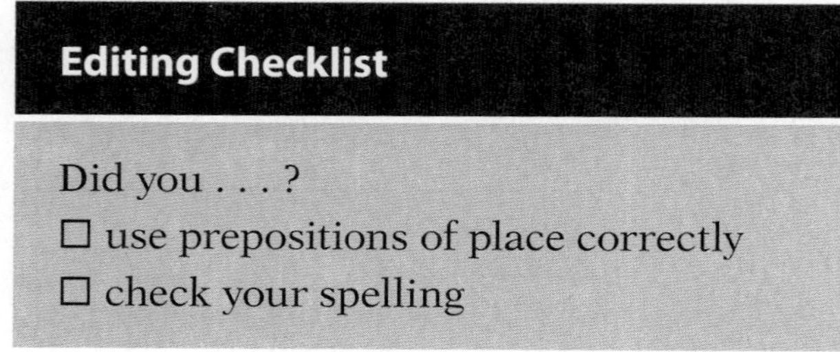

Editing Checklist
Did you . . . ?
☐ use prepositions of place correctly
☐ check your spelling

UNIT 6 Review

Check your answers on page UR-2.
Do you need to review anything?

A | *Look at the picture. Complete the sentences with the words from the box.*

behind	in front of	next to	on	under

1. The book is _______________ the table.
2. The glasses are _______________ the table.
3. The cup is _______________ the book.
4. A watch is _______________ the book.
5. A pencil is _______________ the book.

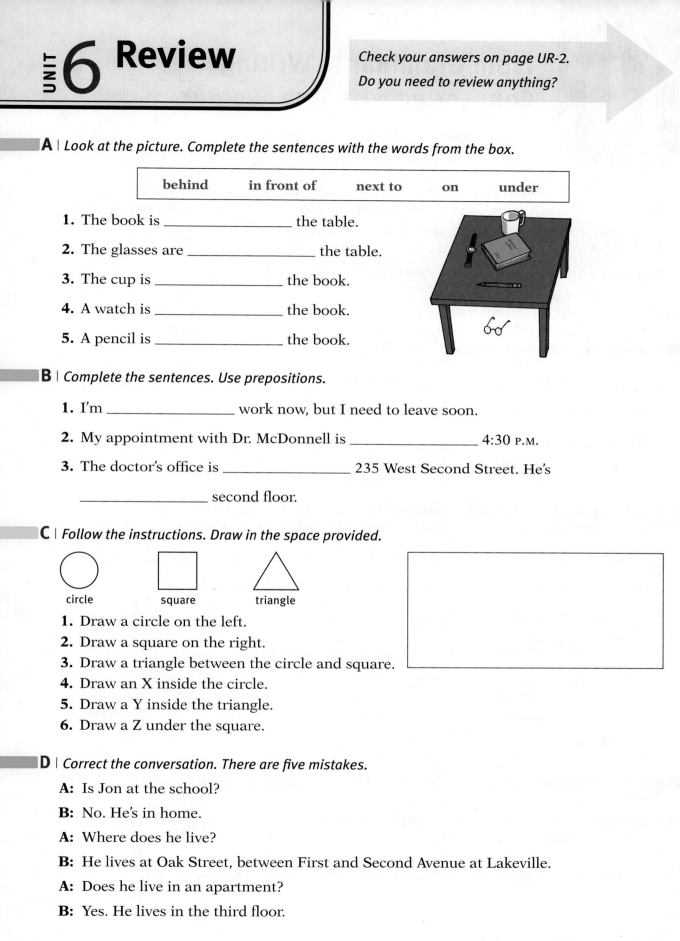

B | *Complete the sentences. Use prepositions.*

1. I'm _______________ work now, but I need to leave soon.
2. My appointment with Dr. McDonnell is _______________ 4:30 P.M.
3. The doctor's office is _______________ 235 West Second Street. He's _______________ second floor.

C | *Follow the instructions. Draw in the space provided.*

circle   square   triangle

1. Draw a circle on the left.
2. Draw a square on the right.
3. Draw a triangle between the circle and square.
4. Draw an X inside the circle.
5. Draw a Y inside the triangle.
6. Draw a Z under the square.

D | *Correct the conversation. There are five mistakes.*

A: Is Jon at the school?

B: No. He's in home.

A: Where does he live?

B: He lives at Oak Street, between First and Second Avenue at Lakeville.

A: Does he live in an apartment?

B: Yes. He lives in the third floor.

From Grammar to Writing

CONNECTING WITH *AND* AND *BUT*

We use the word ***and*** to add information. We use the word ***but*** to show a surprise or contrast. We usually use a comma before ***and*** and ***but*** when they connect two sentences.

EXAMPLES: The book is good, **and** it is easy to understand.
The book is good, **but** it is difficult to understand.

We can use ***and*** or ***but*** to connect two descriptive adjectives.

EXAMPLES: I am hungry **and** tired.
He is tired **but** happy.

1 | *Complete the sentences with* **and** *or* **but.**

1. She's friendly _______________ popular.
2. She's friendly _______________ unpopular.
3. Her last name is long, _______________ it's hard to pronounce.
4. Her last name is long, _______________ it's easy to pronounce.

2 | *Use* **and** *or* **but** *to complete the story about Henry. Then on a separate piece of paper, write a story about someone who made a big change in his or her life.*

Five years ago Henry was a banker. His home was big _______________ (1.) expensive. His car was fast _______________ (2.) fancy. His workday was long, _______________ (3.) his work was stressful. He was rich, _______________ (4.) he was stressed and unhappy.

Today Henry works in a flower shop. His home is small _______________ (5.) inexpensive. His car is old _______________ (6.) small. His workday is short, _______________ (7.) his work is relaxing. He isn't rich, _______________ (8.) he's relaxed and happy.

3 | *On a separate piece of paper, write a story about a big change you made in your life.*

4 | *Exchange papers with a partner. Did your partner follow the directions? Correct any mistakes in grammar and spelling.*

5 | *Talk to your partner. Discuss the mistakes you made. Then rewrite your own paper and make any necessary changes.*

Imperatives and the Simple Present

UNIT	GRAMMAR FOCUS	THEME
7	Imperatives; Suggestions with *Let's, Why don't we . . . ?*	Long Life
8	Simple Present: Affirmative and Negative Statements	Shopping
9	Simple Present: *Yes / No* Questions and Short Answers	Roommates
10	Simple Present: *Wh-* Questions	Dreams

UNIT 7

Imperatives; Suggestions with *Let's, Why don't we . . . ?*

LONG LIFE

STEP 1 GRAMMAR IN CONTEXT

Before You Read

Some people live very long lives. Discuss the questions.

1. Who is the oldest person you know? How old is he or she?
2. What do you think is important for a long life?

Read

Read the online article. Then read the conversation between Joe and Mary on *page 73.*

Secrets to a Long Life

Yiannis Karimalis was 40 years old. He was a bridge painter in the United States. He was sick. His doctor said, "I'm sorry. You have stomach cancer.[1] It is very bad." Yiannis moved back to his hometown in Greece, to the island of Ikaria.

Yiannis is in his 80s and still alive today. His doctor is dead.

Many people in Ikaria live long lives. What are their secrets? Scientist Dan Buettner studies the lifestyle[2] of older people in different parts of the world. As a result of his studies in Ikaria, he offers this advice:

- **Eat** a lot of green vegetables, fresh fruit, olive oil, fish, and Greek honey.
- **Drink** herbal tea and goat milk.
- **Don't worry**.
- **Take naps**.
- **Walk**. **Don't use** a car, a bus, or a train.
- **Call friends** often.
- **Pray**.

Ikaria, Greece

1 ***cancer:*** serious illness in which a growth spreads
2 ***lifestyle:*** the way you live

JOE: Interesting article. But it's too healthy for me.

MARY: Come on, Joe, these suggestions are easy to follow. **Let's try** some of them.

JOE: I have a better idea. **Let's move** to Ikaria!

MARY: Um, **why don't we** just **take** a trip to Greece?

JOE: Stop right there. I'm on the phone with the airlines.

After You Read

A | Practice *PAIRS: Now read the online article and the conversation aloud. Take turns reading each paragraph of the article.*

B | Vocabulary *Complete the sentences with the words from the box.*

advice	dead	island	nap	pray	secret

1. You look very tired. Why don't you take a ________________?
2. Don't tell him. It's a ________________.
3. The flowers are ________________ because nobody watered them.
4. The doctor's ________________ to Mark was, "Walk more. Eat less."
5. We ________________ for peace.
6. Ikaria is a Greek ________________.

C | Comprehension *Circle the correct words to complete the sentences.*

1. At 40, Yiannis Karimalis was **sick / tired**.
2. Karimalis was a **house / bridge** painter.
3. Today Karimalis lives in **the United States / Greece**.
4. Dan Buettner is a **painter / scientist**.
5. Buettner tells people to **take it easy / work hard**.
6. **Mary / Joe** wants to follow Buettner's advice.

STEP 2 GRAMMAR PRESENTATION

THE IMPERATIVE

Affirmative Statements	
Base Form of Verb	
Walk	to work.

Negative Statements		
Don't	**Base Form of Verb**	
Don't	**take**	a bus.

SUGGESTIONS

Affirmative Statements		
Let's	**Base Form of Verb**	
Let's	**use**	olive oil.

Negative Statements			
Let's	***Not***	**Base Form of Verb**	
Let's	**not**	**use**	butter.

Suggestions for You and Another Person		
Why Don't We	**Base Form of Verb**	
Why don't we	**go**	on a bike tour?

Suggestions for Another Person		
Why Don't You	**Base Form of Verb**	
Why don't you	**get**	the cameras?

RESPONSES TO SUGGESTIONS

Agree	Disagree
OK.	No, I don't feel like it.
That's a good idea. OR Good idea.	Why don't we . . . instead.
That sounds good to me. OR Sounds good to me.	Sorry, not today.
Sounds like a plan.	I can't. I . . .

GRAMMAR NOTES

1	The **imperative** uses the **base form of the verb**.	• **Walk** to work.
2	To make an imperative **negative**, use ***don't*** + **base form** of the verb.	• **Don't worry**. • **Don't be** late.
3	In an imperative statement, the subject is always *you*, but we don't say it or write it.	• (You) Be careful.
4	Use the **imperative** to a. give directions and instructions b. give orders c. give advice or suggestions d. give warnings e. make polite requests	 • **Turn** right. • **Stand** there. • **Use** olive oil. **Don't use** butter. • **Be** careful! It's hot. • Please **call** before noon.

5	Use ***please*** to make orders, warnings, and requests more polite. *Please* can come at the beginning or the end of the sentence.	• **Please** be careful. • **Please** call before noon. • Call before noon, **please.**
6	Use ***Let's*** or ***Let's not*** + **base form** for suggestions that include you and another person.	• **Let's go**. • **Let's not eat** there.
7	Use ***Why don't we*** + **base form** for suggestions that include you and another person.	• **Why don't we go** to the pool?
	Use ***Why don't you*** to make a suggestion or give advice to another person.	• **Why don't you look** on the Internet?
	Remember to put a question mark (?) at the end of sentences with *Why don't we* and *Why don't you*.	• **Why don't we meet** at the gym? • **Why don't you call** home?

STEP 3 FOCUSED PRACTICE

EXERCISE 1: Discover the Grammar

*Read the conversations. Next to **line A**, write **I** for the imperative form and **S** for suggestions. Next to **line B**, write **A** when the person agrees. Write **D** when the person disagrees.*

__S__ **1. A:** Let's buy yogurt.

__D__ **B:** I don't like yogurt. Why don't we buy goat cheese?

____ **2. A:** Please get more broccoli. It's on sale.

____ **B:** OK. That's a good idea.

____ **3. A:** Let's not drive to school. The weather is great.

____ **B:** But it's late. Let's walk after school.

____ **4. A:** Call Roberto and invite him to dinner.

____ **B:** Good idea. What's his number?

____ **5. A:** Why don't you take some time off? You look tired.

____ **B:** Don't worry. I'm fine.

____ **6. A:** Maria, don't get those flowers. Some are almost dead.

____ **B:** OK. Thanks for telling me.

EXERCISE 2: Imperative and Suggestions: Affirmative and Negative *(Grammar Notes 1–6)*

Circle the correct words to complete the sentences.

1. The bread is still hot. **Eat / Don't eat** it now.
2. It's cold here. Please **close / don't close** the window.
3. It's a secret. Please **tell / don't tell** your brother about my plan.
4. For information about Dan Buettner, **check / don't check** the Internet.
5. **Let's walk / Let's not walk** to the store. It's not far.
6. **Let's buy / Let's not buy** those doughnuts. They're not very healthy.
7. Please **give / don't give** me directions to the gym. I want to go there today.
8. **Don't try / Try** this herbal tea. It's delicious.
9. **Take / Don't take** a nap now. Help me prepare dinner.
10. **Don't visit / Visit** that island in July. The weather is usually awful at that time.

EXERCISE 3: Imperative for Directions *(Grammar Notes 1, 3–4)*

A | *Read the conversation. Joe gives Mary directions to Gold's gym. Then look at the map and put an* **X** *on the gym.*

MARY: Excuse me . . .Where's Gold's Gym?

JOE: Um, sure . . . The gym is on Second Avenue between 70th and 71st Street.

We're on Third Avenue at 73rd Street. Walk down Third Avenue to 71st Street. That's two blocks from here. Turn left at 71st Street. Walk one block to Second Avenue. Then turn right on Second Avenue. It's right there, on your right.

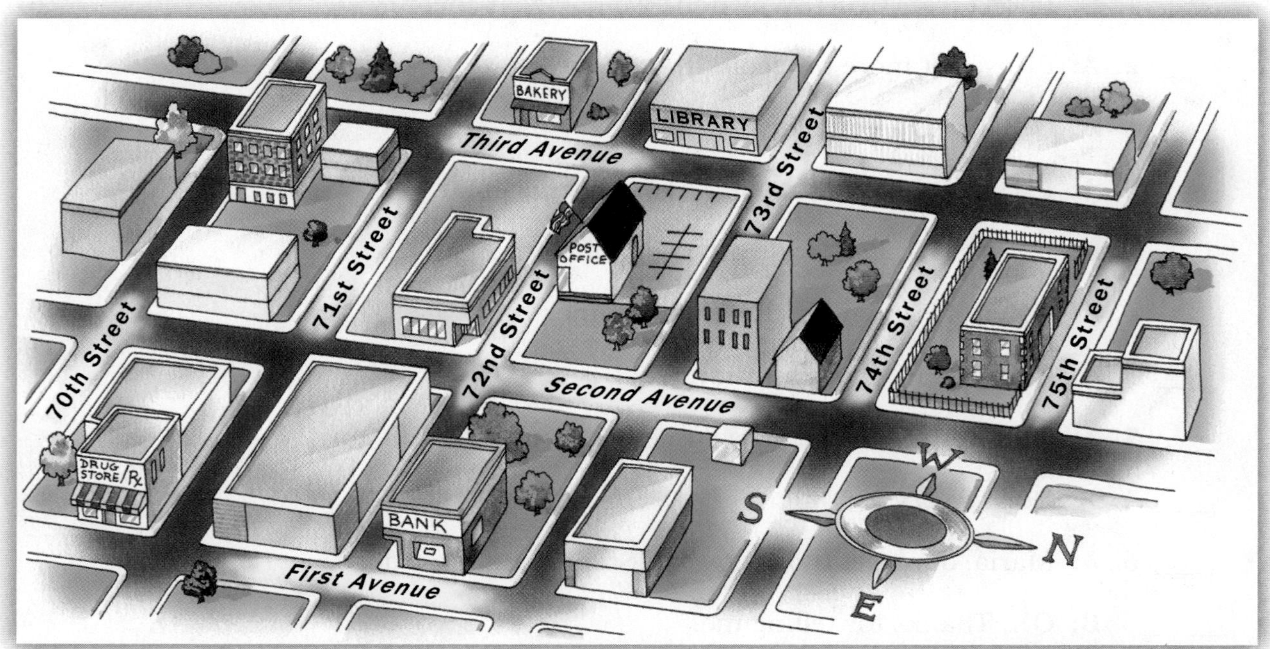

B | *Look at the map again. You are at the drug store. Continue the directions to the library.*

Walk down 71st Street to ______________________. ____________________________

____

EXERCISE 4: Editing

Correct the conversation. There are six mistakes. The first mistake is already corrected. Find and correct five more.

Joe: Let's ~~to~~ go to the movies.

Mary: Why we don't go to the park first? It's a beautiful day.

Joe: OK. But first let have lunch. I'm hungry.

Mary: I'm hungry too. Why don't we have a fruit salad with nuts?

Joe: Good idea.

Mary: But you don't use those apples. They're bad. Throws them away.

Joe: OK.

Mary: And why you don't add honey to the yogurt? It's delicious that way.

Joe: You're right. This is really good.

STEP 4 COMMUNICATION PRACTICE

EXERCISE 5: Listening

A | *Listen. What kind of ad is this? Circle the correct letter.*

a. an ad for a spa

b. an ad for exercise classes

c. an ad for healthy eating

B | *Listen again and check (✓) what the spa offers.*

__✓__ **1.** yoga classes

_____ **2.** tai chi classes

_____ **3.** fresh vegetables

_____ **4.** healthy breakfast

_____ **5.** healthy dinner

_____ **6.** massage and shower

_____ **7.** three weeks free

_____ **8.** two weeks free

EXERCISE 6: Pronunciation

A | *Read and listen to the Pronunciation Note.*

Pronunciation Note

We often **link *don't*** + ***you***. The two words sound like "doncha" **/ doʊnʃə /**

Example: Why don't you try that yogurt?

B | *Listen to the conversations. Notice the pronunciation of* **don't you.**

1. **A:** He's never sick.

   B: Maybe it's his healthy lifestyle. Why don't you try his exercise routine?

2. **A:** It's my mother's birthday tomorrow. I want to get her something.

   B: Why don't you get her Greek soap with olive oil? They say it's really good for the skin.

3. **A:** I don't want fried chicken. It's too fattening.

   B: Why don't you have the fish? It's broiled.

C | *Listen again. Repeat the suggestions with* **why don't you.**

EXERCISE 7: Making Suggestions for Another Person

PAIRS: Take turns. Read a problem. Your partner makes suggestions with **"Why don't you . . ."** *Agree if you like the suggestion. Disagree if you don't like the suggestion.*

1. I'm thirsty. **2.** I'm bored. **3.** I'm hungry. **4.** I'm tired.

Example:
A: I'm thirsty.
B: Why don't you have a soda?
A: Soda? That's not healthy.
B: Well, why don't you have some pineapple juice?
A: OK. That's a good idea.

EXERCISE 8: Making Suggestions for You and Another Person

PAIRS: ***Student A,*** *make a suggestion for a healthy lifestyle.* ***Student B,*** *agree or make another suggestion and give a reason why. Continue until you both agree. Take turns. Use the topics from the list.*

- exercise with friends
- go on a diet together
- go to the gym
- hang out with friends
- sign up for a dance class
- your idea: __________

Example:
A: Let's go to the gym.
B: Why don't we study first?
A: OK. Let's study for an hour and then go to the gym.

EXERCISE 9: Giving Advice

PAIRS: What advice can you give for a healthy lifestyle? Make a list. Use the verbs **drink, eat, meet, nap, pray, walk,** *and* **worry.** *Then read your list to the class.*

EXAMPLE:
- Don't eat a lot of meat.
- Eat . . .

EXERCISE 10: Giving Directions

A | *PAIRS: Look again at the map on page 76. You are at the library. Ask your partner directions to the bank.*

B | *PAIRS: Now give directions to a place on the map from the bakery. Your partner names the place.*

EXERCISE 11: Writing

A | *Write an ad for a hotel on the island of Ikaria. Use imperatives.*

EXAMPLE: For a vacation you won't forget, come to Jean's "Hotel for Life" on the beautiful island of Ikaria. Enjoy a comfortable room with an awesome view of the beach. Eat three delicious and healthful meals in our dining room or on your terrace. Swim in our pool. Jog on the beach. Relax in our jacuzzi. Everything is there for you. Don't delay. Book a room today.

B | *Check your work. Use the Editing Checklist.*

Editing Checklist

Did you . . . ?
- ☐ use imperatives correctly
- ☐ check your spelling

UNIT 7 Review

Check your answers on page UR-2.
Do you need to review anything?

A | *Circle the correct words to complete the sentences.*

1. **Let's get / Let's not get** ice cream. It's on sale this week.
2. **Why don't we invite / Let's not invite** Bob? He's really nice.
3. **Please buy / Don't buy** peppers. I don't like them.
4. **Let's meet / Let's not meet** before 8. I have a lot of work.
5. **Touch / Don't touch** the wall. The paint is still wet.

B | *Complete the instructions with the verbs in parentheses. Use the imperative affirmative or negative form.*

1. ________________ comfortable clothes to tai chi class. They're very important.
   (wear)
2. ________________ tight clothes.
   (wear)
3. ________________ a mat and water.
   (bring)
4. ________________ coffee or soda inside the classroom. You can have those drinks in
   (bring)
   the nearby lounge.
5. Please ________________ by check or cash. We don't accept credit cards.
   (pay)

C | *Write suggestions with the words in parentheses.*

1. ____
   (go to the gym / let's)
2. ____
   (watch a movie this afternoon / let's)
3. ____
   (take a trip together / why don't we)
4. ____
   (hang out with Pietro this weekend / why don't we)

D | *Correct the sentences. There are six mistakes. Check for punctuation.*

1. Why you don't ask Andrij for help?
2. You look really tired. You take a short nap.
3. Let's to walk to work. Let's not drive.
4. Don't ask Boris to fix the car. Asks Mickey.
5. I'm on a diet, so buy yogurt at the store. Don't to buy sour cream.

UNIT 8

Simple Present: Affirmative and Negative Statements

SHOPPING

STEP 1 GRAMMAR IN CONTEXT

Before You Read

A | Kawaii *is the Japanese word for "cute." In Japan, girls like* kawaii *things. In the United States, teens want "cool" things. What do young people say in your country?*

B | *Circle what's true about you.*

1. I **often / don't often** shop for clothes.
2. I look for **bargains / comfortable clothes / trendy clothes**.

Read

Read the online article about teenage shoppers in Japan.

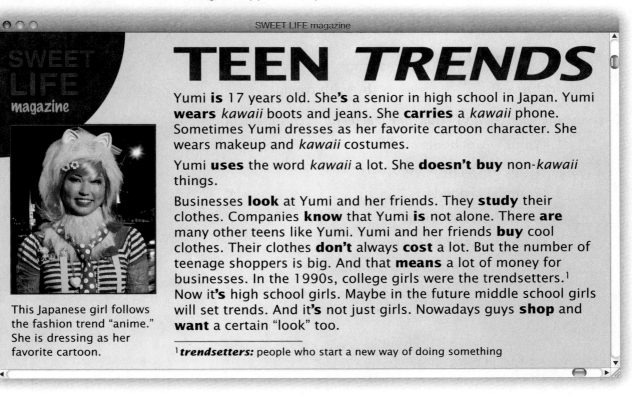

SWEET LIFE magazine

SWEET LIFE magazine

This Japanese girl follows the fashion trend "anime." She is dressing as her favorite cartoon.

TEEN *TRENDS*

Yumi **is** 17 years old. She**'s** a senior in high school in Japan. Yumi **wears** *kawaii* boots and jeans. She **carries** a *kawaii* phone. Sometimes Yumi dresses as her favorite cartoon character. She wears makeup and *kawaii* costumes.

Yumi **uses** the word *kawaii* a lot. She **doesn't buy** non-*kawaii* things.

Businesses **look** at Yumi and her friends. They **study** their clothes. Companies **know** that Yumi **is** not alone. There **are** many other teens like Yumi. Yumi and her friends **buy** cool clothes. Their clothes **don't** always **cost** a lot. But the number of teenage shoppers is big. And that **means** a lot of money for businesses. In the 1990s, college girls were the trendsetters.[1] Now it**'s** high school girls. Maybe in the future middle school girls will set trends. And it**'s** not just girls. Nowadays guys **shop** and **want** a certain "look" too.

[1] ***trendsetters:*** people who start a new way of doing something

After You Read

A | Practice *PAIRS: Now read the article aloud. Take turns reading each paragraph.*

B | Vocabulary *Circle the letter of the best meaning for the words in* **blue.**

1. Yumi is a **senior**. She's in her ________________ year of high school.

   a. first   b. second   c. last

2. She's a **teenager** (or teen). She is between ________________ years old.

   a. 11 and 15   b. 13 and 19   c. 15 and 20

3. Her brother is in **middle school**. Middle school is between ________________.

   a. high school and college   b. primary school and high school   c. kindergarten and first grade

4. Many **companies** study teens. These ________________ believe that teenagers spend a lot of money.

   a. friends   b. businesses   c. families

5. You look **cute** in that photo. You look ________________.

   a. pretty   b. serious   c. funny

6. Many teens **are like** Yumi. They ________________ Yumi.

   a. are in love with   b. are similar to   c. are friends of

7. He lives **alone**. He lives ________________.

   a. by himself   b. with friends   c. with relatives

C | Comprehension *Write* **T (True)** *or* **F (False)** *for each statement.*

____ **1.** Yumi wears boots.

____ **2.** Yumi works for a company.

____ **3.** Yumi has friends.

____ **4.** *Kawaii* means "cute."

____ **5.** Yumi doesn't like costumes.

____ **6.** Teenage boys don't like clothes.

____ **7.** Middle school girls set clothes trends today.

STEP 2 GRAMMAR PRESENTATION

SIMPLE PRESENT: AFFIRMATIVE AND NEGATIVE STATEMENTS

Affirmative Statements		
Subject	**Verb**	
I You* We They	**sell** **have**	jeans.
He She It	**sells** **has**	

Negative Statements			
Subject	***Do not / Does not***	**Base Form of Verb**	
I You* We They	**do not** **don't**	**sell** **have**	jeans.
He She It	**does not** **doesn't**		

**You* is both singular and plural.

GRAMMAR NOTES

1	Use the **simple present** to tell about **things that happen again and again** (habits, regular occurrences, customs, and routines). **Now** **Past** —X—X—+—X—X→ **Future** She shops every Saturday.	• She **wears** boots. • He **shops** at the mall. • They **give** gifts on New Year's Day. • She **buys** her clothes at discount stores.
2	Use the simple present to tell **facts**.	• The word *kawaii* **means** "cute."
3	Use the simple present with **non-action verbs** such as: *be, have, know, like, need, want*.	• She **is** 17 years old. • She **likes** that store. • She **has** an expensive bag.
4	In **affirmative statements**, use the **base form** of the verb for all persons except the third person singular. Add ***-s*** or ***-es*** with *he, she*, or *it*.	• **I want** a new sweater. • **You need** a new suit. • **They have** a car. • **She wants** a new phone. • **He watches** TV every day.
5	In **negative statements**, use ***does not*** or ***do not*** before the base form of the verb. Use the contractions ***doesn't*** and ***don't*** in speaking or in informal writing. **BE CAREFUL!** When ***or*** connects verbs in a negative statement, do not repeat *don't* or *doesn't*.	• He **does not wear** ties. • We **do not shop** there. • He **doesn't wear** ties. • We **don't shop** there. • I **don't smoke** or **drink** coffee. NOT: I don't smoke or ~~I don't~~ drink coffee.

(continued on next page)

6	The **third person singular affirmative** forms of ***have***, ***do***, and ***go*** are irregular. The **third person singular negative forms** of ***have***, ***do***, and ***go*** are regular.	• She **has** a new coat. • He **does** the laundry on Saturday. • He **goes** to the gym at 10:00. • She **doesn't have** a new hat. • He **doesn't do** laundry on Sunday. • He **doesn't go** to the gym at 11:00.
7	**BE CAREFUL!** The verb ***be*** **is irregular.** It has three forms in the present: *is*, *am*, and *are*.	***Be*** / **Regular Verb** • I **am** tired. / I **look** tired. • You **are** tall. / You **look** tall. • He **is** bored. / He **looks** bored.

REFERENCE NOTES

For a fuller discussion of **non-action verbs**, see Unit 17, page 188.
For **spelling and pronunciation rules for the third-person singular** in the **simple present**, see Appendix 6, pages A-6–A-7.
For a complete presentation of the **present tense of verb *be***, see Unit 1, page 5.

STEP 3 FOCUSED PRACTICE

EXERCISE 1: Discover the Grammar

Read the sentences. Underline all examples of the simple present.

1. Sometimes clothes send a message.
2. Sandy doesn't wear leather, and she doesn't eat meat.
3. Pierre and Katrina buy used clothes from thrift shops.
4. Marta makes her own clothes. She's very talented.
5. Ali wears gym clothes every day, and he exercises every day.

EXERCISE 2: Affirmative Sentences

(Grammar Notes 1–4)

Circle the correct word to complete the sentence.

1. My grandfather **work / works** for a big company, and he **wear / wears** a suit to work.
2. My brothers **like / likes** casual clothes. They almost never **wear / wears** suits.
3. His girlfriend **know / knows** about fashion.
4. They **shop / shops** online.
5. The word *cool* **mean / means** different things.
6. You **have / has** a cute hairstyle.

EXERCISE 3: Negative Statements

(Grammar Notes 5, 7)

Underline the verb in the first sentence. Complete the second sentence in the negative. Use the same verb.

1. He shops at flea markets. He ___doesn't shop___ at chain stores.

2. We buy name brands. They ______________ name brands.

3. I like jeans. I ______________ suits.

4. I need a new jacket. I ______________ a new raincoat.

5. My mother wears high heels. She ______________ sneakers.

6. That dress looks good. It ______________ too tight.

7. We are 20 years old. We ______________ teenagers.

8. He is in middle school. He ______________ in high school.

EXERCISE 4: Affirmative and Negative Statements

(Grammar Notes 1–6)

Complete the sentences with the verbs in parentheses. Use the affirmative or negative form.

1. (cost) **a.** It's expensive. It ___costs___ a lot.

b. It's cheap. It ___doesn't cost___ a lot.

2. (need) **a.** I'm hot. I ______________ a sweater.

b. I'm cold. I ______________ a sweater.

3. (want) **a.** His jacket is old. He ______________ a new one.

b. His jacket is new. He ______________ a new one.

4. (like) **a.** We ______________ window shopping. We often look at store windows.

b. They ______________ window shopping. They never look at store windows.

5. (have) **a.** He's rich. He ______________ a lot of money.

b. She's poor. She ______________ a lot of money.

6. (go) **a.** He doesn't like that new department store. He ______________ there.

b. She loves that new department store. She ______________ there every week.

EXERCISE 5: Affirmative and Negative Statements

(Grammar Notes 1–7)

A | *Read this letter from a parent to an advice columnist. Complete the sentences with the verbs in parentheses. Use the correct form.*

Our son ______*is*______ (1. (be)) 14 years old. He ____________ (2. (be)) a good student at his middle school, and he ____________ (3. (have)) a lot of friends. But we ____________ (4. (have)) a problem with him. He ____________ (5. (love)) clothes. He ____________ (6. (wear)) trendy jeans with chains on them. And he ____________ (7. (prefer)) expensive hoodies and brand names. We ____________ (8. (be / not)) poor, but I ____________ (9. (think)) it is wrong to spend a lot of money on clothes, especially for a growing boy. We ____________ (10. (give)) him spending money, but he ____________ (11. (have / not)) enough to buy all the clothes he wants. Now he ____________ (12. (want)) to get a part-time job. I ____________ (13. (want / not)) him to work, but my husband ____________ (14. (think)) it's OK. What do you think?

Rosa Alvarado

B | *Complete the answer to the parent with the words from the box. Use the correct form.*

agree	sound	think	~~want~~	work

Your son is not alone. Most teens ______*want*______ (1.) to look like other teens. It's very normal. And I ____________ (2.) with your husband. When a person ____________ (3.), that person ____________ (4.) about the cost of things. A job for your son ____________ (5.) fine to me.

EXERCISE 6: Editing

Correct the paragraph. There are eight mistakes. The first mistake is already corrected. Find and correct seven more.

Miyuki Miyagi is a teenager. She ~~live~~ lives in Japan. She like clothes, and she shops in the Harajuku District in Tokyo. She say, "My friends and I love fashion. We goes to the stores, but we doesn't always buy much. Clothes are expensive. But we still look good. My friends and I know inexpensive ways to dress "kawaii." For example, sometimes we are make our own clothes. And we mix styles. Sometimes we put on gothic clothes with punk clothes or schoolgirl uniforms. Sometimes we wears lots of makeup. And sometimes we dresses like dolls, or like anime.

STEP 4 COMMUNICATION PRACTICE

EXERCISE 7: Pronunciation

A | *Read and listen to the Pronunciation Note.*

Pronunciation Note

In English, we pronounce the **third person singular ending / s /, / z /**, or **/ ɪz /**.

EXAMPLES:

He lik**es** music. **/ s /**

She pla**ys** golf. **/ z /**

He watch**es** TV every day. **/ ɪz /**

B | *Underline the verb in each sentence. Then listen to each sentence and check (✓) the sound of the verb ending.*

	/ s /	/ z /	/ ɪz /
1. He shops a lot.	✓		
2. She uses that word a lot.			
3. She buys clothes at discount stores.			
4. He knows his business.			
5. It costs a hundred dollars.			
6. He misses her.			
7. She watches fashion shows on TV.			
8. He thinks about his clothes.			

EXERCISE 8: Listening

A | *Listen to the conversation between Elvia and Pedro. What does Elvia want?*

a. something new
b. something black

mannequin

B | *Listen to the conversation again. Complete the sentences.*

1. Elvia wants something for ___Bill's party___.
2. There's a(n) ______________ at the Wrap.
3. She wants a(n) ______________ in a(n) ______________.
4. It costs ______________.
5. Pedro thinks Elvia is a(n) ______________.

EXERCISE 9: Conversation

A | *Check (✓) the sentences that are true for you.*

1.	____ I wear colorful clothes.	____ I don't wear colorful clothes.
2.	____ I like leather jackets.	____ I don't like leather jackets.
3.	____ I buy designer clothes.	____ I don't buy designer clothes.
4.	____ I read fashion magazines.	____ I don't read fashion magazines.
5.	____ I like unusual clothes.	____ I don't like unusual clothes.
6.	____ I wear traditional clothes.	____ I don't wear traditional clothes.
7.	____ I have more than three pairs of jeans.	____ I don't have more than three pairs of jeans.

B | *PAIRS: Discuss the ways you and your partner are alike or different.*

Example: We don't wear colorful clothes. We like dark colors such as black and gray.

EXERCISE 10: Discussion

GROUPS: Talk about clothes customs in different parts of the world. For example, do people wear traditional clothes or Western clothes? Do people remove their shoes when they enter a home? Do people cover their heads?

Example: **A:** In my country, Peru, some people wear colorful woven clothes.
B: What do they look like?
A: They have wide sleeves and full skirts.
B: In Argentina some men who work in the country wear "gaucho" clothing. They wear wide brimmed hats, ponchos, and loose pants in their boots.

EXERCISE 11: Writing

A | *Write about the way you and a relative dress. Use the simple present.*

Example: I usually wear polo shirts and matching slacks to school. Sometimes I wear sneakers, and sometimes I wear boots. I have five polo shirts. They're blue, black, brown, beige, and green. Every day I wear a different shirt. My sister wears bright colors, and her clothes are very unusual. She's pretty, so everything looks great on her.

B | *Check your work. Use the Editing Checklist.*

Editing Checklist

Did you . . . ?

- ☐ use the simple present correctly
- ☐ remember to add ***-s*** or ***-es*** to the third person singular
- ☐ use correct spelling

UNIT 8 Review

Check your answers on page UR-2.
Do you need to review anything?

A | *Circle the correct words to complete the sentences.*

1. John **shop / shops** at The Wrap.
2. He **like / likes** their clothes.
3. My sister and I **don't like / am not like** the clothes at The Wrap.
4. We **go / goes** to Blooms.
5. Blooms **has / have** interesting clothes.

B | *Complete the sentences with the verbs in parentheses. Use the affirmative or negative form.*

1. It's hot today. We ________________ (need) jackets.
2. It's cold and windy today. They ________________ (need) jackets and sweaters.
3. They ________________ (play) soccer. They enjoy the sport.
4. He ________________ (like) sports. He prefers to watch movies or read books.

C | *Complete the sentences with the words from the box. Use the correct form.*

be	be	not wear	wear	work

1. My brother ________________ a fashion designer.
2. He ________________ for a magazine.
3. He ________________ a lot of trendy clothes. People always notice his clothes.
4. I ________________ trendy clothes. I wear old jeans and a white T-shirt.
5. My brother and I ________________ different in other ways too.

D | *Correct the sentences. There are six mistakes.*

1. My son doesn't has a suit.
2. He always wear jeans, T-shirts, and hoodies.
3. He need a suit for my brother's wedding.
4. Suits is expensive, and my son don't like to wear them.
5. We wants to rent or borrow a suit for him.

UNIT 9

Simple Present: *Yes / No* Questions and Short Answers

ROOMMATES

STEP 1 GRAMMAR IN CONTEXT

Before You Read

GROUPS: Do you live alone? Do you have a roommate? Do you share a room with someone? Imagine you are looking for a roommate. What questions are important to ask?

Read

Colleges often use questionnaires to help students find the right roommate. Read the roommate questionnaire. Are Dan and Jon a good match? Why or why not?

Roommate Questionnaire[1]

	Dan		Jon	
	YES	**NO**	**YES**	**NO**
1. **Do** you **wake up** early?	☐	☑	☐	☑
2. **Do** you **stay up** late?	☑	☐	☑	☐
3. **Are** you neat?	☑	☐	☑	☐
4. **Does** a messy room **bother** you?	☑	☐	☑	☐
5. **Are** you quiet?	☐	☑	☑	☐
6. **Are** you talkative?	☑	☐	☐	☑
7. **Does** noise **bother** you?	☐	☑	☐	☑
8. **Are** you outgoing?	☑	☐	☐	☑
9. **Are** you a private person?	☐	☑	☑	☐
10. **Are** you easygoing?	☑	☐	☑	☐
11. **Do** you **listen** to loud music?	☑	☐	☑	☐
12. **Do** you **watch** a lot of TV?	☑	☐	☑	☐
13. **Do** you **study** and **listen** to music at the same time?	☑	☐	☑	☐
14. **Do** you **study** with the TV on?	☑	☐	☑	☐

[1] ***questionnaire:*** a list of questions

After You Read

A | Practice *PAIRS: Now read the questionnaire aloud. Take turns reading the questions.*

B | Vocabulary *Complete the statements with the words from the box. Use the correct form.*

bother	messy	outgoing	stay up
easygoing	neat	private	wake up

1. The room was ________________, so we helped put things away. Now it is ________________.
2. That smell ________________ me. I feel a little sick.
3. We ________________ late on Friday and Saturday nights.
4. She ________________ at seven o'clock on weekdays.
5. He is pretty ________________. He doesn't get upset about most things.
6. I don't know very much about my roommate. He's a very ________________ person.
7. That little girl is very ________________. She's not afraid to talk to anyone.

C | Comprehension *Write* **T** **(True)** *or* **F** **(False)** *for each statement.*

____ **1.** Dan and Jon wake up late.

____ **2.** Dan is neat, but Jon isn't.

____ **3.** Dan and Jon are quiet.

____ **4.** Dan is outgoing, but Jon isn't.

____ **5.** Jon is a private person.

____ **6.** Dan and Jon are both easygoing.

____ **7.** Dan and Jon listen to loud music.

____ **8.** Dan and Jon don't watch TV.

____ **9.** Dan and Jon study and listen to music at the same time.

STEP 2 GRAMMAR PRESENTATION

SIMPLE PRESENT: *YES / NO* QUESTIONS AND SHORT ANSWERS

***Yes / No* Questions**			**Short Answers**					
Do / Does	**Subject**	**Base Form of Verb**	**Affirmative**			**Negative**		
Do	I you* we they	**work?**	Yes,	you I / we you they	**do.**	No,	you I / we you they	**don't.**
Does	he she it			he she it	**does.**		he she it	**doesn't.**

* *You* is both singular and plural.

GRAMMAR NOTES

1	For ***yes / no* questions** in the **simple present**, use ***do*** or ***does*** before the subject. Use the base form of the verb after the subject.	SUBJECT • **Do** you **need** a roommate? • **Does** he **have** a roommate?
2	We usually use **short answers** in conversation. Sometimes we use **long answers**.	**A:** Do you need a roommate? **B:** **Yes.** OR **Yes, I do.** OR **Yes, I need a roommate.** **A:** Does he have a roommate? **B:** **Yes.** OR **Yes, he does.** OR **Yes, he has a roommate.**
3	**BE CAREFUL!** Do not use *do* or *does* for *yes / no* questions with ***be***.	• **Are** you from Ecuador? • **Is** he from France? NOT: ~~Do are you~~ from Ecuador? ~~Does is he~~ from France? ~~Does you~~ from Ecuador?

REFERENCE NOTE

For a discussion of ***yes / no* questions with *be***, see Unit 2, page 17.

STEP 3 FOCUSED PRACTICE

EXERCISE 1: Discover the Grammar

Read about Dan and Jon. Then match the questions and answers on the next page.

In many ways Dan and Jon are alike. Both Dan and Jon like music and sports, but Dan likes popular music, and Jon likes hip-hop. Both Dan and Jon like basketball, but Jon likes soccer and Dan doesn't. Dan and Jon are both neat. They don't like a messy room. They both like to go to bed late—after midnight. They watch about two hours of TV at night, and they study with the TV on. But in one way Dan and Jon are completely different. Dan is talkative, but Jon is quiet. Dan says, "We're lucky about that. It works out nicely. I talk, he listens." Jon says, "Uh-huh."

(continued on next page)

__b__ **1.** Do they both like music and sports?		**a.** It doesn't say.
____ **2.** Do they like to go to bed early?		**b.** Yes, they do.
____ **3.** Does Dan like popular music?		**c.** Yes, he does.
____ **4.** Dan is talkative. Jon is quiet. Does it matter?		**d.** No, they don't.
____ **5.** Do Dan and Jon like movies?		**e.** No, it doesn't.

EXERCISE 2: *Yes / No* Questions and Short Answers

(Grammar Notes 1–2)

Complete the questions with **Do** *or* **Does** *and the verbs in parentheses. Then complete the short answers.*

1. (listen) **A:** __Do__ you __listen__ to music?

B: Yes, __we do__. OR Yes, __I do__.

2. (have) **A:** ________ your roommate ________ a TV?

B: No, she ________.

3. (wake up) **A:** ________ he ________ early?

B: No, ________.

4. (stay up) **A:** ________ they ________ late?

B: Yes, ________.

5. (bother) **A:** ________ the TV ________ you?

B: No, ________.

6. (have) **A:** ________ your room ________ a big window?

B: Yes, ________.

7. (rain) **A:** ________ it ________ a lot in your city?

B: No, ________.

8. (have) **A:** ________ I ________ Internet access?

B: Yes, ________.

9. (go) **A:** ________ she ________ to parties all the time?

B: No, ________.

10. (need) **A:** ________ we ________ another lamp?

B: Yes, ________.

11. (sell) **A:** ________ they ________ gum here?

B: Yes, ________.

EXERCISE 3: *Yes / No* Questions and Short Answers

(Grammar Notes 1–3)

Complete the **yes / no** *questions with* **Do, Does, Am, Is,** *or* **Are**. *Then complete the short answers.*

1. **A:** ___Am___ I late? **B:** No, ___you aren't___.
2. **A:** ______ he come late? **B:** Yes, ______.
3. **A:** ______ you busy? **B:** Yes, we ______.
4. **A:** ______ they have a lot of work? **B:** No, ______.
5. **A:** ______ they roommates? **B:** No, ______.
6. **A:** ______ they live in a dormitory? **B:** Yes, ______.
7. **A:** ______ she your sister? **B:** No, ______.
8. **A:** ______ you live at home? **B:** Yes, I ______.
9. **A:** ______ your roommate play baseball? **B:** No, he ______.
10. **A:** ______ we in the right room? **B:** Yes, you ______.
11. **A:** ______ you friends? **B:** Yes, ______.
12. **A:** ______ you cook well? **B:** No, I ______.

EXERCISE 4: *Yes / No* Questions and Short Answers

(Grammar Notes 1–2)

Complete the conversation. Write questions with the words in parentheses. Then write short answers with **do, does, don't** *or* **doesn't**.

A: So tell me about your new roommate, Edward. ___Do you like___ (1. (you / like)) him?

B: ___Yes, I do___ (2.). He's a really nice guy.

A: Where is he from? He sounds like a native speaker. ______ (3. (he / come)) from England?

B: ______ (4.). He comes from Australia.

A: Cool. What's he studying?

B: Music.

A: Oh, he's a music major. ______ (5. (he / play)) an instrument?

B: Of course. He plays three instruments: violin, cello, and piano.

A: Wow. ______ (6. (you / play)) with him?

B: ______ (7.). I'm not a good musician. But sometimes his cousin plays with him.

(continued on next page)

A: ________________ a lot of family close by?
8. (he / have)

B: ________________. His uncle, his aunt, three cousins, and his grandmother are
9.

10 minutes away. I was at their home last night.

A: Really? ________________ them often?
10. (you / see)

B: ________________. They invite us for a meal at least once a month. They all play music,
11.

and they're interesting people. His uncle is a conductor, and she is an opera singer.

A: ________________ them a small gift when you visit?
12. (you / bring)

B: ________________. I'm a poor student.
13.

A: Hey, you're not that poor.

EXERCISE 5: Editing

Correct the conversations. There are eight mistakes. The first mistake is already corrected. Find and correct seven more.

1. **A:** Does she ~~goes~~ *go* to school?

   B: Yes, she goes.

2. **A:** Does he needs help?

   B: Yes, he does.

3. **A:** Do they are like rock music?

   B: Yes, they do.

4. **A:** Do she live near the museum?

   B: Yes, she lives.

5. **A:** Does he has a roommate?

   B: Yes, he does.

6. **A:** Are you friends?

   B: Yes, we do.

STEP 4 COMMUNICATION PRACTICE

EXERCISE 6: Pronunciation

A | *Read and listen to the Pronunciation Note.*

Pronunciation Note

We **link the** words ***does it*** and ***does he***. The "s" in *does* makes a **/z/** sound.

Join the **/z/** sound in *does* to the vowel sound **/ɪ/** in *it*.

Join the **/z/** sound in *does* to the vowel sound **/i/** in *he*. Do not pronounce the "h" in *he*.

Examples: Does it   Does he

B | *Listen to questions and repeat each question.*

1. Does it have Internet service?
2. Does it come with a desk?
3. Does it have two closets?
4. Does it have windows?
5. Does it have air conditioning?
6. Does he have a roommate?
7. Does he have a test?
8. Does he have a cold?

C | *PAIRS: Take turns. Look at Serge Lafitte's answers to a questionnaire. Ask your partner questions about Serge Lafitte. Remember to link* **Does + he.**

EXAMPLE: **A:** Does he like movies?
B: Yes, he does.

NAME: Serge		
Do you ____________?	**YES**	**NO**
1. like movies	✓	
2. stay up late	✓	
3. have a part-time job		✓
4. study and listen to music	✓	
5. like a clean, neat room		✓

EXERCISE 7: Listening

A | *Listen to the conversation. Why is Andrea talking to Valentina Gold?*

a. to find a roommate **b.** to work out a problem with her roommate

B | *Listen again. Complete the chart with Andrea's answers.*

	Andrea	Leyla
parties		likes parties
music		likes rock
sports		plays basketball, soccer, swims
study habits		studies at night in her room

C | *Compare Andrea and Leyla. Are they a good match? Why or why not?*

____

____

EXERCISE 8: Discussion: Comparing Habits and Personality

PAIRS: Look at the roommate questionnaire again. Answer the questions for yourself. Then compare your answers with a partner's.

	YOU	
	YES	NO
1. Do you **wake up** early?	☐	☐
2. Do you **stay up** late?	☐	☐
3. Are you neat?	☐	☐
4. Does a messy room **bother** you?	☐	☐
5. Are you quiet?	☐	☐
6. Are you talkative?	☐	☐
7. Does noise **bother** you?	☐	☐
8. Are you outgoing?	☐	☐
9. Are you a private person?	☐	☐
10. Are you easygoing?	☐	☐
11. Do you **listen** to loud music?	☐	☐
12. Do you **watch** a lot of TV?	☐	☐
13. Do you **study** and **listen** to music at the same time?	☐	☐
14. Do you **study** with the TV on?	☐	☐

EXERCISE 9: Game: Find Someone Who . . .

Find out about your classmates. Ask these questions and add your own. Take notes. Tell the class something new about three classmates.

Do you . . . ?	Are you . . . ?
cook well	messy
text every day	outgoing
play a musical instrument	a private person
like sports	athletic
watch sports on TV	handy (good at fixing things)
have a lot of brothers and sisters	an only child
have a lot of electronics	interested in art
Your question:	*Your question:*

Example: Ali is handy. He fixes things.
Sara plays the violin. She was in a concert last month.
Mi Young watches sports on TV. She loves the New York Yankees.

EXERCISE 10: Game: What's in Your Backpack?

Work in small groups. Ask questions. Check (✓) the items you have. The first group to check 10 items wins.

EXAMPLE: Do you have keys? OR Does anyone have keys?

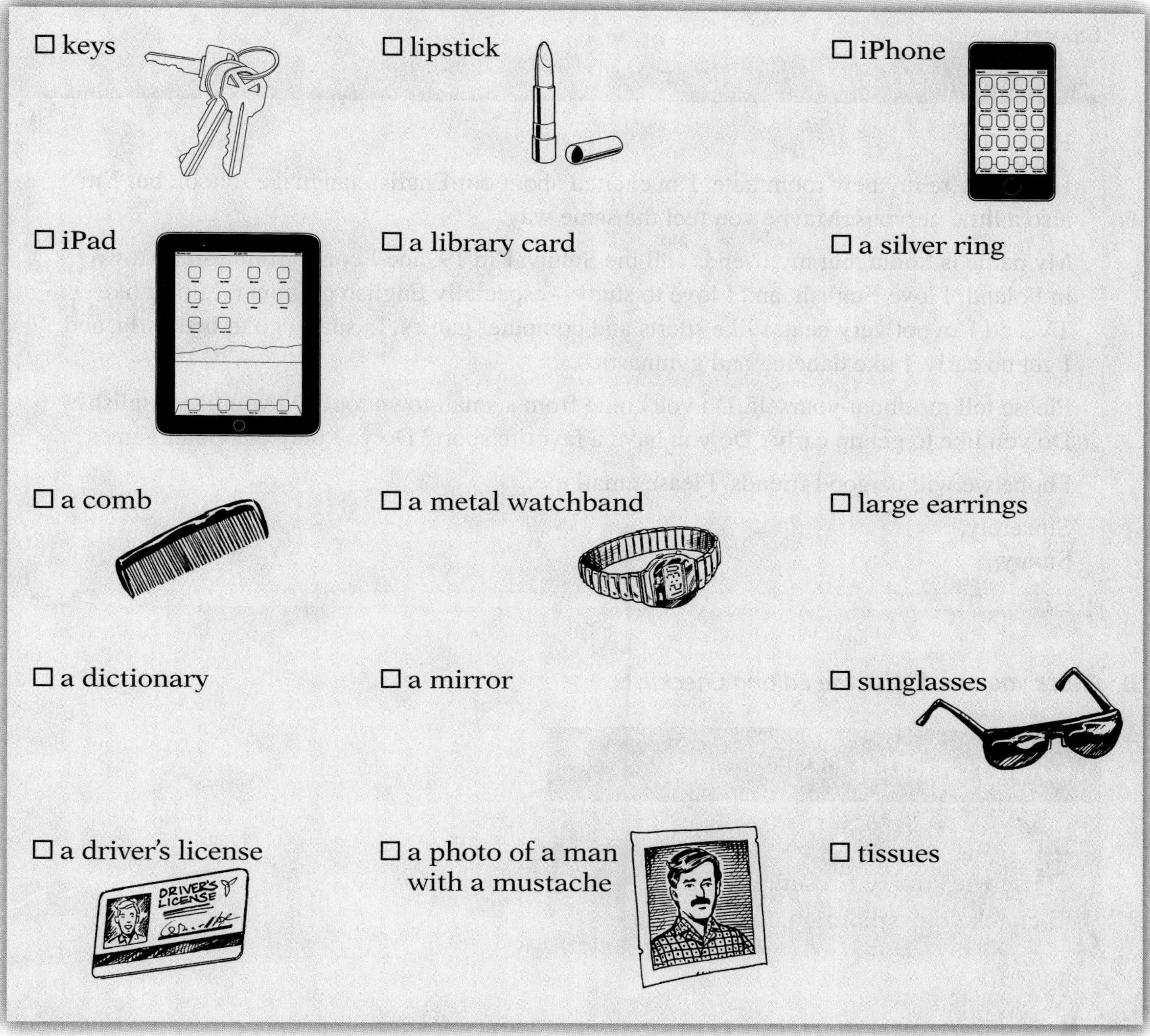

EXERCISE 11: Writing

A | *Imagine you plan to study English at a school for international students. The school has chosen a roommate for you. You do not know the roommate. Write your new roommate an email. Tell about yourself and ask your roommate questions. Use the simple present.*

EXAMPLE:

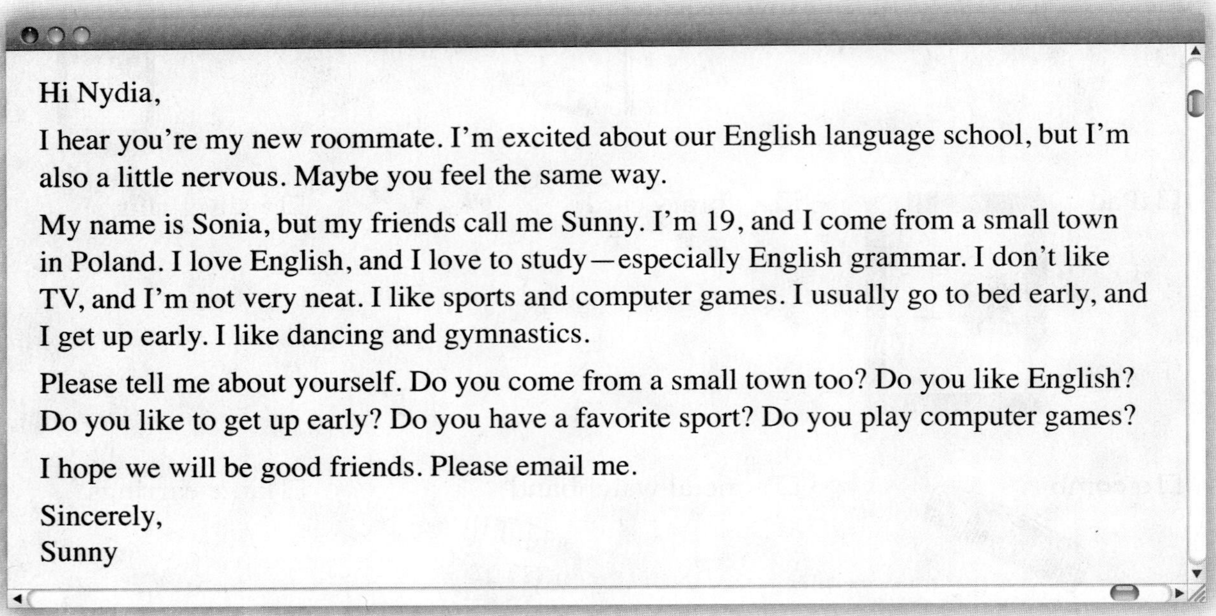

Hi Nydia,

I hear you're my new roommate. I'm excited about our English language school, but I'm also a little nervous. Maybe you feel the same way.

My name is Sonia, but my friends call me Sunny. I'm 19, and I come from a small town in Poland. I love English, and I love to study—especially English grammar. I don't like TV, and I'm not very neat. I like sports and computer games. I usually go to bed early, and I get up early. I like dancing and gymnastics.

Please tell me about yourself. Do you come from a small town too? Do you like English? Do you like to get up early? Do you have a favorite sport? Do you play computer games?

I hope we will be good friends. Please email me.

Sincerely,
Sunny

B | *Check your work. Use the Editing Checklist.*

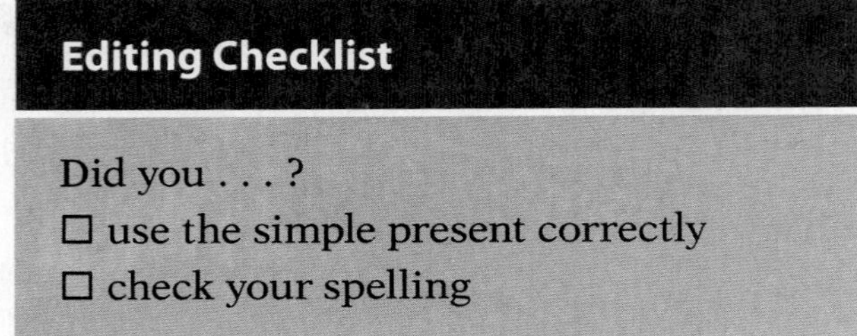

Editing Checklist

Did you . . . ?

☐ use the simple present correctly

☐ check your spelling

UNIT 9 Review

Check your answers on page UR-2.
Do you need to review anything?

A | *Complete the sentences with the words from the box.*

Am	Are	Do	Does	Is

1. ______________ you know his brother?
2. ______________ his brother messy?
3. ______________ he have a lot of friends?
4. ______________ they easygoing?
5. ______________ I your best friend?

B | *Complete the questions with the verbs in parentheses. Use the correct form.*

1. (have) ______________ you ______________ a roommate?
2. (speak) ______________ his roommate ______________ English fluently?
3. (watch) ______________ your roommate ______________ TV at night?
4. (be) ______________ your roommate talkative?
5. (be) ______________ your roommates' parents in the United States?

C | *Write questions about an apartment. Use the words in parentheses.*

1. ____?
   (be / the neighbors / noisy)
2. ____?
   (the apartment building / have / an elevator)
3. ____?
   (be / the apartment / near trains or buses)
4. ____?
   (the bedroom / have / two closets)
5. ____?
   (be / the bedroom / big)

D | *Correct the conversations. There are five mistakes.*

1. **A:** Does he have a big TV in his room?
   B: Yes, he has.

2. **A:** Does she needs help?
   B: No, she don't.

3. **A:** Do you are friends?
   B: Yes, we aren't.

UNIT 10 Simple Present: *Wh-* Questions
DREAMS

STEP 1 GRAMMAR IN CONTEXT

Before You Read

PAIRS: Do you dream? Do you remember your dreams? What do you dream about?

Read

Ask the Expert *is a radio talk show. Today Rob Stevens is talking to dream expert Helena Lee. Read the conversation.*

Dreams

RS: Good afternoon. I'm Rob Stevens. Welcome to *Ask the Expert*. This afternoon my guest is Helena Lee. She's the author of *Sleep and Dreams*. Thank you for coming.

LEE: Thanks, Rob. It's great to be here.

RS: Helena, we have a lot of questions about dreams. Our first question is from Carolina Gomes. She asks, "**Why do we dream?**"

LEE: That's a good question. Actually, nobody really knows why. But I think dreams help us understand our feelings.

RS: OK. . . . Our next question is from Jonathan Lam. He asks, "**Who dreams?** Does everyone dream?"

LEE: Yes, everyone dreams. People dream in every part of the world. And what's more, scientists believe animals dream too.

RS: Wow! That's really interesting. **How do we know?**

LEE: We have machines. They show when people or animals dream. But, of course, no one knows what animals dream about.

RS: Our next question is from Pablo Ortiz. He writes, "People don't remember *all* their dreams. **What dreams do they remember?**"

LEE: People remember their unusual dreams. And, unfortunately, people remember their bad dreams, or nightmares.

RS: Beata Green says, "I have the same dream again and again. **What does that mean?**"

LEE: That dream has special meaning for you. You need to think about it.

RS: Here's a question from Samuel Diaz. "**When do people dream?**"

LEE: They dream during deep sleep. It's called REM sleep. REM means *rapid eye movement.*

RS: I hear REM sleep is important. **Why do we need it?**

LEE: Without it, we can't remember or think clearly.

RS: Our last question for today is from Mike Morgan. He writes, "My roommate doesn't remember his dreams. **Why do I remember my dreams?**"

LEE: Well, a University of Iowa professor says, "Creative[1] people remember their dreams."

RS: Thank you so much, Helena. We look forward to reading your new book.

[1] ***creative:*** able to see things in a new way

After You Read

A | Practice *PAIRS: Now read the conversation aloud.*

B | Vocabulary *Complete the conversations with the words from the box.*

author	guest	nightmares	remember	unfortunately

1. A: Who's the ________ of that book?

B: Helena Lee. She was a(n) ________ on *Ask the Expert*.

2. A: Do you ________ your dreams?

B: No, I don't. ________, I remember my ________ because they wake me up.

C | Comprehension *Write* **T (True), F (False),** *or* **? (it doesn't say)** *for each statement.*

____ **1.** Only creative people dream.

____ **2.** Animals dream about food.

____ **3.** People dream during REM sleep.

____ **4.** REM stands for real eye movement.

____ **5.** A professor believes that smart people remember their dreams.

STEP 2 GRAMMAR PRESENTATION

SIMPLE PRESENT: *WH-* QUESTIONS; SHORT AND LONG ANSWERS

Wh- Questions				Answers	
***Wh-* Word**	***Do / Does***	**Subject**	**Base Form of Verb**	**Short**	**Long**
When	**do**	I	**sleep**?	From 10:00 P.M. to 5:00 A.M.	You sleep from 10:00 P.M. to 5:00 A.M.
Where		you		On the futon.	I sleep on the futon.
Why		we		Because we're tired.	We sleep because we're tired.
What		they	**need**?	Two pillows.	They need two pillows.
Who	**does**	she	**know**?	My brother.	She knows my brother.
How		it	**feel**?	Good.	The blanket feels good.

Wh- Questions about the Subject			Answers
***Wh-* Word**	**Verb**		
Who	**dreams**?		Everyone does.
What	**happens**	during REM sleep?	People dream.

GRAMMAR NOTES

1 ***Wh-* questions** ask for information. Most questions use ***wh-* word** + ***do*** or ***does*** + **subject** + **base form of the verb**.

WH- WORD	*DO / DOES*	SUBJECT	BASE FORM	
• **When**	**do**	you	**go**	to bed?
• **What**	**does**	he	**dream**	about?

2 To ask a **question about the subject**, use ***who*** or ***what*** + **third-person singular form of the verb**.

SUBJECT
- **My brother** sleeps on the sofa.
- **Who sleeps** on the sofa?

SUBJECT
- **Milk** helps me fall asleep.
- **What helps** you fall asleep?

BE CAREFUL! Do not use ***do*** or ***does*** with questions about the subject. Do not use the base form of the verb.

NOT: Who ~~does~~ sleeps on the sofa?
NOT: Who ~~do~~ sleeps on the sofa?
NOT: Who ~~sleep~~ on the sofa?

3		
	Who asks questions about a <u>subject</u>. ***Who*** and ***whom*** ask questions about an <u>object</u>.	SUBJECT • **Who helps** John? Mary does.
		OBJECT • **Who does** Mary **help**? John.
	USAGE NOTE: ***Whom*** is very formal.	OBJECT • **Whom does** Mary **help**? John.

REFERENCE NOTE

For more about ***who***, ***what***, ***where***, ***when***, and ***why***, see Unit 2, page 17.

STEP 3 FOCUSED PRACTICE

EXERCISE 1: Discover the Grammar

Night owls like to stay up late at night. Early birds get up early. Read about a night owl and an early bird. Then match the questions and answers.

Felix is a night owl. He hates to get up in the morning. On weekends he goes to bed at 1:00 A.M. and gets up at noon. Unfortunately for Felix, during the week his first class starts at 8:15, and he needs to get up early.

At 7:00 A.M. Felix's alarm rings. He wakes up, but he doesn't get up. He stays in bed and daydreams. At 7:20 his mom comes in. She has a big smile. She says, "Felix, it's time to get up."

Felix's mother is an early bird. Even on vacations she is up at 6:00 A.M. When his mom wakes him, Felix says, "Leave me alone. I'm tired."

Finally, at about 7:30, Felix gets up. He jumps out of bed, showers, and gets dressed. At 7:50 he drinks a big glass of juice, takes a breakfast bar, and runs to the bus stop. The bus comes at 8:00.

____ **1.** Who hates to get up in the morning?

____ **2.** How does Felix feel in the morning?

____ **3.** Why does Felix run to the bus stop?

 **4.** What does Felix have for breakfast?

 **5.** When does Felix sleep late?

____ **6.** What happens at 7:00?

a. On weekends.

b. Tired.

c. Felix's alarm rings.

d. A glass of juice and a breakfast bar.

e. Because he doesn't want to be late for school.

f. Felix does.

EXERCISE 2: Word Order of *Wh-* Questions

(Grammar Notes 1–3)

Complete the conversations. Read the answers. Then write questions with the words in parentheses.

1. (do / you / usually get up / When)

   A: When do you usually get up?

   B: At 7:00 on weekdays.

2. (Where / come from / your guest / does)

   A: Where dose you guest come from?

   B: She's from Sydney.

3. (at night / they / How / do / feel)

   A: How do they feel at night?

   B: They're never tired at night. They're night owls.

4. (does / Who / he / dream about)

   A: Who dose he dream about?

   B: He dreams about me.

5. (What / she / dream about / does)

   A: What dose she dream about?

   B: Actually, she never remembers her dreams.

EXERCISE 3: *Wh-* Questions about the Subject

(Grammar Note 3)

Complete the conversations. Read the answers. Then write questions with the words in parentheses. Use the correct form.

1. (Who / daydream)

   A: Who daydreams?

   B: John does.

2. (Who / have / nightmares)

   A: Who

   B: Her brother Sam does. What's more, he sometimes screams during a nightmare.

3. (Who / get up / before 6:00 A.M.)

A: ______________________________

B: Grandma Ilene does.

4. (Who / hate / early morning classes)

A: ______________________________

B: Bob, Emiko, and Jill do.

5. (Who / need / more than eight hours of sleep)

A: ______________________________

B: Feng does.

EXERCISE 4: *Wh-* Questions

(Grammar Notes 1–3)

Read the answers. Then ask questions about the underlined words.

1. Sabrina daydreams.

   Who *daydreams* ?

2. Sabrina daydreams during her math class.

   When dose Sabrina day dream ? ?

3. Sabrina daydreams about her boyfriend.

   Who dose She day dream about ? ?

4. Sabrina daydreams during math because she doesn't like the class and doesn't understand the teacher.

   Why dose Sabrina day dream? ?

5. Sabrina's boyfriend is 3,000 miles away in Alaska.

   Where is Sabrina's boy friend ?

6. Sabrina feels lonely.

   How does Sabrina's feel ? ?

7. Sabrina's boyfriend has a good job.

   Who has agood job ?

8. He works for an oil company.

   What dose he do ?

EXERCISE 5: *Wh-* Questions: Subject and Object

(Grammar Notes 2–3)

Label the subject (**S**) *and object* (**O**) *in each sentence. Write one question about the subject and one question about the object. Then answer the questions. Use short answers.*

1. My mother (S) wakes me (O) on weekdays.

   Q: Who wakes you on weekdays? **Q:** Who does your mother wake on weekdays?

   A: My mother. **A:** She wakes me.

2. In a dream Jake meets his boss at a party.

   Q: ______________ **Q:** ______________

   A: ______________ **A:** ______________

3. In a nightmare two giants hit Maya.

   Q: ______________ **Q:** ______________

   A: ______________ **A:** ______________

EXERCISE 6: Editing

Correct the questions. There are ten mistakes. The first mistake is already corrected. Find and correct nine more.

1. Where do they ~~sleeps~~ sleep?
2. Why they need two pillows?
3. Who sleep on the sofa?
4. When does she goes to bed?
5. Who wake you?
6. Who does you dream about?
7. How he feels about that?
8. What you dream about?
9. Where he sleep?
10. How long does she sleeps at night?

STEP 4 COMMUNICATION PRACTICE

EXERCISE 7: Listening

A | *Mia often has the same dream. She tells a doctor about her dream. Listen to their conversation. What is Mia looking for?*

____

B | *Listen again to Mia's dream. Answer the questions.*

1. What important event does Mia have? *She has an important test.*
2. What does the man in the dream say? ______________________________
3. What does Dr. Fox think Mia has? ______________________________
4. What do the two buildings symbolize? ______________________________
5. What does Mia's father want her to study? ______________________________

EXERCISE 8: Pronunciation

A | *Read and listen to the Pronunciation Note.*

Pronunciation Note

Some English words have an ***r*** or ***l*** after another consonant. For example, **/ pr /** as in ***price*** or **/ gl /** as in ***glad***. If it is hard for you to pronounce these two consonants together, try saying the word with the second consonant and then add the first one.

Examples: rice → **price**
lock → **clock**

B | *Listen and repeat the words.*

black	**bright**	**dream**	**free**	**price**
blue	**clock**	**dress**	**great**	**three**

C | *PAIRS: Read a word from Part B. Your partner writes the word in his or her notebook. Take turns.*

D | *Listen and read about Olivia's dream. Underline the words with consonant groups that have an / r / or / l /.*

It was a great dream. Listen. I buy a black dress. The price is only thirty-three dollars. There's a problem with the dress. I bring it back. The salesperson says she's sorry.

She gives me a bright blue dress instead. I try it on. The dress is perfect. I wear the dress to a party. I have a great night out.

EXERCISE 9: Interview

Answer the questions. Then work with a partner. Ask your partner the questions.

	You	Your Partner
When do you go to bed?		
What days do you sleep in?		
Does anyone wake you? If so, who?		
Do you dream? If so, what do you dream about?		
Are you an early bird or a night owl?		

EXERCISE 10: Group Interview

A | *Ask five students these questions about sleep. Take notes on a separate piece of paper.*

EXAMPLE: YOU: Juan, do you snore?
JUAN: No, I don't, but my sister Bianca snores.

1. Who snores?
2. Who gets up before 6:00 A.M.?
3. Who goes to bed after midnight?
4. Who needs more than eight hours of sleep?
5. Who needs less than five hours of sleep?
6. Who dreams in English?
7. Who daydreams?
8. Who has insomnia? (trouble sleeping)
9. Who falls asleep during the day?

B | *Tell the class interesting results.*

EXAMPLE: Juan's sister snores.
Nobody gets up before 6:00 A.M., but sometimes Hasan goes to bed at 5:00 A.M.

EXERCISE 11: Information Gap: Understanding Dreams

PAIRS: **Student A,** *follow the instructions on this page.* **Student B,** *turn to page 112 and follow the instructions there.*

1. Student B often has the same dream. Find out about Student B's dream. Ask these questions.

In your dream:

- Where are you?
- Who do you see?
- Is the person big? little?
- Are you big? little?
- What does the person say?
- What do you do?

2. You have the following dream again and again. Read about your dream. Then answer Student B's questions about it.

> You are on an airplane. The pilot comes to you. He says, "I need your help." You go with the pilot. You fly the plane. You land the plane. Everyone claps. You feel good. You wake up.

3. Talk about your dreams. What do they mean?

EXERCISE 12: Writing

A | *Write about a dream or daydream you often have. Answer the questions:*

- What do you dream or daydream about?
- Where does it take place?
- What happens?
- How often do you have this dream?
- What do you think? Why do you have this dream or daydream?

Example: I often daydream about my family. I daydream about my birthday. I am 14 years old. We are at my grandparents' home. My grandparents' friends are there. They have a granddaughter. She is beautiful. I want to talk to her, but I get nervous. I can't talk. I turn red. Everyone looks at me. Then I run home. I feel very embarrassed.

B | *Check your work. Use the Editing Checklist.*

Editing Checklist

Did you . . . ?

☐ use the simple present correctly

☐ check your spelling

Information Gap for Student B

1. You often have the following dream. Read about your dream. Then answer Student A's questions about it.

> You are in the third grade. You see your third grade teacher. Your teacher is very big. You are small. Your teacher says, "Your schoolwork is great. You are my favorite student." You smile. Then you laugh. Then you wake up.

2. Student A often has the same dream. Find out about Student A's dream. Ask these questions.

In your dream:

- Where are you?
- Who comes to you?
- What does he say?
- What do you do?
- How do you feel?
- What happens?

3. Talk about your dreams. What do they mean?

UNIT 10 Review

Check your answers on page UR-2.
Do you need to review anything?

A | *Complete the* **wh-** *questions with the words from the box.*

how	when	where	who	why

1. **A:** ________________ does she snore? **B:** I don't know why.
2. **A:** ________________ do they get up? **B:** At about 9:00 or 10:00.
3. **A:** ________________ sleeps on the sofa? **B:** Their uncle does.
4. **A:** ________________ do you feel? **B:** Sleepy.
5. **A:** ________________ do you buy sheets? **B:** At Bloom's department store.

B | *Write questions with the words in parentheses. Use the correct form.*

1. ____
   (Who / snore / in your family)
2. ____
   (What / you / dream about)
3. ____
   (What time / your mother / get up)
4. ____
   (What time / you / go to bed)
5. ____
   (Where / your brother / sleep)

C | *Read the statement and answers. Then write the questions.*

John meets his uncle at the diner on Saturdays.

1. **A:** ______________________________ **B:** John does.
2. **A:** ______________________________ **B:** His uncle.
3. **A:** ______________________________ **B:** At the diner.
4. **A:** ______________________________ **B:** On Saturdays.

D | *Correct the questions. There are six mistakes.*

1. Where you live and who you live with?
2. Why he daydreams in class?
3. When does she gets up?
4. How they feel about sleeping pills?
5. Who does you dream about?

From Grammar to Writing

Time Word Connectors: *First, Next, After that, Then, Finally*

1 | *Which paragraph sounds better,* **A** *or* **B***? Why?*

Paragraph A

I like to watch my roommate prepare tea. She boils water and pours the boiling water in a cup with a teabag in it. She removes the teabag and adds sugar. She adds lemon. She adds ice. She sips the tea and says, "Mmm. This tea is just the way I like it."

Paragraph B

I like to watch my roommate prepare tea. First, she boils some water and pours the boiling water in a cup with a teabag in it. Next, she removes the teabag and adds some sugar. After that, she adds some lemon. Then she adds some ice. Finally, she sips the tea and says, "Mmm. This tea is just the way I like it."

You can make your writing clearer by using **time word connectors**. They show the order in which things happen. Some common ones are ***first***, ***next***, ***after that***, ***then***, and ***finally***. We usually use a **comma** after these connectors.

Example: **First**, you add the water. **Next**, you add the sugar.

2 | *Add time word connectors to show the order of things in this paragraph.*

I take a shower. I have breakfast. I drive to the train station. I take a train and a bus. I get to work.

Now write a paragraph about a routine you follow. Use time word connectors. Here are some ideas:

Example: Every Saturday morning . . .
Every New Year's Day . . .
Every year on my birthday . . .

3 | *Exchange papers with a partner. Did your partner follow directions? Correct any mistakes in grammar and spelling.*

4 | *Talk to your partner. Discuss the mistakes you made. Then rewrite your own paper and make any necessary changes.*

There is / There are; Possessives; Modals: Ability and Permission

UNIT 11

There is / There are

SHOPPING MALLS

STEP 1 GRAMMAR IN CONTEXT

Before You Read

PAIRS: Discuss the questions.

1. Do you like big malls? Why or why not?
2. Is there a mall near your school? Where is it? Do you go there? Why or why not?

Read

Read an advertisement for the West Edmonton Mall in Canada.

Come to Edmonton and see its top attraction,

West Edmonton Mall

West Ed Mall is a shopper's dream. **There are** more than 800 stores. They include everything from Old Navy® to Godiva® Chocolates to one-of-a-kind stores. Enjoy the mall's international flavor. **There's** Chinatown, where you can shop in a traditional Chinese marketplace. **There's** Europa Boulevard with its many European specialties. West Ed Mall also has over 110 eating places. And for the young and the young-at-heart **there are** seven world-class attractions including a water park, an amusement park, and an indoor skating rink. So make your travel plans now. **There isn't** a better time to get away.

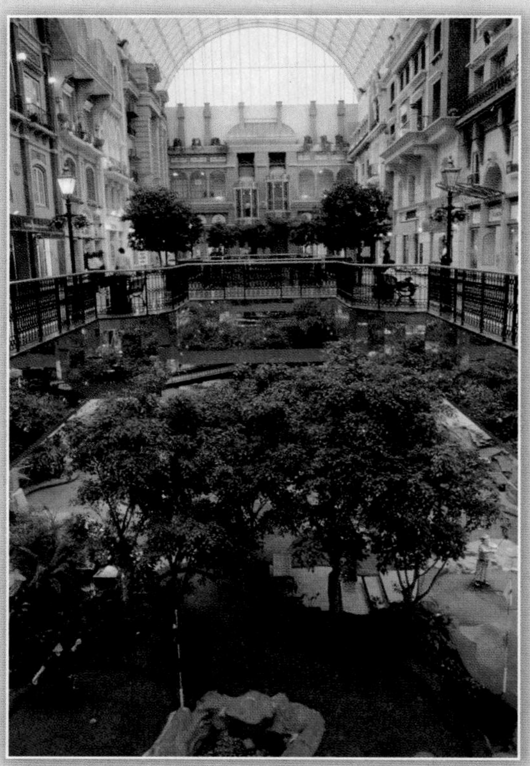

After You Read

A | Practice *PAIRS: Now read the advertisement aloud. Take turns reading sentences.*

B | Vocabulary *Complete the conversations with the words from the box.*

amusement park	**include**	**market**
attraction	**indoor**	**one of a kind**
get away	**international**	

1. **A:** Why do you like that store?

   B: It's ________________. It has unusual things for sale.

2. **A:** Does the bill ________________ the tip at this restaurant?

   B: No. The tip is extra.

3. **A:** What kind of school is it?

   B: It's a(n) ________________ school. Students come from all over the world.

4. **A:** There's a big ________________ in the center of town. You can buy fresh fruit, vegetables, and handmade clothes.

   B: Let's go. It sounds great.

5. **A:** What's the main ________________ at that mall?

   B: The prices. Everything is cheap.

6. **A:** What's your favorite ride at the ________________?

   B: The Hurricane. It's fast and scary. I love it.

7. **A:** Does the school have a(n) ________________ swimming pool?

   B: Yes, it does. The students can swim every day of the year.

8. **A:** He's tired and bored with his job.

   B: He needs to ________________.

C | Comprehension *Read each question about the advertisement. Circle the correct letter.*

1. How many stores are there at the West Edmonton Mall?
   a. more than 80
   b. more than 100
   c. more than 800

2. What does the ad say about the mall?
   a. It has a chocolate flavor.
   b. It has a Canadian flavor.
   c. It has an international flavor.

(Top) Spinner and *(Bottom)* statue at West Edmonton Mall

3. What kind of traditional market is there?
   a. a Mexican market
   b. a Chinese market
   c. a Turkish market

4. How many eating places are there?
   a. more than 80
   b. more than 100
   c. more than 7

5. What does West Edmonton Mall include?
   a. a water park
   b. schools
   c. a golf course

STEP 2 GRAMMAR PRESENTATION

THERE IS / THERE ARE

Affirmative Statements			
There	*Be*	**Subject**	**Place / Time**
There	**is**	a restaurant	on this level.
		a movie	at 6:30.
There	**are**	two restaurants	near the entrance.
		shows	at 7:00 and 9:00.

Negative Statements			
There	*Be + Not*	**Subject**	**Place / Time**
There	**isn't**	a restaurant	on the second level.
There	**aren't**	any movies	at 8:00.

Contractions		
there is	⟶	**there's**
there is not	⟶	**there isn't**
there are not	⟶	**there aren't**

Yes / No Questions			
Be	*There*	**Subject**	**Place**
Is	**there**	a pizza place	on Second Street?
Are	**there**	any banks	nearby?

Short Answers			
Affirmative		**Negative**	
Yes,	**there is.**	No,	**there isn't.**
	there are.		**there aren't.**

GRAMMAR NOTES

1	Use ***there is*** or ***there's*** to state facts about a **person** or **thing**.	• **There is a salesperson** near the door. • **There's a bookstore** next to the electronics store.
2	Use ***there are*** to talk about people or things. We often use *there is* or *there are* to tell the **location** of people or things or the **time** of events. **BE CAREFUL!** Don't confuse *there are* and *they are*.	• **There are five shoe stores** at the mall. • There's a woman's shoe store **on the second level**. (location) • There are concerts **on Friday and Saturday nights**. (time) • **There are two good restaurants.** **They are** on the third level.
3	In the negative, use the contractions ***isn't*** and ***aren't***. The full forms, *is not* and *are not*, are rarely used with *there*. **BE CAREFUL!** Don't confuse *there aren't* with *they aren't*.	• **There isn't** a cloud in the sky. • **There aren't** any gyms near our school. • **There aren't any** gyms here. **There are** three restaurants nearby, but **they aren't** open this late.
4	We often use ***any*** with *yes / no* questions about plural nouns.	• Are there **any** malls nearby?
5	**BE CAREFUL!** ***Here*** and ***there*** are adverbs of place. *Here* is for something nearby, and *there* is for something far. Don't confuse the adverb of place *there* with *there is* or *there are* or with the possessive adjective *their*.	• Last summer we exchanged homes with friends near Banff. We went **there**, and they came **here**. • Banff National Park is good for hiking. **There are** high mountains **there**. • **Their** home is in the mountains.
6	We often use ***There is*** or ***There are*** the first time we talk about people or things. We use ***he***, ***she***, ***it***, or ***they*** to tell more about the people or things.	• **There's a package** in the mail. **It**'s heavy. • **There's a man** at the door. **He** wants to speak to you. • **There are three girls** in the dress store. **They** are choosing dresses for a party.

REFERENCE NOTE

For more about ***any***, see Unit 27, page 311.

STEP 3 FOCUSED PRACTICE

EXERCISE 1: Discover the Grammar

Look at the mall directory. Write **T** (**True**) *or* **F** (**False**) *for each statement.*

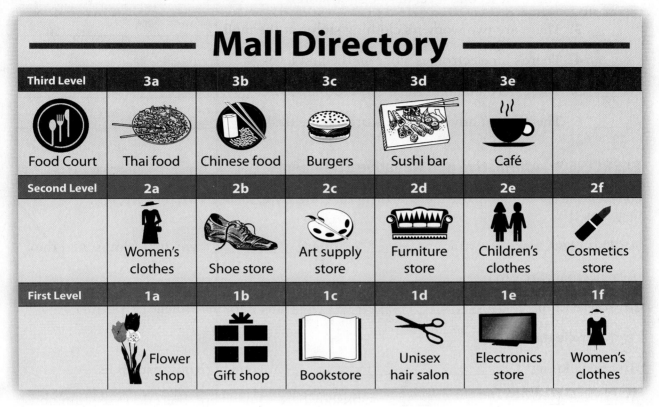

Mall Directory

Third Level	3a	3b	3c	3d	3e	
Food Court	Thai food	Chinese food	Burgers	Sushi bar	Café	
Second Level	**2a**	**2b**	**2c**	**2d**	**2e**	**2f**
	Women's clothes	Shoe store	Art supply store	Furniture store	Children's clothes	Cosmetics store
First Level	**1a**	**1b**	**1c**	**1d**	**1e**	**1f**
	Flower shop	Gift shop	Bookstore	Unisex hair salon	Electronics store	Women's clothes

_T_ **1.** There's a flower shop on the first level.

____ **2.** There's a café on the second level.

____ **3.** There aren't any toy stores.

____ **4.** There are five places to eat.

____ **5.** There isn't any Thai food at this mall.

____ **6.** There's a bookstore on the first level.

____ **7.** There aren't any office supply stores at the mall.

____ **8.** There aren't any jewelry stores at the mall.

____ **9.** There isn't an amusement park at this mall.

____ **10.** There's an art supply store at the mall.

EXERCISE 2: Affirmative and Negative Statements

(Grammar Notes 1–3)

Check (✓) each correct sentence. Change the sentences that don't make sense.

____ **1.** There's a mall in the Chinese restaurant. *There's a Chinese restaurant in the mall.*

____ **2.** There's a second level on the shoe store. ______________________

____ **3.** There are two women's clothing stores at the mall. ______________________

____ **4.** There's an electronics store on the first level. ______________________

____ **5.** There isn't a mall in the men's clothing store. ______________________

____ **6.** There aren't any furniture stores in the desks. ______________________

EXERCISE 3: Affirmative and Negative Statements

(Grammar Notes 1–4, 6)

Complete the conversation. Use **there is, there isn't, there are, there aren't, they are,** *or* **they aren't.**

A: This pizza place is awful. *There aren't* (1.) any tablecloths, and the placemats are dirty.

B: You're right. ______________ (2.) any napkins either.

A: Where is the busboy?

B: I don't know. ______________ (3.) anyone here now except us.

A: ______________ (4.) a busboy here somewhere, but I don't see him now. Well, I need a fork and knife.

B: ______________ (5.) some forks and knives on that table. Oh. ______________ (6.) clean.

A: Oh my gosh. You won't believe this.

B: What is it? Boy, it's hot in here. ______________ (7.) even a fan.

A: ______________ (8.) a mouse over there, near the wall!

B: What? Ugh, ______________ (9.) two mice! Let's leave!

A: What about our food?

B: Let the mice have it. ______________ (10.) hungry, too!

EXERCISE 4: *There is / There are*, *There*, and *They are* (Grammar Notes 1–2, 5)

Complete the conversation. Use **there's, there are, there,** *and* **they're.** *Remember to start sentences with a capital letter.*

A: How about some Chinese food?

B: Well, ___there's___ (1.) only one Chinese food restaurant nearby, but it's not very good. ______________ (2.) a lot of other restaurants though.

A: Today is Sunday. Are they open?

B: ______________ (3.) all open seven days a week.

A: Well, ______________ (4.) a nice Mexican place over ______________ (5.).

B: Where?

A: Over ______________ (6.) next to the diner.

B: That's right. I know the place. I was ______________ (7.) a few months ago. Let's go.

EXERCISE 5: Agreement with *There is / There are* (Grammar Notes 1–2, 6)

Complete the sentences. Use **There's** *or* **There are** *in the first sentence. Use* **He's, She's, It's,** *or* **They're** *in the second sentence.*

1. ___There's___ a good café over there. ___It's___ next to the bookstore.
2. ______________ a salesman behind the counter. ______________ talking to that woman.
3. ______________ a lot of wool sweaters. ______________ in the back of the store.
4. ______________ a scarf on the floor. ______________ your new one, isn't it?
5. ______________ some indoor parking spaces over there. ______________ near the exit.
6. ______________ a small mall on Route 4. ______________ next to the amusement park.
7. ______________ a lot of people in that line. ______________ buying tickets for the movie.

EXERCISE 6: *Yes / No* Questions with *Is there / Are there* (Grammar Notes 1–4, 6)

Look at the calendar. Complete the questions with **is there** *or* **are there**. *Then write answers. Remember to start sentences with a capital letter.*

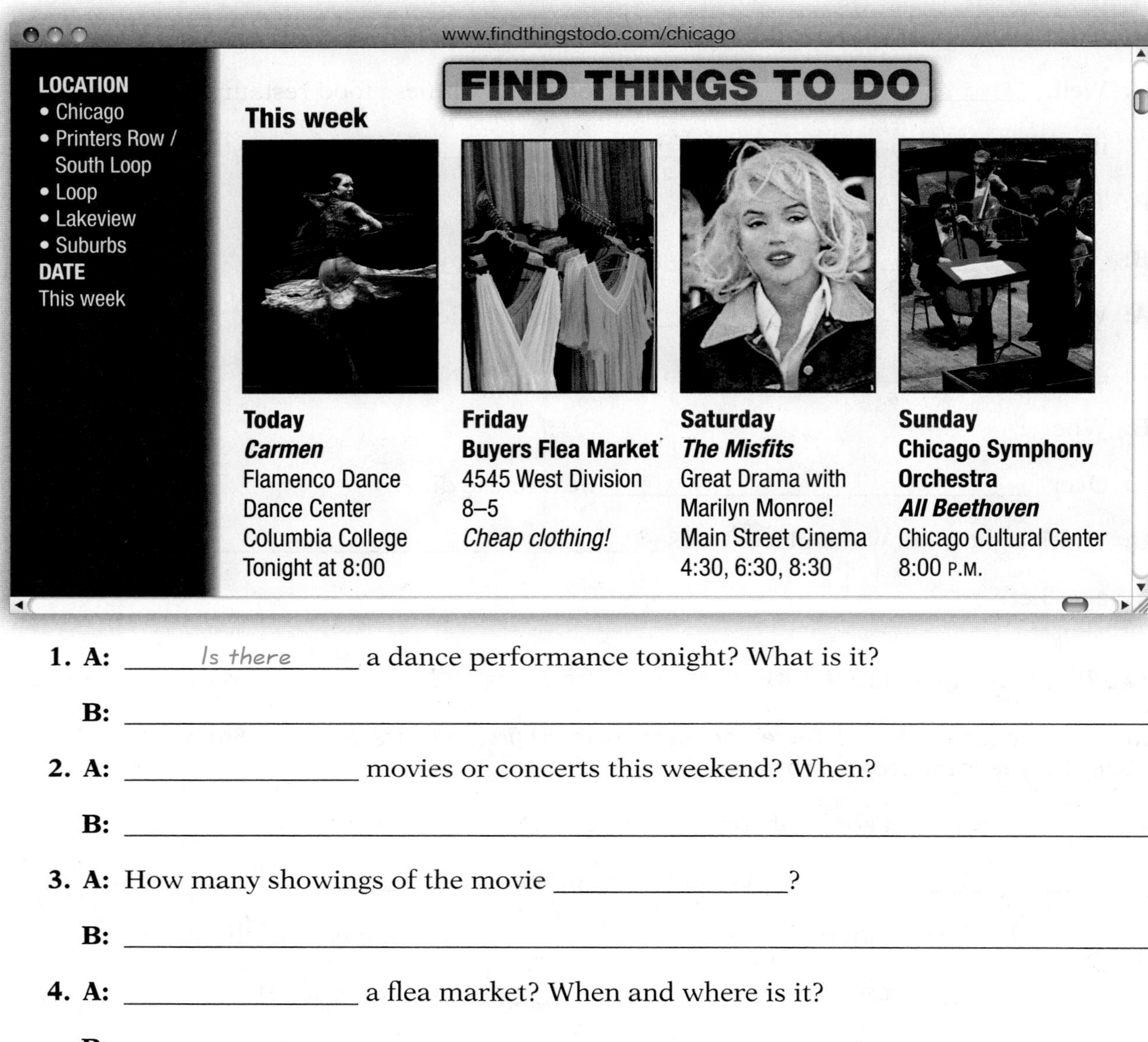

1. **A:** ___Is there___ a dance performance tonight? What is it?

   B: ______________________________

2. **A:** ______________ movies or concerts this weekend? When?

   B: ______________________________

3. **A:** How many showings of the movie ______________?

   B: ______________________________

4. **A:** ______________ a flea market? When and where is it?

   B: ______________________________

EXERCISE 7: Editing

Correct the paragraph. There are six mistakes. The first mistake is already corrected. Find and correct five more.

There ~~be~~ *are* pizza places at almost every mall. The pizzas come in all shapes and sizes. are traditional pizzas with mushrooms, pepperoni, and broccoli. There is also pizzas with curry, red herring, and coconut. In the United States they are over 61,000 pizza places. There represent 17 percent of all restaurants. There are popular with young and old.

STEP 4 COMMUNICATION PRACTICE

EXERCISE 8: Pronunciation

A | *Read and listen to the Pronunciation Note.*

Pronunciation Note

The words ***there***, ***their***, and ***they're*** have the same sound.

B | *Listen to the sentences. Circle the correct letter of the word or words the speaker uses.*

1.	**a.** there (circled)	**b.** their
2.	**a.** There	**b.** There's
3.	**a.** They are	**b.** There are
4.	**a.** There	**b.** There's
5.	**a.** There are	**b.** They are
6.	**a.** There	**b.** They're

EXERCISE 9: Listening

A | *Listen to this conversation between two drivers. What is the speaker's first question?*

Excuse me, ____?

B | *Listen again. Mark the sentences* **Y (Yes), N (No),** *or* **? (it doesn't say).**

__Y__ **1.** Is there a mall up ahead?

_____ **2.** Is the mall crowded?

_____ **3.** Is there a pizza place at the mall?

_____ **4.** Is the food court on the second level?

_____ **5.** Are there at least 10 places where you can eat?

EXERCISE 10: Comparing Pictures

PAIRS: Find 10 differences between Picture A and Picture B.

Example: In Picture A there's a shoe repair shop between the bakery and the pizza place. In Picture B there isn't a shoe repair shop between the bakery and the pizza place. The shoe repair shop is between the pizza place and the flower shop.

Picture A

Picture B

EXERCISE 11: Game: Tic Tac Toe

Use the phrases in the boxes to ask your classmates questions. Begin with **Is there** *or* **Are there any.** *If a student says "yes," write his or her name in the box. When you have three across, down, or diagonally, call out, "Tic Tac Toe!"*

a big mall near your home	an amusement park near your home	an international club in your school
twins in your family	an Italian restaurant near your home	a skating rink near your home
a pizza place on your street	credit cards in your purse or pocket	an indoor pool near your home

EXERCISE 12: Writing

A | *Write about a place where you like to shop. Use* **There is, There isn't, There are,** *or* **There aren't.**

EXAMPLE: There's a small store near my home. It's called "Village Gifts." It's on a street with two other small shops. The owners are a husband and wife. Their gifts include unusual crafts from all over the world. There are some great things to buy—colorful pottery from Mexico, beautiful jewelry from Thailand, traditional rugs from China, and baskets from Jamaica. The owners love the things they sell. There's a story behind every item. That's why I like to shop there. There aren't many shops like that.

B | *Check your work. Use the Editing Checklist.*

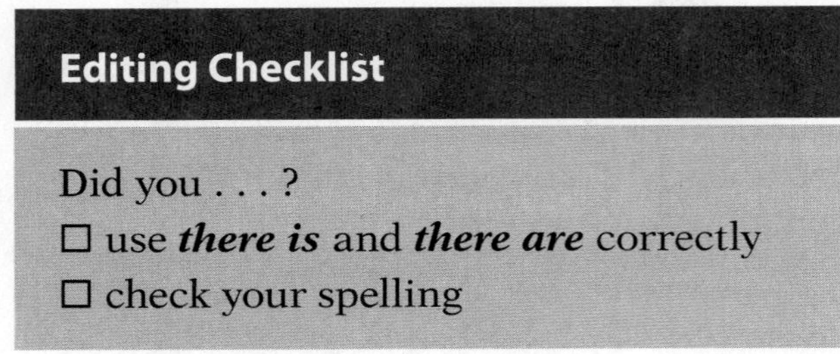

Editing Checklist

Did you . . . ?

☐ use ***there is*** and ***there are*** correctly

☐ check your spelling

UNIT 11 Review

Check your answers on page UR-2.
Do you need to review anything?

A | *Circle the correct words to complete the* **yes / no** *questions and short answers.*

1. **A:** **Are there / Are they** any soda machines in the building?

   B: Yes, **there are / they are**.

2. **A:** **Are there / Are they** any amusement parks near your school?

   B: No, **there aren't / they're not**.

3. **A:** **Is it / Is she** the teacher?

   B: Yes, **she's / she is**.

4. **A:** **Are there / Are they** new students?

   B: No, **they aren't / she isn't**.

5. **A:** **Are there / Is there** a men's room on this floor?

   B: No, **they aren't / there isn't**.

B | *Complete the sentences with* **There's, There are, She's, It's,** *or* **They're.**

1. ________________ a new pizza place on Elm Street. ________________ next to the post office.

2. ________________ a lot of people outside the pizza place. ________________ in a long line.

3. ________________ a great pizza chef there. ________________ funny, and her pizzas are delicious.

C | *Correct the paragraph. There are four mistakes.*

Visit the new Shopper's Mall on Route 290. There's over 100 stores. There a movie theater, and they are ten great places to eat. Come early. Every morning at 10:30 there are a free show for children. The mall is three miles from the Tappan Bridge on Route 290.

UNIT 12

Possessives: Nouns, Adjectives, Pronouns; Object Pronouns; Questions with *Whose*

POSSESSIONS

STEP 1 GRAMMAR IN CONTEXT

Before You Read

A | *Is your handwriting neat? Is it difficult to read?*

B | *Look at Michelle and Rick's handwriting. Whose handwriting is neat? Whose is messy?*

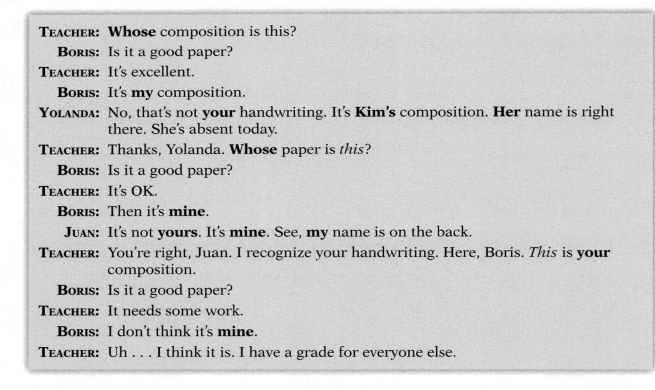

My name is Michelle Young.

My name is Rick M[illegible].

Read

A teacher is returning student compositions. Read the conversation.

TEACHER: **Whose** composition is this?
BORIS: Is it a good paper?
TEACHER: It's excellent.
BORIS: It's **my** composition.
YOLANDA: No, that's not **your** handwriting. It's **Kim's** composition. **Her** name is right there. She's absent today.
TEACHER: Thanks, Yolanda. **Whose** paper is *this*?
BORIS: Is it a good paper?
TEACHER: It's OK.
BORIS: Then it's **mine**.
JUAN: It's not **yours**. It's **mine**. See, **my** name is on the back.
TEACHER: You're right, Juan. I recognize your handwriting. Here, Boris. *This* is **your** composition.
BORIS: Is it a good paper?
TEACHER: It needs some work.
BORIS: I don't think it's **mine**.
TEACHER: Uh . . . I think it is. I have a grade for everyone else.

After You Read

A | Practice *GROUPS OF 4: Now read the conversation aloud.*

B | Vocabulary *Complete the sentences with the words from the box.*

back	composition	grade	handwriting	recognize

1. It's his letter. I can ________________ the ________________.
2. We had to write a ________________ about a favorite childhood possession. Mine was about my blue blanket.
3. Are the answers in the ________________ of the book?
4. What was your ________________ in English? Mine was an A+.

C | Comprehension *Whose compositions are these? Write* **Kim, Juan,** *and* **Boris** *below the correct composition.*

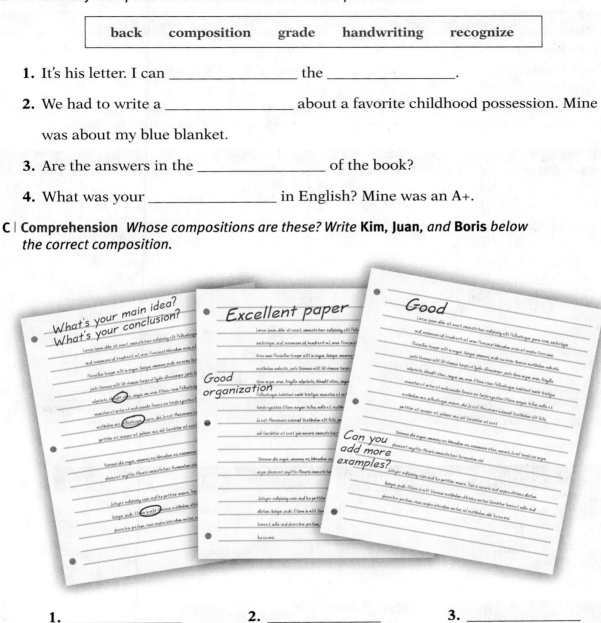

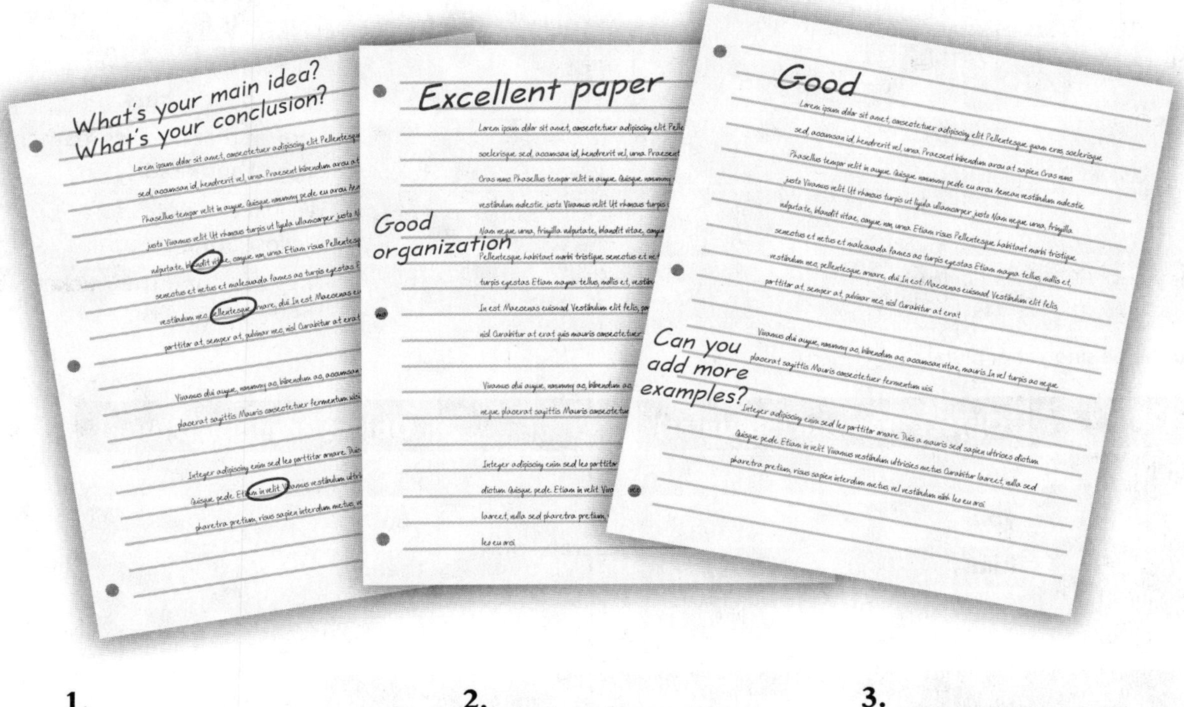

1. ________________ 2. ________________ 3. ________________

STEP 2 GRAMMAR PRESENTATION

POSSESSIVES, OBJECT PRONOUNS; QUESTIONS WITH *WHOSE*

Possessive Nouns	
Singular Nouns	**Plural Nouns**
John's last name is Tamez. **Russ's** last name is Stram.	The **girls'** gym is on this floor.
My **mother's** name is Rita. The **woman's** name is Carmen.	My **parents'** car is in the garage. The **women's** restroom is on the first floor.

Subject Pronoun	Possessive Adjective	Possessive Pronoun	
I	**my**	**mine**	That is **my** book. That book is **mine**.
You*	**your**	**yours**	Do you have **your** key? Do you have **yours**?
He	**his**	**his**	This is **his** car. This car is **his**.
She	**her**	**hers**	That's **her** house. That house is **hers**.
It	**its**		Look at that bird. **Its** feathers are red and gold.
We	**our**	**ours**	We lost **our** notes. We lost **ours**.
They	**their**	**theirs**	They can't find **their** tickets. They can't find **theirs**.

**You* can be singular or plural.

	Object Pronoun (Singular)
Raul likes	**me**.
	you.
	him.
	her.

	Object Pronoun (Plural)
Sarah knows	**us**.
	you.
	them.

Questions with *Whose*	
Questions	**Answers**
Whose hair is long?	Carmen**'s**. Carmen**'s** is. Carmen**'s** hair is long.
Whose eyes are green?	Igor**'s**. Igor**'s** are. Igor**'s** eyes are green.
Whose compositions are finished?	Yoko**'s** and Kaori**'s**. Yoko**'s** and Kaori**'s** are. Yoko**'s** and Kaori**'s** compositions.

GRAMMAR NOTES

1	**Possessive nouns** and **possessive adjectives** show belonging or a relationship.	• **Kim's car** (the car belongs to Kim) • **her aunt** (relationship)
2	To show possession, add: **apostrophe (') +** ***s*** to a **singular noun**. **apostrophe (')** to a **plural noun** ending in ***-s***. **apostrophe (') +** ***s*** to an **irregular plural noun**.	• That's **Juan's** composition. • My **parents'** home is near my home. • The **women's** restroom is on the first floor.
3	**Possessive adjectives** replace **possessive nouns**. Possessive adjectives agree with the possessive noun they replace.	**His** • ~~**My father's**~~ sisters are in Busan and Daegu. **Her** • ~~**My mother's**~~ brother is in Seoul.
4	A **noun** always follows a possessive noun or a possessive adjective.	• Bekir's **book** is new. • His **book** is new.
5	A **possessive pronoun** can replace a **possessive adjective** and **noun**. **BE CAREFUL!** A noun never follows a possessive pronoun. **BE CAREFUL!** The verb after a possessive pronoun agrees with the noun it replaces.	• This isn't **my umbrella**. **Mine** is blue. *(My umbrella is blue.)* • This is my hat. This is **mine**. NOT: This is mine ~~hat~~. • Her **notebook** is blue. = **Hers is** blue. • Her **notebooks** are red. = **Hers are** red.
6	Use ***whose*** for questions about possessions. **BE CAREFUL!** ***Who's*** is short for *who is*.	• **Whose** notebook is this? • **Who's** absent?
7	**BE CAREFUL!** Don't confuse possessive pronouns with **object pronouns**. Object pronouns come after a verb.	• Do you need to see **me**? • The baby loves baths. We give **him** a bath every day.
8	**BE CAREFUL!** A noun + apostrophe (') + *s* may be short for *is* in conversation and very informal writing. Do not confuse ***its*** and ***it's***. **its** = possessive adjective; ***it's*** = ***it is***	• "**Anna's** late." (Anna **is** late.) • This is my turtle. **Its** name is Tubby. • **It's** a hot day.

REFERENCE NOTES

For more rules about possessive nouns, see Appendix 7 on page A-7.
For more about irregular plural nouns, see Appendix 5 on pages A-5–A-6.

STEP 3 FOCUSED PRACTICE

EXERCISE 1: Discover the Grammar

Read the conversations. Then complete the sentences. Circle the correct letter.

Conversation 1:

FENG: Whose book is on the table next to the printer?

LI: It's mine.

1. ***Whose*** refers to ____________.
   (a.) book b. table
2. ***Mine*** means ____________.
   a. my book b. my printer

Conversation 2:

JOSE: Maria, is that your translator?

MARIA: No, it's Marco's. Mine is in my backpack. His is over there.

3. ***Marco's*** means ____________.
   a. Here is Marco. b. Marco's translator
4. ***Mine*** means ____________.
   a. my translator b. my backpack
5. ***His*** means ____________.
   a. Marco's backpack b. Marco's translator

Conversation 3:

SUN HI: How is Mi Young related to you?

JUN: She's my father's brother's wife.

6. My ***father's brother's wife*** is ____________.
   a. my uncle b. my aunt

Conversation 4:

EROL: Where are the workbooks?

AYLA: I put on them on the bookshelves near the door.

7. ***Them*** refers to ____________.
   a. the bookshelves b. the workbooks

EXERCISE 2: Possessive Nouns

(Grammar Notes 1–2)

A | *Read about the Zhang family. Underline the possessive nouns in the reading.*

This is the Zhang family. The older man is Lao Zhang. Lao's wife is Feng. They have two daughters, Hua and Mei. Hua's husband is Gang. They have a son, Bao. Mei's husband is Jinsong. They have a daughter, Ting.

B | *Complete the sentences. Underline the correct noun or possessive noun form.*

1. Ting's **mothers / mother's** mother is Ting's **grandmother / grandmother's**.
2. Hua's **sister / sister's daughter / daughters** is Hua's niece.
3. Gang's **wife / wife's sister / sister's** is his sister-in-law.
4. Bao's **uncle / uncle's** apartment is in Shanghai.
5. Bao and Ting are **cousins / cousin's**. Their **mothers / mother's** are **sisters / sister's**.
6. Lao Zhang is the **families / family's** oldest member.

EXERCISE 3: Possessive Adjectives

(Grammar Notes 1, 3)

Complete the sentences. Use a possessive adjective.

1. My sister studies in Toronto. ____Her____ school is on Victoria Street.
2. She goes to Edgewood University. She likes ________ classes.
3. Carlos's parents work at the United Nations. ________ jobs are interesting. His mother is a translator, and his father is an interpreter.
4. Right now my brother is in Peru, ________ wife is in Belize, and ________ children are in the United States.
5. The children have a rabbit. ________ fur is soft.
6. Does your brother like ________ job?
7. Do you use ________ calculator every day in math class?
8. Does your grandmother like ________ new apartment? Is she happy there?

EXERCISE 4: Possessive Pronouns

(Grammar Note 5)

Replace the underlined words with a possessive pronoun.

1. **A:** Is that your notebook?

   B: No, it's not ~~my notebook~~ mine (a.). It's his notebook (b.). My notebook (c.) is in my book bag.

2. **A:** Is this their house?

   B: No. Their house (a.) is in back of the library.

   A: Whose house is this?

   B: It's our house (b.).

3. **A:** Are those your sunglasses?

   B: No, they're her sunglasses (a.). My sunglasses (b.) are in my bag.

EXERCISE 5: Possessive Adjectives and Possessive Pronouns

(Grammar Notes 1–2, 5, 7)

Complete the conversations with the words in parentheses. Write the correct form.

1. **A:** I think you have my umbrella.

   B: No. This is ___my___ **a. (my / mine)** umbrella. ________ **b. (You / Yours)** is over there. It's next to ________ **c. (her / hers)** translator.

2. **A:** Whose gloves are these? Yours or Julie's?

   B: ________ **a. (Her / Hers)** are black leather. ________ **b. (My / Mine)** are wool.

3. **A:** Where is ________ **a. (their / theirs)** car?

   B: ________ **b. (Their / Theirs)** car is in the garage.

   A: Is ________ **c. (your / yours)** there too?

   B: No. ________ **d. (Our / Ours)** is on the street.

EXERCISE 6: Subject and Object Pronouns, Possessives *(Grammar Notes 1, 3–5, 7)*

Complete the sentences with the words in parentheses. Write the correct form.

1. It's ___mine___ (a. I / my / me / mine). Please give it to ____________ (b. I / my / me / mine). ____________ (c. I / My / Me / I) need it.
2. I don't think ____________ (a. he / him / his) is on the train. I don't see ____________ (b. he / him / his).
3. Our family is from Edmonton. ____________ (a. They / Their / Theirs / Them) family is from Vancouver, but ____________ (b. they / their / theirs / them) live in Edmonton now. We live next door to ____________ (c. they / their / theirs / them).

EXERCISE 7: Possessives: Questions and Verb Agreement *(Grammar Notes 3, 5–6)*

Complete the conversations with the words in parentheses. Write the correct form.

1. **A:** ___Whose___ (Who's / Whose) shoes are these?
   B: They're my shoes. His ____________ (is / are) over there.
2. **A:** ____________ (Who's / Whose) key is this? ____________ (Is / Are) it yours?
   B: No it isn't.
3. **A:** ____________ (Who's / Whose) in room 401?
   B: Florian and David.
   A: ____________ (Is / Are) that their usual classroom?
4. **A:** ____________ (Who's / Whose) books are those? ____________ (Is / Are) they hers?
   B: No, ____________ (they're / it's) his.
5. **A:** ____________ (Who's / Whose) notes are those?
   B: Bob's. His notes are messy. Mine ____________ (is / are) neat.
6. **A:** ____________ (Who's / Whose) that woman?
   B: Her name is Wu-Shen. She's an English teacher.
7. **A:** My parents live in Italy. Hers ____________ (live / lives) in Argentina.

EXERCISE 8: Pronouns and Possessive Adjectives

(Grammar Notes 1–4, 7)

Read and complete the article with the words in parentheses. Write the correct form.

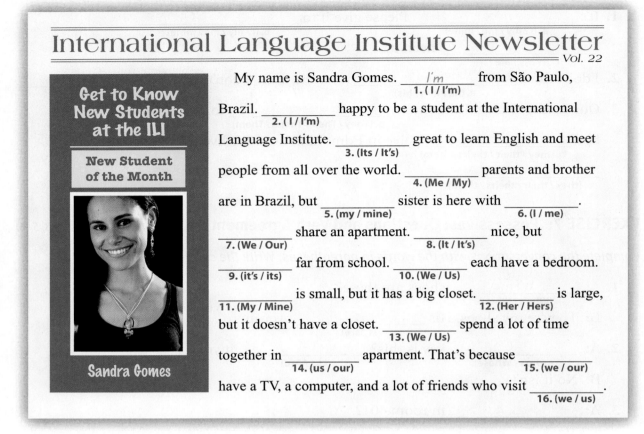

International Language Institute Newsletter

Vol. 22

Get to Know New Students at the ILI

New Student of the Month

Sandra Gomes

My name is Sandra Gomes. ___*I'm*___ (1. (I / I'm)) from São Paulo, Brazil. _________ (2. (I / I'm)) happy to be a student at the International Language Institute. _________ (3. (Its / It's)) great to learn English and meet people from all over the world. _________ (4. (Me / My)) parents and brother are in Brazil, but _________ (5. (my / mine)) sister is here with _________ (6. (I / me)). _________ (7. (We / Our)) share an apartment. _________ (8. (It / It's)) nice, but _________ (9. (it's / its)) far from school. _________ (10. (We / Us)) each have a bedroom. _________ (11. (My / Mine)) is small, but it has a big closet. _________ (12. (Her / Hers)) is large, but it doesn't have a closet. _________ (13. (We / Us)) spend a lot of time together in _________ (14. (us / our)) apartment. That's because _________ (15. (we / our)) have a TV, a computer, and a lot of friends who visit _________ (16. (we / us)).

EXERCISE 9: Editing

Correct the conversations. There are seven mistakes. The first mistake is already corrected. Find and correct six more.

1. **A:** Is that ~~you~~ *your* dictionary?

   B: No. It's his dictionary.

   A: Who's?

   B: Dans.

2. **A:** Is Maria sister here?

   B: No, she's not.

   A: Is Maria here?

   B: No, but his brother is.

   A: Where is Maria?

   B: I think she's with his sister. Their at the movies.

STEP 4 COMMUNICATION PRACTICE

EXERCISE 10: Pronunciation

A | *Read and listen to the Pronunciation Note.*

Pronunciation Note

When you use a possessive, add the sound of **/ z /**, **/ s /** or **/ ɪz /**.

Examples:			
	Lisa	Lisa's	**/ z /**
	Jack	Jack's	**/ s /**
	Ross	Ross's	**/ ɪz /**

B | *Listen to the sentences. Circle the word you hear.*

1. Maria	(Maria's)	Marias		**4.** partner	partner's	partners
2. Maria	Maria's	Marias		**5.** partner	partner's	partners
3. Maria	Maria's	Marias		**6.** partner	partner's	partners

EXERCISE 11: Listening

A | *Listen to the conversation. What are Boris and Jasmine talking about? Circle the correct letter.*

a. bikes **b.** baskets **c.** sales

B | *Listen again. Write the name of the owner above each bicycle. Use the names from the box.*

Amy	**Jasmine**	**Johnny**	**Roger and Ted**

1. ____________ **2.** ____________ **3.** ____________ **4.** ____________

EXERCISE 12: Talking about Family Photos

Bring in photos of family members. Write on the back of the photo how the person is related to you (for example, my sister, my mother, my aunt*). Your teacher collects the photos and gives you a different photo. You and your classmates ask questions about the photos.*

Example: **Anya:** Whose sister is this?
Pablo: I think it's Juan's.
Juan: You're right. She's my sister.

EXERCISE 13: Game: Find Someone Whose / Who's . . .

A | *Complete the questions. Use* **whose** *or* **who's.**

1. ____Whose____ birthday is in December? ________________
2. ____Who's____ good in art? ________________
3. ________________ name means something? ________________
4. ________________ a good athlete? ________________
5. ________________ eyes aren't dark brown? ________________
6. ________________ a good cook? ________________
7. ________________ first name has more than eight letters? ________________
8. ________________ birthday is in the summer? ________________
9. ________________ a good dancer? ________________
10. ________________ handwriting is beautiful? ________________

B | *Look back at Part A. Ask your classmates the questions. Write their names. Report to the class.*

Example: **Maria:** Juan, is your birthday in December?
Juan: No, it's not. Is yours?
Maria: Yes, it is. (Juan writes Maria's name on the line.)

EXERCISE 14: Writing

A | *Look at Exercise 8 on page 138. Write about yourself and your family for a school newsletter. Use pronouns and possessive adjectives.*

Example: I'm from Recife in Brazil. I live with my parents and my younger brother. My older brother, Jose, is married. He is a pilot, and his wife is a pilot too. My mother worries about them, but she is proud of them. My dream is to become a pilot one day too, but it's my secret for now.

B | *Check your work. Use the Editing Checklist.*

Editing Checklist

Did you . . . ?

☐ use possessive adjectives, possessive pronouns, and object pronouns correctly

☐ check your spelling

UNIT 12 Review

Check your answers on page UR-3.
Do you need to review anything?

A | *Cross out the underlined words. Replace them with* **His, Her, Its,** *or* **Their.**

1. The Browns' car is big.
2. My brother's best friend is a history teacher.
3. That bird is injured. That bird's wing is broken.
4. The students' tests are on the teacher's desk.
5. Our aunt's store is on Main Street.

B | *Underline the correct words to complete the conversations.*

1. **A:** You need an umbrella. Take **me / mine**.

   B: I don't want to use **your / yours**.

   A: It's OK. I have **you / your** rain hat.
2. **A: Who / Whose** dictionary is on the floor?

   B: It's **Ali / Ali's**.
3. **A:** Who's talking?

   B: My / Mine children have a parrot. **Its / It's** name is Polly. Polly's talking.
4. **A: Her / Hers** composition is here, but where is **your / yours**?

   B: My / Mine is at home. Sorry.

C | *Correct the conversation. There are five mistakes.*

A: Who's bag is that on the floor?

B: I think it's Maria.

A: No. Her bag is on her arm.

B: Well, it's not mine bag. Maybe it's Rita.

A: Rita, is that bag your?

UNIT 13 Ability: *Can* or *Could*

ABILITIES OF ANIMALS

STEP 1 GRAMMAR IN CONTEXT

Before You Read

GROUPS: Do you have a pet or know someone who has one? What kind? Does it have any unusual talents?

Read

Read the online article about an amazing parrot.

wild nature

WILD NATURE Home | Animal Facts | Photos | Quizzes | Wild TV

A Genius Parrot

Everyone knows parrots **can talk**. By "talk" we mean they **can repeat** words. Most parrots **can't** really **express** ideas.

N'kisi is different. N'kisi is an African gray parrot. He **can say** almost 1,000 words. He **can use** basic grammar. He **can talk** about the present, past, and future. When he doesn't know a form, he **can invent** one. For example, he used the word "flied," not "flew," for the past of the verb "fly."

N'kisi lives in New York City with his owner, Aimee Morgana. He **couldn't talk** much at first. At first he **could** only **say** a few words. But Aimee was a great teacher, and N'kisi was a good student. Now N'kisi talks to anyone near him.

Donald Broom, a professor of Veterinary Medicine at the University of Cambridge, is not surprised. He says that parrots **can think** at high levels. In that way, they are like apes and chimpanzees.

Les Rance of the Parrot Society says, "Most African grays are intelligent. They **can learn** to do easy puzzles. They **can say** 'good night' when you turn the lights off at night. They **can say** 'good-bye' when you put a coat on. But N'kisi **can do** many more things. N'kisi is an amazing[1] bird. He's not just smart. He's a genius."

[1] ***amazing:*** surprising in a good way

After You Read

A | Practice *PAIRS: Read the article again aloud. Take turns reading each paragraph.*

B | Vocabulary *Complete the sentences with the words from the box. Use the correct form.*

be surprised	**genius**	**intelligent**	**invent**	**professor**

1. Monkeys and dolphins are very __intelligent__ animals. They can learn many things.
2. Many people __are surprised__ by the abilities of African gray parrots.
3. Mozart was a __genius__. He wrote great music at the age of six.
4. Try and take his course. He's a very good __professor__.
5. We need to __invent__ a way to learn languages while we sleep.

C | Comprehension *Write* **T (True), F (False),** *or* **? (it doesn't say)** *for each statement.*

__F__ **1.** N'kisi can say more than 1,100 words.
__F__ **2.** N'kisi can't use basic grammar.
__T__ **3.** N'kisi can talk about the past and the future.
__F__ **4.** N'kisi can understand Italian.
__F__ **5.** Parrots can't think at high levels.
__T__ **6.** N'kisi could only say a few words at first.

STEP 2 GRAMMAR PRESENTATION

CAN / CAN'T FOR ABILITY AND POSSIBILITY; *COULD* FOR PAST ABILITY

Affirmative Statements		
Subject	***Can / Could***	**Base Form of Verb**
I You* He We	**can** **could**	**talk.**

Negative Statements		
Subject	***Can't / Couldn't***	**Base Form of Verb**
She It They	**can't** **couldn't**	**talk.**

**You* is both singular and plural.

Yes / No Questions		
Can / Could	**Subject**	**Base Form of Verb**
Can **Could**	you	**understand**?

Short Answers	
Affirmative	**Negative**
Yes, I can.	No, I can't.
Yes, we could.	No, we couldn't.

GRAMMAR NOTES

1	***Can*** expresses **present ability** or **possibility**. It comes before the verb. The verb is always in the **base form**.	• He **can say** 950 words. • We **can teach** your bird to talk.
2	The **negative** of ***can*** is ***can't***. ***Cannot*** is a form of the negative. It is not common.	• I **can't** understand you. • I **cannot** understand you.
3	Reverse the subject and *can* for *yes / no* questions.	• **He can** speak about the past. • **Can he** speak about the past?
4	***Could*** expresses **past ability**. ***Could not*** is the full negative form. The more common form is the contraction, ***couldn't***.	• I **could** run fast in high school. • I **could not** drive five years ago. • I **couldn't** drive five years ago.
5	Reverse the subject and *could* for *yes / no* questions.	• **You could** speak English last year. • **Could you** speak English last year?
6	We usually give short answers to questions with *can, can't, could,* or *couldn't*.	• Can he understand me? **Yes, he can.**

STEP 3 FOCUSED PRACTICE

EXERCISE 1: Discover the Grammar

A | *Read the sentences in column A. Underline* **can, can't,** *or* **couldn't** *and the base form verbs. Circle the negative statements.*

	A		B
____	**1.** N'kisi can invent new words.	**a.**	He's very strong.
____	**2.** We can't understand our professor.	**b.**	She speaks too fast.
____	**3.** I'm sorry. I can't help you now.	**c.**	He was too short.
____	**4.** I can't hear you.	**d.**	They never talk about their feelings.
____	**5.** He can lift 110 pounds (50 kilos).	**e.**	He's a smart bird.
____	**6.** They can't express their love.	**f.**	I'm busy.
____	**7.** The boy couldn't reach the button.	**g.**	It's very noisy here.

B | *Look back at Part A. Match the sentences in column A with the possible reasons in column B.*

EXERCISE 2: *Can* and *Can't*

(Grammar Notes 1–2)

Complete the sentences with **can** *or* **can't** *and the verbs in parentheses.*

1. Many parrots ___can learn___ **(learn)** to speak. My parrot __________ **(say)**, "You're a genius."
2. My dog __________ **(sit)**, but he __________ **(bring)** me my shoes. I'm trying to teach him to bring things to me.
3. My cat __________ **(catch)** mice. He's very good at that. Her cat __________ **(catch)** mice. He just sits and watches them.
4. Her dog __________ **(understand)** two languages, Spanish and English. She speaks to her dog in English, and her husband speaks to the dog in Spanish.
5. Dolphins __________ **(help)** people in trouble. They are smart and show feelings.

EXERCISE 3: *Can / Can't*: *Yes / No* Questions and Answers

(Grammar Note 3)

Read the real conversation between Aimee Morgana and N'kisi, her parrot. Then write **yes / no** *questions with the words in parentheses. Answer the questions.*

N'kisi: Wanna (I want to) go in a car right now.

Aimee: I'm sorry. We can't right now—
maybe we can go later.

N'kisi: Why can't I go in a car now?

Aimee: Because we don't have one.

N'kisi: Let's get a car.

Aimee: No, N'kisi, we can't get a car now.

N'kisi: I want a car.

1. **A:** *Can N'kisi talk?* ______
   (N'kisi / talk)
   B: *Yes, he can.* ______
2. **A:** ______
   (he / ask questions)
   B: ______
3. **A:** ______
   (he / make suggestions)
   B: ______
4. **A:** ______
   (Aimee / buy a car now)
   B: ______
5. **A:** ______
   (N'kisi / ask for things)
   B: ______
6. **A:** ______
   (Aimee and N'kisi / go in a car now)
   B: ______

EXERCISE 4: Past Abilities: *Could / Couldn't*

(Grammar Notes 4–5)

Complete the sentences with **could** *or* **couldn't** *and the verbs in parentheses.*

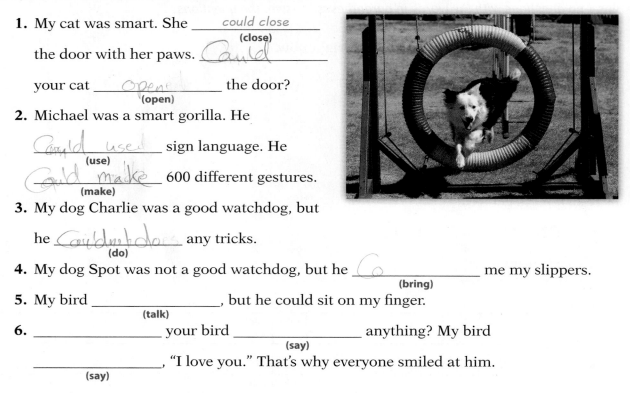

1. My cat was smart. She *could close* (close) the door with her paws. ________ your cat ________ (open) the door?
2. Michael was a smart gorilla. He ________ (use) sign language. He ________ (make) 600 different gestures.
3. My dog Charlie was a good watchdog, but he ________ (do) any tricks.
4. My dog Spot was not a good watchdog, but he ________ (bring) me my slippers.
5. My bird ________ (talk), but he could sit on my finger.
6. ________ your bird ________ (say) anything? My bird ________ (say), "I love you." That's why everyone smiled at him.

EXERCISE 5: Editing

Correct the conversation. There are seven mistakes. The first mistake is already corrected. Find and correct six more. Add **can** *to fix one mistake.*

A: Can you ~~coming~~ *come* to my party? It's next Saturday night. You can to meet my new dog.

B: Yes, I'd love to. How I get to your home?

A: You can to take the train or a taxi.

B: Can you meet me at the train station?

A: I'm sorry. I can't. I no can drive. Maybe Bob can meets you. He has a car, and he can to drive.

STEP 4 COMMUNICATION PRACTICE

EXERCISE 6: Pronunciation

A | *Read and listen to the Pronunciation Note.*

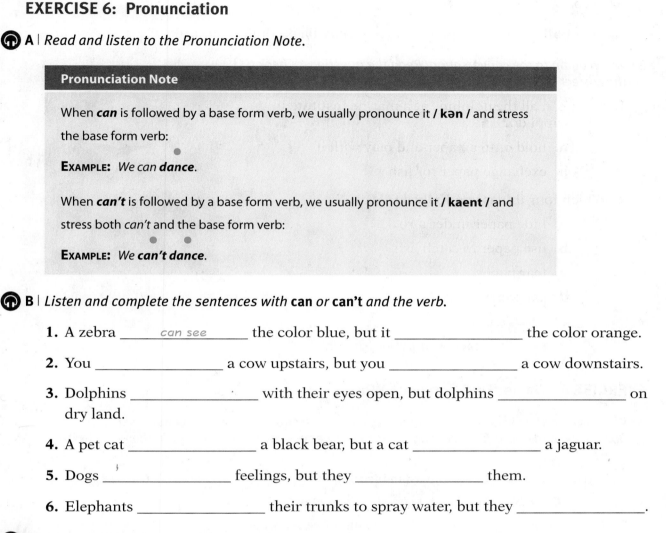

Pronunciation Note

When ***can*** is followed by a base form verb, we usually pronounce it **/ kən /** and stress the base form verb:

EXAMPLE: *We can* ***dance****.*

When ***can't*** is followed by a base form verb, we usually pronounce it **/ kaent /** and stress both *can't* and the base form verb:

EXAMPLE: *We* ***can't dance****.*

B | *Listen and complete the sentences with* **can** *or* **can't** *and the verb.*

1. A zebra ___can see___ the color blue, but it ________________ the color orange.
2. You ________________ a cow upstairs, but you ________________ a cow downstairs.
3. Dolphins ________________ with their eyes open, but dolphins ________________ on dry land.
4. A pet cat ________________ a black bear, but a cat ________________ a jaguar.
5. Dogs ________________ feelings, but they ________________ them.
6. Elephants ________________ their trunks to spray water, but they ________________.

C | *Listen again and repeat the sentences.*

EXERCISE 7: Listening

A | *Listen to a conversation about dolphins. Circle three things the dolphins in Florida could do.*

catch a ball **paint pictures** **play basketball** **talk**

B | *Listen again to the conversation. Read the questions. Check (✓) the correct answers.*

1. What can all the dolphins at a marine institute in Mississippi do?
   ____ **a.** hold onto a paper and play with it
   ____ **b.** exchange paper for fish

2. Which four things can Kelly do?
   ____ **a.** hide paper under a rock
   ____ **b.** use paper to catch fish
   ____ **c.** tear paper
   ____ **d.** eat paper
   ____ **e.** catch a bird
   ____ **f.** exchange pieces of paper for fish

EXERCISE 8: Game: Find Someone Who . . .

A | *Walk around the classroom. Ask your classmates questions with* **can** *or* **could**. *Ask about now and about five years ago. If they answer* **yes**, *write their names in the chart.*

EXAMPLE: **VICTOR:** Can you play an instrument?
CAROLINA: Yes, I can. I can play the guitar.
VICTOR: Could you play the guitar five years ago?
CAROLINA: No, I couldn't.

	Now	Five Years Ago
play an instrument	*Carolina*	
teach a bird to talk		
design a Web page		
ride a motorcycle		
train a dog		

B | *Report your answers to your class.*

EXAMPLE: Erna can play the piano and design a Web page. Five years ago she could play the piano, but she couldn't design a Web page.

EXERCISE 9: Game: What Can Your Group Do?

Work in small groups. Read the questions. When your group can do one of the tasks, raise your hand. The first group to do a task wins.

1. Can you think of 12 different animals that start with 12 different letters of the alphabet?

   EXAMPLE: a = ape   b = bear

2. Can you say "I love you" in more than four languages?
3. Can you name the colors of the flags of six countries?
4. Can you name the capitals of eight countries?

EXERCISE 10: Writing

A | *Write about an interesting pet or other animal. Use* **can** *or* **can't**. *Answer these questions in your paragraph:*

- What kind of animal is it? What does it look like?
- Where does it live?
- Is it your pet? Does it have a name?
- What can this animal do? What can't it do?

EXAMPLE: I have a beautiful parakeet. His feathers are bright green. His name is Chichi. He is two years old. He lives in a cage in the living room. Sometimes he flies around the room. Chichi can sing very beautifully. Chichi couldn't do anything when he was younger. But now he can sit on my finger and eat from my hand. He can't speak, but I'm happy about that. I tell him all my secrets, and he doesn't tell anyone. That's a wonderful quality. I love my Chichi.

B | *Check your work. Use the Editing Checklist.*

Editing Checklist

Did you . . . ?

☐ use ***can*** and ***can't*** correctly

☐ check your spelling

UNIT 13 Review

Check your answers on page UR-3.
Do you need to review anything?

A | *Complete the sentences with* **can, could, can't,** *or* **couldn't** *and the verbs in parentheses.*

1. Last year I _______________ much English. Now I _______________ a lot more.
   (understand) (understand)
2. Jill doesn't have time to exercise these days, so she _______________ fast. In high school she was on a team, and she _______________ a mile in seven minutes.
   (run) (run)
3. I _______________ five years ago. Now I have a driver's license, and I _______________ well.
   (drive) (drive)

B | *Complete the questions and answers. Use* **can, could, can't** *or* **couldn't.**

1. **A:** _______________ you understand your dreams?
   B: Yes, I _______________. They're easy to understand.
2. **A:** _______________ you write reports last year?
   B: No, I _______________, but now I _______________.
3. **A:** _______________ he fix cars?
   B: Yes, he _______________. He's a good mechanic.

C | *Correct the conversation. There are seven mistakes.*

A: Can you to get online?

B: No, I can't not. I couldn't got online last night either.

A: My brother is good with computers. Maybe he can helps.

B: Great. I can no figure out what's wrong.

A: I no can reach him now, but I can to call him after 6 P.M.

UNIT 14 Permission: *Can* or *May*

HEALTH AND DIET

STEP 1 GRAMMAR IN CONTEXT

Before You Read

Foods are mainly made of protein, carbohydrates, and fat. Which category do these foods belong in? Write them below. Then check your answers on page 154.

~~beef~~	~~bread~~	~~butter~~	cake	chicken	fish	oil	pasta	rice

Protein: beef, ______________________

Carbohydrate(s): bread, ______________________

Fat: butter, ______________________

Read

Read the online article about diets. What do you think about them?

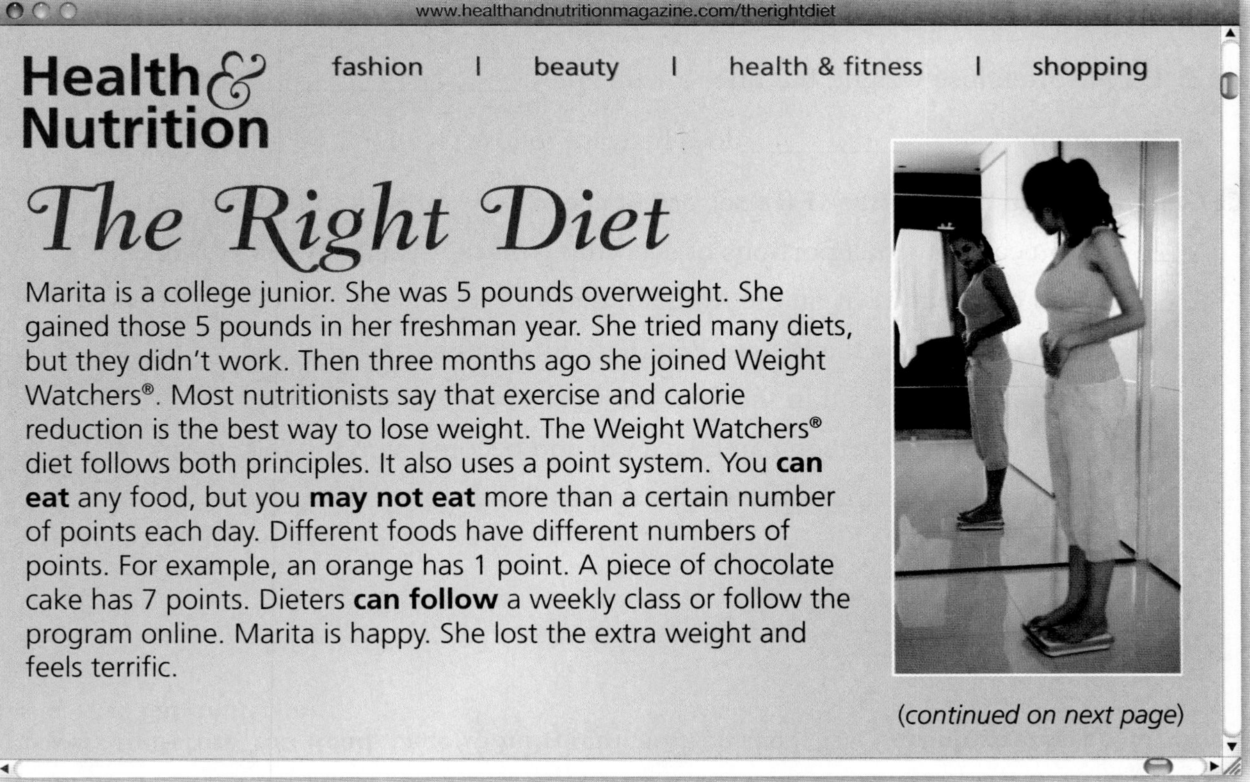

www.healthandnutritionmagazine.com/therightdiet

Health & Nutrition

fashion | beauty | health & fitness | shopping

The Right Diet

Marita is a college junior. She was 5 pounds overweight. She gained those 5 pounds in her freshman year. She tried many diets, but they didn't work. Then three months ago she joined Weight Watchers®. Most nutritionists say that exercise and calorie reduction is the best way to lose weight. The Weight Watchers® diet follows both principles. It also uses a point system. You **can eat** any food, but you **may not eat** more than a certain number of points each day. Different foods have different numbers of points. For example, an orange has 1 point. A piece of chocolate cake has 7 points. Dieters **can follow** a weekly class or follow the program online. Marita is happy. She lost the extra weight and feels terrific.

(*continued on next page*)

www.healthandnutritionmagazine.com/therightdiet

Bill Morgan is a businessman. He eats many meals out. He was 25 pounds overweight. Bill doesn't want to count points, so he's following the Atkins™ diet. In this diet you **may eat** foods high in protein and fat, such as red meat and cheese, but you **can't eat** carbohydrates such as bread, cereal, pasta, and rice. The first two weeks are especially strict. You **can't have** fruit, grains, cereals, bread, or most vegetables. You also **can't drink** any milk or juice. But after three weeks Bill weighs 10 pound less. He's thrilled.

Many people, like Marita and Bill, lose weight on diets, but they don't keep it off. So they have to start all over again. Dieters don't always agree on the best diet, but almost every dieter would like to take a pill one day, become slim the next, and never regain the weight.

Comments (115) Post a comment Share

After You Read

A | Practice *PAIRS: Now read the article aloud. Take turns reading each paragraph.*

B | Vocabulary *Complete the sentences with the words from the box. Use the correct form.*

especially	gain	lose	overweight	pound

1. These days many people eat more than they need, and they become _______________. They need to _______________ weight.

2. That diet is _______________ hard to keep.

3. People often lose weight, but after a while they _______________ it back.

4. How many _______________ does he want to lose?

C | Comprehension *Write* **T (True), F (False),** *or* **? (it doesn't say)** *for each statement.*

____ **1.** You can eat small portions of everything on the Weight Watchers® diet.

____ **2.** You can't eat meat on the Atkins™ diet.

____ **3.** You may follow the Weight Watchers® diet online.

____ **4.** You can't eat cereal in the first two weeks of the Atkins™ diet.

____ **5.** An overweight person can take a pill and become slim the next day.

____ **6.** You may not drink coffee on the Atkins™ diet.

Answers to Before You Read, page 153: Protein: beef, chicken, fish; **Carbohydrates:** bread, cake, pasta, rice; **Fat:** butter, oil

STEP 2 GRAMMAR PRESENTATION

CAN OR *MAY* FOR PERMISSION

Statements			
Subject	***Can / Can't* *May / May Not***	**Base Form of Verb**	
You	**can** **can't**	**start**	today.
He	**may** **may not**	**eat**	nuts.

Yes / No Questions			
Can / May	**Subject**	**Base Form of Verb**	
Can **May**	I	**have**	the day off?

Answers
Yes, you can. **Yes, you may.** **Sure.** **Of course.** **I'm sorry. We're too busy.**

Wh- Questions				
***Wh-* Word**	***Can***	**Subject**	**Base Form of Verb**	
When	**can**	I	**borrow**	the car?
Where		we	**park**?	

GRAMMAR NOTES

1	Use ***can*** or ***may*** to **give permission**. (It's OK to . . .) *Can* and *may* are followed by the base form of the verb. Use ***can't*** or ***may not*** to **deny permission**. (Something is not OK.) There is no contraction for *may not*.	• You **can see** the doctor now. • You **may eat** fish. • You **can't drive** a truck on this road. • You **may not use** my car. NOT: You ~~mayn't~~ drive a car without a license.
2	Use *can* or *may* to **ask for permission**. *May* is more formal than *can*. We respond with a short affirmative response (*Yes, you may*) or a short apology and a reason. (*Sorry, I . . .*)	**A: May** I see the doctor this afternoon? **B: Yes, you may.** OR **No, I'm sorry. The doctor is out.**
3	We use ***Can I help you?*** or ***May I help you?*** to offer help to someone. We thank the speaker or say no thank you and give a reason.	**A: Can I help you?** OR **May I help you?** **B: Thanks**. I'm looking for a winter jacket. OR **No thanks. I'm just looking.**

STEP 3 FOCUSED PRACTICE

EXERCISE 1: Discover the Grammar

A | *Read the conversation. Underline* **can, can't, may,** *or* **may not.** *Then complete Part B.*

__A__ **A:** Can I eat meat?

____ **B:** Yes, you can, but you can only have boiled, grilled, or baked meat.

____ **A:** What about fried chicken? Can I have it? I love fried chicken.

____ **B:** Sorry. You may not have any fried food on this diet.

____ **A:** Can I eat nuts?

____ **B:** Yes, you may, but don't eat too many. And remember, there are many things on this diet that you can eat. You may eat as many green vegetables as you want, and you can drink as much green tea as you want.

A: Well, that sounds good.

____ **B:** If you have any more questions, you can call me weekdays between 11:00 and 1:00.

B | *Look back at Part A. Write* **A** *for sentences that ask for permission,* **G** *for sentences that give permission, and* **D** *for sentences that deny permission.*

EXERCISE 2: *Can* / *May*: Affirmative, Negative, *Yes* / *No* Questions *(Grammar Notes 1–3)*

Complete the conversations with **can** *or* **may** *and the verbs from the box.*

drive	help	~~return~~
eat	keep	see
have	look	take

1. (Can)

A: You're doing great.

B: I feel good too, Dr. Lam. When ___can___ I ___return___ to work?

A: Next week.

B: And when ________________ I ________________?

A: Wait another week. Take the train next week.

B: OK.

A: But remember. Watch your diet. Don't eat heavy food and stay away from dessert.

B: ________________ I ________________ out?

A: Sure. Just watch what you order.

2. (May)

A: ________________ I ________________ you?

B: Thanks. I'd like to make an appointment with Ms. Stein.

A: She's free next Tuesday at 10:00. Here are some booklets about nutrition. You ________________ ________________ them home and read them.

B: Thanks. Do you want them back?

A: No. You ________________ ________________ them.

3. (Can)

A: Your fish comes with a salad.

B: OK. ________________ I ________________ the dressing on the side?

A: Of course.

B: And ________________ we ________________ the dessert menu?

C: Bob, you're on a diet! You can't have dessert.

B: But I ________________ ________________ at the desserts and dream about them.

EXERCISE 3: Permission: *May / Can*

(Grammar Notes 1–3)

Complete the conversation. Write questions with **can** *or* **may** *and the information in parentheses.*

Receptionist: (May) May I help you?
1. (Do you need my help?)

Nuray: Yes, thanks. I'm Nuray Attaturk. I have an appointment with Dr. Lee for 2:00.

Receptionist: Thanks Ms. Attaturk. (May) May I see you health insurance card
2. (~~I~~ want to see your health insurance card.)

Dr. Lee: OK, Nuray. Here's your diet. Any questions?

Nuray: (Can) Can I eat snacks?
3. (Is it OK to eat snacks?)

Dr. Lee: Yes, but you can only have light snacks.

Nuray: (Can) Can I eat ice cream?
4. (Is it OK to eat ice cream?)

Dr. Lee: No, you can't, but you can have low-fat yogurt instead.

Nuray: (May) May I call you with questions?
5. (Is it OK to call you with questions?)

Dr. Lee: Certainly. But don't worry. Everything is on these papers. Just read the diet and follow the directions. You'll feel better in no time.

Nuray: Thanks, Dr. Lee.

EXERCISE 4: Editing

Correct the conversations. There are six mistakes. The first mistake is already corrected. Find and correct five more.

1. A: Can we ~~paid~~ pay in two installments?

B: Yes, you can pays half now and half next month.

2. A: May I speaks to the doctor?

B: I'm sorry. He's with a patient now. Give me your number and he'll call you back.

3. A: Can I to use salt?

B: Yes, but not a lot.

4. A: Can I drink coffee or tea?

B: You may drink tea, but you mayn't drink coffee.

5. A: May I helping you?

B: Thanks. I'd like to make an appointment for next week.

STEP 4 COMMUNICATION PRACTICE

EXERCISE 5: Listening

A | *Listen to a telephone conversation. A patient calls a doctor. What is the woman's problem?*

a. her ankle

b. her elbow

c. her knee

B | *Listen again and answer the questions.*

1. What can she do for the swelling and pain? ______________________________

2. What activities can she do? ______________________________

3. What activities can't she do? ______________________________

EXERCISE 6: Pronunciation

A | *Read and listen to the Pronunciation Note.*

Pronunciation Note

The vowel **/ eɪ /** as in ***lay***, is tense. The vowel **/ ɛ /** , as in ***egg***, is lax. The tongue is higher and the lips are more spread for **/ eɪ /** than for **/ ɛ /** .

B | *Listen and repeat the words with the /* **eɪ** */ sound.*

break **day** **explain** **late** **name** **plate** **play** **say** **scale**

C | *Listen and repeat the words with the /* **ɛ** */ sound.*

egg **get** **guess** **leg** **less** **let** **mess** **met** **stress** **west**

D | *Listen to the sentences. Check (✓) the sound of the underlined word.*

	/ eɪ /	/ ɛ /
1. He drinks eight bottles of water a day.	✓	
2. The doctor can't see you until May.		
3. Can I eat eggs on this diet?		
4. You can have steak on the Atkins™ diet.		
5. They met at a Weight Watchers® session.		
6. May I help you?		
7. The nutritionist's office is on West Street.		

EXERCISE 7: Information Gap

*Work in pairs (**A** and **B**). **Student A,** follow the instructions on this page. **Student B,** look at the Information Gap questions on page 161. Ask Student A the questions.*

1. Read the information for patients of Dr. Green.

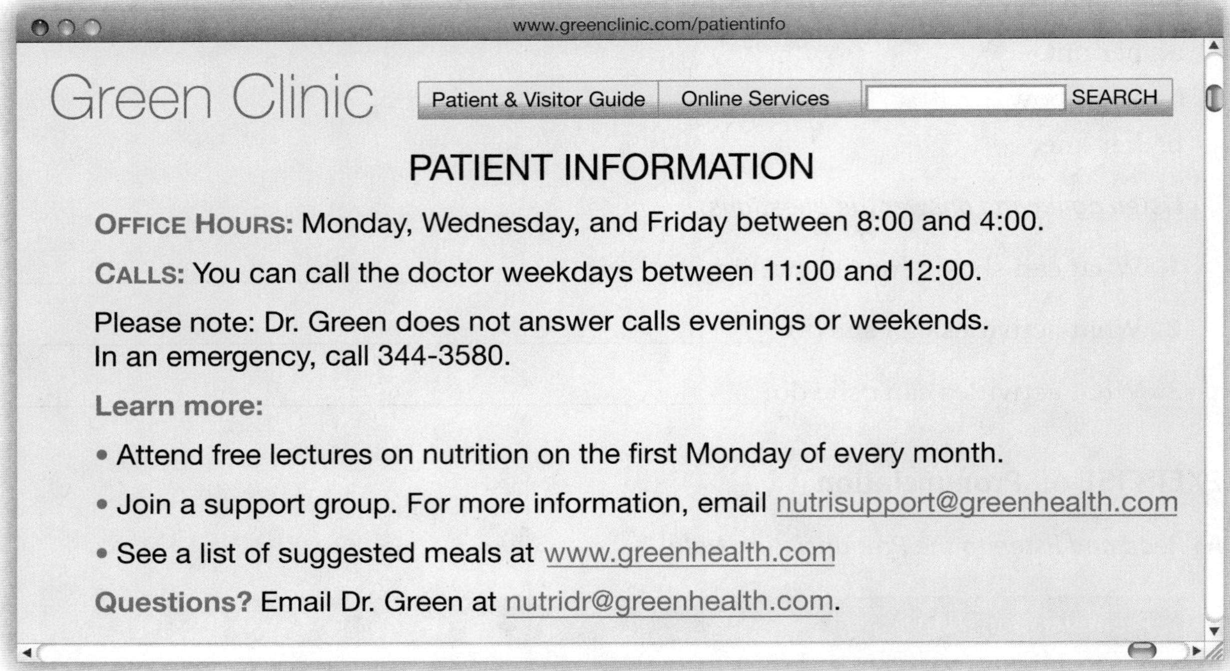

www.greenclinic.com/patientinfo

Green Clinic

Patient & Visitor Guide | Online Services | SEARCH

PATIENT INFORMATION

OFFICE HOURS: Monday, Wednesday, and Friday between 8:00 and 4:00.

CALLS: You can call the doctor weekdays between 11:00 and 12:00.

Please note: Dr. Green does not answer calls evenings or weekends.
In an emergency, call 344-3580.

Learn more:

- Attend free lectures on nutrition on the first Monday of every month.
- Join a support group. For more information, email nutrisupport@greenhealth.com
- See a list of suggested meals at www.greenhealth.com

Questions? Email Dr. Green at nutridr@greenhealth.com.

2. Answer Student B's questions. Use ***can***, ***may***, ***can't***, or ***may not***.

EXERCISE 8: Writing

A | *You and your friend want to lose weight. You found three diets online: The Skinny, 8-Minutes, and The Biggest Loser. Write an email to your friend. Tell your friend the requirements of each diet. Use* **can** *or* **may.**

Can I . . . ?	The Skinny	8-Minutes	The Biggest Loser
Eat out	Yes, often. The Skinny gives advice for foods in restaurants.	Occasionally.	It's difficult.
Drink coffee	Three times a day.	Not too much.	Yes.
Follow a vegetarian diet	Yes. There are many vegetarian possibilities.	Yes.	No. Many suggestions include meat.

EXAMPLE: On the Skinny diet, we can eat out often.

B | *Check your work. Use the Editing Checklist.*

Editing Checklist

Did you . . . ?
☐ use ***may*** and ***can*** for permission
☐ check your spelling

INFORMATION GAP FOR STUDENT B

Ask Student A the questions about the Green Clinic.

1. When can I see the doctor?
2. When can I call her?
3. Can I contact her by email?
4. What can I do in an emergency?
5. Are there any free lectures on nutrition?
6. Can I join a support group?
7. How can I get good meal suggestions?

UNIT 14 Review

Check your answers on page UR-3.
Do you need to review anything?

A | *Complete the paragraph with the words in parentheses. Use the correct form of the affirmative or negative.*

It's a great diet. You ________________ (1. may / eat) whatever you like. You just ________________ (2. can / eat) a lot. For example, for breakfast you ________________ (3. can / have) a slice of toast, an egg, and an orange. You can put jelly on the toast, but you ________________ (4. may / use) butter. You ________________ (5. may / drink) coffee, tea, or milk.

B | *Write John's questions for his doctor. Use* **can** *and the words in parentheses.*

1. ____ (When / I / return to work)
2. ____ (When / I / take a shower)
3. ____ (I / go / to the gym)
4. ____ (I / ride / my bike)

C | *You are taking a language test. Read the rules. Then write sentences with* **may** *or* **may not.**

NO	OK
food	a bottle of water
pencil	a black or blue pen
phone calls	dictionary

1. ____________________ 4. ____________________

2. ____________________ 5. ____________________

3. ____________________ 6. ____________________

D | *Correct the conversation. There are five mistakes.*

A: May I sees a menu?

B: Sure, you might. Here you go.

A: And can we to have some water?

B: I'll be right back with the water. . . . Ready?

A: Yes. I want the chicken with mushroom sauce. But may I has the sauce on the side?

B: You may not. We cook the chicken in the sauce.

A: Oh? Well, then I'll have grilled chicken with rice.

From Grammar to Writing

Punctuation I: The Apostrophe, The Comma, The Period, The Question Mark

1 | *Read this email. Circle all the punctuation marks.*

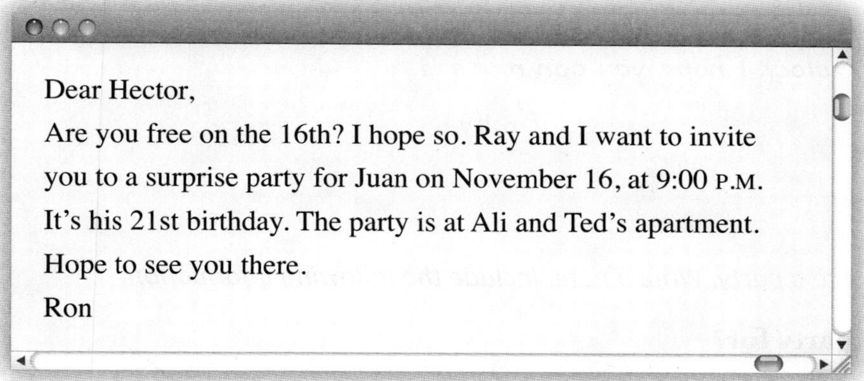

Dear Hector,

Are you free on the 16th? I hope so. Ray and I want to invite you to a surprise party for Juan on November 16, at 9:00 P.M. It's his 21st birthday. The party is at Ali and Ted's apartment.

Hope to see you there.

Ron

2 | *Study these rules of punctuation.*

1	**The apostrophe (')** Use an apostrophe to show possession and to write contractions.	• **Carol's** book is here. • We **aren't** late.
2	**The comma (,)** Rules for commas vary. Here are some places where commas are almost always used: **a.** in a list of more than two things **b.** after the name of a person you are writing to **c.** after *yes* or *no* in a sentence **d.** when you use *and* to connect two sentences.	• He is wearing **a shirt, a sweater,** and a **jacket**. • Dear **John,** • **Yes,** I am. OR **No,** I'm not. • His house is huge**, and** his car is expensive.
3	**The period (.)** **a.** Use a period at the end of a statement. **b.** Use a period after abbreviations.	• We are English language **students.** • The party is on **Nov.** 16.
4	**The question mark (?)** Use a question mark at the end of a question.	• Are you planning a **party?** • Where are you **going?**

3 | *Add punctuation marks to this note.*

Dear Uncle John

Bob and I want to invite you to a party for my parents 25th wedding anniversary Its on Sunday Dec 11

The party is at our home at 23 Main St Its at three o'clock I hope you can make it

Emily

4 | *Invite a friend to a party. Write a note. Include the following information.*

Who is the party for?

Who is giving the party?

What is the occasion?

When is the party?

Where is the party?

5 | *Exchange papers with a partner. Did your partner follow the directions? Correct any mistakes in grammar and spelling.*

6 | *Talk to your partner. Discuss the mistakes you made. Then rewrite your own paper and make any necessary changes.*

PRESENT PROGRESSIVE

UNIT	GRAMMAR FOCUS	THEME
15	Present Progressive: Affirmative and Negative Statements	High School
16	Present Progressive: *Yes / No* and *Wh-* Questions	Movies
17	Simple Present and Present Progressive; Non-Action Verbs	Smartphones

UNIT 15 Present Progressive: Affirmative and Negative Statements

HIGH SCHOOL

STEP 1 GRAMMAR IN CONTEXT

Before You Read

PAIRS: Answer the questions.

1. How many hours a day do high school students spend in school?
2. Were you very busy during your high school years?
3. Is a very busy schedule good for high school students? Why or why not?

Read

Read the online article about two cousins.

www.nineteen.com/lifestyle

Nineteen | quizzes & games | fashion | lifestyle | celebrities | guys |

Mi Young and Julie are cousins. Mi Young lives in Seoul, and Julie lives in New York City. Both teens are *juniors*[1] in high school. It's the second week of the semester.

It's 10:00 at night. Mi Young is still in school. She**'s working** on some tough math problems. She's tired, but she**'s not giving up**. Mi Young goes to public school from 8:00 to 3:00. Then she goes to a private study school from 3:30 to 10:00. Her friends are in the study school with her. Like Mi Young, they**'re hoping to** go to a top college. There is a lot of competition and pressure to get into top schools. These private schools—or "cram" schools—are popular with middle class[2] and wealthy families all over East Asia.

12 hours later

It's 10 P.M. in New York City. Julie is in her family's apartment. She**'s texting** her friend. They**'re making plans** to study together. Julie goes to school from 9:00 to 3:00. She swims on the school swimming team. Then she does her homework. Julie and her friends **are** all **working** hard this year. They**'re going** to school. They**'re preparing** for the SATs.[3] They**'re playing** on teams, and they**'re doing** a lot of other extra-curricular activities. They**'re not getting** enough sleep. They**'re feeling** a lot of pressure.[4] Julie only takes a break[5] once in a while.

Just like Mi Young and her friends, they**'re doing** all this work because they want to attend a top-rated college.

But is a "top" school really so important? What are they learning and what are they missing?

---

1 ***juniors:*** students in their third year of high school
2 ***middle class:*** the group of people in a society who are not rich and not poor
3 ***SAT:*** a test students take to get into many colleges
4 ***pressure:*** things in your life that make you worry
5 ***take a break:*** rest

After You Read

A | Practice *PAIRS: Now read the online article aloud. Take turns reading each paragraph.*

B | Vocabulary *Match the words from the article with their meaning.*

____ **1.** tough	**a.** in addition to school work
____ **2.** give up	**b.** people trying to be better than others
____ **3.** extracurricular	**c.** stop doing something
____ **4.** top	**d.** rich
____ **5.** competition	**e.** best
____ **6.** wealthy	**f.** difficult

C | Comprehension *Look back at the online article. Complete the chart. Check (✓) what is true about Mi Young and Julie or both. It's 10* P.M.

	Mi Young	Julie
1. in school		
2. at home		
3. working hard		
4. hoping to get into a top college		
5. texting a friend		
6. feeling a lot of pressure		
7. doesn't have a lot of free time		

STEP 2 GRAMMAR PRESENTATION

PRESENT PROGRESSIVE

Affirmative Statements		
Subject	***Be***	**Base Form of Verb + *-ing***
I	**am**	**relaxing.**
He	**is**	
She		
It		
We	**are**	
You*		
They		

Negative Statements			
Subject	***Be***	***Not***	**Base Form of Verb + *-ing***
I	**am**	**not**	**sleeping.**
He	**is**		
She			
It			
We	**are**		
You			
They			

**You* can be both singular and plural subjects.

GRAMMAR NOTES

1	Use the **present progressive*** to talk about an **action** that is or is not **happening now**. Now Past ———X———→ Future We can use the time expressions ***now***, ***right now***, and ***at the moment*** with the present progressive. **BE CAREFUL!** We don't usually use non-action verbs in the present progressive.	• I **am** driving • We **are not** walking. • The machine **isn't working now**. • **Right now** she**'s resting**. • **At the moment** he**'s talking** on the phone. • The textbook costs $80. NOT: ~~The textbook is costing $80~~.
2	Use **contractions** in speaking and informal writing.	• **I'm** not studying. **I'm** resting. • Luis **isn't** playing a game. **He's** reading. • We **aren't** playing a game. **We're** practicing.
3	Do not repeat the verb ***be*** when the subject is doing two things.	• They**'re singing** and **dancing**. NOT: ~~They're singing and are dancing~~.
4	If a verb ends in a silent ***-e***, drop the final ***-e*** and add ***-ing***.	• She's **driving** home. (drive) • I'm **taking** a test. (take)
5	We sometimes use the present progressive for an action that is taking place at this time, but may not be happening at this moment.	• **These days** Julie **is working** hard.

*The present progressive is also called present continuous.

REFERENCE NOTES

See Unit 17, page 188 for a discussion of non-action verbs.
See Appendix 8, page A-8 for more spelling rules for the present progressive.

STEP 3 FOCUSED PRACTICE

EXERCISE 1: Discover the Grammar

A | *Read about Mi Young and Julie. Underline the present progressive.*

1. 6:00 A.M. Mi Young is getting ready for school. She's putting on her school uniform. Julie is still sleeping.

2. 7:00 A.M. Mi Young and her classmates are taking the bus to school. Julie is washing her face and combing her hair.

3. 3:30 P.M. Mi Young is studying English. Julie is swimming at her high school pool.

4. 7:00 P.M. Mi Young is having dinner with her classmates. Julie is eating at home.

5. 11:00 P.M. Mi Young is riding home on the bus. Julie is studying physics.

B | *Write the base form of the words you underlined in Part A.*

1. get	4. ______	7. ______	10. ______
2. ______	5. ______	8. ______	11. ______
3. ______	6. ______	9. ______	12. ______

EXERCISE 2: Present Progressive Statements

(Grammar Notes 1–4)

Write about Julie's day with the words in parentheses. Use the present progressive.

1. It's 9:00 A.M. on Saturday morning.

   (Julie / get / up) Julie is getting up. She's late.

   (She / not / eat breakfast) ______

2. 9:40 A.M.

   (Julie / take the bus) ______ to her SAT prep class.

3. 1:00 P.M. Julie is at her school for a swimming competition.

   (Julie / compete) ______ against 20 swimmers.

   Three swimmers are ahead of Julie.

   (Julie / not / give up) ______

4. 4:00 P.M. Julie is home.

   (She / study / physics) ______

5. 8:00 P.M.

   (Julie / hang out) ______ with some friends.

   (They / not / study) ______

   (They / not / compete) ______

   (They / relax and have fun) ______

EXERCISE 3: Present Progressive Statements

(Grammar Notes 1–2, 4)

It's 10:00 P.M. at Julie's home. Complete the sentences with the words from the box. Use the present progressive form.

chat	go / not	sleep / not	study / not	~~turn~~
do / not	hang out	study	take	worry

1. Julie's brother Jay ___is turning___ off his computer. He's tired. He __________ any more homework.
2. Julie's sister Grace __________ her notes for biology class. She has a test tomorrow. She's tired, but she __________ to bed.
3. Julie __________ a short break from studying math. Julie and her friend __________ online.
4. Julie's mom __________ about her children. Julie and Grace __________ enough. They're always tired. Jay __________ enough. He doesn't care about school. Most of the time he __________ with his friends, instead.

EXERCISE 4: Present Progressive Statements

(Grammar Notes 1–5)

Complete the paragraph with the verbs in parentheses. Use the present progressive.

Hye Won is the manager of an international company. This week she ___is traveling___ (1. travel) on business. She __________ (2. meet) with clients in Spain. It's 8:00 in the evening. Hye Won __________ (3. have) dinner with a manager and a client. They __________ (4. eat) at a top restaurant in Madrid. Hye Won __________ (5. learn) about Spanish customs from the client. On this business trip, Hye Won and the other manager __________ (6. spend) two days in Madrid and two days in London.

Hye Won loves her job and her lifestyle. She says, "I'm glad I'm not married. School was hard. Now I __________ (7. enjoy) my freedom, and I __________ (8. earn) a lot of money. I __________ (9. save) for the future. I __________ (10. look / not) for a husband right now, maybe later." Hye Won's parents __________ (11. begin) to worry, but Hye Won is very happy.

EXERCISE 5: Editing

Correct the journal entry by a high school student. There are eight mistakes. The first mistake is already corrected. Find and correct seven more.

sitting
I'm ~~sit~~ in the park. It's a beautiful day. The leaves changing color. Today there are a lot of children in the park. They laughing and are playing. They no are studying. They're lucky. It's hard to study on a beautiful day.

I trying to memorize vocabulary words for the SATs. I'm wait for my friend Grace. She's in my Saturday SAT prep class. We planning to study together all afternoon and evening.

STEP 4 COMMUNICATION PRACTICE

EXERCISE 6: Listening

A | *Listen to a telephone conversation. Where is the mother calling from?*

She's ______________________________.

B | *Listen again and answer the questions.*

1. What's the father doing?

   He's cooking.

2. What's Jay doing?

   ____

3. What's Julie doing?

   ____

4. Where's Grace?

   ____

5. What time will the mother arrive?

   ____

EXERCISE 7: Pronunciation

A | *Read and listen to the Pronunciation Note.*

Pronunciation Note

When we use the present progressive, we do not stress the ***-ing*** ending. The *-ing* is unstressed.

EXAMPLES: She's **wait**ing for Janet. He's **study**ing for finals.

B | *Read and listen to the sentences. Then listen and repeat.*

1. She's taking a test.
2. He's not giving up.
3. We're trying out for the play.
4. We're studying together.
5. He's driving home.
6. They're watching the news.

EXERCISE 8: Game: Describing a Photo

A | *GROUPS: You have 10 minutes. Look at the photo. Write as many affirmative and negative statements as you can. Use the present progressive.*

B | *Now compare the class in the photo to your own class.*

EXERCISE 9: Writing

A | *Look at people in a school cafeteria, a park, a mall, or on a train or a bus. Write about two people. Answer these questions. Use the present progressive.*

- Where are you? What time is it?
- What are the people doing? What are they wearing?

EXAMPLE: I'm in our school cafeteria. It's 12:30 P.M. Two girls are paying for their food. One girl is very tall. The other is not. The tall girl is wearing black pants and a black T-shirt. The shorter girl is wearing jeans and a red sweater. They're carrying a lot of books. The tall girl isn't smiling. She's carrying a tray with a cup of yogurt and a salad. The shorter girl is carrying a tray with a sandwich, a salad, an apple, and cookies. She's talking a lot. The tall girl is listening. She isn't saying a word. I think they're in the same class. I don't think they're close friends.

B | *Check your work. Use the Editing Checklist.*

Editing Checklist

Did you . . . ?

☐ use the present progressive correctly

☐ check your spelling

UNIT 15 Review

Check your answers on page UR-3.
Do you need to review anything?

A | *Circle the correct words to complete the sentences.*

1. I'm **not getting / no am getting** enough sleep.
2. We **are prepare / 're preparing** for the SATs now.
3. She **isn't playing / no is playing** tennis now.
4. They **doing / 're doing** a lot of extracurricular activities.
5. He **is feel / 's feeling** a lot of pressure.

B | *Complete the sentences with the words from the box. Use the present progressive form.*

carry	**drive**	**listen to**	**run**	**stand and talk**

1. A man ________________ music on his iPod.
2. Two women ________________ on a street corner.
3. Some children ________________ to catch their school bus.
4. A young man ________________ a red sports car.
5. An older man ________________ a briefcase.

C | *Complete the sentences with the verbs in parentheses. Use the affirmative or negative form of the present progressive.*

1. John ________________ (text) his friend. He ________________ (call) him. John says texting is faster.
2. Mary and Lulu ________________ (work) on some tough physics problems. The problems are difficult, but they ________________ (give up).
3. Julie ________________ (swim) fast. She ________________ (try) to win a race.

D | *Correct the paragraph. There are four mistakes.*

My classmates and I am sitting in a computer lab. One student writing a composition. Two students are check their email. A teacher is helps a student. The other students are surfing the Internet.

UNIT

16 Present Progressive: *Yes / No* and *Wh-* Questions

MOVIES

STEP 1 GRAMMAR IN CONTEXT

Before You Read

A | *Where do you like to watch movies? Check (✓) your favorite place:*

- ☐ on a flat-screen TV
- ☐ at the theater
- ☐ on your computer
- ☐ on your phone

Movie theater in India

B | *Look at the stamps that show famous movies. Do you like these kinds of movies? Check (✓) the types that you like.*

☐ Fantasy/Adventure

☐ Romance

☐ Action

C | *Look at the list of other kinds of movies. Check (✓) each kind of movie you like.*

☐ animation ☐ crime / horror ☐ mystery

☐ comedy ☐ drama ☐ science fiction

Read

Abby has a cold. Her co-worker Greg is calling to see how she is. Read their conversation.

Abby: Hello.

Greg: Hi, Abby. **How are you feeling?** Any better?

Abby: Uh-huh. I'm coughing less, and the fever is going down.

Greg: Good. **Are you resting?**

Abby: Yes, and I'm watching a DVD.

Greg: Oh? **What are you watching?**

Abby: *The Wizard of Oz.*[1]

Greg: *The Wizard of Oz*?

Abby: I know its a kid's movie, but I really like it.

Greg: So **what part are you watching? What's happening?**

Abby: I'm watching the scene where Dorothy meets the Tin Man.

Greg: **Is Dorothy giving the Tin Man oil?**

Abby: Yes, she's putting oil in his mouth.

Greg: **Is he talking?**

Abby: No, not yet. Dorothy and the Scarecrow are talking to him, but he can't talk.

Greg: I remember the scene. It's amazing. The film is still popular after so many years.

Abby: Well, it's a classic. **So what's going on at work?**

Greg: Same old same old.[2] We're working on ten things at once.

Abby: **Is Mr. Brooks going crazy?**[3]

Greg: Uh-huh. And tomorrow he'll be worse.

Abby: Why?

Greg: I'll be out. I think I'm catching your cold.

---

[1] ***The Wizard of Oz:*** 1939 film about a Kansas farm girl. Her house goes up in the air during a storm and she lands in a magical place called Oz.

[2] ***same old same old:*** nothing new

[3] ***going crazy:*** feeling very upset because many things are happening all at once

After You Read

A | Practice *PAIRS: Now read the conversation aloud.*

B | Vocabulary *Complete the sentences with the words from the box.*

catching a cold	classic	coughing	favorite	fever	scene

1. In this ______________ Dorothy meets the Tin Man.
2. I don't feel well. I think I'm ______________.
3. Do you feel hot? Do you have a ______________.
4. Take this medicine. But if you're ______________ a lot, maybe you should see a doctor.
5. The movie *Casablanca* is a ______________. It's still popular after more than 60 years.
6. Eddie Murphy is my ______________ actor. I watch every comedy he is in.

Eddie Murphy

C | Comprehension *Correct the false statements to make them true.*

1. Abby is staying home from work because her daughter has a cold and fever.
2. Greg is taking care of Abby.
3. Greg and Abby are watching *The Wizard of Oz*.
4. Dorothy is giving the Tin Man water.
5. The Tin Man is talking.
6. Greg's boss, Mr. Brooks, isn't going crazy.

STEP 2 GRAMMAR PRESENTATION

PRESENT PROGRESSIVE: *YES / NO* QUESTIONS AND *WH-* QUESTIONS

Yes / No Questions		
Be	**Subject**	**Base Form of Verb + *-ing***
Am	I	**resting**?
Are	you	
Is	he she it	
Are	we you they	

Short Answers					
Affirmative			**Negative**		
Yes,	you	**are**.	**No,**	you**'re**	**not**.
	I	**am**.		I**'m**	
	he she it	**is**.		he**'s** she**'s** it**'s**	
	you we they	**are**.		you**'re** we**'re** they**'re**	

Wh- Questions				
***Wh-* Word**	***Be***	**Subject**	**Base Form of Verb + *-ing***	
Why	**are**	you	**staying**	home?
What			**watching?**	
Where		they	**going?**	
Who	**is**	she	**meeting?**	

Answers
I'm sick.
The Wizard of Oz.
To the movies. They're going to the movies.
Her teacher. She's meeting her teacher.

Wh- Questions about the Subject		
***Wh-* Word**	***Be***	**Base Form of Verb + *-ing***
Who	**is**	**reading?**
What		**happening?**

Answers
My friend (is).
They're singing.

GRAMMAR NOTES

1	Use the **present progressive** to ask about **something that is happening now**. Reverse the subject and *be* when asking a ***yes / no*** question.	**I'm singing** in the rain. • He is singing. • Is he singing?
2	Most ***wh-*** **questions** in the present progressive use the same word order as *yes / no* questions. Use *whom* only for formal English.	• **Where is** he **working**? • **What are** they **doing**? • **Who are** you **meeting**? • **Whom** is the president meeting?
3	***Who*** and ***What*** **questions about the subject** use statement word order.	STATEMENT • Dorothy is singing. *WH-* QUESTION • Who is singing? What is happening?

STEP 3 FOCUSED PRACTICE

EXERCISE 1: Discover the Grammar

A | *Read the conversation again on page 175. Write the three other* **yes / no** *questions.*

1. *Are you resting?*
2. ______
3. ______
4. ______

B | *Look at the conversation again. Write the four other* **wh-** *questions in the charts.*

Wh- word + *be*	Subject	Base Form of Verb + *-ing*
1. *How are*	*you*	*feeling?*
2.		
3.		

Wh- word + *be*	Base Form of Verb + *-ing*
4.	
5.	

EXERCISE 2: Present Progressive: *Yes / No* and *Wh-* Questions

(Grammar Note 1)

Write questions with the words in parentheses. Use the present progressive. Then match the questions with the answers below.

__b__ **1.** (you / watch / a movie) *Are you watching a movie?*

____ **2.** (what / Johnny Depp / do / now?) ________________

____ **3.** (you / watch / it / on your DVD) ________________

____ **4.** (you / tape / it / for me) ________________

a. No, sorry, but it will be on again.

b. Yes. I'm watching *Pirate of the Caribbean: Curse of the Black Pearl* with Johnny Depp.

c. No. It's on TV.

d. He's standing on the deck of his ship.

EXERCISE 3: Present Progressive: *Yes / No* and *Wh-* Questions

(Grammar Notes 1–3)

Abby and Greg are talking on the telephone. Complete their conversation with the words in parentheses. Use the present progressive.

Abby: Hi, Greg. *How are you feeling* ? ________________ ?
1. (How / you / feel) **2. (you / feel / any better)**

Greg: No, I'm not.

Abby: ________________ ?
3. (you / take / the medicine)

Greg: Yes, I am. ________________ ?
4. (Where / you / call from)

Abby: I'm at an Italian restaurant. Greg. Listen to this. Meryl Streep is eating here.

Greg: No kidding! ________________ ?
5. (Who / she / eat / with)

Abby: I think she's with her daughter. I'm not sure.

Greg: ________________ ?
6. (people / ask for her autograph)

Abby: No. Nobody's bothering her, but everyone knows she's there.

Greg: Well, when you pass her table, say, "Bon appétit!" That was my favorite line in *Julie and Julia*.

EXERCISE 4: Common Two-Word Verbs

(Grammar Notes 1–2)

Complete the questions with the words from the box. Use the present progressive.

listen to	look at	look for	~~wait for~~

1. **A:** Is that *Shrek 3*?

   B: No. I *'m waiting for* *Shrek 3* to start. I'm watching a preview of some other film.

2. **A:** ______________ you ______________ a good movie to watch?

   B: Yes, I am. Why? Do you have an idea?

3. **A:** What ______________ she ______________?

   B: She's looking at some online movie reviews.

4. **A:** What ______________ they ______________?

   B: The music from *The Wizard of Oz*.

EXERCISE 5: Editing

Correct the conversations. There are six mistakes. The first mistake is already corrected. Find and correct five more.

1. **A:** Excuse me, who^'s collecting tickets?

   B: He isn't here now. Wait a minute. He'll be right back.

2. **A:** What you doing?

   B: I'm turning off my cell phone.

3. **A:** Is Dad buy popcorn?

   B: Yes, he is.

4. **A:** What taking him so long?

   B: He's waiting in a long line.

5. **A:** Excuse me, is someone sits here?

   B: No, no one sitting here. Please sit down.

STEP 4 COMMUNICATION PRACTICE

EXERCISE 6: Listening

A | *Listen to the conversation. What is Dan shopping for? Circle the correct letter.*

a. an HDTV **b.** a DVD player **c.** a DVR player

B | *Listen again and answer the questions.*

1. Who is Dan getting a gift for? for his dad
2. What's the occasion? ____________
3. When can he use the gift? ____________
4. What does Dan's friend tell him to buy? ____________
5. What's happening at Goodbuys this week? ____________

EXERCISE 7: Pronunciation

A | *Read and listen to the Pronunciation Note.*

Pronunciation Note

When letters are used in abbreviations, we usually stress the last syllable.

Examples:

MTV PC

B | *Listen and repeat the abbreviations.*

CD DVD DVR TV ISBN BA

C | *Change the underlined words to abbreviations. Then take turns reading the sentences. Stress the last letter of each abbreviation.*

1. We're buying a new <u>digital video disc</u> player. (DVD)
2. That 50-inch flat screen <u>television</u> is on sale.
3. Do you have an extra <u>compact disc</u>?
4. Give me the <u>international standard book number</u>.
5. We want to get a <u>digital video recorder</u> so we can record shows.
6. He has a <u>bachelor of arts</u> in film.

D | *Listen to the sentences in Part C. Then repeat the sentences.*

EXERCISE 8: Role Play

PAIRS: Write a telephone conversation with your partner. Student A is watching a movie when Student B calls. Student B, ask Student A questions about his or her movie. Use the present progressive. Continue the conversation.

B: Hi, ________________? This is ________________. Are you busy?

A: Oh, hi, ________________. I ________________ a movie.
(watch)

B: What ________________?
(watch)

A: ________________.

B: What's happening?

A: ____.

EXERCISE 9: Describing Pictures

A | *PAIRS: On a separate piece of paper, write questions about the picture. Use the present progressive. Ask another pair your questions.*

B | *Draw a picture. Include four people or more and a basket. Use four of these actions:* **sing, dance, wear, look at, look for, carry.** *Do not show your partner your picture.*

C | *PAIRS: Ask your partner questions about his or her picture. Then try to draw the picture your partner describes. Answer your partner's questions about your picture. Compare pictures.*

EXAMPLE: **A:** Who is singing?
B: Two girls are singing.
A: What are they wearing?

EXERCISE 10: Writing

A | *PAIRS: Interview each other about your favorite movies. Ask some questions with the present progressive:*

- What's the name of the movie? Who's the director? Who's the star? What language is it in?
- What do you like best about the movie?
- What's your favorite in the scene?
- Where is it taking place? When?
- What are the people doing?

B | *Now write about the movie you talked about. Use the present progressive when possible.*

Example: The movie is *Avatar*. The director is James Cameron. It's a science fiction fantasy. It takes place in a world called Pandora. The digital art is the best part of the movie. In this scene the hero Jake is an avatar. He's flying on Pandora with his girlfriend. He is helping her people and trying to save Pandora from greedy people from Earth.

C | *Check your work. Use the Editing Checklist.*

Editing Checklist

Did you . . . ?

☐ use the present progressive correctly

☐ check your spelling

UNIT 16 Review

Check your answers on page UR-3.
Do you need to review anything?

A | *Complete the conversations with the verbs in parentheses. Use the present progressive.*

1. **A:** The kids are screaming. ________ they ________ (watch) a horror show?

   B: Yes, ________.

2. **A:** What ________ you ________ (do)?

   B: I ________ (listen) to my favorite CD.

3. **A:** What ________ (happen) outside?

   B: Uncle John ________ (put) up a new fence.

B | *Write* **yes** / **no** *questions with the words in parentheses. Use the present progressive.*

1. ________________________ (you / work)
2. ________________________ (he / buy tickets online)
3. ________________________ (they / watch a mystery)
4. ________________________ (she / enjoy the movie)

C | *Write* **wh-** *questions in the present progressive with the words in parentheses.*

1. ________________________ (Where / they / go)
2. ________________________ (What music group / perform)
3. ________________________ (Where / they / play)
4. ________________________ (Why / Bob stay home)

D | *Correct the conversations. There are four mistakes.*

1. **A:** Is it's raining outside?

   B: Yes. I hope it stops.

2. **A:** Are they playing soccer?

   B: No, they not. They're playing rugby.

3. **A:** You watching a good movie?

   B: It's OK.

4. **A:** What they doing?

   B: They're fixing the cabinets.

UNIT 17

Simple Present and Present Progressive; Non-Action Verbs

SMARTPHONES

STEP 1 GRAMMAR IN CONTEXT

Before You Read

Do you have a cell phone? How many ways do you use it?

Read

Read the online article about today's phones.

ARTS | SCIENCE | POLITICS | TECHNOLOGY | SEARCH:

Cell Phone Mania | Technology Today

More than 4½ million people **have** them. People under 30[1] **don't know** a world without them. They **come** in all colors and shapes. Some **are** waterproof and shockproof.[2] What **are** they? Cell phones.

Today's cell phones **have** many different features. Take Xavier. He**'s** at a picnic in a park. He **needs** a ride to a party that evening. He**'s texting** a friend. The couple in the car were in a minor accident. The man **is taking** a photo with his phone. And John **is checking** email from his phone.

It**'s** easy to understand the popularity of these phones. People **want** to connect with others, and at the same time, they **want** to be *mobile*.[3] Cell phones **make** it possible to do both. Cell phones **are** big business, and the technology **is** constantly **improving**. What about the future? What will it bring? Nobody **knows**, but here **are** the wishes of two people.

Emily, age 15, **says**, "I often **forget** to charge my phone. I **want** a phone with endless power."

Robert, a college freshman **says**, "I **want** a phone that can teach me a foreign language while I **sleep**."

Well, Emily may get her wish a lot sooner than Robert. But of course, with the speed at which things **are changing**, you never **know** what the future will bring.

---

[1] ***under 30:*** less than 30 years old
[2] ***shockproof:*** doesn't break when it falls
[3] ***mobile:*** able to move around

After You Read

A | Practice *PAIRS: Now read the article aloud. Take turns reading each paragraph.*

B | Vocabulary *Circle the best meaning for the words in* **blue**.

1. We **connect** through Facebook®.

a. join **b.** make contact

2. That watch is **waterproof**. You can swim with it on.

a. not hurt by water **b.** dry

3. That new computer comes with a lot of **features**.

a. parts that make it better **b.** memory

4. He calls her **constantly**. Is he in love?

a. all the time **b.** from time to time

5. Your work is **improving**.

a. getting better **b.** changing.

6. There's a **minor** problem with my computer.

a. serious **b.** small

C | Comprehension *Complete the sentences. Circle the correct letter.*

1. More than ________________ people have cell phones today.

a. 450,000 **b.** 4,500,000 **c.** 4,500,000,000

2. The man in the car accident is using the phone as a ________________.

a. radio **b.** camera **c.** computer

3. Telephone technology is ________________.

a. making phones harder to use **b.** using video **c.** improving all the time

4. Emily wants her phone to ________________.

a. have power all the time **b.** have a beeper **c.** teach her a language

STEP 2 GRAMMAR PRESENTATION

SIMPLE PRESENT AND PRESENT PROGRESSIVE

The Simple Present	The Present Progressive
I **eat** at eight o'clock.	I'**m eating** now.
He **eats** at 8:00 too.	He'**s eating** now.
She **doesn't eat** with me.	She **isn't eating** with him.
They **don't eat** with us.	They **aren't eating** with us.
Does he **eat** meat?	**Is** he **eating** chicken?
Do you **eat** in the cafeteria?	**Are** you **eating** chicken?

NON-ACTION (STATIVE) VERBS

State of Being	Emotion	Sense / Appearance	Need / Preference	Mental Action	Possession	Measurement
be	love hate like dislike	hear see feel taste smell sound look	want need prefer	agree disagree guess understand know remember believe think mean worry	have own belong	cost weigh owe

GRAMMAR NOTES

1	Use the **simple present** to tell or ask about **habits, customs, routines**, or **facts**. **Now** **Past** —X—X—+—X—X→ **Future** *She shops every Saturday.*	• I **check** Facebook® every morning. • **Do** you **check** Facebook® in the morning?
2	Use the **present progressive** to tell or ask about an action happening **right now** or **these days**. **Past** ———X———→ **Future** **Now**	• He**'s checking** email now. • **Is** Enrique **checking** email? • Jon **is teaching** computer science this year.
3	Some verbs do not describe actions. These verbs are called **non-action** or **stative verbs**.	• I **have** a great idea. • This **belongs** to me. • They **love** that phone.
4	**Non-action verbs** do the following: **a.** express emotion **b.** describe sense or appearance **c.** express a need or preference **d.** describe a thought **e.** show possession **f.** give a measurement **g.** *Be* expresses a state of being.	 • We **like** that computer. • The music **sounds** relaxing. • I **prefer** email. • Jennifer **knows** you. • It **belongs** to me. • It **costs** a lot of money. • I **am** tired now.
5	We usually do not use non-action verbs in the present progressive (*-ing*) form.	• I **own** a smartphone • It **costs** a lot. NOT: ~~I'm owning~~ a smartphone. It~~'s costing~~ a lot.

STEP 3 FOCUSED PRACTICE

EXERCISE 1: Discover the Grammar

Underline the simple present. Circle the present progressive. Underline twice all non-action verbs.

Raisa has a new phone with a lot of great features. She likes her phone a lot. Her phone keeps her in touch with her friends wherever she is. Right now Raisa is texting friends. They are making plans for the evening. She and her friends often text. They don't talk much on the phone. They also connect through Facebook®. Raisa often adds new friends to her site. Sometimes she doesn't know them very well. Raisa's mother, Olga, worries about that. Olga doesn't use social networks. She prefers to talk on the phone or connect through email.

EXERCISE 2: Simple Present; Non-Action Verbs; Present Progressive *(Grammar Notes 1–5)*

Complete the conversation with the words in parentheses. Use the simple present or present progressive. Use contractions when possible.

A: What ____*are*____ (1.) you ____*doing*____ (2. (do))?

B: I ________ (3. (check)) my messages. Look. That's my friend from high school. She ________ (4. (have)) three kids now. They ________ (5. (sing)) happy birthday to their father.

A: Oh. That's nice.

B: ________ (6.) you ________ (7. (use)) social networking sites?

A: No, I ________ (8.). I ________ (9. (prefer)) to email my friends. I ________ (10. (think)) it's more personal. Also, I ________ (11. (know)) there are privacy features in social networking sites, but I ________ (12. (worry)) about my privacy.

EXERCISE 3: Simple Present; Non-Action Verbs; Present Progressive *(Grammar Notes 1–5)*

Complete the conversation with the words in parentheses. Use the simple present or present progressive. Use contractions when possible.

A: I'm worried about Tim. This term he ___is___ (1. be) always online or _______________ (2. text) friends. He _______________ (3. do / not) well in school. I _______________ (4. think) he _______________ (5. fail) Spanish.

B: Oh. What _______________ (6.) he _______________ (7. say)?

A: Nothing. Right now he _______________ (8. play) some new game. He _______________ (9. love) computer games. I _______________ (10. think) he _______________ (11. become) a computer addict.

EXERCISE 4: Simple Present; Non-Action Verbs; Present Progressive *(Grammar Notes 1–5)*

Complete the paragraph with the verbs from the box. Use the correct form. Use contractions.

answer	ask	be	talk	think	want	~~work~~

Phuong is a fisherman. He ___is working___ (1.) on a boat. His old phone is broken. Phuong _______________ (2.) a new phone. He _______________ (3.) about getting a waterproof smart phone with a lot of features. Right now he _______________ (4.) to a saleswoman in a wireless phone store. He _______________ (5.) a lot of questions. The saleswoman _______________ (6.) his questions. She _______________ (7.) very helpful.

EXERCISE 5: Editing

Correct the paragraph. There are six mistakes. The first one has been corrected for you. Find and correct five more.

I ~~hates~~ hate cell phones. My boss is thinking he can call me anytime, even on weekends. I'm dislike email for the same reason. People in my company work all the time. There's no "off" time. Look at John over there. It's his lunchtime, but he answering calls and is checking email. This wasn't possible in my parents' day. I don't think it's right. Technology great in some ways, but it's awful in other ways.

STEP 4 COMMUNICATION PRACTICE

EXERCISE 6: Listening

A | *Listen to the phone messages. Which calls are from co-workers? Which calls are from family? Check (✓)* **co-worker** *or* **family** *next to the call.*

Phone Message	Co-worker	Family	Message
1.			Please send me a copy of the Smith report.
2.			She's ______________________.
3.			She needs to ______________________.
4.			She's looking for ______________________.

B | *Look back at Part A. Listen again. Complete the messages.*

EXERCISE 7: Pronunciation

A | *Read and listen to the Pronunciation Note.*

Pronunciation Note

We can use intonation to express emotions such as surprise or anger.

Examples: I'm surprised at you! (surprised)   I'm surprised at you! (angry)

B | *Listen to this conversation. How does the woman sound? Circle the correct letter.*

a. surprised   **b.** angry

C | *Listen to this conversation. How does the woman sound? Circle the correct letter.*

a. surprised   **b.** angry

D | *PAIRS: Practice the conversation. Take turns reading each part. Practice showing surprise. Then practice showing anger.*

A: I have a call coming in. It's my boss.

B: But it's 2:00 A.M.! Why is he calling now?

EXERCISE 8: Conversation

PAIRS: Read about these people. Guess why they're doing something different today.

1. Paul and Ana usually shop at Electronics Plus for their electronics. Today they're shopping at Goodbuys.

   Example: Paul and Ana are shopping at Goodbuys today because there is a big sale.

2. Maria usually texts friends. Today she's calling and speaking to them.
3. Joaquin usually wears jeans and a T-shirt in class. Today he's wearing a suit.
4. Ali usually brings his lunch to work. Today he's eating out.

EXERCISE 9: Survey

A | *GROUPS: Match the pictures and sentences. Write the correct letter.*

1. ___d___

2. ________

3. ________

4. ________

5. ________

a. She's checking her messages.
b. He's texting a friend
c. They're reading e-books.
d. He's using a landline.
e. He's using a desktop computer.

B | *Complete the survey for yourself. Write your preference and a reason why.*

Which do you prefer?	I prefer______.
using email or Facebook®	*Facebook®. I think it's more fun. It's easy to connect with everyone at once.*
texting or talking on the phone	
ebooks or printed books	
cell phones or landlines	
laptops or desktop computers	

C | *GROUPS: One student asks the others for their preferences and takes notes. Another student reports the results to the class.*

EXAMPLE: **Juan:** Marta, do you prefer social network sites or email?

Marta: I prefer email.

Juan: Emiko, what about you? Do you prefer . . .

Paul: In our group four people prefer social networking sites, and two prefer email.

EXERCISE 10: Writing

A | *Look at the pictures. Write about the people. They are doing many things at once. What are they doing? Use the present progressive.*

EXAMPLE: The man is drinking a cup of tea . . .

B | *Now write about times when you do many things at once. Use the simple present.*

EXAMPLE: I'm always busy in the morning. I usually walk to school. Sometimes I look at the other people and I wonder about their lives.

C | *Check your work. Use the Editing Checklist.*

Editing Checklist

Did you . . . ?

☐ use simple present, present progressive and non-action verbs correctly

☐ check your spelling

UNIT 17 Review

Check your answers on page UR-4.
Do you need to review anything?

A | *Complete the sentences with the words in parentheses. Use the affirmative or negative form of the simple present.*

1. They ______________________ a car.
   (own / not)
2. He ______________________ to drive.
   (like / not)
3. She ______________________ a new bike.
   (have)
4. She ______________________ a lock for it.
   (need)
5. They ______________________ to buy bikes too.
   (want)

B | *Complete the paragraph with the verbs in parentheses. Use the simple present or present progressive.*

John ________________ his new computer now. He ________________ the
1. (use) 2. (surf)
Internet. He ________________ information about events in his area. His computer
3. (get)
________________ a lot of great features. John ________________ to learn how to use
4. (have) 5. (want)
all of them.

C | *Complete the conversation with the words in parentheses. Use the simple present or present progressive.*

A: What ________________ Tom ________________?
1. (do)
B: He ________________ to fix his printer again.
2. (try)
A: What ________________ the problem now?
3. (be)
B: I ________________.
4. (know / not)
A: ________________ he ________________ a new printer? This one is pretty old!
5. (need)

D | *Correct the conversations. There are five mistakes.*

1. **A:** Where you calling from?
   B: Downtown. I walk along Second Street.
2. **A:** Is she play tennis at West Park?
   B: No, she's not. She no like those courts.
3. **A:** Does he understands Greek?
   B: Yes, he does. He was in Greece for a year.

From Grammar to Writing

Subjects and Verbs

1 | *What's wrong with these sentences?*

1. He a handsome man.
2. She a red skirt.
3. I from Argentina.
4. Am wearing blue pants.
5. Are tired?
6. Is a cool day.

Sentences 1–3 are missing a verb. Sentences 4–6 are missing a subject.

2 | *Study the information about subjects and verbs.*

Every sentence needs a subject and verb.	SUBJECT VERB My **mother works**.
The **subject** is a noun or pronoun. It tells who or what the sentence is about.	• **John** is running. • **They** are watching TV.
The **verb** tells the action or links the subject with the rest of the sentence.	• It **is raining**. • He **is** a doctor.

3 | *Correct this paragraph. Then underline the subject and circle the verb in each sentence.*

I in Central Park. It a sunny day in September. Is crowded. Some children soccer. They're laughing and shouting. Some people are running. Three older women on a bench. Are watching the runners and soccer players. A young man and woman are holding hands. Are smiling. Are in love. Central Park a wonderful place to be on a beautiful day.

4 | *Imagine you are in one of these places. Write a paragraph about the people you see.*

an airport **a busy street** **a park** **a train station**

5 | *Exchange papers with a partner. Did your partner follow the directions? Correct any mistakes in grammar and spelling.*

6 | *Talk to your partner. Discuss the mistakes you made. Then rewrite your own paper and make any necessary changes.*

SIMPLE PAST

UNIT	GRAMMAR FOCUS	THEME
18	Simple Past: Affirmative and Negative Statements with Regular Verbs	Travel
19	Simple Past: Affirmative and Negative Statements with Irregular Verbs	You Never Know
20	Simple Past: *Yes / No* and *Wh*-Questions	Interviews

UNIT 18

Simple Past: Affirmative and Negative Statements with Regular Verbs

TRAVEL

STEP 1 GRAMMAR IN CONTEXT

Before You Read

Discuss the question.

- In which countries are these tourist attractions? (See answers on page 202.)

Read

Read a message from Karen to Dahlia and Dahlia's answer. What city did Karen visit? *(See answer on page 202.)*

WALL
FRIENDS
PHOTOS

Karen van der Broek

Hi Dahlia,

You were so right! This city is awesome.

Yesterday morning Julian and I **watched** foot-volley on Ipanema Beach. The players were great. Then in the afternoon we **visited** Sugarloaf. What a view! In the evening we **enjoyed** a delicious meal at a churrascuria (a barbecued meat restaurant).

Our flight here was the only bad part of the trip. It was bumpy, and we **didn't land** until 11:30 at night. But someone from the hotel **picked** us **up**, and we **arrived** at the hotel before 1:00 A.M. Everyone here is helpful, and our room is beautiful. The weather is great. I **didn't need** to pack my umbrella or my jacket.

Say hi to everyone at the office.

Love, Karen

WALL
FRIENDS
PHOTOS

Dahlia Gold

Hey Karen,

I'm glad *you're* having such a great time. It's freezing here. Yesterday it **snowed** all day, and last week it **rained**.

I **stayed** late Monday and Tuesday preparing for the spring conference. I **dined** on sandwiches from the vending machines downstairs. Then guess what happened? Mr. Grimes **canceled** the conference.

So enjoy every minute of your vacation.

—Miss you.

Love, Dahlia

After You Read

A | Practice *PAIRS: Now read the messages aloud. Take turns.*

B | Vocabulary *Complete the sentences with the words from the box.*

bumpy	canceled	freezing	landed	picked / up

1. Our flight was very ________________. I felt sick during the flight.
2. Our airplane ________________ on time. I was glad the flight was over.
3. Someone from the hotel ________________ us ________________.
4. It's ________________ in this room. I need a sweater.
5. I ordered french fries and a shake but then I ________________ my order because I need to diet.

C | Comprehension *Make the false statements true.*

1. Karen and Julian ~~played~~ *watched* foot-volley on Ipanema Beach.
2. Karen and Julian enjoyed dessert at a café.
3. Karen and Julian's plane arrived in the afternoon.
4. The people at the hotel were unhelpful.
5. Mr. Grimes attended the spring conference.

STEP 2 GRAMMAR PRESENTATION

THE SIMPLE PAST: STATEMENTS WITH REGULAR VERBS

Affirmative Statements	
Subject	**Base Form of Verb + *-ed***
I He She It We You* They	land**ed**. arriv**ed**. cri**ed**.

Negative Statements		
Subject	***Did Not***	**Base Form of Verb**
I He She It We You* They	**did not** **didn't**	**land**. **arrive**. **cry**.

**You* can be both singular and plural subjects.

Past Time Markers		
Yesterday	***Ago***	***Last***
yesterday **yesterday** morning **yesterday** afternoon **yesterday** evening	two days **ago** a week **ago** a month **ago** a year **ago** a couple of days **ago**	**last** night **last** Monday **last** week **last** summer **last** year

GRAMMAR NOTES

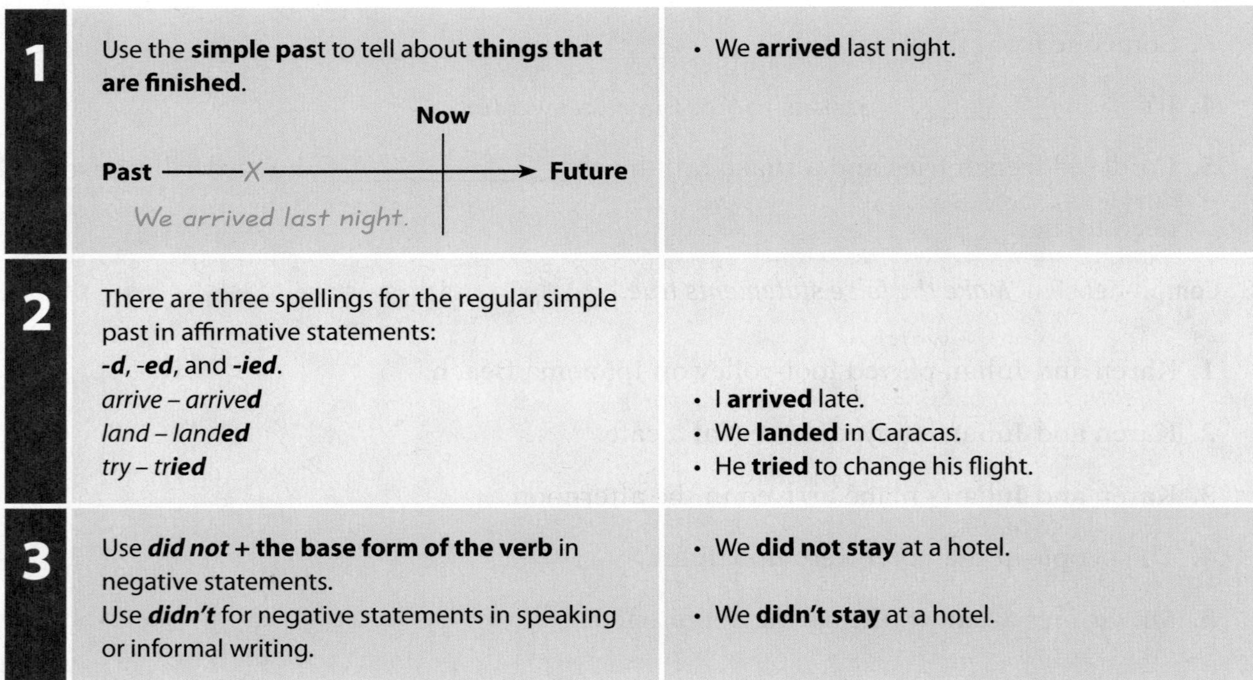

1	Use the **simple past** to tell about **things that are finished**. Past ——X——|——→ Future (Now) *We arrived last night.*	• We **arrived** last night.
2	There are three spellings for the regular simple past in affirmative statements: ***-d***, ***-ed***, and ***-ied***. *arrive – arrive**d*** *land – land**ed*** *try – tr**ied***	• I **arrived** late. • We **landed** in Caracas. • He **tried** to change his flight.
3	Use ***did not*** + **the base form of the verb** in negative statements. Use ***didn't*** for negative statements in speaking or informal writing.	• We **did not stay** at a hotel. • We **didn't stay** at a hotel.

4	The **verb form** is the **same for all subject pronouns**.	• **I visited** Seoul. • **She visited** Mexico City. • **They visited** Madrid.
5	**Time markers** usually come at the beginning or end of a sentence. You can use ***yesterday*** alone. You can also use it before *morning*, *afternoon*, or *evening*. Use ***ago*** after a length of time. Use ***last*** before words like *night*, *week*, or *year*.	• **Yesterday** I studied. • I studied **yesterday**. • I visited my friends **yesterday**. • I visited my friends **yesterday evening**. • I started this class a month **ago**. • I arrived here **last** month.

REFERENCE NOTE

For complete simple past spelling and pronunciation rules, see Appendix 10 on page A-10.

STEP 3 FOCUSED PRACTICE

EXERCISE 1: Discover the Grammar

A | *Underline the simple past affirmative verbs. Circle the simple past negative verb. Then write the base form of the verb next to each sentence.*

Base Form

1. We arrived in Washington, D.C., last Friday. *arrive*
2. Yesterday afternoon we walked around the National Zoo. ________
3. Some friends invited us for dinner last night. ________
4. Ana baked a cheesecake yesterday morning. ________
5. The cheesecake didn't look good, but it tasted delicious. ________, ________
6. Miguel cooked enchiladas. ________
7. The enchiladas looked delicious, but they didn't taste good. ________, ________
8. We visited Dupont Circle with Ana and Miguel. ________
9. An hour ago I called and thanked them for a wonderful evening. ________, ________

B | *Write the six time markers in Part A.*

________________, ________________, ________________,

________________, ________________, ________________

EXERCISE 2: Affirmative Statements

(Grammar Notes 1, 2, 4)

Complete the sentences with the verbs from the box. Use the simple past form.

~~borrow~~	cook	land	walk
cancel	hug	visit	watch

1. We ___borrowed___ a guidebook from our friends.
2. His plane ________________ on time.
3. Yesterday she ________________ the art museum.
4. He ________________ a meal for us. It was terrific.
5. I'm tired. I ________________ up a lot of hills in San Francisco this morning.
6. The airlines ________________ many flights because of bad weather.
7. Two nights ago they ________________ a movie.
8. Everyone ________________ and kissed us when we left.

EXERCISE 3: Negative Statements

(Grammar Notes 3–4)

Underline the verb in the first sentence. Then complete the second sentence with the negative simple past form of the verb.

1. He <u>stayed</u> with friends. He ___didn't stay___ at a hotel.
2. I wanted coffee. I ________________________________ tea.
3. It rained in the morning. It ________________________________ in the afternoon.
4. She only invited you. She ________________________________ your whole family.
5. He helped you. He ________________________________ me.
6. I watched a movie. I ________________________________ the news.
7. He picked her up from the airport. He ________________________________ her ________________________________ from the train station.

Answers to Before You Read, page 198: (From left to right): France, China, Peru
Answers to Read, page 198: Brazil

EXERCISE 4: Affirmative and Negative Statements *(Grammar Notes 2–3)*

Complete Camila's travel notes with the verbs in parentheses. Use the simple past.

Carlos and I ____arrived____ (1. arrive) in San Francisco last Wednesday night at 9:00. The next day it ________ (2. rain), but the weather ________ (3. stop / not) us from sightseeing. We ________ (4. carry) our umbrellas and ________ (5. shop) at Fisherman's Wharf. Then the rain ________ (6. stop), so we ________ (7. climb) Telegraph Hill. We ________ (8. walk) around there a bit, and then we ________ (9. board) a bus to Baker Beach. We ________ (10. watch) the sun set next to the Golden Gate Bridge, and we ________ (11. listen) to the ocean waves. I was so tired. I ________ (12. want / not) to stay out. I ________ (13. want) to go back to our hotel. On the way home we ________ (14. need) to eat, though. Chinatown was the perfect spot. We ________ (15. order) a "bird's nest" and red bean soup. It was delicious. Everything in San Francisco was amazing.

EXERCISE 5: Past Time Markers *(Grammar Note 5)*

Complete the conversations. Use **last** *or* **ago,** *or* **yesterday.**

1. **BEN:** Were you away?

   SAM: Yes, I was in Mexico City ____last____ (a.) week.

   BEN: Oh. I was there a couple of months ________ (b.). By the way, Ian called me ________ (c.) night. He wants us to meet for lunch.

2. **STEVE:** Where is Demetrios? I never see him anymore!

   ALLY: I know. He's always traveling. He was in Montreal ________ (a.) weekend. He was in Prague ________ (b.) month. And two months ________ (c.) he visited his family in Greece.

   STEVE: Where is he now?

   ALLY: I'm not sure. I called him ________ (d.) but he didn't answer.

EXERCISE 6: Simple Past and Simple Present Statements *(Grammar Notes 1–6)*

Complete the conversations with the words in parentheses. Use the simple past or simple present.

1. **A:** When do you usually travel?

   B: We usually ___travel___ (travel) in the summer, but last year we ________ (travel) in the fall.

2. **A:** Does John like guided tours?

   B: No. He ________ (like / not) most guided tours, but he ________ (like) the one yesterday in Chicago.

3. **A:** When does that restaurant open?

   B: It usually ________ (open) at 7:00 A.M., but it ________ (open / not) until 7:30 today.

4. **A:** Do you travel on business a lot?

   B: No, I don't. I usually ________ (travel / not) on business, but last month I ________ (travel) twice on business.

5. **A:** When do you start work?

   B: I usually ________ (start) at 9:00, but I ________ (start) at 8:00 this morning because I was very busy.

6. **A:** Does Jade always take the bus?

   B: She usually ________ (take) a bus or train, but this week she ________ (use / not) public transportation. She ________ (rent) a car.

7. **A:** Where do you have lunch?

   B: I usually ________ (bring) something from home, but last Friday was a co-worker's birthday, so five of us ________ (ate) in a Thai restaurant.

EXERCISE 7: Editing

Correct the postcard. There are six mistakes. The first mistake is already corrected. Find and correct five more.

Dear Ilene,

Paris is unbelievable at night! It's 10 P.M., and I'm writing to you from a café. We arrived here ~~ago two days~~ two days ago. Paul's friend Pierre picks us up. We toured the city during the day, and at night we did walked along the Seine River. Today we dining in Montmartre, and we visited the Louvre Museum. I not like the food in Montmartre, but I did loved the area.

We hope all is well with you. Don't work too hard.

Love,

Michelle and Paul

To:
Ilene Carson
85 Maple Street
Plymouth, DE 19905
USA

STEP 4 COMMUNICATION PRACTICE

EXERCISE 8: Listening

A | *Listen to the conversation. Write* **T** (**True**) *or* **F** (**False**) *for each statement. Then correct the false statements.*

ryokan

F 1. Marta visited ~~Mexico~~ Japan.

____ 2. Marta stayed with friends.

____ 3. Marta stayed at a traditional Japanese inn.

____ 4. Marta rented a car.

____ 5. Marta didn't enjoy her trip.

B | *Listen again. Write the amount of time.*

1. Marta was in Japan: ________________
2. Marta stayed in a ryokan: ________________
3. Marta visited Kyoto: ________________
4. Marta and her friend talked about Marta's trip: ________________

EXERCISE 9: Pronunciation

A | *Read and listen to the Pronunciation Note.*

Pronunciation Note

Regular simple past verbs end in three sounds: / **d** /, / **t** /, or / **ɪd** /.

Examples: He arriv<u>ed</u> late. **/ d /**
They work<u>ed</u> at a hotel. **/ t /**
We wait<u>ed</u> a long time. **/ ɪd /**

B | *Listen to the sentences. Check (✓) the final sound of each verb.*

Last weekend, . . .	/ t /	/ d /	/ ɪd /
1. I watched TV.	✓		
2. I rented a movie.			
3. I listened to music.			
4. I played a sport.			
5. I visited friends.			
6. I worked.			

C | *PAIRS: Ask your partner what he or she did last weekend. Then tell your partner what you did. Use the verbs in Part B or other regular simple past verbs.*

Example: **A:** What did you do last weekend, Zofiya?
B: I listened to music at a concert in the park.

EXERCISE 10: Game: Truths and Lies

A | *On a separate piece of paper, write five things you did on your last trip. Four of them are true, and one is a lie. Use five verbs from the unit. Use the past tense.*

Example: On my last trip, . . .

1. I toured Seattle.
2. I rented a car.
3. I stayed with friends.
4. I visited the Space Needle.
5. It rained every day.

B | *GROUPS: Take turns reading your sentences. Guess which one is not true.*

Example: **A:** On my last trip, I toured Seattle. I rented a car. I stayed with friends. I visited the Space Needle. It rained every day.
B: I think "I rented a car" is not true. You don't drive!

EXERCISE 11: Writing

A | *Write about a city you would like to visit. Imagine you traveled to that city last summer. Write a postcard to a classmate about the trip. Use the words from the box, the simple past, and at least two time markers.*

arrive	like	shop	travel	walk
enjoy	rent	stay	visit	watch

EXAMPLE:

Hola Jack,

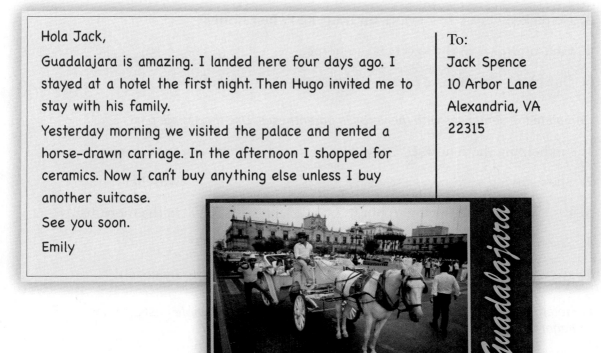

Guadalajara is amazing. I landed here four days ago. I stayed at a hotel the first night. Then Hugo invited me to stay with his family.

Yesterday morning we visited the palace and rented a horse-drawn carriage. In the afternoon I shopped for ceramics. Now I can't buy anything else unless I buy another suitcase.

See you soon.

Emily

To:
Jack Spence
10 Arbor Lane
Alexandria, VA
22315

B | *Check your work. Use the Editing Checklist.*

Editing Checklist

Did you . . . ?

☐ use the simple past with regular verbs correctly

☐ check your spelling

UNIT 18 Review

Check your answers on page UR-4.
Do you need to review anything?

A | *Circle the correct words to complete the sentences.*

1. I **watch / watched** TV last night.
2. We **did visit / visited** Chile last summer.
3. He picked her up from work **an hour ago / last hour**.
4. **Last night / A night ago** I stayed home.
5. Our plane **didn't land / no landed** on time.

B | *Complete the sentences with the verbs in parentheses. Use the simple past.*

1. I'm helping them now. I ____________________ (help) them last week too.
2. She's staying with me. Last year I ____________________ (stay) with her.
3. It snowed during the night, but it ____________________ (snow / not) in the morning.
4. She only asked you. She ____________________ (ask / not) him.
5. We wanted to fly first class. We ____________________ (want / not) to fly coach.

C | *Complete the sentences with the verbs from the box. Use the simple past affirmative or negative.*

cancel	enjoy	play	rain	stay

1. My boss ____________________ the conference. He's trying to save money.
2. She ____________________ late at work. She needed to get home to her children.
3. I didn't need my umbrella. It ____________________.
4. We ____________________ soccer for three hours. It was a lot of fun.
5. He ____________________ the movie. It was very boring.

D | *Read the paragraph. Find the five mistakes.*

Hello from London. Our friends did invited us here for a week. We're having a great time. Yesterday we visit Big Ben, and we tour the Royal Palace. This morning we watch the Changing of the Guard. We wanted to shop this afternoon, but we didn't. The prices were high, but we are enjoyed looking at the store windows.

UNIT 19 Simple Past: Affirmative and Negative Statements with Irregular Verbs

YOU NEVER KNOW

STEP 1 GRAMMAR IN CONTEXT

Before You Read

Some people say, "In life, you never know what will happen." What does that mean?

a. Life never changes. **b.** Life has surprises.

Read

Read this Chinese folktale.

YOU NEVER KNOW WHAT WILL HAPPEN

A long time ago there lived a poor Chinese peasant.[1] One day a beautiful horse appeared on his farm. When the peasant's friends **saw** the horse they **said**, "How lucky you are!"

The peasant answered, "You never know what will happen."

Two days later the horse **ran** away. The peasant's friends **came** and **said**, "What a terrible thing. How unlucky you are! The fine horse **ran** away." The peasant **didn't get** excited. He simply **said**, "You never know what will happen."

Exactly one week later the horse returned. And it **brought** three other horses. When the peasant's friends **saw** the horses they **said**, "Oh. You are so lucky. Now you have four horses to help you." The peasant looked at them and once again **said**, "You never know what will happen."

The next morning the peasant's oldest son **was** in the field.[2] Suddenly one of the horses **ran** into him, and the boy **fell** to the ground. He **was** badly hurt. He **lost** the use of his leg. Indeed, this **was** terrible, and many people **came** to the peasant and expressed their sadness for his son's misfortune. But again the peasant simply **said**, "You never know what will happen."

[1] ***peasant:*** person who works on a farm

[2] ***field:*** large grassy area

A month after the accident, soldiers **rode** into the village. They shouted, "There is a problem along the border! We are taking every healthy young man to fight." The soldiers **took** all the other young men, but they **didn't take** the peasant's son. All the other young men **fought** in the border war, and they all died. But the peasant's son lived a long and happy life. As his father **said**, you never know what will happen.

After You Read

A | Practice *PAIRS: Read the folktale again aloud. Take turns reading paragraphs.*

B | Vocabulary *Complete the sentences with the words from the box.*

appeared	border	lucky	shouted	suddenly	terrible

1. I didn't like the story because it had a(n) ________________ ending.
2. He showed his passport to cross the ________________ into Mexico.
3. We didn't expect the rain. The weather changed ________________.
4. It's a folktale about a(n) ________________ man. Good things always happen to him.
5. He ________________, but nobody heard him.
6. A beautiful red bird ________________ on my window sill.

C | Comprehension *Number the events in the order they occurred* (1 to 6).

_____ A week later the horse came back with three other horses.
__1__ A horse appeared on a peasant's land. Two days later it ran away.
_____ The next morning one of the horses ran into the peasant's son; he was hurt.
_____ A month later soldiers rode into the village.
_____ The other young men died. The peasant's son lived a long, happy life.
_____ The soldiers took all the healthy young men to fight, but they didn't take the peasant's son.

STEP 2 GRAMMAR PRESENTATION

SIMPLE PAST: IRREGULAR VERBS—AFFIRMATIVE AND NEGATIVE STATEMENTS

Affirmative Statements		
Subject	**Verb**	
I You He We	**bought** **rode** **saw**	the horses.

Negative Statements			
Subject	***Did Not / Didn't***	**Base Form of Verb**	
I You He We	**did not** **didn't**	**buy** **ride** **see**	the horses.

Be: Affirmative Statements		
Subject	***Was / Were***	
She	**was**	lucky.
They	**were**	unlucky.

Be: Negative Statements		
Subject	***Was / Were not***	
I	**was not**	home.
We	**were not**	nearby.

Contractions
was not → **wasn't**
were not → **weren't**

GRAMMAR NOTES

1	Many common verbs are irregular. **Irregular past verbs** do not add *-ed*. They often look different from the base form.	• We **saw** a beautiful horse. (**see**) • They **went** to work. (**go**) • She **came** late. (**come**) • He **brought** a friend to school. (**bring**) • He **ate** a big lunch. (**eat**)
2	For **negative statements** in the past, use ***did not*** + **base form of the verb** (except for *be*). Use the short form ***didn't*** for speaking and informal writing. **BE CAREFUL!** Do not use the simple past form after *didn't.*	• They **did not see** him. • She **did not eat** lunch. • They **didn't** see him. NOT: They didn't ~~saw~~ him. They didn't ~~ate~~ lunch.
3	The **past tense of *be*** is ***was*** or ***were***. The **negative** is ***was not*** or ***were not***. Use ***wasn't*** and ***weren't*** for speaking and informal writing.	• I **was** at the library last night. • They **were not** home this morning. • It **wasn't** late. • They **weren't** in Mexico City.
4	We use ***was*** or ***were*** + ***born*** to tell when or where people were born.	• I **was born** in Nicaragua. • She **was born** in 1989.

REFERENCE NOTES

See Appendix 11, page A-11 for a list of irregular past forms.
See Unit 3, page 28 for a discussion of the past of *be*.
See Unit 18, pages 200–201, and Unit 20, pages 222–223 for more about the simple past.

STEP 3 FOCUSED PRACTICE

EXERCISE 1: Discover the Grammar

Circle the verbs in the past. Then write the verbs and the base form of each verb in the chart.

I have two brothers. My older brother was a great student. He brought home prizes and won awards. My younger brother felt bored by school. He never did well. My parents worried about him. Then in his second year of high school, he had a great chemistry teacher. He became interested in chemistry. He began to study hard. He's now a chemistry professor at a university. So, you never know what will happen.

Past	Base Form
was	be
brought	bring

EXERCISE 2: Simple Past: Irregular Verbs

(Grammar Notes 1–3)

Complete the paragraph with the words in parentheses. Use the simple past.

Abe ___was___ (1. be) nine when his mother died in 1818. His family ________ (2. have) very little money and lived in a log cabin with one room. Still, Abe ________ (3. go) to school. He ________ (4. grow) strong and very tall. He ________ (5. split) wood for money, then he ________ (6. teach) himself the law and ________ (7. begin) a law firm. For a short time, he ________ (8. be) a soldier, but he ________ (9. see / not) any action. He ________ (10. come) home, ________ (11. give) speeches, and ________ (12. run) for political office. People ________ (13. make fun) of him because he was so tall, but he ________ (14. let / not) it bother him. He ________ (15. become) president of the United States and ________ (16. lead) the country during a difficult civil war. His army ________ (17. win) the war. He ________ (18. become) one of the most admired American presidents in history. His name, as you guessed, ________ (19. be) Abraham Lincoln.

EXERCISE 3: Simple Past: Irregular Verbs

(Grammar Notes 1–4)

Complete the paragraphs with the words in parentheses. Use the simple past.

James Earl Jones ___was born___ **1. (be born)** in Mississippi in 1931. At five his family moved to Michigan. Soon after that, he ______________ **2. (begin)** to stutter. For many years he ______________ **3. (say / not)** more than a few words. In high school a teacher tried to help him. After Jones ______________ **4. (write)** a poem, this teacher ______________ **5. (make)** him read it aloud. Jones ______________ **6. (know)** the poem by heart, and he ______________ **7. (say)** it without stuttering. It ______________ **8. (be)** his first success at public speaking. Later, Jones ______________ **9. (got)** a scholarship to the University of Michigan. At first, he studied medicine, but then he changed to theater.

After college, he ______________ **10. (go)** to New York. He ______________ **11. (have / not)** money, and he ______________ **12. (do)** all sorts of jobs to pay his bills. After a few years, people ______________ **13. (see)** his talent. He ______________ **14. (become)** a famous and admired actor. Maybe you know his deep, powerful voice. It is the voice of Darth Vader in the *Star Wars* movies and Mufasa in *The Lion King*.

In 2009 Jones ______________ **15. (win)** a Lifetime Achievement Award of the Screen Actors Guild. Jones's life is amazing when you think that as a child, speaking ______________ **16. (be)** his biggest challenge. So in life you never know what will happen.

EXERCISE 4: Simple Past: Irregular Verbs

(Grammar Notes 1–4)

Complete each paragraph with the words from the box. Use the simple past.

~~be born~~	become	begin	be / not	read

Joanne Kathleen ___was born___ (1.) in 1965 in England. She ________________ (2.) writing at the age of five, and she always ________________ (3.) a lot. She majored in French at the university and ________________ (4.) a bilingual secretary. But she ________________ (5.) very good at it.

begin	go	have	teach

At 26, she ________________ (6.) to Portugal. She ________________ (7.) English there. At this time she first ________________ (8.) working on a story about a boy with special powers named Harry. She met a journalist in Portugal. They married and ________________ (9.) a daughter in 1993. Unfortunately, the marriage ended in divorce.

be	give	have / not	sell	want / not	write

She moved to Scotland to be near a sister and finish her book. In Scotland life ________________ (10.) hard because she ________________ (11.) much money. She tried to sell her book, but the publishers ________________ (12.) it. She finally ________________ (13.) her book for about $4,000. Several months later, an American company ________________ (14.) her money to write full time. Soon her book became a bestseller. She ________________ (15.) several more Harry Potter books. Today, J. K. Rowling is rich and famous. So you never know what will happen.

Actor Daniel Radcliffe, star of *Harry Potter*

EXERCISE 5: Editing

Correct the sentences. There are nine mistakes. The first mistake is already corrected. Find and correct eight more.

My grandfather ^was^ born in Peru. He had an older brother and sister. Their dad (my great-grandfather) were a dreamer. The family have not much money. When my grandfather was 13, his mother did died and his dad remarried. My grandfather no like his stepmother so he move in with his sister and her husband. All three leave for America. They did begin a small business. They worked hard, and the business grow. Today my sister and I direct the company.

STEP 4 COMMUNICATION PRACTICE

EXERCISE 6: Listening

A | *Listen to Paul's story. Answer the question. Circle the correct letter.*

The story is about ______________________.

a. a father and son **b.** a man and his grandfather

B | *Listen again and complete the sentences.*

1. Paul's grandfather gave him a(n) ___blanket___.
2. After a couple of years it ____________ ____________ good.
3. Paul's mother made it into a(n) ____________ ____________.
4. Then the ____________ ____________ tore.
5. His mother made it into a(n) ____________ ____________.
6. Paul ____________ the ____________.
7. He felt ____________.
8. His friends said, "____________ ____________ ____________."
9. Paul didn't ____________ about it. He ____________ about it instead.
10. Many years later Paul's ____________ found the story.

EXERCISE 7: Pronunciation

A | *Read and listen to the Pronunciation Note.*

Pronunciation Note

The **/ æ /** sound, as in ***have***, is slightly more open than the **/ ɛ /** sound, as in ***bed***.

To pronounce the **/ ɛ /** sound, keep your mouth open and your lips spread. Keep your tongue low in your mouth. Touch the lower front teeth lightly with the tip of your tongue.

B | *Listen to the / æ / sound in the underlined words. Then repeat the sentences.*

1. The story happened in China.
2. A Chinese peasant's horse ran away.
3. It came back with three more horses.
4. The son lived a happy life.
5. The peasant laughed and said, "You never know what will happen."

C | *Listen. Check (✓) if the underlined word has the / æ / sound or the / ɛ / sound.*

	/ æ /	/ ɛ /
1. They had a hard life.	☑	☐
2. The boy's head hurt from his fall.	☐	☐
3. He told us the end of the story.	☐	☐
4. We liked the story and the movie.	☐	☐
5. The man was lucky.	☐	☐
6. The men fought on the border.	☐	☐

EXERCISE 8: A Memory Game

GROUPS: Sit in a circle. Take notes. The first student tells one thing he or she did last weekend. The next student tells what the first one did and then what he or she did. Continue until every student speaks.

EXAMPLE: **ANN:** I went to the movies.

JOE: Ann went to the movies, and I read a book.

EXERCISE 9: Discussion

SMALL GROUPS: Tell about a wonderful day and a terrible day. Use **First, Then,** *and* **After that.**

Example: I had a wonderful day. First, I saw my grandmother. Then, I went to the park. After that, I rented a video.
Yesterday I had a terrible day. First, I got up late. Then, I broke my glasses. After that, I lost my keys.

EXERCISE 10: Writing

A | *Write your autobiography. The year is now 2066. Think about these questions as you write.*

- Where and when were you born?
- Where did you go to school?
- What did you do in your free time?
- What did you become? (businessperson, etc.) Why?
- Where did you live?
- Did you marry? Did you have children?
- Did you travel?
- Did you become rich or famous?
- Did you make a difference in the world?
- Were you happy?

Example: Right now I'm celebrating my eightieth birthday with my four children, their children, and their children's children. I am a lucky man. I was born in 1980 in Korea. My family didn't have much money, but we were hardworking. I was the fourth of five children. My parents were . . .

B | *Check your work. Use the Editing Checklist.*

Editing Checklist

Did you . . . ?
☐ use the simple past of irregular and regular verbs correctly
☐ check your spelling

UNIT 19 Review

Check your answers on page UR-4.
Do you need to review anything?

A | *Complete the sentences with the verbs in parentheses. Use the simple past.*

1. One day a fox ________________ (see) some delicious grapes.
2. He ________________ (be) hungry, and he ________________ (want) the grapes.
3. He ________________ (try) to reach the grapes, but they were too high.
4. He ________________ (get) angry and said, "I really ________________ (want / not) them anyway."

B | *Complete the paragraph with the verbs from the box. Use the simple past.*

become	find	keep	steal	use / not

A lucky man ________________ a pot of gold. He ________________ the pot of gold in a hole in the ground of his garden. A jealous worker ________________ the gold from the man. The man ________________ upset. But a neighbor laughed because the man ________________ the gold. He just enjoyed counting it.

C | *Complete the sentences with the verbs in parentheses. Use the affirmative or negative form.*

1. The concert was terrible. I ________________ (stay) until the end.
2. He ________________ (lose) his keys. He needs to get a new set of keys.
3. We ________________ (run) 5 miles yesterday. We're practicing for a big race.
4. We ________________ (see) him in school. Was he sick?
5. It ________________ (take) him a long time to get to school. I wonder why?

D | *Correct the sentences. There are four mistakes.*

1. William Sidney Porter born in North Carolina in 1862.
2. He was a famous American short story writer. He wrote under different names, but he did became best known as O. Henry.
3. His stories were had surprise endings.
4. O. Henry had many talents, but he did get into trouble and spent time in prison.

UNIT

20 Simple Past: *Yes/No* and *Wh-* Questions

INTERVIEWS

STEP 1 GRAMMAR IN CONTEXT

Before You Read

PAIRS: Read these lines by the greatest writer in the English language. Who wrote these famous lines? In what play did he write them?

- "Romeo, Romeo! Wherefore art thou Romeo?"
- "Parting is such sweet sorrow."

William Shakespeare wrote these words in the play *Romeo and Juliet*. Altogether Shakespeare wrote between 37 and 38 plays and many poems.

Leonardo DiCaprio starred in the 1996 movie version of *Romeo and Juliet*

Read

Read a radio talk show interview between English professor Robert Gibbons and Carla Jonas.

CARLA: Thank you for coming today Professor Gibbons. I see your new book ***Who Wrote the Greatest Plays of All?*** is out. It's about Shakespeare, right?

PROFESSOR GIBBONS: Yes, it is. It's about Shakespeare and the time period he lived in.

CARLA: So, **why did you write the book?**

PROF: I wanted to explore some questions we have about Shakespeare and his life. Shakespeare probably wrote all the plays and poems that we say he did, but we don't know for sure. You see, Shakespeare's life is a mystery. There are many things we don't know about him. And the questions are interesting.

(continued on next page)

CARLA: Well, what can you tell us about him? **When was Shakespeare born?**

PROF: He was born in 1564 in Stratford-on-Avon, but we don't know the exact date.

CARLA: What about his family?

Juliet's castle, Castle Vecchio

PROF: His father was a landowner and a town leader. His mother was the daughter of a wealthy landowner. But his father was illiterate.[1]

CARLA: **Did Shakespeare go to school?**

PROF: Yes, but we don't know too much about Shakespeare's education because there is no paper trail.[2] We think he went to grammar school.[3] But he did not attend a university. He probably studied Latin and Greek. But . . . **was his education good enough? How did Shakespeare learn to write so well? Did he really write the plays himself**, or **did someone else write them for him?**

CARLA: What do you mean?

PROF: At that time, many people wrote under a different name, a pen name. Some people think that Shakespeare's friend, Ben Jonson, wrote the plays.

CARLA: That's interesting. I have a question about Shakespeare. He wrote many plays about English kings and queens. **How did he know so much about the life of royalty?**[4] He wasn't in that class.[5]

PROF: That's a good question. We think he read about them. We're pretty sure the story of *Macbeth* and parts of *King Lear* came from a book by Raphael Holinshed. That book tells all about English, Scottish, and Irish kings. Still . . . we don't know, **was Shakespeare the writer?** And could one person write so many great works? Most scholars[6] believe Shakespeare was the author. We think he was a man of great genius and imagination . . . but perhaps it was someone else. We may never know for certain.

CARLA: Such interesting points! I'm looking forward to reading your book, Professor. For those of you who like a good mystery, buy Professor Mark Gibbons's new book, *Who Wrote the Greatest Plays of All?* And Professor, thank you for coming here today.

PROF: And thank you, Carla, for inviting me.

---

[1] ***illiterate:*** not able to read or write

[2] ***paper trail:*** a written record

[3] ***grammar school:*** basic English schooling for boys in the 1500s

[4] ***royalty:*** a king, queen, and their family

[5] ***class:*** a group of people classified by income and education

[6] ***scholar:*** someone who studies a subject deeply

After You Read

A | Practice *PAIRS: Now read the interview aloud.*

B | Vocabulary *Complete the sentences with the words from the box.*

author	be out	mystery	play	poem

1. Shakespeare wrote the _______________ *Romeo and Juliet* between the years 1591 and 1595.
2. Shakespeare is the _______________ of between 37 and 38 plays.
3. Nobody knows Shakespeare's exact birthday. It's a(n) _______________.
4. The words in that _______________ are beautiful, but they don't rhyme.
5. When will that new book about *Romeo and Juliet* _______________? I'd like to read it.

C | Comprehension *Read the questions. Circle the correct letter.*

1. Where was Shakespeare born?
   a. London **b.** Stratford-on-Avon
2. When was he born?
   a. 1654 **b.** 1564
3. Did his parents come from poor families?
   a. Yes, they did. **b.** No, they didn't.
4. Did Shakespeare attend a university?
   a. Yes, he did. **b.** No, he didn't.
5. What was *Macbeth* the name of?
   a. a play by Shakespeare **b.** a town in England
6. Do most scholars believe that Shakespeare wrote all of his plays?
   a. Yes, they do. **b.** No, they don't.

Stratford-on-Avon

STEP 2 GRAMMAR PRESENTATION

THE SIMPLE PAST: *YES / NO* AND *WH-* QUESTIONS AND ANSWERS

***Yes / No* Questions**		
Did	**Subject**	**Base Form of Verb**
Did	I you he she it we they	**help?**

Short Answers					
Affirmative			**Negative**		
Yes,	you I he she it you they	**did.**	**No,**	you I he she it you they	**didn't.**

***Wh-* Questions**				**Answers**
***Wh-* Word**	***Did***	**Subject**	**Base Form of Verb**	
What	**did**	I	**ask**?	You asked about his name.
Where		you	**go**?	I went to the library. (To the library.)
When		he	**write**?	He wrote at night, after work. (At night, after work.)
Why		we	**leave**?	We went someplace else.
Who		you	**call**?	We called the doctor. (The doctor.)
How long		they	**stay**?	They stayed for an hour. (For an hour.) (An hour.)

***Wh-* Questions about the Subject**			**Answers**
***Wh-* Word**	**Past Form of Verb**		
Who	**wrote**	*Romeo and Juliet*?	William Shakespeare did.
What	**happened**	in the play?	Romeo and Juliet fell in love.

GRAMMAR NOTES

1	***Yes / No* questions** in the **simple past** have the same form (***Did*** + **subject** + **base form**) for regular and irregular verbs. The verb ***be*** is the one exception.	REGULAR VERB • **Did** you **call** your classmate? IRREGULAR VERB • **Did** you **write** your report? • **Was** Shakespeare an actor?
2	Most ***wh-* questions in the past** begin with the **question word** followed by ***did*** + **the subject** + **the base form** of the verb.	• **What did** he **write**? • **Why did** he **write**? • **Where did** he **write**? • **Who did** he **work** for?

3	*Wh-* questions in the past **do not use *did*** when the **question is about the subject**.	SUBJECT • Shakespeare wrote *Romeo and Juliet*. **Q: Who wrote *Romeo and Juliet*?** **A:** William Shakespeare. NOT: **Q:** Who ~~did write~~ *Romeo and Juliet*?
4	We usually give **short answers** to *yes / no* and *wh-* questions, but we can also give **long answers**. **NOTE:** ***Yes / No* questions** use **rising** intonation. ***Wh-* questions** use **falling** intonation.	**Q:** Did you work yesterday? **A:** Yes. OR Yes, I did. OR Yes, I worked yesterday. • Did you hear the story? • What did you think about it?

REFERENCE NOTE

See Unit 3, page 28 for more about the past of *be*.

STEP 3 FOCUSED PRACTICE

EXERCISE 1: Discover the Grammar

A | *Underline all the base form verbs.*

1. Did you watch a Shakespeare play last summer?
2. What did you see?
3. Did anyone go with you?
4. Did you understand it?
5. Did you enjoy it?
6. Did you read the whole play?

B | *Match the questions with the responses from the box. Write the responses.*

a. I read *Hamlet*.	**c.** Yes, I saw it three times.
b. William Shakespeare.	**d.** No, I didn't. I got it at the library.

1. **A:** What did you read for English class?
   B: ______________________________
2. **A:** Who wrote it?
   B: ______________________________
3. **A:** Did you buy the book?
   B: ______________________________
4. **A:** Did you see the movie?
   B: ______________________________

EXERCISE 2: Simple Past: *Yes / No* Questions

(Grammar Note 1)

*Write **yes / no** questions in the simple past. Use the verb from the first sentence.*

1. I read all his plays. ___Did___ you ___read___ them too?
2. We enjoyed the movie. ______________ you ______________ it too?
3. The movie had good acting. ______________ it ______________ a good story?
4. I didn't understand everything. ______________ she ______________ everything?
5. We didn't like the ending. ______________ he ______________ the ending?
6. I expected a happy ending. ______________ you ______________ a happy ending?
7. We saw a review online. ______________ they ______________ the review online?

EXERCISE 3: Simple Past: Short Answers

(Grammar Note 4)

Complete the conversations with the simple past. Write affirmative or negative short answers.

1. **A:** Did you finish your homework?

   B: ___Yes, I did.___ I finished it before dinner.

2. **A:** Did they go to the movies?

   B: ______________________. They stayed home and watched TV.

3. **A:** Did I call too late?

   B: ______________________. I'm usually up at this hour.

4. **A:** Did we get any mail?

   B: ______________________. We got our tickets for *King Lear*.

5. **A:** Did the package arrive?

   B: ______________________. It just came.

6. **A:** Did you buy the DVD?

   B: ______________________. I plan to buy it next weekend.

7. **A:** Did she lose her phone?

   B: ______________________. She thinks she left it on the bus.

EXERCISE 4: Simple Past Questions

(Grammar Notes 1–3)

Sherryl Woods is a best-selling romance and mystery writer. She has written more than 100 books that are available in over 20 countries. Read the interview. Complete the questions with the words in parentheses. Use the simple past.

I = INTERVIEWER

SW = SHERRYL WOODS

When will David ask me to marry him? Only Sherryl Woods knows!

I: ___When did you write___ your first book?
1. (When / you / write)

SW: In 1980. It came out in 1982.

I: ______________________ to be a writer?
2. (you / always / want)

SW: No, I didn't. For many years I wanted to be a graphic artist.

I: ______________________ always good at writing?
3. (be / you)

SW: Well, my first-grade teacher wrote, "Sherryl is good at everything except making up stories."

I: ______________________ your first-grade teacher?
4. (you / like)

SW: I can't remember.

I: ______________________ to write?
5. (When / you / start)

SW: After I graduated from college, I became a journalist.

I: ______________________ as a journalist?
6. (How long / you / work)

SW: I worked for newspapers for 14 years.

I: ______________________ writing romance novels?
7. (Why / you / start)

SW: Romances were new when I started. I read one and said, "I can do this too."

I: ______________________ the most?
8. (Who / help / you)

SW: My agent did. She was there for me from the beginning.

I: ______________________ when your books became popular?
9. (How / you / feel)

SW: I felt terrific. I remember the first time I saw someone with my book. I said, "That's my book." The woman looked at me and said, "No, it's not. It's mine." I said, "No, no, no. It's my book. I wrote it."

EXERCISE 5: Editing

John Steinbeck was a great American writer. Correct the questions and answers about him. There are ten mistakes. The first mistake is already corrected. Find and correct nine more.

Q: When ^was John Steinbeck ~~was~~ born?

A: He born in 1902.

Q: Where he was born?

A: He was born in Salinas, California.

Q: Where did he studied writing?

A: He studied writing at Stanford University.

Q: He graduate from Stanford?

A: No, he didn't.

Q: Does he marry?

A: Yes, he did. He married in 1930.

Q: When he published *Tortilla Flat*?

A: In 1936.

Q: What year did *The Grapes of Wrath* come out?

A: In 1938. It was his best book.

Q: What were it about?

A: It was about a family who lost their farm and became fruit pickers in California.

Q: Did he won many prizes?

A: Yes, he did. He won a Pulitzer Prize and a Nobel Prize in Literature.

Q: When did he died?

A: He died in New York in 1968.

STEP 4 COMMUNICATION PRACTICE

EXERCISE 6: Pronunciation

A | *Read and listen to the Pronunciation Note.*

Pronunciation Note

When you pronounce **/ dʒ /** as in ***jump***, place the tip of your tongue high and pulled back from the teeth.

When you pronounce **/ y /** as in ***young***, the center of your tongue slides up toward the front of your mouth.

Examples: **/ dʒ /** jet
/ y / yet

B | *Listen and repeat the sentences.*

1. I like yellow.
2. I like Jell-O.™
3. He's going to Yale.
4. He's going to jail.
5. There's no juice.
6. There's no use.

C | *PAIRS: Your partner says a sentence from Part A. Read a sentence from the list below that follows your partner's sentence.*

1. Why? Did he rob a bank?
2. I do too. It's delicious.
3. Do I need to buy some?
4. You mean we can't change anything?
5. That's a great university.
6. It's my favorite color, too.

D | *Listen to the sentences. Underline the* **/ dʒ /** *sounds and circle the* **/ y /** *sounds that you hear.*

1. His initials are J. S.
2. He's good at storytelling, and some say he's a genius.
3. Does the J stand for Jack or John?
4. What year was he born?
5. We saw the movie *The Grapes of Wrath* yesterday.
6. At what age did he write his first book?
7. The language is not so difficult to understand.
8. Steinbeck wrote, "A journey is like marriage."

EXERCISE 7: Listening

A | *Listen to the conversation between Jon and Elena. Then read the questions. Circle the correct letter.*

1. What movie did Jon see last night?
- **a.** *I Love Shakespeare* **b.** *Shakespeare in Love*

2. Where did it take place?
- **a.** in London **b.** in Rome

3. When did it take place?
- **a.** in the 1500s **b.** in the 1600s

B | *Listen again. Complete the sentences about the play* Romeo and Juliet.

Romeo and Juliet fell ____________________. They couldn't ____________________ because ____________________. In the last scene, they ____________________.

EXERCISE 8: Describing a Performance or Event

PAIRS: Name a play, a movie, a concert, a TV show or an athletic event you attended. Your partner asks **wh-** *questions and* **yes** / **no** *questions about the event.*

EXAMPLE: **A:** I saw the play *West Side Story*.
B: What was it about?
A: It was a play about two people who fell in love.
B: When did it take place?
A: In the 1950s.

EXERCISE 9: Writing

A | *Work in small groups. Complete the chart with names of famous people from the past.*

Artists	Writers	Musicians	Scientists / Inventors	Actors	Athletes

B | *Write 10 questions about one of the people from Part A. Use the words in parentheses.*

1. Where was Leonardo diCaprio born?
(Where / he or she / born?)

2. ______________________________
(When / he or she / born?)

3. ______________________________
(Where / he or she / grow up?)

4. ______________________________
(What / he or she / do in his or her free time?)

5. ______________________________
(he or she / have / a happy childhood?)

6. ______________________________
(he or she / travel?)

7. ______________________________
(he or she / work hard?)

8. ______________________________
(he or she / make a lot of money?)

9. ______________________________
(YOUR QUESTION)

10. ______________________________
(YOUR QUESTION)

C | *Check your work. Use the Editing Checklist.*

Editing Checklist

Did you . . . ?
☐ use ***yes/no*** and ***wh-*** questions with the simple past correctly
☐ check your spelling

UNIT

20 Review

Check your answers on page UR-4.
Do you need to review anything?

A | *Write* **yes / no** *questions with the verbs in parentheses. Use the simple past.*

1. ________________________________ (they / go to the theater)
2. ________________________________ (she / get there by bus)
3. ________________________________ (you / have good seats)
4. ________________________________ (he / understand everything)
5. ________________________________ (we / miss the beginning)
6. ________________________________ (it / have a happy ending)

B | *Complete the questions with the words in parentheses. Use the simple past.*

1. ________________________________? (what play / see / you)
2. ________________________________? (where / you / see / it)
3. ________________________________? (how long / be / the show)
4. ________________________________? (you / enjoy / the performance)
5. ________________________________? (who / be / the stars)
6. ________________________________? (you / go out / after the show)
7. ________________________________? (Where / you / go)
8. ________________________________? (What / you / order)

C | *Correct the sentences. There are six mistakes.*

1. Where he did go last night?
2. What saw he?
3. Did he enjoyed it?
4. Who he met?
5. When they go?
6. Who did pay for it?

From Grammar to Writing

Punctuation II: The Exclamation Point (!), The Hyphen (-), Quotation Marks ("...")

1 | *What's wrong with the sentences? Discuss them with a partner.*

1. You're kidding
2. She's 21 years old
3. He said I love you
4. He worked for many years before he became rich. Then he invest

   ed his money and became even richer.

2 | *Study this information about punctuation.*

The exclamation point (!) Use the exclamation point after **strong, emotional statements**. (Don't use it too often.)	• What a surprise! • You're kidding! • How wonderful!
The hyphen (-) **a.** Use a hyphen in **compound numbers** from twenty-one to ninety-nine. **b.** Use a hyphen **at the end of a line** when dividing a word. Words must be divided by syllables. (Check your dictionary if you are unsure.)	• There were **twenty-two** students in the class. • We visited them at the **begin-ning** of the year.
Quotation marks ("...") Use quotation marks **before** and **after the exact words** of a speaker. Use a comma before the quote.	• She said, "I just love your new sweater."

3 | *Add the correct punctuation to the sentences in Exercise 1.*

4 | *Read the story. Circle the exclamation marks. Add quotation marks where necessary.*

Whose Baby Is It?

Solomon was a king. He lived about 3,000 years ago. Everyone came to Solomon because he was very wise.

One day two women approached King Solomon. One carried a baby. The woman said, We live nearby and had our babies three days apart. Her baby died in the night, and she changed it for mine. This baby is really mine.

The other woman said, No! That woman is lying. That's my baby.

The two women started arguing. They continued until King Solomon shouted, Stop!

He then turned to his guard and said, Take your sword and chop the baby in two. Give one part to this woman and the other to that one. The guard pulled out his sword. As he was about to harm the baby, the first woman screamed, No! Don't do it. Give her the baby. Just don't kill the baby.

King Solomon then said, Now I know the real mother. Give the baby to the woman who has just spoken.

5 | *Work in small groups. Follow the steps.*

1. Think about these questions. Take notes.
   - What was your favorite story as a child?
   - When did you first hear it? Who told it to you? Why did you like it?
2. Tell your story to your group.
3. Write your story. When you are finished, read your story twice. First pay attention to the story. Next pay attention to the grammar and punctuation.

6 | *Exchange papers with a partner. Did your partner follow the directions? Correct any mistakes in grammar and spelling.*

7 | *Talk to your partner. Discuss the mistakes you made. Then rewrite your own paper and make any necessary changes.*

8 | *Hang your story on the wall. Go around and read the stories of your classmates.*

PART

VII

VERB REVIEW AND CONTRAST AND EXPANSION

UNIT	GRAMMAR FOCUS	THEME
21	Simple Past Review	Biographies
22	Gerunds and Infinitives	Careers and Abilities
23	Simple Present, Present Progressive, and Simple Past	Creativity

UNIT

21 Simple Past Review

BIOGRAPHIES

STEP 1 GRAMMAR IN CONTEXT

Before You Read

PAIRS: Look at the words in the box. Tell your partner about people or pets with these qualities. Tell why.

generous	innovative	loyal	powerful
hardworking	loving	passionate	understanding

EXAMPLE: My cousin is very passionate about his work. He's an architect and spends hours working on projects.

Read

Read the article about a very unusual dog.

A Loyal Friend

Many people say dogs are loving and loyal. For one dog named Hachiko that description is especially true. He **won** the hearts of people all over the world because of his love and faithfulness to his master.

Hachiko **was** an Akita Inu dog. Akita Inus are large dogs from Japan. Hachiko **was born** in 1923. His owner, Ueno, **was** a professor at Tokyo University. Every morning Ueno and Hachiko **walked** to the Shibuya train station together. Every evening Hachiko **met** Ueno at the station. This routine **continued** for a couple of years. One evening, however, Hachiko **went** to the station, but Ueno **didn't get** off the train. That day, Ueno **was** at work when he suddenly **had** a cerebral hemorrhage[1] and died.

Hachiko **didn't know** what to do. He **looked** everywhere for Ueno. He **was** very sad, and he **missed** his master a lot. Every day for nine years he **went** to the train station and **waited** for his master's return. After a while people at the station **noticed** the dog and **began** to bring him food. They **admired** his loyalty. In 1934 they **hired** a well-known sculptor to build a statue of Hachiko. Hachiko **was** there when the statue was unveiled. A year later, in 1935, Hachiko **died**.

After Hachiko's death, Ueno's students **wrote** articles about the amazing dog. People **wrote** books about him. In 2004 Leslie Newman **wrote** and Machiyo Kodaira **illustrated** *Hachiko Waits*. This book **received** many awards. In 2009 Richard Gere **starred** in a movie based on Hachiko's life.

These days when people are near the Shibuya train station in Tokyo, they often say, "Let's meet at the statue of Hachiko!"

One thing is certain. Hachiko's life will not be forgotten.

[1]***cerebral hemorrhage:*** bleeding in the brain

After You Read

A | Practice *PAIRS: Now read the article aloud. Take turns reading each paragraph.*

B | Vocabulary *Circle the letter of the best meaning for the words in* **blue.**

1. I **noticed** that he had a good memory.
   a. forgot b. saw
2. When I'm away from home, I **miss** my brothers.
   a. wish to be with b. don't think about
3. He **illustrated** a children's book.
   a. wrote b. drew pictures for
4. The movie **is based on** the book.
   a. comes from ideas in b. is different from
5. I **admire** his ability in art. He is a very good sculptor.
   a. think highly of b. admit
6. There is a stone **statue** of our first president in front of the park.
   a. figure that looks like a person b. painting that looks like a person

C | Comprehension *Read the questions. Circle the correct letter.*

1. What kind of dog is Hachiko?
   a. a Collie b. an Akita Inu
2. What did Hachiko's master do?
   a. He was a professor. b. He was a train conductor.
3. When was Hachiko born?
   a. in 1934 b. in 1923
4. Where did Hachiko wait for his master every evening?
   a. at the university b. at the train station
5. What did Hachiko do after Ueno died?
   a. He waited for Ueno at the train station. b. He looked for Ueno at the university.
6. Why did people admire Hachiko?
   a. He was loyal and patient. b. He was strong and powerful.
7. What is *Hachiko Waits*?
   a. a story based on Hachiko's life b. a TV show based on Hachiko's life

STEP 2 GRAMMAR PRESENTATION

THE SIMPLE PAST

Affirmative Statements (All Verbs Except *Be*)		
Subject	**Verb**	
I	**stayed**	home.
We	**went**	

Affirmative Statements with *Be*		
Subject	**Verb**	
I	**was**	at home.
We	**were**	

Negative Statements (All Verbs Except *Be*)			
Subject	***Did Not (Didn't)***	**Base Form of Verb**	
I	**did not**	**stay**	with them.
We	**didn't**	**go**	

Negative Statements with *Be*		
Subject	**Verb**	
I	**was not** **wasn't**	at work.
We	**were not** **weren't**	

Yes / No Questions (All Verbs Except *Be*)		
Did	**Subject**	**Base Form of Verb**
Did	she	**leave**?
	they	

Yes / No Questions with *Be*		
Was / Were	**Subject**	
Was	he	home last night?
Were	they	

Wh- Questions (All Verbs Except *Be*)			
***Wh-* Word**	***Did***	**Subject**	**Base Form of Verb**
When	**did**	you	**arrive**?
Where		he	**work**?
How		it	**begin**?
Why		he	**leave**?
Who(m)		they	**help**?

Wh- Questions with *Be*			
***Wh-* Word**	**Past Form**	**Subject**	
When	**was**	she	there?
Where		he	from?
How	**were**	his	tests?
Why		you	late?
Who(m)		they	with?

Wh- Questions About the Subject (All Verbs Except *Be*)		
***Wh-* Word**	**Past Form**	
Who	**walked**	to the station?
What	**happened**	to him?
How many people	**waited**	there?

Wh- Questions About the Subject with *Be*		
***Wh-* Word**	**Past Form**	
Who	**was**	his friend?
What		his last name?
How many people	**were**	there?

GRAMMAR NOTES

1	Use the **simple past** to tell about **something that happened in the past**. For all verbs except *be*, the simple past form is the same for all persons.	• **He liked** that book. • **We liked** that book. • **I liked** that book.
2	**Regular verbs** end in ***-d***, ***-ed***, or ***-ied***. Many common verbs are **irregular** in the past.	• They **noticed** the dog. • He **missed** his master. • He **worried** about him. • She **wrote** a book. • He **had** a special dog.
3	For **negative statements** use ***did not (didn't)*** + **the base form of the verb**.	• He **did not know** him. • He **didn't know** him.
4	For ***yes / no*** **questions** use ***Did*** + **subject** + **the base form of the verb**.	*DID* SUBJECT BASE FORM • **Did** you **see** the dog? • **Did** they **go** to work?
5	Most ***wh-*** **questions** use a *wh-* question word and *yes / no* question order.	*WH-* WORD *DID* SUBJECT BASE FORM • **What** did he do? • **Where** did she go? • **Who** did he marry? • **How** did he do it?
6	**Questions about the subject** use statement word order. They do not use *did*.	SUBJECT VERB SUBJECT • **Who helped** him? His **friend** did. NOT: Who ~~did~~ helped him? NOT: Who ~~did help~~ him?
7	The verb ***be*** has **different forms** from all other verbs. **BE CAREFUL!** Do not use *did* or the base form of the verb for questions or negative statements with *be*.	**STATEMENTS** • He **was** happy. • They **weren't** happy. **QUESTIONS** • **Was** he in a movie? • **Were** you in the audience? • Where **were** they? Who **was** on TV? NOT: ~~Did they were~~ famous? NOT: He was ~~be~~ a loyal dog.

REFERENCE NOTES

For a more complete discussion of the past, see Unit 3, page 28, Unit 18, page 201, Unit 19, page 211, and Unit 20, page 222.
For more about the past of *be*, see Unit 2, page 17.
For a list of irregular verbs see Appendix 11, page A-11.
For pronunciation and spelling rules for the simple past of regular verbs, see Appendix 10, pages A-10–A-11.

STEP 3 FOCUSED PRACTICE

EXERCISE 1: Discover the Grammar

Read the conversation. Then write the sentences (both statements and questions) that use the past on the lines below.

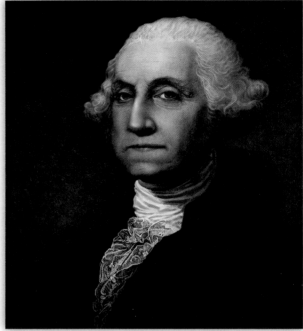

BORIS: Who's the man in the picture?

TEACHER: George Washington. He was the first president of the United States.

BORIS: When was that?

TEACHER: He became the president in 1789.

RODRICA: How long was he president?

TEACHER: For eight years.

RODRICA: Was he a good leader?

TEACHER: Yes, he was. And before he became president, he led the army during the American Revolution.

BEKIR: He sounds a lot like Ataturk. Kemal Ataturk was the father of modern Turkey. He was also a great soldier and leader. He gave Turkey many things including a modern alphabet. Now spelling is easy in Turkish.

TEACHER: Well, George Washington didn't do anything about the English alphabet. Spelling is still hard in English.

EUN YOUNG: King Sejong gave Korea an alphabet. He was one of Korea's greatest leaders.

JOSÉ: In South America, Simón Bolívar led many countries to independence. He didn't change our alphabet, but spelling is not so hard in Spanish.

Sentences with *Be* in the Past

1. *George Washington was the first president of the United States.*
2. ______
3. ______
4. ______
5. ______
6. ______
7. ______

Sentences with Other Verbs in the Past

1. *He became the president in 1789.*
2. ______
3. ______
4. ______
5. ______
6. ______
7. ______

EXERCISE 2: Affirmative and Negative Statements

(Grammar Notes 1–2, 7)

Complete the paragraph with the words in parentheses. Use the correct form of the simple past.

Pierre Omidyar ___was born___ (1. be / born) in Paris, France. His parents ________ (2. be) from Iran. His mother ________ (3. be) a professor, and his father ________ (4. practice) medicine. His family ________ (5. move) to the United States when Omidyar ________ (6. turn) six years old. He ________ (7. go) into the field of computer science. At age 28, Omidyar ________ (8. write) the computer code for eBay. eBay ________ (9. become) extremely successful. In July 2008, eBay ________ (10. have) shares that were worth $4.45 billion. In 2004 Omidyar ________ (11. start) the Omidyar Foundation. In 2005, Omidyar and his wife ________ (12. give) $100 million to the foundation. The money will help poor people in developing countries. In 2010, Omidyar ________ (13. join) 40 billionaires. They all ________ (14. promise) to give away at least half of their money before they die.

EXERCISE 3: Affirmative and Negative Statements

(Grammar Notes 1–3, 7)

Read the article. Complete the sentences with the words in parentheses. Use the correct form of the simple past.

Recluse Leaves Millions

Anne Schreiber ___was___ (1. be) a recluse. Recluses live apart from other people. Anne Schreiber never ________ (2. marry). She also never ________ (3. have) close friends. She ________ (4. live) alone in a tiny studio apartment and ________ (5. wear) the same outfit every day—a black coat and a black hat. For many years she ________ (6. work) for the tax department of the U.S. government. She ________ (7. be) an auditor. She ________ (8. make) sure people paid their taxes. However, she ________ (9. like / not) to pay taxes. She ________ (10. like / not) to pay for anything.

(continued on next page)

As a young woman, Anne ______________ (11. follow) the suggestions of a brother and ______________ (12. invest) all her money in his company. His company ______________ (13. go) bankrupt, and she ______________ (14. lose) her life savings. She ______________ (15. forgive / not) her brother. Anne ______________ (16. start) investing again in 1944 when she ______________ (17. be) 49 years old. This time she ______________ (18. use) her own ideas. By investing well, she ______________ (19. turn) $5,000 into $22,000,000. She ______________ (20. do) better than the biggest businessmen. But she ______________ (21. want / not) her relatives to know she had so much money because she ______________ (22. want / not) to give them any of it. And she didn't. Anne Schreiber ______________ (23. die) in 1995 at the age of 101. She ______________ (24. leave) her money to universities to help poor, bright women get an education.

EXERCISE 4: Simple Past: Questions and Answers

(Grammar Notes 1–7)

A | *Read the article. On the next page, write* **wh-** *questions that the underlined words answer.*

When you think of basketball, do you think of Michael Jordan, LeBron James, Shaquille O'Neal . . . or Dr. James Naismith? Dr. Naismith? Who was he? What did he do for basketball?

James Naismith was born in Ontario, Canada (1.), in 1861 (2.). He was a good athlete and a good student. He always loved school (3.).

Dr. Naismith earned four (4.) degrees, including one in medicine. But his biggest contribution to the world did not come from his work as a medical doctor. In the winter of 1891 (5.) he worked as a gym instructor in Massachusetts.

Basketball team around 1900

His students were active and hard to control (6.). He wanted them to play an indoor sport because it was too cold to play outdoors (7.). He invented the game of basketball (8.). It became an instant success in the United States. Soon it spread to other countries.

1. Where was James Naismith born?

2. ______________________________

3. ______________________________

4. ______________________________

5. ______________________________

6. ______________________________

7. ______________________________

8. What game ______________________________?

B | *Write **yes** / **no** questions about James Naismith with the given words. Use the correct form. Then write short answers.*

1. be / he good at sports?

   Q: Was he good at sports?

   A: Yes, he was.

2. be / he a good student?

   Q: ______________________________

   A: ______________________________

3. he / finish college?

   Q: ______________________________

   A: ______________________________

4. he / become a lawyer?

   Q: ______________________________

   A: ______________________________

5. he / invent the game of volleyball?

   Q: ______________________________

   A: ______________________________

EXERCISE 5: Editing

Correct the conversation. There are eleven mistakes. The first mistake is already corrected. Find and correct ten more.

1. **Q:** Who ^was Elizabeth Blackwell?

   A: She was the first woman physician in the United States.

2. **Q:** Where she was born?

   A: She was born in England.

3. **Q:** When was she born?

   A: She born in 1821.

4. **Q:** When she did come to the United States?

   A: She did come to the United States in 1833.

5. **Q:** Was it hard for her to become a doctor?

   A: Yes, it were. Most medical schools didn't want women.

6. **Q:** How was her grades in medical school?

   A: She was an outstanding student. Her grades were excellent.

7. **Q:** When she graduate?

   A: In 1849.

8. **Q:** What did Dr. Blackwell fight for?

   A: She did fight for the admission of women to medical schools.

9. **Q:** Where did she goes in 1869?

   A: She returned to London. She worked and wrote there for many years.

10. **Q:** When she die?

    A: She died in 1910.

STEP 4 COMMUNICATION PRACTICE

EXERCISE 6: Pronunciation

A | *Read and listen to the Pronunciation Note.*

Pronunciation Note

The words ***work*** and ***walk*** are sometimes hard to pronounce correctly. Listen to the difference between the vowel sound / ɝ / in *work* and / ɔ / in *walk*. Also remember the / **kt** / ending in words like ***work****ed* and ***walk****ed* is one sound.

B | *Listen and repeat the words.*

work **works** **worked** **walk** **walks** **walked**

C | *Listen to the sentences and repeat.*

1. I walked fast.
2. I worked fast.
3. Do you walk after school?
4. Do you work after school?
5. Who works with you?
6. Who walks with you?

EXERCISE 7: Listening

A | *Two people are watching TV. Listen to their conversation. Then circle the letter of the correct answer to the question.*

What kind of a TV show are they watching?
a. a quiz show **b.** a talk show

B | *Listen again. Complete the questions. Write the answers.*

1. Q: Who ___painted___ *The Night Watch*? **A:** Rembrandt.

2. Q: In what century ________________? **A:** The ________________ century.

3. Q: Where ________________? **A:** In ________________.

4. Q: What is ________________? **A:** Rembrandt van Rijn.

5. Q: Who ________________ Yoko Ono? **A:** ________________

6. Q: What ________________ of John Lennon's ________________? **A:** ________________

7. Q: Where ________________? **A:** ________________

8. Q: When ________________ their last appearance together? **A:** ________________

EXERCISE 8: A Quiz Show

SMALL GROUPS: Prepare a quiz show. On a separate piece of paper, write questions in the past. Choose a host or hostess from your group. Choose classmates in other groups to be contestants.

Examples: Who starred in the *Twilight* movies?
What was the *Titanic*?
Who wrote *One Hundred Years of Solitude*?

EXERCISE 9: What Were You Like As a Child?

PAIRS: Ask your partner what he or she was like as a child. Use boxes A and B for ideas.

Example: **A:** When you were a child, were you talkative?
B: Yes. Once my teacher wrote a note to my mother, "Bernie never stops talking. He's smart, but he needs to give other children a turn." What about you? What were you like? Did you study hard?
A: No, I didn't. I began to study hard in high school.

A: Were you ________?	B: Did you ________?
athletic / uninterested in sports	study hard
naughty / well behaved	listen to your parents
stubborn / easygoing	watch a lot of TV
talkative / quiet / shy	play a lot of computer games
cheerful / moody	like music / art / dance

EXERCISE 10: Information Gap: Guess the Musician

Work in pairs (A and B). Student A, follow the instructions on this page. Student B, turn to page 246 and follow the instructions there.

1. Read about the life of the musician Ray Charles. Do not tell your partner his name. Your partner will ask you questions about the person and guess. Answer your partner's questions.

He was born in Albany, Georgia, in 1930. His family was very poor. He became blind at the age of seven. He learned to read Braille and play music at the St. Augustine School for the Deaf and the Blind in Florida. His mother died when he was a teenager. He left school at 15 and began his career as a musician. He moved to Seattle and started his rise to fame. He started out as a jazz and blues pianist and singer, but over more than 50 years he built a career that combined many types of music. In 2004, he died in Beverly Hills, California. He was 73 years old.

2. Now you will ask your partner questions about a different musician. First, write questions with the words given and the simple past.

   1. When / he / born _When was he born?_______________________
   2. Where / he / born ________________________________
   3. What / he / teach himself to play________________________
   4. Where / he / begin his career __________________________
   5. Who / discover him ______________________________
   6. Where / be / he from 1958 to 1960 _______________________
   7. What / he / appear in after that _________________________
   8. When / die ___________________________________

3. Ask your partner the questions from Part 2 and then guess who the musician is.

EXERCISE 11: Writing

A | *Write a short biography of a musician. Use the simple past. Read your biography to a partner.*

B | *Check your work. Use the Editing Checklist.*

Editing Checklist

Did you . . . ?

☐ use the simple past correctly

☐ check your spelling

Information Gap for Student B

1. You will ask your partner questions about a musician. First, write questions about the person. Use the words given and the simple past.

   1. Where / be / born *Where was he born?*
   2. When / he born ______
   3. What / happened to him at the age of seven ______
   4. Where / he / go to school ______
   5. What / he / learn at school ______
   6. Where / he / move ______
   7. How many years / he / be / in the music business ______
   8. When / he / die ______

2. Ask your partner the questions from Part 1 and then guess who the musician is.

3. Now read about the life of the musician Elvis Presley. Do not tell your partner his name. Your partner will ask you questions about the person and guess. Answer your partner's questions.

> He was a popular singer. He was born in Tupelo, Mississippi, in 1935. He began singing in a local church, and he taught himself to play the guitar. Sam Phillips, the president of Sun Records, discovered him in 1953. By 1956 he was the most popular performer in the United States. Soon after that he became popular all over the world. His music combined country and western music with rhythm and blues. He spent two years, from 1958 to 1960, in the army. He appeared in several movies, but none were very successful. He died in 1977. He is known as the King of Rock and Roll.

UNIT 21 Review

Check your answers on page UR-4.
Do you need to review anything?

A | *Complete the sentences with the verbs in parentheses. Use the correct form and the simple past.*

1. Craig Newmark ____________________ on December 6, 1952.
   (be born)
2. He ____________________ in New Jersey.
   (grow up)
3. He ____________________ Morristown High School.
   (attend)
4. He ____________________ to college in Ohio.
   (go)
5. In 1995 he ____________________ an email list.
   (start)
6. It ____________________ a Web-based service in 1996.
   (become)
7. It ____________________, and today almost everyone knows about Craigslist®.
   (expand)

B | *Write questions with the words in parentheses. Use the simple past.*

1. ______________________________
   (when / she / go to college)
2. ______________________________
   (who / they / meet)
3. ______________________________
   (where / he study)
4. ______________________________
   (how long / they live in Canada)

C | *Complete the questions with* **be** *or* **do.** *Use the correct form and the simple past.*

1. ______________ you late yesterday?
2. ______________ they work last night?
3. ______________ he at the park with his son?
4. ______________ she marry him?
5. ______________ he move?

D | *Correct the paragraph. There are four mistakes.*

Steve Paul Jobs did start college in 1970, but he no did finish it. In 1976 Jobs and his friend begin to make their own computers. They worked in the Jobs' garage. That was the beginning of Apple® Computers. Their company become a big success. Apple® changed the field of computers, and by the age of 30, Jobs was a multimillionaire.

UNIT 22

Gerunds and Infinitives

CAREERS AND ABILITIES

STEP 1 GRAMMAR IN CONTEXT

Before You Read

Look at the photos. Why do people choose a particular career? For example, why do people become fashion designers, makeup artists, or models? Would you like these jobs? Or others?

Read

To get the right job and be successful, you need to know yourself. Read these people's comments and the jobs that match their needs.

1. I **like to learn** new things. I **hope to continue** learning throughout my career.

   doctor, software developer, scientist, teacher

2. I **enjoy working** with my hands.

   auto mechanic, chef, carpenter, farmer

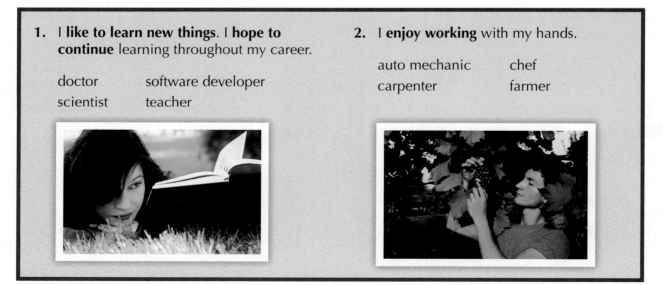

3. I don't like routine work. I **expect to do** something different every day. I don't like things to be predictable.

actress — musician
fire fighter — police officer

4. I'm very competitive. I **hate losing**. People say I have a type A personality.

attorney — politician
investment banker — professional athlete

5. I love the outdoors. I **can't stand wearing** a suit. I **avoid wearing** formal clothes.

anthropologist — gardener
farmer — park ranger

6. I **enjoy interacting** with people. I **love helping** them with their problems.

hotel manager — psychologist
physical therapist — social worker

After You Read

A | Practice *PAIRS: Now read the comments aloud. Take turns reading the comments.*

B | Vocabulary *Circle the letter of the best meaning for the words in* **blue.**

1. He's not good at math. He **avoids** working with numbers.
   a. tries not to **b.** is afraid of

2. He **can't stand** speaking with angry customers.
   a. is good at **b.** hates

3. He always does the same thing. He's **predictable**.
   a. not surprising; expected **b.** suprising

4. Everyone likes her. She has a pleasant **personality**.
   a. way of behaving **b.** way of smiling

5. She needs **formal** clothes for her brother's graduation and her sister's wedding.
   a. dresses **b.** dress clothes

6. He hates losing. He's **competitive**.
   a. wants to play sports **b.** wants to win

C | Comprehension *Read the descriptions. Circle the letter of the career that* ***doesn't belong.***

1. You expect to make a lot of money. You always want to win.
   a. lawyer **b.** investment banker **c.** social worker

2. You often need to wear a suit.
   a. banker **b.** farmer **c.** lawyer

3. You're a "people person." You enjoy interacting with others.
   a. teacher **b.** physical therapist **c.** computer programmer

4. Your work routine changes every day.
   a. chef **b.** artist **c.** actress

5. You don't wear formal clothes at work.
   a. teacher **b.** carpenter **c.** politician

STEP 2 GRAMMAR PRESENTATION

GERUNDS AND INFINITIVES

Subject	Verb	Gerund (Verb + *-ing*)
I	**enjoy**	**dancing**.

Subject	Verb	Infinitive
She	**wants**	**to sing**.

Subject	Verb	Infinitive or Gerund
They	**like**	**driving**.
		to drive.

Verb + Gerund	Verb + Infinitive		Verb + Infinitive or Gerund
avoid	agree	refuse	hate
enjoy	decide	want	like
finish	expect		continue
keep	hope		love
keep on	intend		prefer
regret	need		try
think about	plan		

GRAMMAR NOTES

1	A **gerund** is a noun that is formed by the **base form of a verb + *-ing***. Some verbs, such as *enjoy*, *finish*, and *keep*, can be followed by a gerund.	• I **enjoy singing**. • We **finished studying** at 8:00. • She **keeps asking** about the job.
2	An **infinitive** is ***to*** **+ the base form of the verb**. Some verbs, such as *want* and *need*, can be followed by an infinitive.	• I **want to work**. • She **needs to write** a résumé. • He **wants** to change jobs.
3	Some verbs, such as *like* and *hate*, can be followed by a gerund (*-ing* form) or an infinitive (*to* + base form).	• I **like writing**. • I **like to write**.

STEP 3 FOCUSED PRACTICE

EXERCISE 1: Discover the Grammar

Write **I (verb + infinitive)** *or* **G (verb + gerund)** *for each statement.*

__G__ **1.** I enjoy working with people.

____ **2.** He needs to get a job.

____ **3.** She prefers to work at night.

____ **4.** I prefer working in the daytime.

____ **5.** I avoid wearing a suit.

____ **6.** He refused to work late.

____ **7.** They hope to move in July.

____ **8.** They finished eating at 10:00.

EXERCISE 2: Infinitives

(Grammar Note 2)

Complete the sentences with the words from the box. Use infinitives.

complete	~~find~~	leave	move	send	work

1. John's looking for a job. He hopes ___to find___ a job in this city.

2. He likes this city. He doesn't want ________________ away.

3. He sees his friends every weekend. He refuses ________________ on weekends.

4. He plans ________________ out some letters of application this afternoon.

5. In two years he intends ________________ his job and go to business school.

6. He hopes ________________ his M.B.A. in four years.

EXERCISE 3: Gerunds

(Grammar Note 1)

Complete the sentences with the words from the box. Use gerunds.

apply	do	go	leave	~~take~~	work

1. He finished ___taking___ final exams last week.

2. He is thinking about ________________ for a part-time job for the summer.

3. He enjoys ________________ sales work.

4. He doesn't like ________________ with his hands.

5. He regretted ________________ his part-time job, but he needed time to study.

6. He avoided ________________ out with friends for a month before his final exams.

EXERCISE 4: Gerunds and Infinitives

(Grammar Notes 1–3)

Complete the conversation. Use gerunds or infinitives with the verbs in parentheses. One verb can be used with both a gerund or an infinitive.

Elena: Do you enjoy ___acting___ (1. act)?

Julian: Yes. I love ________ (2. act).

Elena: Is it hard to find work as an actor?

Julian: Very hard. Many people want ________ (3. become) actors. You need ________ (4. have) talent, patience, and luck.

Elena: Do you ever want ________ (5. change) careers? Do you ever regret ________ (6. spend) so much time looking for work?

Julian: No. I refuse ________ (7. give up) my dream. I keep ________ (8. try out) for new parts. I think I'm a great actor, and I plan ________ (9. show) the world!

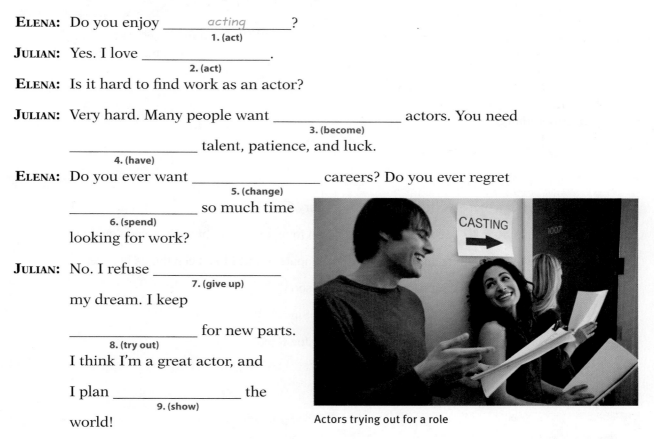

Actors trying out for a role

EXERCISE 5: Gerunds and Infinitives

(Grammar Notes 1–2)

Complete the sentences with the words from the box. Use infinitives and gerunds.

get	look	meet	study	tell	~~work~~

1. Do you enjoy ___working___ with children?
2. Do you plan ________ an advanced degree?
3. He hoped ________ with the president of the company. Instead he met with the vice president.
4. I regret ________ him about my problem with my previous employer.
5. He keeps ________ at his watch. I hope he isn't bored.
6. Many people decide ________ law after watching courtroom dramas.

EXERCISE 6: Editing

Correct the letter. There are seven mistakes. The first mistake is already corrected. Find and correct six more.

35 Main Street, Apt. 6
New Hope, New Jersey 07675

May 27, 2012

Head Librarian
Kennedy Library
7 West Street
New Hope, New Jersey 07675

To Whom It May Concern:

I want ^to apply for a part-time job at Kennedy Library. I am in my senior year of high school. I expect attend State College next year, and I plan to majoring in library science. I enjoy to read and to work with the public. I'm good at computers, and I like keep things in order. I've enclosed a résumé. I hope hearing from you soon.

Sincerely,

Joe Reed

STEP 4 COMMUNICATION PRACTICE

EXERCISE 7: Pronunciation

A | *Read and listen to the Pronunciation Note.*

Pronunciation Note

Of is usually pronounced with the unstressed sound **/ əv /**. When *of* comes after a consonant sound, we link the consonant with *of.*

Example: out of ice cream

B | *Listen and repeat.*

1. out of town
2. out of everything
3. out of juice
4. out of eggs
5. out of order

C | *PAIRS: Answer the questions. Use the phrases in Part B.*

1. **A:** Do we have any orange or grape juice?

   B: No, we're ______________________________.

2. **A:** Does the copy machine work?

   B: No, it's ______________________________.

3. **A:** Is he in town?

   B: No he's ______________________________.

4. **A:** Do we have any eggs?

   B: No, we're ______________________________.

5. **A:** Where are you going?

   B: Shopping for food. We're ______________________________.

EXERCISE 8: Listening

A | *Listen to a conversation between two friends. When do the friends meet?*

a. every week **b.** for the first time in years

B | *Listen again. Write* **T** (**True**) *or* **F** (**False**) *for each statement. Change the false statements to make them true.*

_____ **1.** Ken plans to go back to school for more training.

_____ **2.** Cindy got tired of working for a big company.

_____ **3.** Cindy plans to write a book.

_____ **4.** Cindy enjoys planning conventions.

_____ **5.** Cindy likes to work with animals.

_____ **6.** Ken wants to have lunch with Cindy on Saturday.

EXERCISE 9: Discussion: Likes

PAIRS: For each category, write something that you enjoy doing. Then tell your partner. Use infinitives and gerunds. Your partner then agrees or tells about something he or she prefers.

EXAMPLE: **A:** I like playing golf.
B: I do too. OR I prefer to play tennis.

1. sports: ___*golf*___ **3.** books: ____________ **5.** desserts: ____________

2. movies: ____________ **4.** music: ____________ **6.** cars: ____________

EXERCISE 10: Game: What Do I Do?

SMALL GROUPS: Each group thinks of an occupation and gives the other groups hints. Use only the verbs in the chart on page 251.

EXAMPLE: **MOHAMMED:** You want to help people.
TATIANA: You need to study for many years.
HECTOR: (Student from another group): Are you thinking about a doctor?
MOHAMMED: Yes, we are.

EXERCISE 11: Problem Solving: Finding the Right Job

PAIRS: Ask your partner the questions. Talk about possible jobs.

- Do you enjoy working with people?
- Do you want to make a difference in the world?
- Do you want to be rich?
- Do you dislike traveling?
- Do you want to be famous?
- Do you want a safe job (one that you can keep when times are bad)?
- Do you want to help others?
- Do you like to "do your own thing"?

EXERCISE 12: Writing

A | *Write about your future career goals. Use gerunds and infinitives.*

EXAMPLE: I enjoy window shopping and studying all the latest fashions. I also love to draw. I hope to combine my two passions and become a fashion designer. I plan to study art and fashion in college this year. I hope to get an internship with a design company in the summer. I expect to graduate in four years. In 10 years I hope to have my own fashion design business.

B | *Check your work. Use the Editing Checklist.*

Editing Checklist

Did you . . . ?
☐ use infinitives and gerunds correctly
☐ check your spelling

UNIT 22 Review

Check your answers on page UR-5.
Do you need to review anything?

A | *Underline the correct words to complete the sentences.*

1. Do you regret **to start / starting** a business?
2. I hope **to sell / selling** my business next year.
3. She decided **to return / returning** to school.
4. She hopes **to become / becoming** a pilot.
5. She enjoys **to fly / flying** and **to see / seeing** the world.
6. Her parents plan **to help / helping** her reach her goal.

B | *Complete the sentences with the words in parentheses. Use the correct form.*

1. She doesn't want __________________ evenings.
   (work)
2. Her boss refuses __________________ her hours.
   (change)
3. She's thinking about __________________ her job and __________________ back to school.
   (quit) **(go)**
4. She wants __________________ computer science.
   (study)
5. She enjoys __________________ Web design.
   (do)

C | *Correct the paragraph. There are eight mistakes.*

Carol volunteers at a hospital. She enjoys to take care of patients. Some patients refuse do exercise, but Carol keeps to push them. Carol intends study physical therapy in college. She needs taking a lot of science courses. She expects to went to college next fall. She hopes get a degree in physical therapy in five years. She prefers to working with teenagers, but she will work with adults too.

UNIT 23 Simple Present, Present Progressive, and Simple Past

CREATIVITY

STEP 1 GRAMMAR IN CONTEXT

Before You Read

A | *GROUPS: What can you do with the items below? Write as many ideas as you can. Be as creative as possible.*

aluminum foil **hairdryer** **straws** **Ziploc® bag**

EXAMPLE: You can wrap your hair with aluminum foil to make it curly.

B | *Share your ideas with the class. Now vote. Which ideas were the most interesting?*

Read

Read the online article about creativity.

ARTS | SCIENCE | POLITICS | TECHNOLOGY | SEARCH:

What does it **mean** to be creative? To be creative **means** to see things in a new way. New inventions often **come** from old ideas. **Do** you **know** a new invention that **came** from an older one?

Glue **is** a very old invention, from 250,000 B.C., but Krazy Glue® **is** a new kind of glue. It **is** extremely strong. In fact, it **can glue** your fingers together. Dr. Harry Coover **invented** this kind of glue in 1942. He **wanted** to use it for airplanes, but it **didn't work**. Later, in 1962, scientists **realized** they could use the glue in surgery.[1] They **used** it to save lives in wars. Nowdays doctors **are** still **using** a kind of Krazy Glue® during surgery.

How do new inventions **come** about? Sometimes, a new invention **is** the result of two old ideas combined. The motorcycle, for example, **is** a combination of a car and bicycle. New inventions can also **happen** over time, in steps. One creative idea **comes** after another, and the invention **changes**—adjustments **take** place—and the invention **improves**. We **see** this in today's computers and phones, which **are changing** all of the time.

New ideas **do not** always **meet** with public approval at first. Often it **takes** time for people to accept new ways of thinking. In France, in the late 1800s, painters **came up with** a style of painting called Impressionism. At first people **disliked** this art and **rejected** the style, but later they **accepted** and **admired** it. And in this century, the public first **rejected**, and then **began** to accept ebooks.

Picturephone, 1965

[1] ***surgery:*** medical treatment in which a doctor cuts open the body to fix or remove something inside

These days we **are learning** more about creativity through a recent invention. The MRI[2] **takes** pictures of the body which **are** more powerful and accurate than X-rays. Scientists **are** now **using** MRIs to study the human brain. MRIs **show** them what happens in the brain when a person **is thinking** creative thoughts. So in the future, we may have a deeper understanding of the creative process. One day scientists may even invent a pill for creativity. Would you try such a pill?

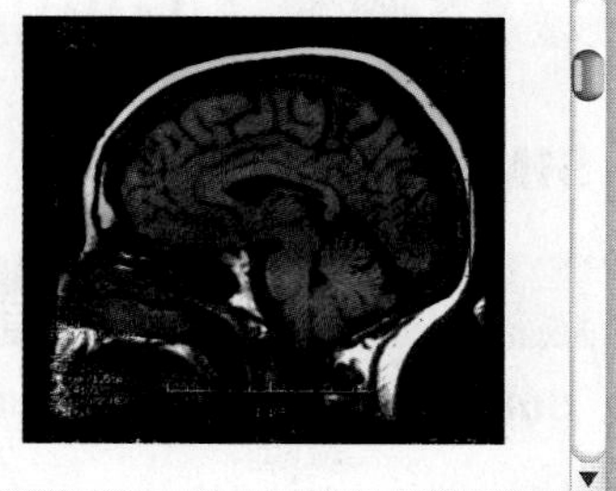

[2] ***MRI:*** magnetic resonance imaging

After You Read

A | Practice *PAIRS: Now read the article aloud. Take turns reading each paragraph.*

B | Vocabulary *Complete the sentences with the words from the box.*

accepted	came up with	comes after	invented	rejected

1. Who ________________ with the idea for Krazy Glue®?

2. What number ________________ 9,999?

3. At first, they ________________ his suggestion, but later they agreed to it.

4. We ________________ his invitation to the party.

5. Thomas Edison ________________ the lightbulb.

C | Comprehension *Read the statements. Write* **T (True)** *or* **F (False)**.

____ **1.** To be creative means that you are an artist.

____ **2.** Glue is not a new invention.

____ **3.** Krazy Glue® is not used by doctors any more.

____ **4.** Sometimes a new invention is a combination of two older ones.

____ **5.** The art movement Impressionism ended around 1800.

____ **6.** It took people time to like Impressionism.

____ **7.** Scientists are using MRIs to understand the human brain and creativity.

STEP 2 GRAMMAR PRESENTATION

SIMPLE PRESENT

Affirmative Statements		
Subject	**Verb**	**Time Marker**
I	**paint**	sometimes.
He	**paints**	
They	**paint**	

Negative Statements		
Subject	**Verb**	**Time Marker**
I	**don't paint**	often.
He	**doesn't paint**	
They	**don't paint**	

PRESENT PROGRESSIVE

Affirmative Statements		
Subject	**Verb**	**Time Marker**
I	**'m painting**	now.
He	**'s painting**	
They	**'re painting**	

Negative Statements		
Subject	**Verb**	**Time Marker**
I	**'m not painting**	now.
He	**'s not painting** **isn't painting**	
They	**'re not painting** **aren't painting**	

SIMPLE PAST

Affirmative Statements		
Subject	**Verb**	**Time Marker**
I	**painted**	last week.
He		
They		

Negative Statements		
Subject	**Verb**	**Time Marker**
I	**didn't paint**	last week.
He		
They		

GRAMMAR NOTES

1	**REMEMBER:** Use the **simple present** to tell about **things that happen again and again** or to **tell facts**. Use the simple present with **non-action verbs** even when something is happening now.	• He **goes** to work every day. • Some doctors **use** glue during surgery. • I **like** your idea.
2	**REMEMBER:** Use the **present progressive** to talk about **an action that is happening now or nowadays**.	• He **is looking** at your MRI now. • Scientists **are studying** the brain these days.
3	**REMEMBER:** Use the **simple past** to tell about **things that are finished**.	• He **had** a good idea. • At first people **rejected** his work.

STEP 3 FOCUSED PRACTICE

EXERCISE 1: Discover the Grammar

Read the conversation. Underline the present progressive verbs once. Underline the simple present verbs twice. Circle the simple past verbs.

A: What are you doing?

B: I'm looking at a plan of my apartment. It's really tiny. Now with a baby we need more space. I'm trying to redo it.

A: Check out Gary Chang of Hong Kong. He's an architect. He lives in a 333-square-foot apartment, but he divided his small apartment into 24 rooms.

B: Are you kidding?

A: I'm not kidding. I read about it online. And I even saw it on YouTube.™

EXERCISE 2: Simple Present and Simple Past *(Grammar Notes 1, 3)*

Complete the conversation with the verbs in parentheses. Use the correct form.

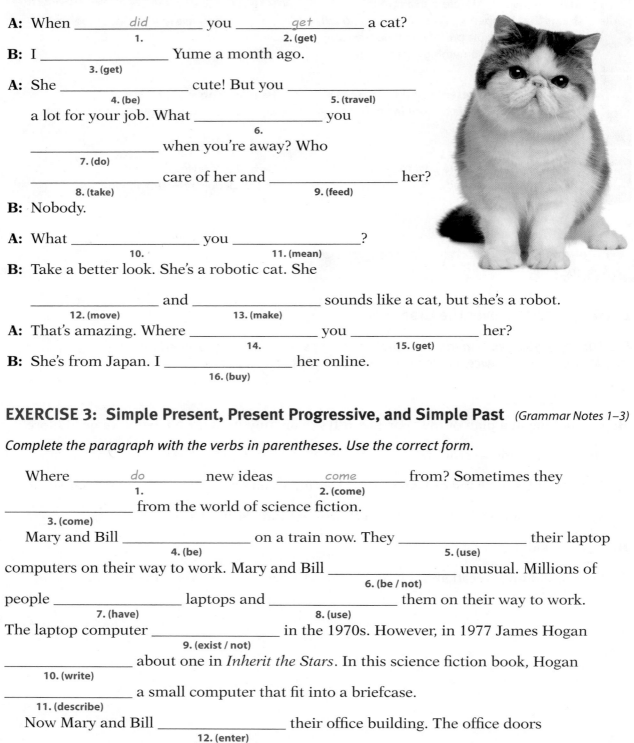

A: When ___did___ (1.) you ___get___ (2. get) a cat?

B: I __________ (3. get) Yume a month ago.

A: She __________ (4. be) cute! But you __________ (5. travel) a lot for your job. What __________ (6.) you __________ (7. do) when you're away? Who __________ (8. take) care of her and __________ (9. feed) her?

B: Nobody.

A: What __________ (10.) you __________ (11. mean)?

B: Take a better look. She's a robotic cat. She __________ (12. move) and __________ (13. make) sounds like a cat, but she's a robot.

A: That's amazing. Where __________ (14.) you __________ (15. get) her?

B: She's from Japan. I __________ (16. buy) her online.

EXERCISE 3: Simple Present, Present Progressive, and Simple Past *(Grammar Notes 1–3)*

Complete the paragraph with the verbs in parentheses. Use the correct form.

Where ___do___ (1.) new ideas ___come___ (2. come) from? Sometimes they __________ (3. come) from the world of science fiction.

Mary and Bill __________ (4. be) on a train now. They __________ (5. use) their laptop computers on their way to work. Mary and Bill __________ (6. be / not) unusual. Millions of people __________ (7. have) laptops and __________ (8. use) them on their way to work. The laptop computer __________ (9. exist / not) in the 1970s. However, in 1977 James Hogan __________ (10. write) about one in *Inherit the Stars*. In this science fiction book, Hogan __________ (11. describe) a small computer that fit into a briefcase.

Now Mary and Bill __________ (12. enter) their office building. The office doors __________ (13. open) automatically. In 1899 doors __________ (14. not / open) automatically. But H. G. Wells __________ (15. write) about such doors in his novel *When the Sleeper Wakes*.

These are just two examples in which science fiction showed us the future.

EXERCISE 4: Editing

Correct the paragraph. There are seven mistakes. The first mistake is already corrected. Find and correct six more.

> Jay Leno is a comedian. He also ~~love~~ *loves* to collect cars. One of his cars needs not gas. It's a Baker electric car. Baker invent an electric car in 1909. In the early 1900s, electric cars was popular in the United States. Then Henry Ford did produce inexpensive cars that used gas. People stopped buying electric cars. But nowadays people is trying to keep the air clean. So electric cars are become popular once again.

STEP 4 COMMUNICATION PRACTICE

EXERCISE 5: Listening

A | *Listen to a talk about X-rays. Then circle the correct letter.*

Doctors, dentists, and ________________ use X-rays.

a. airline companies **b.** baggage companies **c.** airplane manufacturers

B | *Listen again. Read the questions. Circle the correct letter.*

1. Where was Wilhelm Roentgen from?

(**a.**) Germany **b.** Austria

2. When did he discover X-rays?

a. 1859 **b.** 1895

3. Whose hand did he first X-ray?

a. his hand **b.** his wife's hand

4. How did people learn about X-rays?

a. from Roentgen **b.** from newspapers

5. What did Roentgen win?

a. the Nobel Prize **b.** the Pulitzer Prize

6. What did Roentgen's friends tell him to call X-rays?

a. X-rays **b.** Roentgen rays

EXERCISE 6: Pronunciation

A | *Read and listen to the Pronunciation Note.*

Pronunciation Note

Compound nouns are two nouns we put together as one. They can be two words or one word. We **stress** the **first noun**.

EXAMPLES: credit card
notebook

B | *Listen and repeat these compound nouns.*

1. bike trip
2. office building
3. houseboat
4. motorbike
5. library book
6. wedding ring

C | *PAIRS: Student A, choose a sentence. Student B, say the compound noun Student A is thinking of. Remember to stress the first noun. Take turns.*

EXAMPLE: **A:** I'm thinking of a trip by bicycle.
B: A bike trip.

1. I'm thinking of a building with offices.
2. I'm thinking of a bicycle with a motor.
3. I'm thinking of book you can borrow from the library.
4. I'm thinking of a ring you wear when you are married.

EXERCISE 7: Information Gap

Work in pairs (A *and* B). **Student A,** *follow the instructions on this page.* **Student B,** *turn to page 266. Follow the instructions on that page.*

1. Ask your partner questions to complete your chart.

EXAMPLE: **Student A:** Who invented the ATM?
Student B: Don Wetzel invented the ATM.
Student A: When did he invent it?
Student B: In 1968.
Student A: Where is he from?
Student B: He's from the United States.

Invention	Inventor	Year	Country
ATM	Don Wetzel	1968	United States
credit card			
dishwasher			
eyeglasses			
fork			
paper money			
subway			
YouTube™			

2. Now your partner will ask you questions. Answer the questions with information from the chart.

Answers to Student B's Questions

Invention	Inventor	Year	Country
bicycle	Baron Karl von Drais de Sauerbrun	1818	Germany
disposable diapers	Marion Donovan	1950	U.S.
mirror (glass)	the Venetians	c. 1200	Italy
paper	Ts'ai Lun	c. 105	China
pencil	Conrad Gessner	1565	Switzerland
satellite	Soviet Space program	1957	Russia
thermometer	Galileo	1592	Italy
World Wide Web	Tim Berners-Lee	1989	U.K.

3. GROUPS: Talk about the inventions. Are they still good? Are there newer and better inventions?

EXERCISE 8: Writing

A | *Imagine you are living in the future. Choose the year. Write about life in that year. Write about something you're doing now and something you did. Include the simple present, present progressive, and simple past.*

EXAMPLES: It's 3010. As usual the weather is sunny and 65 degrees. It never rains or snows. Sometimes people complain. They say, "We want some bad weather."

I live in France, but I go to school in Spain. Right now I'm flying to school in my new aeromobile. It's a lot of fun. I'm flying across the border and looking at the beautiful mountains below.

Last month two exciting things happened. On the first of the month, scientists announced a cure for the cold. Finally. On the 15th of last month, my great granddad celebrated his 150th birthday. The whole family met, and we had a party for him in his new home on the bottom of the ocean.

B | *Check your work. Use the Editing Checklist.*

Editing Checklist

Did you . . . ?

☐ use correct forms of the simple present, present progressive, and simple past

☐ check your spelling

Information Gap for Student B

1. Your partner will ask you questions. Answer the questions with information from the chart.

Answers to Student A's Questions

Invention	Inventor	Year	Country
ATM	Don Wetzel	1968	U.S.
credit card	Frank McNamara, Ralph Schneider	1950	U.S.
dishwasher	Josephine Cochrane	1886	U.S.
eyeglasses	Salvino degli Armati or Alessandro di Spina	1280s	Italy
fork	—	2000 B.C.E.	China
paper money	—	late 900s	China
subway	Sir John Fowler	1863	U.K.
YouTube	Steven Chen, Chad Hurley, and Jawed Karim	2005	U.S.

2. Now ask your partner questions to complete your chart.

Example: **Student B:** Who invented the bicycle?
Student A: Baron Karl von Drais de Sauerbrun.
Student B: When did he invent it?
Student A: In 1818.
Student B: Where was he from?
Student A: Germany.

Invention	Inventor	Year	Country
bicycle	*Baron Karl von Drais de Sauerbrun*	*1818*	*Germany*
disposable diapers			
mirror (glass)			
paper			
pencil			
satellite			
thermometer			
World Wide Web			

3. GROUPS: Talk about the inventions. Are they still good? Are there newer and better inventions?

UNIT 23 Review

Check your answers on page UR-5.
Do you need to review anything?

A | *Complete the sentences with the verbs in parentheses. Use the simple present, present progressive, or simple past.*

1. My brother _______________ (take) a sculpture class now.
2. Each week the students _______________ (make) sculptures out of recycled materials.
3. Last month he _______________ (make) a sculpture out of soda cans.
4. He really _______________ (like) the class.

B | *Complete the paragraph with the verbs in parentheses. Use the simple present, present progressive, or simple past.*

Whitcomb Judson _______________ (1. invent) a zipper in 1893. His zipper _______________ (2. work / not), and nobody _______________ (3. want) it. Later the B. F. Goodrich company _______________ (4. become) interested in a zipper for rain shoes, and Judson's zippers _______________ (5. start) to sell. Today we still _______________ (6. use) zippers. Right now factory workers _______________ (7. sew) zippers in clothes, bags, shoes, and many other things.

C | *Complete the questions with the words in parentheses. Use the correct form.*

1. ____ (Where / you / go / last weekend)
2. ____ (How / you / get there)
3. ____ (What / you / see / at the museum)
4. ____ (How / be / the museum)
5. ____ (you / often/ go there)

D | *Correct the sentences. There are four mistakes.*

1. Last night I did watch a movie about fish.
2. The fish were beautiful, and I enjoy the movie.
3. My brother is watching the movie now, but he don't like it.
4. He is only liking action films.

From Grammar to Writing

Organization: Time Sequence Markers

1 | *Look at these sentences. Which words show the time?*

1. He studies at home in the evening.

2. At present I live on Bleeker Street.

2 | *Study the information about time sequence markers.*

You can organize your writing by using **time sequence markers**. Some common markers for the time of day are ***in the morning***, ***in the afternoon***, ***in the evening***, and ***at night***.

Example:

Monique works **in the morning**.

Some common markers for the past, present, and future are ***in the past***, ***at present***, and ***in the future.***

Example:

At present, I'm a student.

3 | *Read this story about a country doctor. Underline the time sequence markers. Then write about a day in the life of someone you know well.*

Michelle Hirch-Phothong is a country doctor. Her day begins at 6:30 in the morning. At seven o'clock she is at the hospital. She visits her patients and discusses their problems with the nurses and other doctors. Michelle enjoys talking to her patients. She listens carefully and never rushes.

In the afternoon Michelle works at a clinic. The clinic is busy, and patients are often worried about their health. Michelle and the other doctors try to help them.

At six o'clock in the evening Michelle leaves the clinic. She goes home and relaxes. Every evening at seven o'clock Michelle goes to Bangkok in the Boondocks. That's my restaurant, and Michelle is my wife. Michelle and I usually enjoy a delicious Thai dinner alone.

Sometimes, however, people come to the restaurant and tell Michelle their medical problems. I say, "Tell them to go to the clinic." But Michelle never sends them home without listening to their problems and offering advice. Michelle is a wonderful doctor.

4 | *Exchange papers with a partner. Did your partner follow the directions? Correct any mistakes in grammar and spelling.*

5 | *Talk to your partner. Discuss the mistakes you made. Then rewrite your own paper and make any necessary changes.*

PART VIII

THE FUTURE

UNIT	GRAMMAR FOCUS	THEME
24	*Be going to* for the Future	City and Campus Planning
25	*Will* for the Future; Future Time Markers	The Future
26	*May* or *Might* for Possibility	Weather

UNIT

24 *Be going to* for the Future

City and Campus Planning

STEP 1 GRAMMAR IN CONTEXT

Before You Read

PAIRS: Do you ever read or write letters to the editor of a newspaper? Tell your partner about a letter you remember.

EXAMPLE: This city is going to increase the cost of transportation. Last week there was a letter against the increase. I agree with the writer.

Read

Read the letters from students to the editor of their school newspaper.

www.dailycolumbus.com/letters_to_the_editor

DAILY COLUMBUS

The website of Columbus College

Home | Campus | City | Sports | Classifieds

LETTERS TO THE EDITOR

To the Editor:

Last week President Clark talked about plans for a new fitness center[1] for our college. The center sounds great. It**'s going to have** a beautiful gym, a track for running, an Olympic size pool, saunas, steam rooms, a basketball court, exercise machines, and weight-lifting equipment.[2] But this fitness center **is going to cost** a lot of money.

Where is the money **going to come** from? You guessed it. Most of the money **is going to come** from us. Our tuition **is going to increase**. That's why I'm against the plan. With a tuition increase, more students **are going to need** to work while they go to school. We**'re not going to have** time to enjoy the fitness center. We**'re not going to have** time to study.

Why is President Clark doing this? He only wants a fitness center because other schools have them. He thinks more students **are going to come** to our school if we have a fancy fitness center. But we're here for a good education, not to enjoy a state-of-the-art fitness center.

—Joe Molina

To the Editor:

A week ago President Clark announced plans for a new fitness center for our college. I love the idea. It**'s going to give** us a chance to relax and unwind[3] before and after classes. College is not just a time to sit in a library and study. It's a time for us to make our bodies *and* our minds stronger.

When the gym is built, I**'m going to go** there every day. Yes. We**'re going to pay** for it. There **is going to be** a tuition hike.[4] But in my opinion, it's worth it. It**'s going to improve** our lives.

Last month a study showed that most students gain 10 pounds in their freshman year. I'll bet that**'s not going to happen** once we have our new fitness center.

—Alison Meadows

---

[1] ***fitness center:*** a place to exercise
[2] ***equipment:*** machines
[3] ***unwind:*** to relax and feel no stress
[4] ***hike:*** an increase

After You Read

A | Practice *PAIRS: Read the Letters to the Editor again aloud. Take turns reading each paragraph.*

B | Vocabulary *Circle the letter of the best meaning for the words in* **blue.**

1. Is the **tuition** at your school the same as it was last year?

a. work　　**b.** money for school

2. Our teacher **announced** that there will be a school party next Thursday.

a. said　　**b.** answered

3. They **increased** the number of students from 22 to 25 per class.

a. raised　　**b.** changed

4. The train is two dollars more than the bus. **Is it worth it?**

a. How much is the train?　　**b.** Is there value in paying extra for the train?

5. I am **against** the idea of raising taxes.

a. not for　　**b.** worried about

6. **In my opinion** students need a fitness center.

a. I know　　**b.** I think

C | Comprehension *Read the sentences. Is the statement for or against the fitness center? Write the letter in the correct box.*

a. "It's going to cost a lot of money."
b. "It's going to be a place to relax and unwind."
c. "It's going to keep students in good shape."
d. "More students are going to need to work during the school year."
e. "Tuition is going to increase."
f. "It's going to attract more students."

For the Fitness Center	Against the Fitness Center
	a

STEP 2 GRAMMAR PRESENTATION

BE GOING TO FOR THE FUTURE

Affirmative Statements			
Subject + *Be*	***Going to***	**Base Form of Verb**	
I'm He**'s** We**'re** You**'re*** They**'re**	**going to**	**study**	tonight.
It**'s**		**rain**	

Negative Statements			
Subject + *Be*	***Not***	***Going to***	**Base Form of Verb**
I**'m** He**'s** We**'re** You**'re** They**'re**	**not**	**going to**	**sleep**.
It**'s**			**rain**.

**You're* can be both singular and plural subjects.

Yes / No Questions				
Be	**Subject**	***Going to***	**Base Form of Verb**	
Am	I	**going to**	**drive**	tomorrow?
Are	you			
Is	he			

Short Answers	
Affirmative	**Negative**
Yes, you are.	No, you're not.
Yes, I am.	No, I'm not.
Yes, he is.	No, he's not.

Wh- Questions						Short Answers
***Wh-* Word**	***Be***	**Subject**	***Going to***	**Base Form of Verb**		
What	**is**	she	**going to**	**do**?	there?	Meet her friend.
Where	**are**	they		**go**?		To the library.
How	**am**	I		**get**		By bus.

GRAMMAR NOTES

1

There are different ways to express **the future**.

USAGE NOTE: In speaking, *be going to* is more common than *will*.

- We **are going to buy** a car.
- We **are buying** a car next month.
- We **will buy** a car.

2

One way to express the future is with a form of ***be*** + ***going to*** + **the base form of the verb**.

- He **is going to start** at 9:00.
- They **are going to start** at 9:00.

Use **contractions** of ***be*** in speaking and informal writing.

- He**'s going to start** at 9:00.
- They**'re going to start** at 9:00.

Remember to use a form of *be* before *going to*. Remember to use the base form of the verb after *going to*.

NOT: He ~~going to~~ start at 9:00.
NOT: He's going to ~~starts~~ at 9:00.

3	Use *be going to* + base form • **to state facts about the future** • **to make predictions** • **to talk about plans**	• The politicians **are going to meet** in Rome. • There **is going to be** a change in the climate. • I can't go to the restaurant. **I'm going to take** my friend to the airport.
4	Use ***probably*** with *be going to* to say that **you think something will happen, but you are not sure**.	• We're **probably** going to start at 9:00. • It's **probably** going to rain.
5	**Future time markers** usually come at the beginning or the end of a sentence. Some common future time markers are: ***tomorrow***, ***next week***, ***next month***, ***this weekend***, and ***in 2100***.	• They are going to start construction **next week**. • **Next week** they are going to start construction.
6	Sometimes we use **the present progressive** + **a future time marker** to talk about the future. This is especially true with the verb *go* and verbs such as *drive* or *fly*. We do not use the present progressive with non-action verbs to talk about the future.	• We**'re going** there **next week**. • He**'s driving** to the country **this weekend**. • He**'s going to need** a new car next year. NOT: ~~He's needing~~ a new car next year.

STEP 3 FOCUSED PRACTICE

EXERCISE 1: Discover the Grammar

A | *Read the sentences. Underline all examples of* **be going to** *and the base form of the verb that follows.*

1. Last week Mayor Jonas talked about building a sports stadium. It's going to seat 300,000 people.
2. They're going to build a garage for the stadium. It's going to have spaces for 5,000 cars.
3. The mayor is giving a speech on Wednesday here at our school. She's going to talk about raising money for the stadium.
4. They're going to build stores around the stadium. The stores are going to provide jobs for a lot of people.
5. Some people don't want the city to build a new stadium. They're against it because the city is going to destroy some historic buildings when they build the stadium.

B | *Look at Part A. Circle the sentence that uses present progressive for the future.*

EXERCISE 2: *Be going to* for the Future

(Grammar Notes 2–4)

Complete the sentences with **be going to** *and the verbs in parentheses.*

A: The city needs money.

B: What ___is___ (1.) the mayor ___going to do___ (2. (do)) about it?

A: He ______________ (3. (increase)) taxes.

B: ______________ (4.) he ______________ (5. (lay off)) city workers?

A: No. Two thousand city workers ______________ (6. (retire)). The city ______________ (7. (hire / not)) new police or teachers.

B: That's not good. Crime ______________ (8. (probably / increase)).

A: I agree.

B: And children ______________ (9. (probably get / not)) a good education.

A: I ______________ (10. (write)) a letter to the mayor.

B: What ______________ (11.) you ______________ (12. (say))?

A: I ______________ (13. (tell)) him to bring more business to the city.

B: How ______________ (14.) he ______________ (15. (do)) that?

A: Tourism. That's the answer.

EXERCISE 3: *Be going to* for the Future: *Wh-* Questions

(Grammar Notes 2–5)

Read the news announcement. Write questions with **be going to** *and the words in parentheses on the next page. Then answer the questions. Use short answers.*

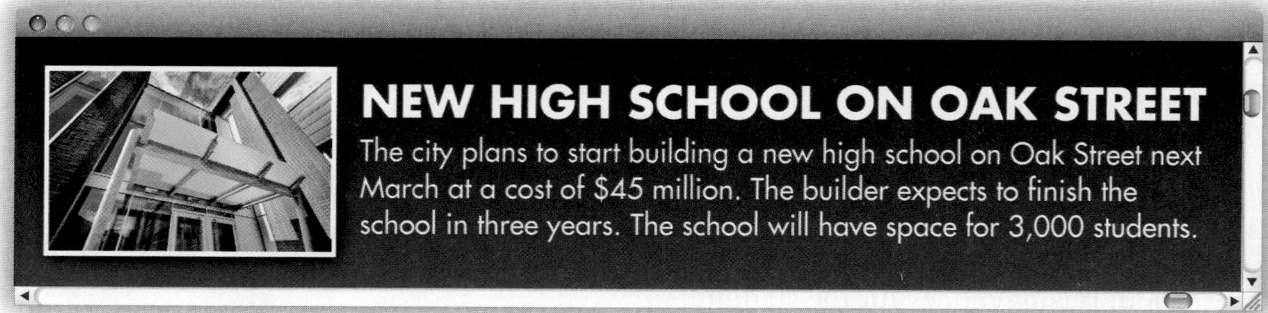

NEW HIGH SCHOOL ON OAK STREET
The city plans to start building a new high school on Oak Street next March at a cost of $45 million. The builder expects to finish the school in three years. The school will have space for 3,000 students.

1. (What / city / build)

A: What's the city going to build?

B: A new high school.

2. (Where / it / be)

A: ______________________________

B: ______________________________

3. (When / the builders / start)

A: ______________________________

B: ______________________________

4. (How much / it / cost)

A: ______________________________

B: ______________________________

5. (How long / it / take)

A: ______________________________

B: ______________________________

EXERCISE 4: *Be going to* for the Future

(Grammar Notes 1–3)

The West Street Association is against the construction of a new building on West Street. Complete their letter to the editor with the affirmative or negative form of **be going to.**

To the Editor:

Mr. Romp wants to build a 20-story building on West Street. The West Street Association is against the plan. It's going to change (1. (change)) the area. All the buildings on West Street are only four or five stories high. A very tall building ______________ (2. (look)) good. The new building ______________ (3. (have)) garage spaces for 50 cars, but there ______________ (4. (be)) 200 apartments. There ______________ (5. (probably / be)) enough parking spaces. There ______________ (6. (be)) a lot more traffic in the area and ______________ (7. (look)) terrible. Let's stop construction of the Romp Tower!

EXERCISE 5: Simple Past, Simple Present, *Be going to*

(Grammar Notes 1–4)

Complete the conversations with the verbs in parentheses. Use the simple past, the simple present, or **be going to** *for the future.*

CONVERSATION A

INEZ: ___Did___ (1.) you ___listen___ (2. (listen)) to the weather report?

ROBERTO: Yes. It ________ (3. (be)) sunny and warm today and tomorrow.

INEZ: Good. There ________ (4. (be)) a town meeting outdoors in East Park tomorrow.

CONVERSATION B

DANIEL: The mayor ________ (1. (want)) to close Maple Street to cars next month. He ________ (2. (make)) it a place for people to walk. No cars will be allowed.

ALISA: How ________ (3.) you ________ (4. (know)) about it?

DANIEL: The mayor ________ (5. (announce)) it last night on his weekly radio show.

ALISA: I ________ (6. (think)) it's a great idea.

DANIEL: Well, storeowners aren't happy. They say they ________ (7. (lose)) business.

ALISA: What else ________ (8.) the mayor ________ (9. (say)) last night?

DANIEL: In the next five years he ________ (10. (turn)) this city into a center for the arts.

ALISA: How ________ (11.) he ________ (12. (do)) that?

DANIEL: He ________ (13. (offer)) cheap housing for artists. He ________ (14. (build)) a concert hall, and he ________ (15. (put)) artwork in the park.

EXERCISE 6: Present Progressive for the Future

(Grammar Note 6)

Look at the mayor's schedule for next Monday and Tuesday. Write questions with the given words. Use the **present progressive for the future.** *Then write short answers.*

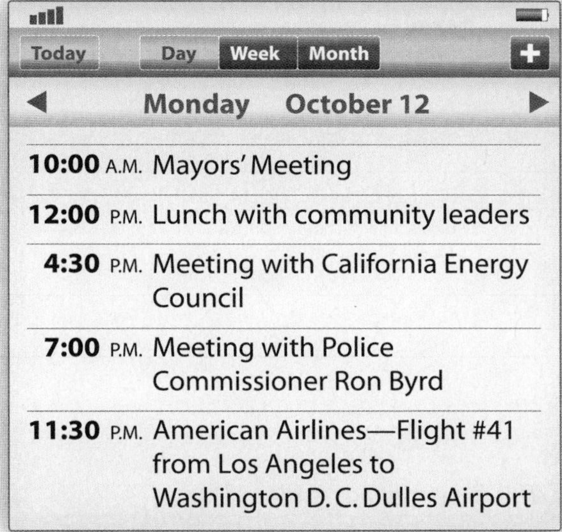

Today
Day
Week
Month
Monday October 12
10:00 A.M. Mayors' Meeting
12:00 P.M. Lunch with community leaders
4:30 P.M. Meeting with California Energy Council
7:00 P.M. Meeting with Police Commissioner Ron Byrd
11:30 P.M. American Airlines—Flight #41 from Los Angeles to Washington D.C. Dulles Airport

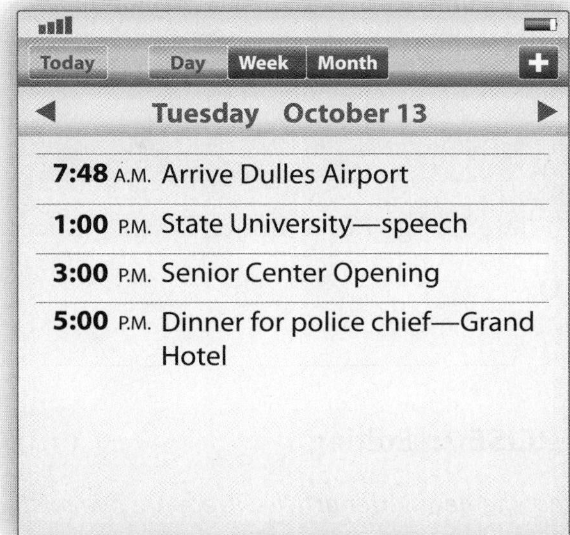

Today
Day
Week
Month
Tuesday October 13
7:48 A.M. Arrive Dulles Airport
1:00 P.M. State University—speech
3:00 P.M. Senior Center Opening
5:00 P.M. Dinner for police chief—Grand Hotel

1. Who / he / have lunch with on Monday?

   Q: *Who is he having lunch with on Monday?*

   A: *He's having lunch with community leaders.*

2. What / he / do / Monday afternoon?

   Q: ______________________________

   A: ______________________________

3. Who / he / meet / at 7:00 P.M. on Monday?

   Q: ______________________________

   A: ______________________________

4. What time / he / fly home from Los Angeles?

   Q: ______________________________

   A: ______________________________

(continued on next page)

5. Where / he / speak/ in Washington, D.C.?

Q: ______________________________

A: ______________________________

6. When / he speak to the senior citizens?

Q: ______________________________

A: ______________________________

7. Where he / go / to a dinner for the police chief?

Q: ______________________________

A: ______________________________

EXERCISE 7: Editing

Correct the newsletter article. There are five mistakes. The first mistake is already corrected. Find and correct four more.

VILLAGE GREEN APARTMENTS

Dear Residents:

Last week the mayor talked about building a sports stadium in our neighborhood. I think it's a terrible idea. It's going ^to^ cost taxpayers millions of dollars. It going to mean traffic jams. Parking is being difficult, and it's going to bringing noise to the area.

Next Monday at 7:00 P.M. the mayor is goes to answer questions at the public library. Please come out and speak out against the new stadium.

Sincerely,
Dale Ortiz
President, Residents' Association

STEP 4 COMMUNICATION PRACTICE

EXERCISE 8: Pronunciation

A | *Read and listen to the Pronunciation Note.*

Pronunciation Note

In informal speaking, ***going to*** is often pronounced **"gonna"** when it comes before a verb.

EXAMPLE: We're "gonna" win this race. (***going to*** + **verb**)

Do not pronounce *going to* as "gonna" when *going* comes before the preposition ***to*** + **a place**.

EXAMPLE: We're going to the movies. (***going to*** + **place**)

B | *Listen to the sentences. Check (✓) when you hear* **going to** *and when you hear* **"gonna."**

going to	"gonna"
1.	
2.	
3.	
4.	
5.	
6.	
7.	

C | *Listen and repeat the sentences.*

1. He's going to a concert.
2. They're going to be late.
3. It's going to rain.
4. We're going to the library.
5. I'm going to think about it.

EXERCISE 9: Listening

A | *Listen to a conversation about a new building. Circle the correct letter.*

Why does the man want to buy the newspaper?

a. He wrote a letter and wants to see if his letter is in the paper.

b. He wants to see if the paper is for the new building.

B | *Listen again. Answer the questions.*

1. What are two reasons for building the new apartment building?

a. ______________________________

b. ______________________________

2. What are two reasons against building it?

a. ______________________________

b. ______________________________

3. Is the man for or against the new building? ______________________________

EXERCISE 10: Conversation: Changes in Your Life

PAIRS: Tell about an upcoming change in your life or the life of someone you know well. For example, a move or a new job. Your partner asks questions about the change. Then talk about a good and a bad thing about the change. Take turns.

EXAMPLE: **A:** My sister is moving away from the city.
B: Why is she moving?
A: She needs a larger home. She has two children. She's going to have more space, but she and her husband are going to have a long commute to work.

EXERCISE 11: Writing

A | *GROUPS: Read the changes in the chart for Columbus College and the city of Columbus. Choose one school change and one city change. Discuss reasons why you are for or against the change.*

School Changes	City Changes
50% of courses will be online.	No cars on Main Street on weekends
No tests, just written reports	Higher taxes on clothes and entertainment to pay for better schools
No smoking on college campus	Restaurants need to show calorie and fat content of all food on menus.

EXAMPLE: Fifty percent of classes will be online courses.
A: I think that's a terrible idea. Online courses will be boring.
B: I disagree. In my opinion, we're going to have great online discussions.

B | *Write an email letter to the editor. Explain why you are for or against one of these changes. Explain what the change is going to mean. Use* be going to *for the future.*

EXAMPLE:

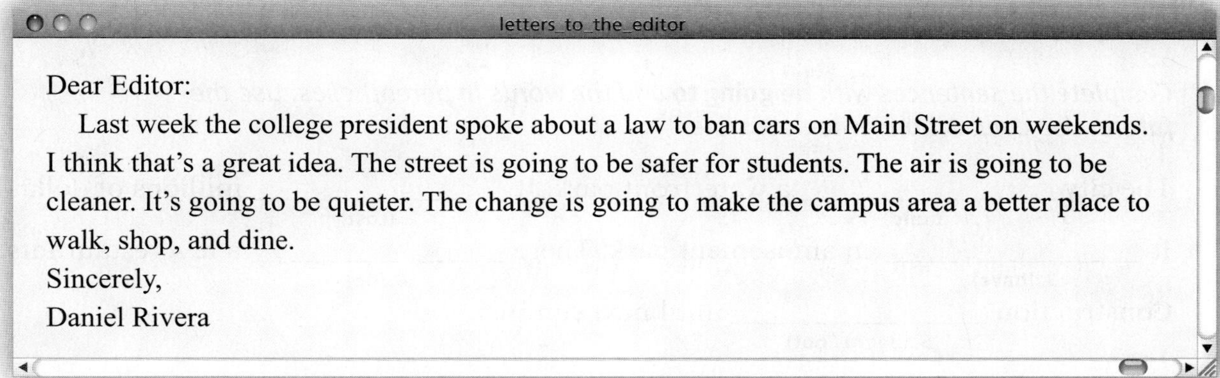

letters_to_the_editor

Dear Editor:

Last week the college president spoke about a law to ban cars on Main Street on weekends. I think that's a great idea. The street is going to be safer for students. The air is going to be cleaner. It's going to be quieter. The change is going to make the campus area a better place to walk, shop, and dine.

Sincerely,

Daniel Rivera

C | *Check your work. Use the Editing Checklist.*

Editing Checklist

Did you . . . ?

☐ use correct forms of ***be going to*** for the future

☐ check your spelling

UNIT 24 Review

Check your answers on page UR-5.
Do you need to review anything?

A | *Complete the sentences with* **be going to** *and the words in parentheses. Use the future. Use contractions when possible.*

The city ______________ (1. build) a waterfront park. It ______________ (2. cost) millions of dollars. It ______________ (3. have) an amusement park. There ______________ (4. be) a few restaurants. Construction ______________ (5. begin / not) until next summer.

B | *Complete the sentences with* **be going to** *and the words in parentheses. Use the future and the affirmative or negative form. Use contractions when possible.*

1. Everyone is happy. Taxes ______________ (increase). No one likes to pay taxes.
2. It's raining hard. We ______________ (play) soccer in the park.
3. John is in the hospital. We ______________ (visit) him. Do you want to come?
4. It's Mary's last year. She ______________ (retire) in December and move away.
5. I'm tired and it's late. I ______________ (do) any more work.

C | *Look at Eun Young's schedule. Write questions with the words in parentheses. Use the present progressive for the future. Write short answers.*

MONDAY: dentist 5:30 TUESDAY: meet Yu Chen Pappa Pizza 6:30

1. (When / she / go to the dentist)

   Q: ______________ **A:** ______________

2. (Where / she / meet / Yu Chen)

   Q: ______________ **A:** ______________

3. (she / meet / Yu Chen / on Monday)

   Q: ______________ **A:** ______________

D | *Correct the paragraph. There are four mistakes.*

This city going to change under our new mayor. People's going to ride bikes, and they're gonna use public transportation. They're no going to drive big cars. There are probably going to be higher tolls on bridges and more bike paths on the roads.

UNIT 25

Will for the Future; Future Time Markers

THE FUTURE

STEP 1 GRAMMAR IN CONTEXT

Before You Read

What do you think will be different by the year 2025? 2050? By 2100?

EXAMPLE: I think people will travel to the past and the future.

Read

Future Science Magazine *asked scientists to make predictions for the year 2050. How will we look? How will we travel? How long will we live? Read their predictions.*

www.futuresciencemag.com

FUTURE SCIENCE

What's in Store[1] for Us in 2050?

1. More people **will be** vegetarians. They **won't eat** any meat or fish.
2. People **will look** bigger than people today.
3. People **will read** each other's thoughts.
4. They **will take** memory pills.
5. Cars **will run on** solar[2] energy.
6. Private planes **will be** common.
7. Travel to the moon **will be** common.
8. Robots **will cook** our meals. We **won't spend** a lot of time in the kitchen.
9. On average, people **will weigh** 11 pounds (5 kilograms) more, and they **will be** about 5 inches (12.5 centimeters) taller.
10. People **will live** to be 100 years old on average, and the majority of people **will be** over 60.
11. People **won't need** so many tissues. There **will be** a cure for the common cold.
12. Paper money and coins[3] **will disappear**. People **will use** credit cards for all their purchases.

[1]***be in store:*** to be about to happen to someone
[2]***solar:*** from the sun
[3]***coins:*** metal money such as quarters or dimes

After You Read

A | Practice *PAIRS: Read the predictions again aloud. Take turns reading each prediction.*

B | Vocabulary *Complete the sentences with the words from the box.*

common	disappear	meal	spend time	vegetarian

1. He never eats meat. He's a ________________.
2. In the future, travel to the moon will be ________________.
3. Did the moon ________________ behind a cloud?
4. What's your favorite ________________ of the day?
5. We like to ________________ in the laboratory.

C | Comprehension *Read the questions. Circle the letter of the correct answers based on the article in* Future Science Magazine. *There may be more than one correct answer.*

1. How will people look?

   a. taller b. shorter c. smaller

2. Where will people travel?

   a. to the moon b. to Mars c. to the past

3. What will increase?

   a. the number of vegetarians b. the average life span c. the number of colds

4. What will be common in 2050?

   a. coins b. private planes c. travel to the moon

STEP 2 GRAMMAR PRESENTATION

WILL FOR THE FUTURE

Affirmative Statements			
Subject	***Will / 'll***	**Base Form of Verb**	**Time Marker**
I You* He She It We They	**will** **'ll**	**leave**	tomorrow.

Negative Statements			
Subject	***Will Not / Won't***	**Base Form of Verb**	**Time Marker**
I You* He She It We They	**will not** **won't**	**leave**	tonight.

**You* is both singular and plural.

Yes / No Questions			
Will	**Subject**	**Base Form of Verb**	**Time Marker**
Will	I you he she it we they	**arrive**	tonight?

Short Answers					
Affirmative			**Negative**		
Yes,	you I he she it we they	**will.**	No,	you I he she it we they	**won't.**

Future Time Markers	
today tonight tomorrow	
this	morning afternoon evening
tomorrow	morning afternoon evening night
Saturday	night

Future Time Markers with *Next* and *In*	
next	week month year Monday weekend
in	2020 the 22nd century 20 years two weeks a few days

GRAMMAR NOTES

1	Use ***will*** + **the base form of the verb** to talk about things that will take place in the future. **BE CAREFUL!** Use the base form of the verb after *will* or *won't*. Remember, the base form does not change.	• The class **will begin** on November 2. • We **will meet** tomorrow at 10:00 A.M. • The plane **will arrive** at 6:00 P.M. Not: The plane will ~~to arrive~~ at 6:00 P.M. Not: The plane will ~~arrives~~ at 6:00 P.M.
2	Use **contractions** of *will* **with pronouns** in speaking and informal writing. **BE CAREFUL!** Do not use contractions in affirmative short answers.	• **We'll** be there before 3:00. **A:** Will they be there? **B:** Yes, they will. Not: Yes, ~~they'll~~.
3	Use *will* to make **predictions**. **USAGE NOTE:** In writing, we often use *will* in one sentence and *be going to* in the next sentence.	• In 2050 there **will be** more megacities. Those cities **are going to be** very crowded.
4	Use *will* to make a **promise** or **give assurance**.	• I**'ll be** back in five minutes. • I **won't do** that again.
5	Use *will* to **ask for** or **offer** something.	**A: Will** you **help** me? **B:** Don't worry. I**'ll help**.
6	***Won't*** is the contraction of ***will*** + ***not***. It has two meanings. Use *won't* to mean the **negative future**. Use *won't* to mean "**refuse(s) to**."	 • He **won't be** in school tomorrow. • The child **won't eat** carrots.
7	To say that something is not definite, use ***probably*** with *will* for the future.	• People will **probably** take more vacations.
8	Some **time markers** are used only for the future. Other time markers can be used for the past or the future.	FUTURE • She won't be home **tomorrow**. FUTURE • She'll be home **this afternoon**. PAST • She was at the library **this afternoon**.

STEP 3 FOCUSED PRACTICE

EXERCISE 1: Discover the Grammar

*Read the sentences. How is **will** used? Match the sentences with the descriptions.*

b 1. I won't do it. I think it's wrong.
____ 2. Will you show me how to use that computer?
____ 3. I'll be back by 9:00.
____ 4. There won't be any meeting on February 8.
____ 5. By 2020 people will fly to the moon for fun.

a. predicts something
b. refuses to do something
c. promises to do something
d. asks for something
e. tells about something that is not going to happen

EXERCISE 2: *Will* for the Future

(Grammar Notes 1–7)

*Complete the conversations with **will** or **won't** and the verbs in parentheses.*

1. **A:** Mom, when will dinner be (be) ready?
   B: Robot Bob says it ________ (be) ready in 22 minutes.
2. **A:** Do you really think scientists ________ (find) a cure for the cold?
   B: I hope so. It ________ (save) a lot of money. People ________ (miss) work so often.
3. **A:** Dr. Smith, my great grandmother ________ (take) her memory pills. She says they taste bad. ________ you ________ (give) her some that taste good?
   B: Don't worry. I ________ (give) her some that taste like candy.
4. **A:** When do you think we ________ (send) astronauts to the planet Mars?
   B: No one knows. Right now we're spending less money on space exploration. So it ________ (probably / take) longer than we thought.
5. **A:** Where ________ the wedding ________ (take place)?
   B: The wedding ________ (be) on the moon.
   A: And where ________ you ________ (go) for your honeymoon?
   B: We ________ (probably / go) to Mars.

EXERCISE 3: *Will* for the Future

(Grammar Notes 1–7)

Complete the conversation with **will** *and the verbs in parentheses.*

A: So, Laura, when ___will___ (1.) you ___finish___ (2. (finish)) the article about the future?

B: It ____________ (3. (not / be)) ready until 4:00 P.M., but I think you ____________ (4. (like)) it.

A: You interviewed Dr. Reicher, right?

B: Yes, I did. He says computers ____________ (5. (help)) us stay healthy.

A: Oh, yeah? How's that?

B: In the future, we ____________ (6. (have)) computers inside our bodies. They ____________ (7.) constantly ____________ (8. (check)) things such as our blood sugar and blood pressure.

A: ____________ (9.) diabetes and heart disease ____________ (10. (disappear))?

B: No, but people ____________ (11. (probably / die / not)) from those diseases so often, and people ____________ (12. (live)) longer.

A: And when ____________ (13.) this ____________ (14. (happen))?

B: By 2030.

A: That's really not so far away.

EXERCISE 4: *Will* for the Future

(Grammar Notes 2–3, 8)

Look at the chart of predictions. Write questions about Fogville with the words in parentheses. Use **will** *for the future. Answer the questions.*

Predictions for Fogville in 2050	
The cost of housing ↓	Crime →
The cost of health care ↓	The percent of people under 25 ↑
Taxes ↓	The percent of people over 65 →

Key
Increase = ↑
Stay the same = →
Decrease = ↓

1. **A:** *Will the cost of housing increase?*
   (the cost of housing / increase)

   B: *No, it won't. The cost of housing will decrease.*

2. **A:** ________________________________
   (the cost of health care / stay the same)

   B: ________________________________

3. A: ______________________________
(taxes / stay the same)

B: ______________________________

4. A: ______________________________
(the percent of people under 25 / decrease)

B: ______________________________

5. A: ______________________________
(the percent of people over 65 / decrease)

B: ______________________________

EXERCISE 5: Review of Present, Past, Future

(Grammar Notes 3–4, 6–8)

Complete the conversation. Use the verbs in parentheses. Use the simple present, the simple past, or the future with **will**. *Use contractions where possible.*

A: ___Did___ (1.) you ___hear___ (2. (hear)) the lecture last week?

B: No, what __________ (3. (be)) it about?

A: The future. According to Professor Johns, by the year 2100 there __________ (4. (be)) cities in the ocean, we __________ (5. (take)) trips to the moon, and we __________ (6. (learn)) everything from computers.

B: By 2100? We __________ (7.) all __________ (8. (be)) gone by then. __________ (9. (like)) the people __________ (10.) his lecture?

A: Yes, they did. They always do. He __________ (11. (know)) how to make any subject fascinating.

EXERCISE 6: Editing

Correct the conversation. There are six mistakes. The first mistake is already corrected. Find and correct five more.

A: What did he say?

B: He said there ^will be an increase in the population. Many young people will moves to the area. Taxes will increases. The value of homes will also to increase.

A: How about crime? Will it increases?

B: No, it doesn't.

A: Well, it sounds like a great place to live.

STEP 4 COMMUNICATION PRACTICE

EXERCISE 7: Pronunciation

A | *Read and listen to the Pronunciation Note.*

Pronunciation Note

In conversation we often **link** the **subject pronoun** (*I, you, he, she, it, we,* OR *they*) and ***will***. The final vowel sound of *will* often sounds like **/ əl /**.

EXAMPLES: I'll she'll it'll we'll

B | *Listen and repeat the contractions.*

I'll **you'll** **he'll** **she'll** **it'll** **we'll** **they'll**

C | *Now listen and repeat the sentences.*

1. You'll fly to the moon.
2. He'll visit you on the moon.
3. They'll be there too.
4. She'll help you fly the spaceship.
5. I'll be with you shortly.
6. It'll cost a lot of money.
7. We'll see them the following year.

EXERCISE 8: Listening

A | *Listen to a conversation between a TV news reporter and two people. Read the question. Circle the correct letter.*

Why is the man talking to the two people?

a. They made a lot of money. **b.** They won a lot of money.

B | *Listen again. Answer the questions.*

1. What will the woman do with her money?

a. ____

b. ____

2. What will the man do with his money?

____

3. What does the man mean when he says, "They'll get over it."

____

EXERCISE 9: Class Survey

SMALL GROUPS: Look at the predictions in the Future Science *article on page 283. Do you agree? What are your predictions? Discuss your answers. Report to the class.*

Example: We all think paper money will disappear. People will use credit cards or check cards to pay for everything. Coins are heavy, and bills are not clean. These cards are the way of the future.

EXERCISE 10: Survey: In the Future

A | *Complete the information.*

1. Write the name of something that is very popular today.

____

2. Write the name of a country and a time in the future.

____

B | *Complete the questions below with your answers from Part A. Then survey five classmates. Ask them the questions.*

1. Will _______________ still be popular in _______________?

2. Will _______________ be a popular tourist destination in _______________?

C | *Report your results to the class.*

Example: I asked five people this question: "Will DVDs still be popular in 10 years?" Four out of six students said, "No."

EXERCISE 11: Making Predictions

A | *Make predictions about these fields for the year 2050. Tape them on the wall.*

environment **health** **jobs** **medicine** **sports** **technology**

Example: Nobody will be hungry.

B | *Number all the predictions. Go around and read each prediction. Choose four predictions. Tell if you agree or disagree with them.*

EXERCISE 12: Writing

A | *GROUPS: Talk about how life will be in the future. Use these topics:*

education **fashion** **food** **homes** **tourism** **travel**

Example:
A: I think people will wear paper clothes.
B: I disagree. People will worry about the environment. They won't wear throwaway clothes.
C: I think people will wear special clothes in the summer. They will be light, but they will protect them from the sun.
D: And in the winter they will wear clothes that are light in weight, but very warm.

B | *Choose a year. Choose a topic from Part A. Write about how things will be different. Use* **will** *for the future and* **be going to** *for the future.*

Example: TRAVEL IN 2050
In 2050 people will have new ways to travel. First of all, people will have their own wings. They're going to use them to fly distances of 50 miles or less. The wings won't take up much space, so people won't have to "park" their wings. People will also travel with flying cars. These cars will go up to 200 miles an hour. People are going to use their flying cars to travel 200 to 400 miles. There will be regular planes and jets, and there will be spaceships for trips to other planets.

C | *Check your work. Use the Editing Checklist.*

Editing Checklist

Did you . . . ?

- ☐ use ***will*** for the future correctly
- ☐ use ***be going to*** for the future correctly
- ☐ check your spelling

UNIT 25 Review

Check your answers on page UR-5.
Do you need to review anything?

A | *Write questions with* **will** *and the words in parentheses.*

1. ______________________________
   (Where / people / travel / in 20 years)
2. ______________________________
   (people / fly / to the moon)
3. ______________________________
   (How / they / get around)
4. ______________________________
   (the climate / change)
5. ______________________________
   (people / look / different)

B | *Circle the correct word to complete the sentences.*

1. He doesn't like hats. He **will / won't** wear them.
2. I'm busy tomorrow morning. I **will / won't** be at work until noon.
3. He's good at computers. He probably **will / won't** be able to fix your computer.
4. The sale ends today, but there **will / won't** be a sale next month.
5. I need more time. I **will / won't** be ready for at least a half an hour.

C | *Write questions with* **will**. *Use the same ideas in all sentences.*

1. Yesterday was hot. Today is hot. _____________ it _____________ tomorrow too?
2. Last week he had a test. This week he has a test. _____________ he _____________ next week too?
3. Last September there was a storm. This September there was a storm. _____________ there _____________ next September too?
4. Yesterday it rained. Today it rained. _____________ it _____________ tomorrow too?
5. He worked late yesterday. He worked late today. _____________ he _____________ tomorrow too?

D | *Correct the paragraph. There are five mistakes.*

I usually bring my lunch to work, but tomorrow I no will bring it because it's my birthday. My co-workers will takes me out to a restaurant. We'll to order a few different dishes, and we'll share them. They'll singing "Happy Birthday," and they'll give me a small gift. I'm sure it will is a lot of fun.

UNIT 26 *May* or *Might* for Possibility

WEATHER

STEP 1 GRAMMAR IN CONTEXT

Before You Read

Answer the questions.

1. How do you know what the weather will be? (*I watch TV, check my phone or computer, listen to the radio, read the newspaper*)
2. How often do you think the weather report is wrong? (*rarely, sometimes, often, almost always*)

Read

Read the conversation and TV weather report.

MOTHER: Shh. The weather report is **coming on.**[1]

ANNOUNCER: It's Sunday, May 15. The time is 9:00 A.M. And now here's the weather forecast with Luis Malina.

METEOROLOGIST: Good morning, everyone. If you plan to be outdoors today or Monday, wear a warm jacket and bring an umbrella. The weather will continue to be unseasonable.[2] Today will be cold and windy. And heavy rain will begin

[1] ***coming on:*** starting

[2] ***unseasonable:*** unusual for the time of year

tonight or tomorrow. For your morning commute, there **may be** flooding on the highways.

So, if you can, take public transportation. And don't put away those umbrellas too soon because we'll have more rain on Tuesday and Wednesday. By Thursday the weather **may become** milder with only a 20 percent chance of showers.[3] We **might** even **see** some sun. But until then, my friends, my best advice is stay indoors with a good book or movie.

ALEX: I guess that means no soccer tomorrow.

MOTHER: Don't be too sure. You **may** still **have** a game. The meteorologist[4] is often wrong. Remember last Friday. He predicted a beautiful day, but it was awful. And last week he said we **might have** a major[5] storm. It turned out to be sunny and dry.

ALEX: Maybe.

MOTHER: I just hope you don't play in the rain.

ALEX: We **might**. The last time it rained we played the entire game. Playing in the mud was great! And we won!

---

[3] ***chance of showers:*** a short period of heavy rain
[4] ***meteorologist:*** weather reporter
[5] ***major:*** big

After You Read

A | Practice *GROUPS OF THREE: Now read the conversation aloud.*

B | Vocabulary *Complete the sentences with the words from the box.*

commute	entire	flooding	highways	mild	predicted	storm

1. They canceled the game because they expected rain the ________________ day.
2. He lives outside the city. His ________________ to work is an hour and a half each way.
3. There is always ________________ on that street when it rains. The city needs to fix the problem.
4. The meteorologist ________________ beautiful weather for the next three days.
5. There is bad traffic on all the major ________________. I think we should wait to go home.
6. The ________________ is getting worse. They may close the airport.
7. I want to live someplace where the weather is sunny and ________________.

C | Comprehension *Circle the correct weather for each day, according to the forecast.*

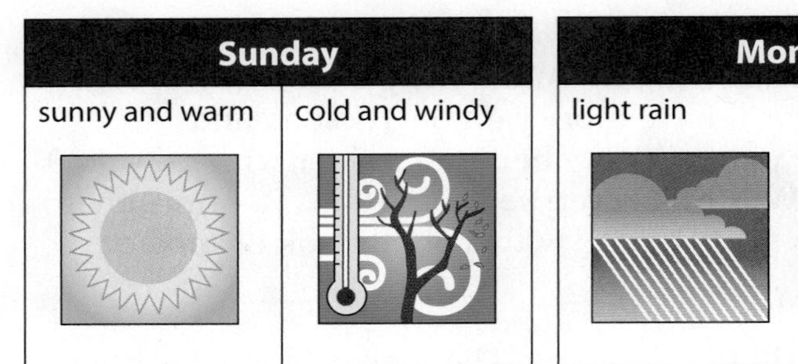

Monday
light rain
heavy rain
Tuesday
rainy
sunny

Thursday
sunny—no chance of rain
sunny—20% chance of rain

STEP 2 GRAMMAR PRESENTATION

MAY OR *MIGHT* FOR POSSIBILITY

Affirmative Statements			
Subject	***May / Might***	**Base Form of Verb**	
I You* He She We They	**may** **might**	**play**	soccer.
It	**may** **might**	**rain**	tonight.

Negative Statements				
Subject	***May / Might***	***Not***	**Base Form of Verb**	
I You* He She We They	**may** **might**	**not**	**play**	soccer.
It	**may** **might**	**not**	**rain**	tonight.

**You* is both singular and plural.

GRAMMAR NOTES

1	Use ***may*** or ***might*** to express **possibility** about the present or the future.	**A:** Where's John? **B:** I don't know. He **may be** on vacation. **A:** What are you going to do this weekend? **B:** We **might go** to a movie.
	May and *might* have almost the same meaning, but *may* means something is a little more possible than *might*.	• It **might** rain. *(It's possible.)* • It **may** rain. *(It's more possible.)* • It**'ll probably** rain. *(It's likely.)* • It **will** rain. *(It's definite.)*
2	*May* and *might* are **followed** by the **base form of the verb**.	• He **might go** to the movies. NOT: He might ~~goes~~ to the movies. NOT: He might ~~to go~~ to the movies.
	There are no contractions for *may* or *might*.	He might not go to the movies. NOT: He ~~mightn't~~ go to the movies.
3	**USAGE NOTE:** We usually use ***will*** or ***be going to***, not *may* or *might*, to **ask *yes / no* questions about the future**.	**A: Will** you **go** to the party? **B:** I might. OR I may. **A: Are** you **going to see** that movie tonight? **B:** We might. OR We may. NOT: ~~May~~ you go to the party?
4	We use ***I think I might*** for possibility. We use ***I'm sure*** + **subject** + ***will*** for certainty.	• **I think I might** have the flu. • **I'm sure I will** be there. NOT: I'm sure I ~~might~~ buy that book.
	We use ***I think I will*** for something that is likely.	• **I think I'll call** the doctor.
5	*May* and *might* are modals. ***Maybe*** is an adverb. It means "there's a possibility." ***Maybe I will*** has a similar meaning to *I might* or *I may*.	**Maybe I'll go** to the party. = **I might go** to the party. OR **I may go** to the party. **A:** Are you going to the game? **B: Maybe.** = **I may.** OR **I might.**
6	We use ***it might*** or ***it may*** to talk about the weather.	• **It might** rain tonight. • **It may** snow tomorrow.

STEP 3 FOCUSED PRACTICE

EXERCISE 1: Discover the Grammar

Match the sentences. Write the correct letter.

__d__ **1.** It's definitely going to rain.
____ **2.** There's an 80 percent chance of rain.
____ **3.** There's about a 50 percent chance of rain.
____ **4.** There's a 10 percent chance of rain.
____ **5.** It's definitely not going to rain.

a. It probably won't rain.
b. It'll probably rain.
c. It won't rain.
d. It will rain.
e. It may rain.

EXERCISE 2: Affirmative of *May* or *Might*

(Grammar Notes 1–2, 4)

Complete the conversations with **may** *or* **might** *and the verbs from the box. Use the affirmative or negative form.*

be	cancel	have	leave	~~rain~~	take

1. A: Take your umbrella. I think it ____might rain____ this afternoon.

B: Really? The forecast was for sun.

2. A: Start dinner without me. It ________________ me a long time to get home. The rain is causing flooding on the highway.

B: That's OK. We'll wait.

3. A: Sandy looks upset.

B: She is. She ________________ her trip. Her sister is in the hospital.

4. A: Why are you so worried?

B: The kids are camping tonight, and the forecast is for unusually cold weather. They ________________ enough clothes.

5. A: Where's John? The meeting will start in a few minutes.

B: He ________________ late. All flights are delayed because of the wind.

6. A: How are you feeling now?

B: Terrible. I ________________ the office early.

EXERCISE 3: *May/ Might / Will / Will probably*

(Grammar Notes 1–3)

Read today's weather forecast. Complete the sentences with the correct words in parentheses.

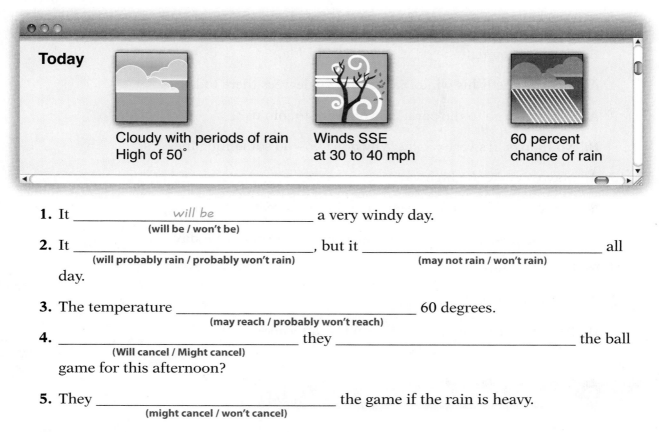

Today

Cloudy with periods of rain
High of 50°

Winds SSE
at 30 to 40 mph

60 percent
chance of rain

1. It ____*will be*____ a very windy day.
   (will be / won't be)
2. It ________________, but it ________________ all day.
   (will probably rain / probably won't rain) **(may not rain / won't rain)**
3. The temperature ________________ 60 degrees.
   (may reach / probably won't reach)
4. ________________ they ________________ the ball game for this afternoon?
   (Will cancel / Might cancel)
5. They ________________ the game if the rain is heavy.
   (might cancel / won't cancel)

EXERCISE 4: *Maybe* and *May / Might*

(Grammar Note 5)

Replace **maybe** *with* **may** *or* **might**. *In some cases you may need to add a subject or a subject and a verb.*

1. **A:** Do you have an extra umbrella?

   B: I'm not sure. ~~Maybe I have one~~ *I may have one* in that closet.

2. **A:** Where are the baby's shoes?

   B: Maybe they are in the top drawer.

3. **A:** Are they going to cancel the barbecue?

   B: Maybe. The forecast is for heavy rain.

4. **A:** Where will you meet if it rains?

   B: Maybe we'll meet at the mall.

5. **A:** Will she bring her daughter in the rain?

   B: Maybe.

EXERCISE 5: Editing

Correct the conversations. There are six mistakes. The first mistake is already corrected. Find and correct five more.

1. **A:** Where's Bill?

   B: ~~I'm sure~~ *I think* he might be on vacation in Florida.

   A: He may needs his winter jacket. It's 40 degrees there today.

2. **A:** We maybe go to the park. Do you want to join us?

   B: No thanks. It's very windy. Why don't you do something indoors?

3. **A:** May you take the highway?

   B: Yes, I may. It's usually faster than the city streets.

4. **A:** Are you going to finish your paper on climate change today?

   B: I want to, but I mightn't have enough time.

5. **A:** What's the weather report?

   B: It's sunny now, but it may to rain this afternoon.

STEP 4 COMMUNICATION PRACTICE

EXERCISE 6: Pronunciation

A | *Read and listen to the Pronunciation Note.*

Pronunciation Note

For numbers that end in ***-ty*** such as *thirty, forty, fifty,* etc., we stress the **first syllable** of the word. For numbers that end in ***-teen***, we usually stress the **second syllable**.

B | *Listen and circle the word you hear.*

1. 16 60
2. 13 30
3. 19 90
4. 15 50
5. 18 80

C | *Now listen and complete the conversations. Write the words you hear. Then practice the conversation with a partner.*

1. **A:** This tornado has winds of _______________ miles an hour.

   B: Did you say 115 or 150?

   A: _______________.

2. **A:** It's _______________ degrees.

   B: Was that 60 or 16?

   A: _______________.

3. **A:** There are _______________ inches of snow.

   B: Was that 14 or 40?

   A: _______________.

4. **A:** It's _______________ degrees below zero.

   B: Did you say 13 or 30?

   A: _______________.

Tornadoes have wind speed from 40 to 300 miles an hour.

EXERCISE 7: Listening

A | *A couple is taking a trip to Oregon. Listen to their conversation. What is the conversation about? Circle the correct letter.*

a. The things the man is taking with him on the trip

b. The things the man is going to do on the trip

B | *Listen again. What reason does the man give for packing these things in his suitcase?*

1. boots _They may go mountain climbing._
2. a raincoat _______________
3. two hats _______________
4. two books _______________
5. a sports jacket _______________

EXERCISE 8: Discussion

PAIRS: Take turns asking about your partner's plans for tonight. Use **may, might,** *and* **will probably** *in your answers. Use the ideas in the list or your own. Explain your answer.*

- stay indoors
- listen to the weather report
- go running
- watch a movie
- study English
- eat out
- cook dinner

EXAMPLE: **A:** Are you going to stay indoors?
B: I think so. I'll probably stay home and watch a movie tonight. How about you?
A: I might eat out. I may try that new Korean restaurant. My friend says it's very good.

EXERCISE 9: Writing

A | *You are a reporter for UpToDateWeather.com. Write a weather report for the next three days for your region. Look at pages 294–295 for ideas. Use* **may** *and* **might** *where possible.*

EXAMPLE: Good evening. This is Hye Won Paik with the three-day forecast. Tomorrow you will want to take out your running shoes. We're going to have perfect weather. It's going to be sunny and warm. On Wednesday, it will still be warm, but we may see some clouds. Then on Thursday, temperatures will drop, and we might have a shower in the evening.

B | *Check your work. Use the Editing Checklist.*

Editing Checklist

Did you . . . ?
☐ use ***may*** and ***might*** correctly
☐ check your spelling

UNIT 26 Review

Check your answers on page UR-5.
Do you need to review anything?

A | *Circle the correct words to complete the sentences.*

1. She may **to go / go** to the library.
2. He may **buy / buys** a new car.
3. It **mightn't / might not** rain tonight.
4. They **maybe / may** return the TV.
5. **Will / Might** you go to the party?

B | *Complete the sentences with* **may** *or* **might** *and the verbs from the box. Use the affirmative or negative form.*

get	need	see	snow	stay

1. Take your boots. It ________________ this afternoon.
2. Start dinner without me. I ________________ home from work until 10:00 P.M.
3. Karina is upset. The doctor says she ________________ surgery.
4. Here's a gift. I ________________ you before your birthday.
5. Traffic is heavy now. I ________________ here for a while.

C | *Rewrite the sentences. Replace* **Maybe** *with* **may** *or* **might** *and the correct word order.*

1. Maybe there's a restroom in the library. ________________________________
2. Maybe he's the director. ________________________________
3. Maybe the plane is late. ________________________________
4. Maybe they are cousins. ________________________________
5. Maybe it's his coat. ________________________________

D | *Correct the sentences. There are five mistakes.*

1. He might goes on vacation next week.
2. He may works late tomorrow.
3. They might to visit him tomorrow. Are you free?
4. I might not help him. I might to help her instead.
5. She maybe take a yoga class.

From Grammar to Writing

Time Clauses with *When*

1 | *Study this information about time clauses.*

1. I was six years old. I loved to play with dolls.

____

2. I graduate next year. I will work for a bank.

____

2 | *Combine the sentences using* **when**. *Look at the chart below for help.*

1	We can combine two sentences that tell about time by using a **time clause** and a **main clause**. *When I was six* is a **time clause**. It is not a sentence and can never stand alone. It needs a main clause.	• I was six. I started school. TIME CLAUSE / MAIN CLAUSE • **When** I was six, I started school.
2	When we use **present time clauses**, the verbs in both the time clause and the main clause are written in the **present**.	PRESENT TIME CLAUSE / MAIN CLAUSE • When I **get** home, I **have** dinner.
3	When we use **past time clauses**, the verbs in both the time clause and the main clause are written in the **past**.	PAST TIME CLAUSE / MAIN CLAUSE • When I **got** home, I **had** dinner.
4	When we use a **future time clause**, the future time clause uses the **simple present**. The main clause uses the **future**.	FUTURE TIME CLAUSE / MAIN CLAUSE • When I **get** home, I **will have** dinner. (First I'll get home. Then I'll have dinner.)
5	You can begin a sentence with the time clause or the main clause. When the time clause begins the sentence, put a **comma** before the main clause. There is no comma when the main clause begins the sentence.	PRESENT TIME CLAUSE / MAIN CLAUSE • When I get home**,** I will have dinner. MAIN CLAUSE / PRESENT TIME CLAUSE • I will have dinner when I get home.

3 | *Rewrite this paragraph using three time clauses.*

My Dream

I was a child. I loved to play "make-believe" games. Sometimes I was a cowboy, and sometimes I was a prince. I became a teenager. I got a job at a video store. I saw many movies. I also made a couple of videos, and I acted in all the school plays. Now I'm studying film and acting at school. I will finish college next year. I will move to Hollywood. I hope to become a movie star.

4 | *Write a paragraph about yourself at different times of your life. Include a part about your future.*

5 | *Exchange papers with a partner. Did your partner follow the directions? Correct any mistakes in grammar and spelling.*

6 | *Talk to your partner. Discuss the mistakes you made. Then rewrite your own paper and make any necessary changes.*

COUNT / NON-COUNT NOUNS; *MUCH* / *MANY*; QUANTIFIERS

UNIT	GRAMMAR FOCUS	THEME
27	Count and Non-Count Nouns, Quantifiers, Articles	Restaurants and Food
28	*How much* / *How many*, Quantifiers, *Enough*, Adverbs of Frequency	Desserts, Cooking, and Baking
29	*Too much* / *Too many*, *Too* + Adjective	The Right Place to Live

UNIT 27 Count and Non-Count Nouns, Quantifiers, Articles

RESTAURANTS AND FOOD

STEP 1 GRAMMAR IN CONTEXT

Before You Read

What do you usually look for in a restaurant? Check (✓) three things that are important to you. Put an **X** *next to three things that are not important.*

____ unusual food	____ a quiet place
____ polite service	____ a lively place
____ fast service	____ low prices
____ a beautiful atmosphere	____ food I like
____ an unusual atmosphere	____ big portions

Read

Read the online restaurant reviews.

www.kassandrasfoodreview.com

Kassandra's Food Reviews

Al Hambra ★★★★

Rich **spices** are the **draw**[1] at **Al Hambra**. The **flavor** of **ginger**, **garlic**, **cumin**, and **lemon** make the **chicken** in a **tagine** (**ceramic pot**) our favorite **choice**. Another great **choice** for the main **course** is the **lamb** with **ginger**. Note: There isn't **much beef** on the **menu**, and there isn't **any pork**. However, there are **many choices** of fresh **fish**, **chicken**, and **lamb**. All the **appetizers** are great. We especially like an **appetizer** called ***zaalouk***. This is a **salad** made of **eggplant and tomato**. For **dessert** we recommend **the** almond **cookies**. There aren't **many tables** at Al Hambra, so be sure to make a **reservation** well in advance.

[1]***draw:*** attraction

www.kassandrasfoodreview.com

Topkapi ★★★

Topkapi serves Turkish **food** in a colorful **atmosphere**. The **mirrors**, **lights**, and yellow and red **colors** give this **restaurant a** warm, inviting **look**. The **food** is delicious. Try the vegetable **combo**[2] to begin. The pita **bread** with **hummus**, **yogurt**, and **tahini** is excellent. For the main **course** I suggest the lamb **kebab** with rice and salad. The best **dessert** is the **baklava**. This is **a** sweet **pastry** made with pistachios or walnuts. Enjoy your **baklava** with Turkish **coffee**. But beware, Turkish **coffee** is very strong.

Note: You may need to wait **a few minutes** even with a **reservation**, but the **atmosphere**, **food**, and **service** are worth the **wait**.

[2]*combo:* combination

After You Read

A | Practice *PAIRS: Now read the restaurant reviews aloud.*

B | Vocabulary *Complete the sentences with the words from the box.*

atmosphere	delicious	main course	menu	reservation	service

1. The food was ________________. We will definitely go back to that restaurant.
2. Everything on the ________________ is fresh and tasty. Order whatever you like.
3. I ordered steak for my ________________. My friend ordered a pasta dish.
4. All the servers are polite and helpful. The ________________ was excellent.
5. The restaurant has soft lights, slow music, and beautiful flowers everywhere. The ________________ is romantic.
6. Be sure to make a ________________ in advance. That restaurant is always crowded.

C | Comprehension *Read the descriptions of the restaurants. Write* **AH (Al Hambra)** *or* **T (Topkapi)** *for each statement.*

____ **1.** People come here for the spices.

____ **2.** There is no pork on the menu.

____ **3.** They serve chicken cooked in a ceramic pot.

____ **4.** The reviewer recommends the lamb kebab.

____ **5.** The best dessert is the baklava.

STEP 2 GRAMMAR PRESENTATION

COUNT AND NON-COUNT NOUNS; QUANTIFIERS, ARTICLES

Affirmative Statements

Singular Count Nouns		
	Article or *One*	**Singular Noun**
She wants	**a**	**banana.**
	an	**apple.**
	one	**banana.** **apple.**

Plural Count Nouns		
	Number or Quantifier	**Plural Noun**
He owns	**seven**	**restaurants.**
	a few	
	some	
	a lot of	
	many	

Non-count Nouns		
	Quantifier	**Non-count Noun**
Carol needs	**a little**	**help.** **coffee.**
	some	
	a lot of	

Negative Statements

Singular Count Nouns		
	Article or *One*	**Singular Noun**
I didn't buy	**a**	**pear.**
	an	**apple.**
	one	**pear.** **apple.**

Plural Count Nouns		
	Number or Quantifier	**Plural Noun**
I didn't buy	**two**	**pears.**
	any	
	many	
	a lot of	

Non-count Nouns		
	Quantifier	**Non-count Noun**
I didn't buy	**any**	**milk.**
	much	
	a lot of	

The Definite Article *The*		
Count Noun	**Plural Count Noun**	**Non-count Noun**
I need **the menu.**	She has **the napkins.**	He has **the butter.**

GRAMMAR NOTES

1	***A***, ***an***, and ***the*** are **articles.** An article comes before a noun. It can also come before an adjective + noun.	• **The** pears are delicious. • **a** pear / **a** juicy pear • **an** avocado
2	There are two kinds of nouns: **count nouns** and **non-count nouns.** **Count nouns** are ones that we can count. We cannot count **non-count nouns.**	• **Count:** a pear, an apple • **Non-count:** milk, water, salt

3	Use ***a***, ***an***, or ***one*** before a singular count noun. Use ***a*** before a **consonant sound**. Use ***an*** before a **vowel sound**. **BE CAREFUL!** Do not put *a*, *an*, or a number before a non-count noun. Do not add *-s* or *-es* to a non-count noun.	• **a salad**, **an onion**, **one olive** • **a c**upcake • **an a**vocado • There's **salt** on the table. NOT: There's ~~a salt~~ on the table. NOT: There's ~~salts~~ on the table.
4	***A*** and ***an*** are **indefinite** articles. ***The*** is a **definite** article. We use *a* or *an* to talk about a person or thing for the first time, or when it is not clear which person or thing you mean. We use *the* when it is clear which person or thing you mean.	• (You're hungry. You are looking for a restaurant. You see one and say, "There's **a** restaurant.") I want to go to a **Thai restaurant**, but I don't know a good one. • We ate chicken and rice. **The chicken** was good, but **the rice** was bad.
5	You can use the **definite article *the*** before singular count nouns, plural nouns, and non-count nouns.	• **The restaurant** is open. • **The menus** are there. • **The soup** is delicious.
6	Use ***some*** before plural count nouns and non-count nouns in affirmative statements. Use ***any*** before plural count nouns and non-count nouns in negative statements. We usually use ***any*** in *yes / no* questions. We can also use ***some*** in *yes / no* questions when we offer something or ask for something.	• He wrote **some invitations.** • He drank **some juice**. • He didn't mail **any invitations**. • He didn't drink **any soda**. **YES / NO QUESTIONS** • Did you buy **any** milk? • Did you buy **any** bananas? **AN OFFER** • Would you like **some** juice? **A REQUEST** • Can I have **some** more coffee?
7	Use ***a few*** for small amounts and ***many*** for large amounts with count nouns. Use ***a little*** for small amounts and ***much*** for large amounts with non-count nouns. **BE CAREFUL!** *Much* is not usually used in affirmative statements. We usually use *a lot of* instead.	• I ate **a few peanuts**. • I ate **many grapes**. • I used **a little salt**. • I didn't use **much pepper**. • I drank **a lot of water**. NOT: I drank ~~much water~~.

(continued on next page)

8	Some nouns can be <u>both</u> **count** and **non-count nouns**.	COUNT NOUN • He bought three **cakes** for the party. NON-COUNT NOUN • He ate some **cake**.
	USAGE NOTE: In informal speaking, some non-count nouns are used as count nouns.	• I'd like **two coffees** and **two sodas**. *(I'd like two cups of coffee and two cans of soda.)*

REFERENCE NOTES

See Unit 4, page 43 for count nouns and the indefinite article *a/an*.
See Appendix 5 on page A–5 for spelling and pronunciation rules for plural nouns.
See Appendix 12 on page A–12 for a list of common non-count nouns.

STEP 3 FOCUSED PRACTICE

EXERCISE 1: Discover the Grammar

A | *Read the sentences. Circle the noun in each sentence. Then check (✓) whether the noun is used as a singular count noun, a plural count noun, or a non-count noun.*

	Singular Count Noun	Plural Count Noun	Non-count Noun
1. We ate a little (chicken.)	☐	☐	☑
2. I need some information.	☐	☐	☐
3. There's a menu over there.	☐	☐	☐
4. There aren't many customers.	☐	☐	☐
5. We ate some bread.	☐	☐	☐
6. We need one more napkin.	☐	☐	☐
7. There was one server there.	☐	☐	☐
8. It's about 6 miles (10 kilometers) from here.	☐	☐	☐
9. The coffee is expensive.	☐	☐	☐
10. There aren't any rolls.	☐	☐	☐
11. There isn't any food left.	☐	☐	☐
12. The people here are very kind.	☐	☐	☐

B | *Read the situations. Circle the correct letter.*

1. You're in a restaurant. You need a napkin. Your friend sees one and says,

________________.

a. "Here's a napkin." **b.** "Here's the napkin."

2. You ask about a person's job. Someone says, ________________.

a. "He's the lawyer." **b.** "He's a lawyer."

3. It's your child's 10th birthday. You ask her what she wants for her party. She says,

________________.

a. "Please bake a cake." **b.** "Please bake some cake."

4. You're at a restaurant. You say, ________________.

a. "Please pass some salts." **b.** "Please pass the salt."

EXERCISE 2: *A, An, The*

(Grammar Notes 3–4)

Complete the conversation with **a, an,** *or* **the.**

A: Where's ___the___ (1.) party?

B: At Rectangles Restaurant.

A: Are ________ (2.) Garcias coming?

B: Yes, they are.

A: He's ________ (3.) chef, right?

B: Yes, he is. His wife is ________ (4.) chef too.

A: I hope they like ________ (5.) food at Rectangles.

B: I'm sure they'll like ________ (6.) atmosphere and ________ (7.) service.

A: Where do they work?

B: She works at ________ (8.) Spanish restaurant, and he works at ________ (9.) Peruvian one.

A: Where are their restaurants?

B: ________ (10.) Spanish restaurant is in downtown Manhattan. ________ (11.) Peruvian restaurant is on Queens Boulevard in Rego Park in New York.

EXERCISE 3: *A, An, The*

(Grammar Notes 3–5)

Correct this paragraph. Add **a, an,** *or* **the.** *There are 10 more missing articles.*

Kel Warner is ^a college student. He's English major. He has great part-time job. He writes for school paper. He's food critic. Kel goes to all restaurants in his town and writes about them. He can take friend to restaurants, and school newspaper pays bill. Kel really has wonderful job.

EXERCISE 4: *Some, Any*

(Grammar Note 6)

Complete the conversation with **some** *or* **any.**

Man: Could you bring ___some___ (1.) more bread, please?

Server: Certainly. . . . Here you go. Anything else?

Man: ____________ (2.) water, please. With ice.

Server: Would you like ____________ (3.) water too, ma'am?

Woman: No thanks, I don't feel like having ____________ (4.) water. Hmm, maybe . . . how about a glass of ginger ale?

Server: Sure.

Woman: Also, could we have ____________ (5.) more butter?

Server: Of course.

Man: Do you have ____________ (6.) fish dishes? I don't eat meat, and I don't see ____________ (7.) fish on the menu.

Server: I'm sorry—we don't have fish, but we have ____________ (8.) delicious vegetarian dishes.

EXERCISE 5: *Many, Much*

(Grammar Note 7)

Complete the sentences with **many** *or* **much.**

1. Boston's South End has ___many___ good restaurants.
2. You can find ____________ delicious dishes from different parts of the world including Brazil, France, Italy, Ethiopia, the Middle East, and Korea.

3. There isn't ______________ parking on Saturday night, so it's better to use public transportation.

4. If you don't have ______________ time, try Falafel King. The service is fast, and the food is tasty.

5. If you don't have ______________ money, try the Bakery Café. There are ______________ delicious choices at reasonable prices.

6. ______________ of the best restaurants are on Tremont Street. ______________ people call that street "restaurant row."

EXERCISE 6: *Many, Much*

(Grammar Note 7)

Complete the conversations. Use **much** *or* **many** *and the words from the box.*

choices	people	time
information	restaurants	~~traffic~~

1. **A:** How long did it take you to get to the South End?

   B: There wasn't ______much traffic______, but it still took us an hour to get there.

2. **A:** It was a holiday. Were ______________________ open?

   B: Yes, we had a lot of choices.

3. **A:** Was your boyfriend with you?

   B: Yes, but he didn't have ______________________. He had to leave at 9:00, and we only got to Tremont Street at 8:15.

4. **A:** How ______________________ were you with?

   B: There were six of us. We chose a small Italian restaurant.

5. **A:** How was the food?

   B: Delicious, but there weren't ______________________.

6. **A:** Did you find out about the area from your hotel concierge?

   B: No, he didn't have ______________________. I got everything from the Internet.

EXERCISE 7: *A few*, *A little*, *Much*, or *Many*

(Grammar Note 6)

Complete the sentences with **a few, a little, much,** *or* **many.**

1. We need to get some more apples. We only have ___a few___ left.
2. There's ______________ pea soup in the refrigerator. I didn't finish it all.
3. There's just ______________ milk. We need to stop for more.
4. I want to buy ______________ onions for an onion soup.
5. We don't have ______________ cheese. Let's add that to the list.
6. We don't have ______________ rolls. I'll stop at the bakery and buy some more.
7. Hurry. There isn't ______________ time. The supermarket will close in half an hour.

EXERCISE 8: Editing

Correct the paragraph. There are nine mistakes. The first one is already corrected. Find and correct eight more.

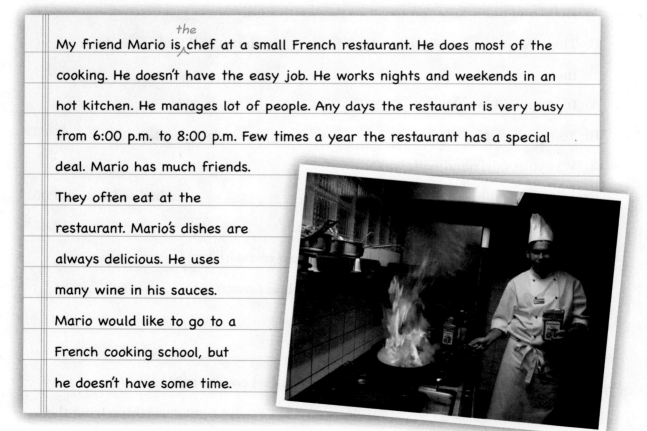

My friend Mario is ^the^ chef at a small French restaurant. He does most of the cooking. He doesn't have the easy job. He works nights and weekends in an hot kitchen. He manages lot of people. Any days the restaurant is very busy from 6:00 p.m. to 8:00 p.m. Few times a year the restaurant has a special deal. Mario has much friends. They often eat at the restaurant. Mario's dishes are always delicious. He uses many wine in his sauces. Mario would like to go to a French cooking school, but he doesn't have some time.

STEP 4 COMMUNICATION PRACTICE

EXERCISE 9: Pronunciation

A | *Read and listen to the Pronunciation Note.*

Pronunciation Note

The indefinite article ***a*** is usually unstressed and sounds like **/ ə /** .

EXAMPLE: a little sugar

B | *Listen and repeat the phrases.*

a delicious dish	**a little butter**	**a little salt**
a few eggs	**a little cheese**	
a few minutes	**a little pepper**	

C | *Now listen and complete the recipe. Then listen again and repeat each sentence.*

1. Put ______________________ in a frying pan.
2. Heat the pan and add ______________________ and ______________________.
3. Scramble the eggs for ______________________.
4. Add ______________________ and ______________________.
5. Enjoy ______________________ of scrambled eggs.

EXERCISE 10: Listening

A | *Listen to a conversation. Miguel helps Theresa prepare for a party. Circle the food Miguel buys.*

cheese	**ice**	**nuts**	**soda**
chips	**ice cream**	**salsa**	**tuna**

B | *Listen again. Answer the questions.*

1. What's the problem?

____

2. Why is Miguel upset?

____

EXERCISE 11: Presentation

A | *Imagine that you are a TV chef. Think of an appetizer, a main course, and a dessert. Write notes on the steps for your presentation. Remember to include articles and quantifiers.*

B | *Now tell about the meal you will prepare. The class asks questions about the meal.*

Example: Good afternoon and welcome to Pietro's Cooking Class. Today I will prepare a meal fit for a king. I'll begin with the salad. It's easy to make. The salad will have a lot of lettuce, a few pieces of carrot, a few walnuts, and some mango. I'll add a little creamy Italian dressing. Next I'll show how to make some carrot soup. Then for the main course I'll prepare lamb shish kebab with rice and some mixed vegetables.

Example: **Student A:** What will you make for dessert?
Student B: For dessert, I will prepare an orange almond cake.

EXERCISE 12: A Restaurant

A | *Think of a restaurant you know. Complete the sentences with true statements about the restaurant. Use the suggestions from the box or your own ideas.*

big selection	fast service	lower prices	organic ingredients
cool design	free parking	music	tables outside
desserts	garden	new drinks	vegetarian choices

Name of restaurant: ____________________

There's a(n) ____________________

There aren't any ____________________

There aren't many ____________________

There isn't any ____________________

There isn't much ____________________

It doesn't have any ____________________

B | *SMALL GROUPS: Tell your group about the restaurant.*

Example: The name of my restaurant is Tiramisu Restaurant.
There's a beautiful garden in the back of Tiramisu Restaurant.
There aren't any rooms for private parties.

EXERCISE 13: Writing

A | *Write a review of the restaurant you described in Exercise 12 or any other restaurant, coffee shop, or cafeteria. Rate the restaurant and give the address and phone number. Tell about the food, the atmosphere, and the prices.*

EXAMPLE:

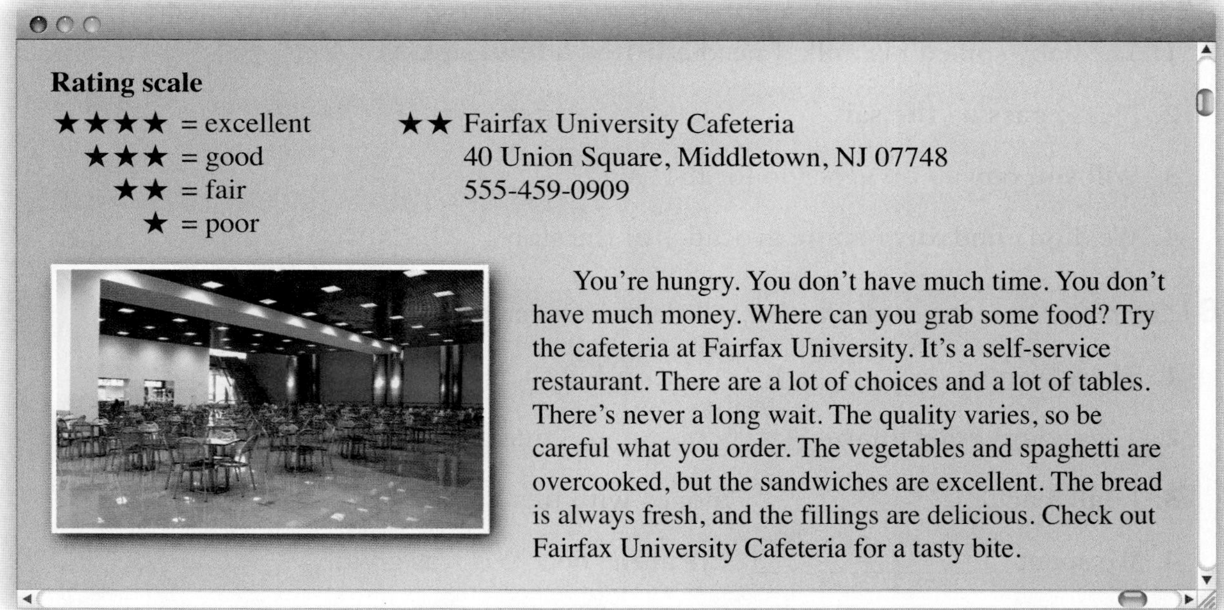

Rating scale

★★★★ = excellent
★★★ = good
★★ = fair
★ = poor

★★ Fairfax University Cafeteria
40 Union Square, Middletown, NJ 07748
555-459-0909

You're hungry. You don't have much time. You don't have much money. Where can you grab some food? Try the cafeteria at Fairfax University. It's a self-service restaurant. There are a lot of choices and a lot of tables. There's never a long wait. The quality varies, so be careful what you order. The vegetables and spaghetti are overcooked, but the sandwiches are excellent. The bread is always fresh, and the fillings are delicious. Check out Fairfax University Cafeteria for a tasty bite.

B | *Check your work. Use the Editing Checklist.*

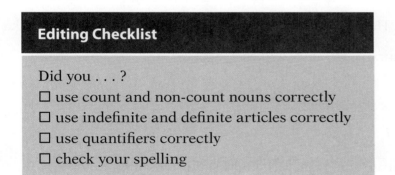

Editing Checklist

Did you . . . ?

- ☐ use count and non-count nouns correctly
- ☐ use indefinite and definite articles correctly
- ☐ use quantifiers correctly
- ☐ check your spelling

UNIT 27 Review

Check your answers on page UR-6.
Do you need to review anything?

A | *Circle the correct words to complete the sentences.*

1. The baby spilled his milk. I need **a little / a few** napkins.
2. Please pass **a / the** salt.
3. Will you buy **a / an** avocado for the salad?
4. We didn't find **any / some** avocados at the store.

B | *Complete the sentences with* **a few, a little, many** *or* **much.**

1. There weren't _________________ people at the party, only 10 or 12.
2. These days I don't have _________________ free time. I work and study.
3. I only had _________________ money with me. I couldn't pay for everyone.
4. We spent _________________ days at the beach. It was great.

C | *Complete the sentences with* **a, an,** *or* **the.**

We bought grandpa ____1.____ watch and ____2.____ tie. I hope he liked ____3.____ watch. He didn't like ____4.____ tie. Next year we'll take him to ____5.____ restaurant. He always likes ____6.____ good meal.

D | *Correct the conversations. There are six mistakes.*

1. **A:** What are you looking for?

   B: I need a little stamps. I wrote any postcards, and I want to mail them.

2. **A:** There isn't some yogurt in the refrigerator. There's only half a container.

   B: There isn't much eggs either. We need to go shopping, but we don't have many time.

UNIT 28 *How much / How many*, Quantifiers, *Enough*, Adverbs of Frequency

DESSERTS, COOKING, AND BAKING

STEP 1 GRAMMAR IN CONTEXT

Before You Read

PAIRS: Ask your partner these questions.

- Do you have a favorite dessert? What is it?
- Where is it from?
- Do you know the recipe?
- How often do you eat it?

Read

Read the conversation. Each month Robert Fertita's English class has a party. A student brings a typical dessert from his or her country and tells the class about it.

WASANA: Carlos, try some of my dessert. It's very popular in Thailand. It's a mango and rice dessert.

CARLOS: No thanks, Wasana. I'm not that hungry.

WASANA: Just try **a little.** I think you'll like it.

CARLOS: OK, but just **a little**. That's **enough**. . . . Hmm. It's not bad.

WASANA: What do you mean, not bad. It's delicious.

CARLOS: Actually, it is pretty good. It's just that color . . . I don't **usually** eat purple rice. **How often** do you have it?

WASANA: My mom **often** makes it when mangoes are in season.

CARLOS: What's in it?

WASANA: Well, there's white rice and black rice, coconut milk, sugar, salt, and mangoes. It's not so hard to prepare.

CARLOS: Maybe I'll try to make it. **How much rice** do you use?

WASANA: A cup of white rice and a cup of black rice. The black rice gives it that dark color.

CARLOS: **How much coconut milk**?

WASANA: Two cups.

CARLOS: And **how many mangoes**?

(continued on next page)

Wasana: Three.

Carlos: I have an idea, Wasana. How about if I buy the ingredients, and I watch you prepare the dessert? Then I'll really know how to make it.

Wasana: OK. But then you have to show me how to make those delicious cookies from your country.

Carlos: You mean the ones with the *dulce de leche* filling?

Wasana: Yes. They were wonderful.

Carlos: Um. I er . . . I just went to the grocery store and bought them. They sell them all over my neighborhood.

After You Read

A | Practice *PAIRS: Now read the conversation aloud.*

B | Vocabulary *Complete the sentences with the words from the box.*

ingredients	in season	neighborhood	prepare	pretty good	taste

1. This lemon chicken has an amazing ________________.
2. Peaches are not ________________ right now, so I bought apples.
3. It takes a long time to ________________ that dish.
4. There are two good fruit and vegetable stores in my ________________.
5. This cake is ________________, but I prefer the ice cream.
6. Do you know the ________________ of this cake? I want to make it.

C | Comprehension *Make the false statements true based on the conversation.*

1. Wasana doesn't want Carlos to try her dessert.
2. Wasana's dessert is popular in Turkey.
3. Carlos likes the look of Wasana's dessert.
4. Wasana's dessert has two kinds of fruit.
5. Carlos brought fruit from his country.

STEP 2 GRAMMAR PRESENTATION

HOW MUCH / HOW MANY, QUANTIFIERS, *ENOUGH*

Questions with *How Much*		
How Much	**Non-count Noun**	
How much	**milk**	do you need? did she buy?

Answers
Quantifier
A lot. (A lot of milk.) **Two quarts.** (Two quarts of milk.) **A carton.** (A carton of milk.) **A glass.** (A glass of milk.) **A cup.** (A cup of milk.) **A little.** (A little milk.)

Questions with *How Many*		
How Many	**Plural Count Noun**	
How many	**apples**	do we need? did he buy?

Answers
Quantifier
A lot. (A lot of apples.) **One bag.** (One bag of apples.) **Two pounds.** (Two pounds of apples.) **One or two.** (One or two apples.) **A few.** (A few apples.)

Statements with *Enough*			
		Enough	**Noun (Plural Count or Non-count)**
We	have don't have	**enough**	**vegetables**. **meat**.

Questions with *Enough*			
		Enough	**Noun (Plural Count or Non-count)**
Do you Does he	have	**enough**	**vegetables**? **milk**?

QUESTIONS ABOUT FREQUENCY

Questions with *How Often*			
How often	**do**	I you we they	**bake**? **cook**?
	does	he she	
		it	**break**?

Answers
Three times a day. Every (Sunday). Once a week. Rarely. Once in a while. Never.

ADVERBS AND EXPRESSIONS OF FREQUENCY

Adverbs of Frequency			
Subject	**Adverb**	**Verb**	
I	**usually** **almost never**	**cook**	on Tuesdays.
He She It		**cooks**	
We You* They		**cook**	

Adverbs of Frequency with *Be*			
Subject	***Be***	**Adverb**	
I	**am**	**usually** **almost never**	busy.
He She It	**is**		
We You* They	**are**		

**You* is both singular and plural.

Adverbs of Frequency	
always	100%
almost always	
frequently	
usually / often	
sometimes	50%
rarely / seldom	
almost never	
never	0%

Expressions of Frequency	
Emiko cooks	every day. twice (a day). three times (a month). several times (a year). once in a while.

GRAMMAR NOTES

1	Use ***how much*** or ***how many*** to ask about quantity. Use ***how much*** with non-count nouns. Use ***how many*** with count nouns. Use ***a little*** with non-count nouns. Use ***a few*** with count nouns.	**A: How much** juice do you have? **B: A little.** OR I have **a little juice**. **A: How many** lemons do you need? **B: A few.** OR We need **a few** lemons.
2	It is not necessary to repeat the noun after *how much* or *how many* if the noun was named before or if the noun is understood.	**A: How much** does it cost? *(How much money is it?)* **B:** Ten dollars. **A:** I bought some cupcakes. **B: How many did you buy**? *(How many cupcakes did you buy?)*
3	You can **count non-count nouns** by using **measure words** or **containers**. Measure words include *a quart, a liter, an ounce, a kilogram, a teaspoon*, and *a tablespoon*. Containers include *a cup, a glass, a can, a jar*, and *a box*.	• Please get me **one quart of milk**. • He drank **two glasses of water**.

4	***Enough*** means the amount you need. Use *enough* before plural count nouns and non-count nouns. ***Not enough*** means less than the amount you need. Use *not enough* before plural count nouns and non-count nouns.	• We have **enough eggs**. *(We need six eggs, and we have six eggs.)* • We have **enough juice**. • There **aren't enough apples**. • There **isn't enough milk**.
5	***How often*** asks questions about **frequency**. *How often* is usually used with the simple present or simple past. It is rarely used with the present progressive.	• **How often** do you bake? NOT: How often ~~are you baking?~~
6	**Adverbs** and **expressions of frequency** tell **how often** we do something. Adverbs and expressions of frequency are often used with the simple present. They rarely occur with the present progressive.	• Tim **always** shops at the Farmer's Market. • Marta goes to class **every day**. • They **usually** open the market at 9:00. NOT: They ~~are usually opening~~ the market at 9:00.
7	Adverbs of frequency usually come **after the verb *be***. They usually come **before other verbs** in the simple present. ***Sometimes***, ***usually***, and ***often*** can also come at the beginning of a sentence. **BE CAREFUL!** Don't begin a sentence with ***never*** or ***always***. **BE CAREFUL!** Don't use negative adverbs of frequency (*rarely, seldom, almost never*) in negative sentences.	• Yoko **is usually** on time. She **isn't usually** late. • She **rarely eats** dessert. • She **doesn't often eat** dessert. • He **sometimes goes** to the bakery. • **Sometimes** he **goes** to the bakery. • I **never** cook. NOT: ~~Never~~ I cook. NOT: I ~~rarely don't~~ cook.
8	**Expressions of frequency** are time markers. They usually come at the beginning or at the end of a sentence.	• He eats an orange **every day**. • **Every week** she goes to the bakery.

REFERENCE NOTES

See Unit 35 page 411 for a discussion of *enough* after an adjective.
See Appendix 12, page A-12 for a list of quantity expressions.

STEP 3 FOCUSED PRACTICE

EXERCISE 1: Discover the Grammar

A | *Underline the noun in each phrase. Then check (✓) the category.*

	Singular Count Noun	Plural Count Noun	Non-count Noun
how much milk			✓
how many eggs			
a lot of raisins			
enough sugar			
a little juice			
a lemon			

B | *Underline the adverbs of frequency. Circle the expressions of frequency.*

1. He almost always cooks.

2. She usually bakes.

3. Once in a while he bakes.

4. Every weekend they go to a café.

5. They often meet friends there.

6. It is frequently crowded.

EXERCISE 2: *How much / How many / How often* *(Grammar Notes 1–2, 4)*

Complete the conversations with **How much, How many,** *or* **How often.** *Complete the answers with* **much, many,** *or* **often.**

1. A: ___How many___ meals do you prepare in a week?

B: Not ________________. I eat breakfast and lunch at school.

2. A: ________________ does he eat out?

B: Not ________________. He likes to eat at home.

3. A: On average ________________ time does it take you to prepare dinner?

B: Not ________________. Only about 15 or 20 minutes.

4. A: ________________ times a week do you shop for food?

B: Not ________________. We usually shop once or twice a week.

5. A: ________________ do they spend on food each week?

B: Not ________________. They shop when there are sales.

6. A: ________________ do you bake?

B: Not ________________. There's a great bakery in our neighborhood.

EXERCISE 3: Word Order: Adverbs and Expressions of Frequency
(Grammar Notes 5–7)

Write sentences with the words in parentheses.

1. (chocolate / Hugo / and / Every afternoon / has coffee / a piece of)

   Every afternoon Hugo has coffee and a piece of chocolate.

2. (hot / is / always / The coffee)

   ____

3. (almost always / dark / is / The chocolate)

   ____

4. (never / It / white chocolate / is)

   ____

5. (Hugo / never drinks / in the evening / coffee)

   ____

6. (hot chocolate / drinks / usually / He)

   ____

7. (drinks / Sometimes / he / ginger tea)

   ____

EXERCISE 4: *Enough*
(Grammar Note 4)

Complete the sentences with **enough** *and the words from the box.*

chairs	cupcakes	drinks	ice	plates	room	~~time~~

1. We can't bake a cake. There isn't ___enough time___. People will be here soon.
2. People get thirsty. Are there ____________________?
3. Is there ____________________ for the drinks? The drinks aren't cold.
4. You can't put those cupcakes on that table. There isn't ____________________.
5. There aren't ____________________ for everyone. Why don't you cut them in half?
6. People won't want to stand. Are there ____________________?
7. People will want to put their dessert on something. Are there ____________________?

EXERCISE 5: Containers

(Grammar Note 3)

Complete the conversation with the words in parentheses. Write the correct words.

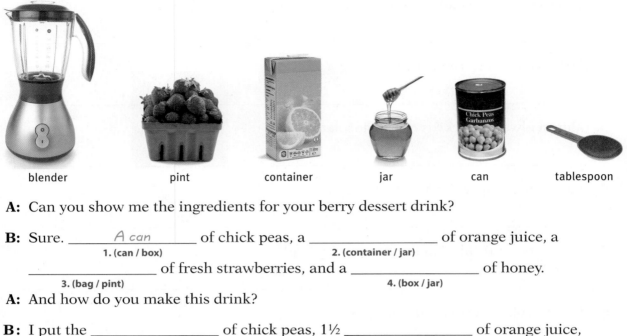

blender pint container jar can tablespoon

A: Can you show me the ingredients for your berry dessert drink?

B: Sure. ___A can___ (1. (can / box)) of chick peas, a ________ (2. (container / jar)) of orange juice, a ________ (3. (bag / pint)) of fresh strawberries, and a ________ (4. (box / jar)) of honey.

A: And how do you make this drink?

B: I put the ________ (5. (can / box)) of chick peas, 1½ ________ (6. (cups / bags)) of orange juice, 2 ________ (7. (cups / cans)) of strawberries, and 2 or 3 ________ (8. (tablespoons / cans)) of honey in a blender. When it's smooth, I add six ice cubes. Then I blend it again. Delicious!

EXERCISE 6: Editing

Correct the conversations. There are seven mistakes. The first mistake is already corrected. Find and correct six more.

1. **A:** How ~~much~~ many cookies are there in the box?

   B: Only one. Mary ate the rest.

2. **A:** How often do you bake?

   B: Always I bake on the weekend.

3. **A:** Do we have cake enough for everyone?

   B: Yes, we do.

4. **A:** How many flour do you need?

   B: Two cups.

5. **A:** How many egg are there in the cake? And how much sugars?

   B: Four eggs and three cup of sugar.

STEP 4 COMMUNICATION PRACTICE

EXERCISE 7: Pronunciation

A | *Read and listen to the Pronunciation Note.*

Pronunciation Note

Sometimes when people get hurt they say, "Ow." That's the **/ aʊ /** sound in words such as ***how*** or ***flour***.

B | *Listen and underline the / aʊ / sound in the sentences.*

1. Now, add the eggs.
2. How much brown sugar do you need?
3. You need about two cups of sugar.
4. How many pounds of flour did you buy?
5. Take the cupcakes out of the oven.
6. How many ounces of milk does this need?

C | *Listen again and repeat the sentences.*

EXERCISE 8: Listening

A | *Listen to a conversation. Write* **T** (**True**) *or* **F** (**False**) *for each statement.*

____ 1. Robert is giving Laura a recipe.

____ 2. Laura thinks Robert's red velvet cupcakes are good.

____ 3. Robert doesn't want to give Laura the recipe.

____ 4. Laura writes down the recipe.

B | *Listen again and check (✓) the ingredients in the recipe.*

✓ flour	____ butter	____ red food color
____ cocoa powder	____ eggs	____ vanilla extract
____ baking soda	____ sour cream	____ cream
____ salt	____ milk	____ sugar

EXERCISE 9: Survey

Survey five students. Report the results to the class. Ask "How often do you ________________________________?" with the activities in the list.

bake   cook   do dishes   eat dessert   eat out   go to a bakery

EXAMPLE: Mi Young frequently eats dessert. But she rarely bakes or cooks. So she often eats out. Sometimes she eats at a bakery.

EXERCISE 10: Information Gap

Work in pairs. **Student A,** *follow the instructions on this page.* **Student B,** *turn to page 332* *and follow the instructions there.*

1. Look at the list of ingredients. Ask your partner questions to find out how much you need of each ingredient to make chocolate chip cookies. Write the amounts.

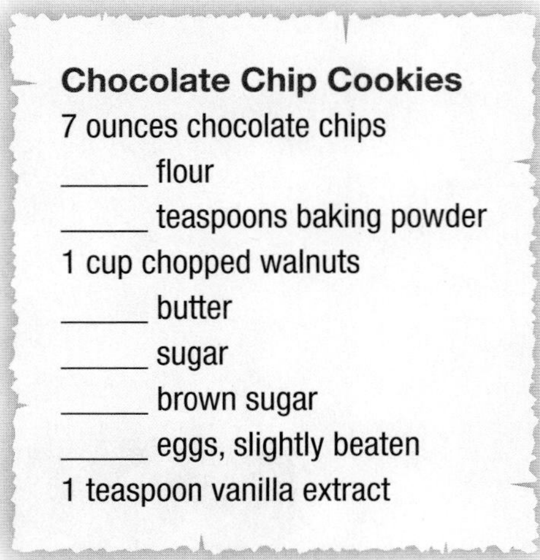

Chocolate Chip Cookies
7 ounces chocolate chips
_____ flour
_____ teaspoons baking powder
1 cup chopped walnuts
_____ butter
_____ sugar
_____ brown sugar
_____ eggs, slightly beaten
1 teaspoon vanilla extract

EXAMPLE: STUDENT A: How much flour do you use for the chocolate chip cookies?
STUDENT B: Two and half cups.

2. Now look at the list of ingredients for apple pie. Answer your partner's questions.

Apple Pie

The Crust
2 cups flour
1 teaspoon salt
2/3 cup shortening
5 tablespoons cold water

The Filling
1/3 cup sugar
1/4 cup flour
1/2 teaspoon ground cinnamon
1/2 teaspoon ground nutmeg
a pinch of salt
8 medium-size apples
2 tablespoons butter

EXAMPLE: STUDENT B: How much flour do you use in the apple pie crust?
STUDENT A: Two cups of flour.

EXERCISE 11: Group Presentation

GROUPS: You are preparing dessert for 50 people. Decide what you will serve and how much. Be specific and include different kinds of desserts. Each student talks about one or two of the desserts. Suggestions: nuts, cheese, fruit, dessert drinks, cakes, cookies, mocha ice cream, and flan.

EXAMPLE: STUDENT A: I'm going to buy a variety of nuts. I'm going to get a pound of salty cashews and a pound of unsalted peanuts. I'm also going to buy some almonds and raisins. I like the combination of a salty and sweet dessert.

STUDENT B: I'm going to bake 30 red velvet cupcakes. I'm going to frost half of them and leave half of them without frosting.

STUDENT C: I'm going to buy fresh fruit. I'm going to buy pears, grapes, and strawberries.

EXERCISE 12: Writing

A | *Describe the desserts your group bought for the party in Exercise 11. Use quantity expressions where possible.*

EXAMPLE: We prepared desserts for 50 people. We served nuts, cakes, cookies, fresh fruit, cheese, and crackers. We brought 3 pounds of mixed nuts. Sonia baked a chocolate cake and Ana made three dozen chocolate chip cookies. Mohammed brought fresh fruit. He brought 2 pounds of pears, apples, and two pineapples. Pierre brought a lot of different kinds of cheese and crackers.

B | *Check your work. Use the Editing Checklist.*

Editing Checklist

Did you . . . ?

☐ use quantity expressions correctly

☐ check your spelling

Information Gap for Student B

1. Look at the list of ingredients for chocolate chip cookies. Answer your partner's questions.

Chocolate Chip Cookies
7 ounces of chocolate chips
2 1/2 cups flour
3 teaspoons baking powder
1 cup chopped walnuts
1 cup butter
3/4 cup sugar
3/4 cup brown sugar
2 eggs, slightly beaten
1 teaspoon vanilla extract

Example: **Student A:** How much flour do you use for the chocolate chip cookies?
Student B: Two and a half cups.

2. Now look at the list of ingredients. Then ask your partner questions to find out how much you need of each ingredient to make apple pie. Write the amounts.

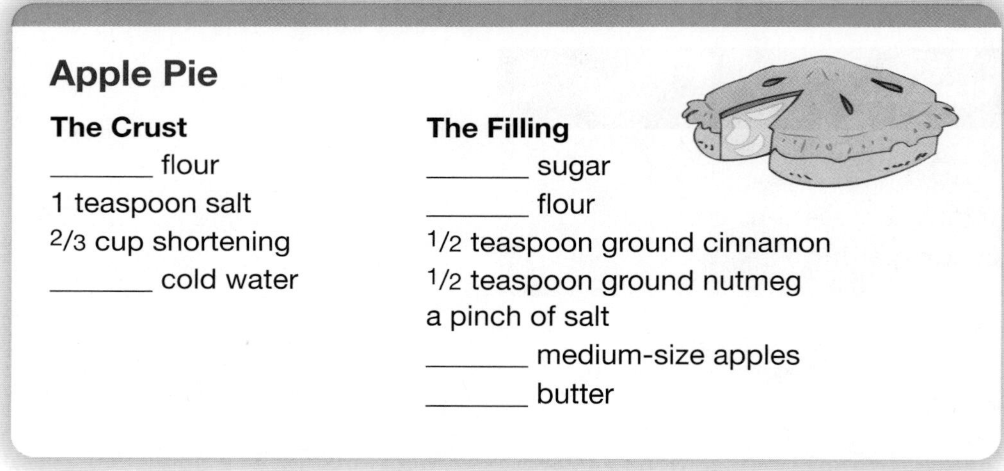

Apple Pie

The Crust
_______ flour
1 teaspoon salt
2/3 cup shortening
_______ cold water

The Filling
_______ sugar
_______ flour
1/2 teaspoon ground cinnamon
1/2 teaspoon ground nutmeg
a pinch of salt
_______ medium-size apples
_______ butter

Example: **Student B:** How much flour do you use in the apple pie crust?
Student A: Two cups of flour.

UNIT 28 Review

Check your answers on page UR-6.
Do you need to review anything?

A | *Complete the sentences with* **How many** *or* **How much.**

1. ____________ people went to the party?
2. ____________ noise was there?
3. ____________ servers did they hire?
4. ____________ bread did he eat?
5. ____________ desserts did they bring?

B | *Write questions with the words in parentheses. Begin with* **How many, How much,** *or* **How often.**

1. ____________
   (you / go to the movies)
2. ____________
   (close friends / you have)
3. ____________
   (time / you spend online)
4. ____________
   (people / live in your home)
5. ____________
   (you / check email)

C | *Write sentences with the words in parentheses.*

1. ____________
   (usually / I / a few times a week / bake)
2. ____________
   (in the house / They / have / food / never / enough)
3. ____________
   (soccer / we / Every weekend / play / in the park)
4. ____________
   (a / He / glass / spilled / of grape juice)
5. ____________
   (salt / She / a little / added / to the soup)

D | *Correct the sentences. There are five mistakes.*

1. Never I eat breakfast at home.
2. She once in a while bakes.
3. Do you have milk enough?
4. How much tomatoes did they buy?
5. I rarely don't cook.

UNIT 29 *Too much / Too many, Too* + Adjective

THE RIGHT PLACE TO LIVE

STEP 1 GRAMMAR IN CONTEXT

Before You Read

Does your city or town have any of these problems? Check (✓) them.

- ❑ too much noise or traffic
- ❑ not enough jobs
- ❑ too few parking spaces
- ❑ too much crime
- ❑ too few parks
- ❑ too hot or too cold

Read

Read the online article about three U.S. cities. Which of these cities would you want to live in most?

DREAM LOCATIONS

Home | Lifestyle | Photos

Miami Beach

Some call my town *The American Riviera*. Others say it's the *Latin Hollywood*. For me, it's the best place to live. We have sunny weather, beautiful sandy beaches, and graceful palm trees. From January to March the sky is mostly blue, and the temperature is in the 70s almost every day. There are a lot of water activities, and the night life is great. It is a cosmopolitan area with people from all over the world. But the climate isn't perfect.

In the summer months the weather is **too hot** and **humid**, and storms are common. Public transportation isn't very good. There are **too few busses**, and there isn't a subway, so there's **too much traffic**. It's hard to find a good job. Unemployment is high, and most salaries are low. Some say they pay you here in sunshine. But if you have a job, and you like warm weather, sandy beaches, and a rich nightlife, Miami Beach is a great place to live.

urban living

Times Square, New York City

Some say this city is the capital of the world. It has a rich cultural life and offers lots of things to do. There are great theaters, restaurants, museums, sports stadiums, and a wonderful nightlife. There are job opportunities, good health care, and a truly multicultural atmosphere with people from all over the world. It's called the city that never sleeps.

But housing is much **too expensive**. You pay a fortune to live in an apartment the size of a closet. The schools are often **too crowded**. There is a good subway system, but there is **too much traffic**. Still, this is a city of opportunity, and I'd rather live here with 8 million other New Yorkers than any other place on earth.

Kenai Peninsula, Alaska

I find most cities **too busy**, **too dirty** with **too much traffic**, **pollution**, and **crime**. They also have **too many people**, and **too few animals**. That's why I love my town of Kenai in the Kenai Peninsula of Alaska. Here the air is clean, and you can hike and fish and see the stars at night. Of course, it's **too cold** for some people, and there's **too little sunlight** for others. But I'm happy here in this small town far away from the hubbub[1] of big city life.

[1]***hubbub:*** confusion

After You Read

A | Practice *PAIRS: Read the article again aloud. Take turns reading each section.*

B | Vocabulary *Complete the sentences with the words from the box.*

climate	crime	free time	housing	pollution	unemployment

1. The ________________ here is awful. Summers are too hot, and winters are too cold.
2. The ________________ from the factories is causing health problems among children in the area.
3. That's a very safe area. There is almost no ________________.
4. The government is building ________________ for the poor of the city.
5. We're working too much. We have no ________________.
6. ________________ is low here, so he expects to find a good job soon.

C | Comprehension *Read the statements. Write* **MB (Miami Beach), NYC (New York City),** *or* **K (Kenai),** *based on the reading. Some statements are true for more than one place.*

_______ **1.** There's a lot of traffic.

_______ **2.** It has a great nightlife.

_______ **3.** It's great for hiking.

_______ **4.** There are many wild animals.

_______ **5.** Housing is very expensive.

_______ **6.** The transportation system is poor.

_______ **7.** People here feel close to nature.

_______ **8.** This city has a lot of opportunities.

STEP 2 GRAMMAR PRESENTATION

TOO MUCH / TOO MANY / TOO + ADJECTIVE

	Too Many / Too Few	Plural Count Noun
There are	**too many**	**cars**.
	too few	**parking spaces**.

	Too Much / Too Little	Non-count Noun
There is	**too much**	**noise**.
	too little	**light**.

	Too	Adjective
It's	**too**	**hot**.
		cold.

GRAMMAR NOTES

1 ***Too many*** and ***too much*** mean "more than the right amount." These words usually have a negative meaning. Use *too many* before plural count nouns. Use *too much* before non-count nouns.
Too few is the opposite of *too many*.
Too little is the opposite of *too much*.
Both *too few* and *too little* mean "not enough." These words usually have a negative meaning. Use *too few* with count nouns. Use *too little* with non-count nouns.

- **Too many** students registered for that course. *(There was room for 10 students. Fifteen people registered.)*
- It costs **too much** money. *(We can't afford it.)*
- There were **too few** books. *(There were books for five people, but seven people needed books.)*
- There was **too little** time. *(We couldn't finish.)*

2 Use ***too*** + **adjective** to say that something has a negative result.

- The water is **too cold**. *(We can't swim here.)*

REFERENCE NOTE

See Unit 35, page 411 for more about *too* + adjective and *very*.

STEP 3 FOCUSED PRACTICE

EXERCISE 1: Discover the Grammar

Underline the adjectives that follow **too.** *Circle the nouns that follow* **too much, too many, too few,** *and* **too little.**

1. Housing is too expensive there. Let's not move there.
2. They're building a new school. This school is too crowded.
3. The commute to work was too long. It took two hours each way.
4. There are too many cars on the highway. Let's take a different route.
5. I have too little information about that neighborhood. I don't want to rent a place without more information.
6. There's too much crime in that area.
7. There are too few jobs in that city. People are moving away.

EXERCISE 2: *Too much / Too many*

(Grammar Note 1)

Complete the sentences with **too many** *or* **too much** *and the words from the box.*

crime	noise	pollution	rats	storms	~~unemployment~~

1. Jobs are hard to find. There's *too much unemployment* in this town.
2. The climate isn't good. There are ____________________.
3. The streets aren't safe. There's ____________________.
4. It's often hard to breathe here. There's ____________________.
5. There's ____________________ in that neighborhood. We won't be able to sleep at night.
6. There are ____________________ in that area. They should do something to get rid of them.

EXERCISE 3: *Too* + Adjective

(Grammar Note 2)

Add **too** *before the adjective in each sentence.*

1. Homes are ^too expensive in that area. That's why people can't afford to live there.
2. We don't want to move there. The commute is long. It's two hours to downtown.
3. The train is crowded at this time. Let's take a later train.
4. That house is small for you. There are six people in your family. How will you manage?
5. It's not small for us. We love the location. We can manage.
6. I don't like that area. Winters are long.

EXERCISE 4: *Too few / Too little*

(Grammar Note 1)

Complete the conversations. Use **There is, There are,** *or* **There was,** *and* **too few** *or* **too little** *and the ideas in parentheses.*

1. **A:** What's the problem?

   B: ____There are too few doctors____ in that hospital. The hospital
   (not enough doctors)
   administration needs to hire more doctors or people's health will suffer.

2. **A:** Why is the grass brown?

   B: ________________________ this past summer.
   (not enough rain)

3. **A:** Why are so many people moving?

   B: ________________________ in this area.
   (not enough jobs)

4. **A:** Why are all those people moving so far out?

   B: ________________________ in the center of town.
   (not enough affordable housing)

5. **A:** ________________________ this area.
   (not enough schools)

   B: That's true, but the city is planning to build two new schools.

6. **A:** ________________________ around here.
   (not enough parks)

   B: I agree. The city planners need to build more parks.

EXERCISE 5: *Too much / Too many / Too few / Too little / Too* *(Grammar Notes 1–2)*

Complete the conversations with **too, too many, too much, too few,** *or* **too little.**

1. **A:** What's wrong with Middletown?

   B: The climate. It gets ___too much___ rain and humidity. It's damp most of the year.

2. **A:** Why don't you want to move to Rockford?

   B: The climate there is OK, but the health care is terrible. There are ______________ doctors and hospitals.

3. **A:** How about moving to Newtown?

   B: It's boring. There are ______________ things to do.

4. **A:** How was the new restaurant on Spring Street?

   B: It was ______________ dark. I wasn't able to read the menu or see my food. There was ______________ light.

5. **A:** Do you go to that beach?

   B: Not in the summer. There are ______________ people at that time of year. It's ______________ crowded.

6. **A:** Did you take the job?

   B: No. The salary was ______________ low, and there were ______________ holidays and sick days.

7. **A:** Am I ______________ late for the talk about the environment?

   B: Yes, it began an hour ago.

8. **A:** Which car did you buy, the Cruiser or the Mercedes?

   B: Neither. The Mercedes was ______________ expensive, and the Cruiser had ______________ problems.

EXERCISE 6: Editing

Correct the conversations. There are seven mistakes. The first mistake is already corrected. Find and correct six more.

1. **A:** I'd like to move to the suburbs. The city is ^too^ noisy for me.

   B: Not me. I think the suburbs are quiet.

2. **A:** What's wrong with that company?

   B: There are too many managers and too little workers.

3. **A:** Did you buy that apartment?

   B: No. It was too money for too few space.

4. **A:** Don't go by bus. It will take too many time. Take the train. It's a lot faster.

   B: Yes, but it's too much expensive. The bus is half the price.

STEP 4 COMMUNICATION PRACTICE

EXERCISE 7: Pronunciation

A | *Read and listen to the Pronunciation Note.*

Pronunciation Note

- To pronounce **/ t /** as in ***time***, touch the upper gum ridge with your tongue.
- To pronounce **/ θ /** as in ***three*** or **/ ð /** as in ***this***, place your tongue tip between your upper and lower front teeth.
- The **/ t /** and **/ θ /** sounds are not voiced. The vocal cords do not vibrate.
- The **/ ð /** sound is voiced. The vocal cords vibrate.

B | *Listen. Then place your hand on your throat and repeat the words.*

/ t / not voiced	/ θ / not voiced	/ ð / voiced
ten		then
tear		there
tease		these
tree	three	
taught	thought	
tin	thin	

C | *Listen and underline the / **t** / sound. Underline the / **θ** / sound twice. Circle the / **ð** / sound.*

1. I thought Ted taught about the environment.
2. There are three trees in front of their house.
3. Is it true that the technician went through the house in only thirty minutes?

D | *Listen again and repeat each sentence.*

EXERCISE 8: Listening

A | *A couple looked at three apartments. Listen to their conversation with a real estate salesperson. Which apartment did the couple like the most? Circle the correct letter.*

a. the first one **b.** the second one **c.** the third one

B | *Listen again and complete the chart.*

	What They Liked	What They Didn't Like
First apartment		
Second apartment		
Third apartment		

EXERCISE 9: Role Play

Act out a situation with a partner. Use **too, too much, too many, too few,** *or* **too little,** *in your conversation.*

Situation 1:

A salesperson is trying to convince a customer to rent a tiny apartment that is far from everything.

Situation 2:

Two friends live in the same big city. One friend wants to move away from the city. The other wants to stay.

EXAMPLE: **A:** I want to move to Australia for a few years.
B: Don't move! It's too far away!

EXERCISE 10: Describe Your City

SMALL GROUPS: Write four good things and four bad things about the city or town you are in. Use **too, too much, too many, too few,** *and* **too little.**

EXAMPLE:

Good	**Bad**
There's a wonderful concert hall here.	There are too few parking spaces.
There isn't much pollution here.	There are too few bicycle paths.

EXERCISE 11: Writing

A | *Write an email to a newspaper. Complain about one aspect of life in your city. Use two of the following:* **too, too much, too many, too few,** *or* **too little.**

EXAMPLE: Young people are the future of this city, but there are too few jobs for them here. Too many young people have nothing to do. The city needs to help them find jobs. In the past, the city spent too much money on roads and highways and too little on job training. Many young people don't have good workplace skills. The city needs to offer job training and practical skills. The city should offer courses in how to write a resumé, take an interview, and get and keep a job. This newspaper complained that too many young people are getting into trouble. With good jobs, young people will stay out of trouble.

B | *Check your work. Use the Editing Checklist.*

Editing Checklist

Did you . . . ?

☐ use ***too many***, ***too much***, ***too little***, ***too few***, and ***too*** correctly

☐ check your spelling

UNIT 29 Review

Check your answers on page UR-6.
Do you need to review anything?

A | *Add* **too, too much,** *or* **too many** *to each sentence. Use a ^ symbol.*

1. That movie was long. I didn't enjoy it.
2. We have homework. We can't go to the movies today.
3. I bought milk. Who's going to drink it?
4. There are trucks on that road. Let's take another route.
5. It takes time to get there by bus. Let's take the train.

B | *Complete the sentences with* **too, too much, too many, too little,** *or* **too few.**

1. That desert town is ________________ hot, and it gets ________________ rain.
2. Unemployment is high in that area. There are ________________ jobs.
3. That town is not safe. There is ________________ crime.
4. This area has ________________ dishonest politicians.

C | *Rewrite the sentences with* **too little** *or* **too few.**

1. There's not enough rain. ____
2. There aren't enough subways. ____
3. There's not enough sunlight. ____
4. There aren't enough traffic lights. ____
5. There isn't enough water. ____

D | *Correct the paragraph. There are five mistakes.*

The climate here is terrible. It gets too much hot in the summer and too cold in the winter. There's too many snow and ice. Winters are to long. There are too little comfortable days with mild temperatures and blue skies. Also, there's too many air pollution from all the traffic on the streets. I want to move.

From Grammar to Writing

A Business Letter

1 | *PAIRS: When we write a business letter, we follow a certain style. We use this style for all letters that are not to friends or relatives. Look at the business letter and answer the questions.*

Rua Rio de Janeiro 12 (1)
São Paulo, Brasil

March 12, _______ (2)

Lee Spencer, Director (3)
International English Language Institute
Hunter College
New York, New York 10021

Dear Mr. Spencer: (4)

I am interested in attending Hunter College's (5)
International English Language Institute in the fall.

Would you please send me an application and a catalog of your courses?

Thank you for your prompt attention to this request. (6)

Sincerely yours, (7)
João Lima (8)
João Lima

1. Where does your address belong?

____

____

2. Where does the date belong?

____

____

3. Where does the name and the address of the person you are writing to belong?

____

____

4. How do you address the person you are writing to?

____

____

5. What do you do in the first sentence?

____

6. What does the last line of the letter say?

____

7. How do you end the letter?

____

8. What do you write last?

____

2 | *Read the rules we use to write a business letter.*

1. Write your address at the top left of the page.
2. Write the date below your address.
3. Skip at least two lines. Write the name and address of the person you are writing to on the left margin below the date.
4. When you write a letter, it's best to write to a person by name. If you don't know the person's name, you may write "Dear Sir / Madam:" or "To Whom It May Concern:"; be sure to use a colon (:) after the name.
5. In your first sentence, explain what you want.
6. In the last line of your letter, you usually thank the person you are writing to.
7. You may end a letter with "Sincerely yours" or "Yours truly."
8. Finally, write your signature, and write your name below your signature.

3 | *Write one of the following business letters. Follow the rules in Part 2.*

1. Ask for a bulletin of courses and an application for a language program.
2. Ask for a list of moderately priced apartments near the college.

4 | *Exchange letters with a partner. Did your partner follow the directions? Correct any mistakes in grammar and spelling.*

5 | *Talk to your partner. Discuss the mistakes you made. Then rewrite your own paper and make any necessary changes.*

Modals: Requests, Advice, Necessity

UNIT	GRAMMAR FOCUS	THEME
30	Advice: *Should, Ought to, Had better*	Dos and Don'ts of the Business World
31	Requests, Desires, and Offers: *Would you, Could you, Can you . . . ?, I'd like . . .*	Neighbors
32	Necessity: *Have to, Don't have to, Must, Mustn't*	Rules at School

UNIT 30

Advice: *Should, Ought to, Had better*

DOS AND DON'TS OF THE BUSINESS WORLD

STEP 1 GRAMMAR IN CONTEXT

Before You Read

PAIRS: Look at the photo of Angelina Jolie and Cambodian Prime Minister Hun Sen. In the United States, a firm handshake is important in business. Is it important in other countries too? Discuss with your partner.

Read

Read the online article about doing business in Chile and Egypt.

Global Business

BUSINESS NEWS | MONEY MARKETS | POLITICS | SMALL BUSINESS | SEARCH:

GLOBAL BUSINESS

It's always a good idea for business people to know the customs of people in the place they are doing business. If you don't know the customs, you might insult someone and lose a business deal. Here is some advice for anyone headed for[1] Chile.

First of all, when **should** you go? Chileans usually take vacations in January and February so you **should not plan** a business trip during those two months. Many offices will be closed for the summer vacation.

Next, how **should** you greet people at business meetings? When attending a business meeting in Chile, you **ought to greet** and **shake hands** with everyone. Later at business dinners and receptions, men sometimes greet other men with hugs. Women often hug and touch cheeks while kissing the air. You **should not be** surprised to get a hug or kiss from a Chilean you know. During a meal, you **should keep** your hands on the table, not in your lap.

In Chile, an open palm upward with the fingers separated means "stupid." You **should avoid** making this gesture. And beware[2]! Slapping your right fist[3] into your left open palm[4] is very impolite. You**'d better not make** that gesture, or you may insult or anger someone.

[1] ***headed for:*** going to
[2] ***beware:*** be on guard against
[3] ***fist:*** a hand with fingers closed tightly together
[4] ***palm:*** the inside of hand

Now in Egypt, you **should not expect** to do business on Fridays. It is the Muslim day of rest. Also, throughout the Arab world, people use the Islamic calendar (also called Muslim calendar or Hijri calendar) and the Western calendar. To avoid confusion, you **should put** two dates on paperwork—the Hijri (Islamic) date and the Gregorian (Western) date.

If you're invited for a meal, you **should eat** with your right hand. In many countries with large Muslim and Hindu populations, people consider the left hand unclean. In Egypt leaving a little food is a sign that you are full, so you **shouldn't eat** everything on your plate. Also, you**'d better not add** salt to your food or you might insult the cook.

What do you know about sitting in Egypt? You **should** never **sit** with legs crossed or **show** the sole[5] of your shoe. In Arab culture, it is a big insult to show the bottom of the foot.

So remember, before you go to another country to do business, learn about the culture. And remember when you're in that country, try and "do as the Romans do."[6]

In the Middle East, it is not polite to cross legs.

[5] ***sole:*** the bottom of foot or shoe

[6] ***"do as the Romans do":*** copy the people in the place you are visiting

After You Read

A | Practice *PAIRS: Now read the article aloud. Take turns reading each paragraph.*

B | Vocabulary *Complete the sentences with the words from the box.*

business receptions	confusion	consider	customs	insult

1. Business people should know the ________________ of the countries they visit.
2. At Chilean ________________, men greet other men with hugs.
3. To avoid ________________, put the Western and Islamic date on this paperwork.
4. People in the United States ________________ a firm handshake is important.
5. It is an ________________ to show the bottom of your foot in the Middle East.

C | Comprehension *Write* **T (True)** *or* **F (False)**.

_____ **1.** Chileans often take vacations in July and August.

_____ **2.** Offices in Chile are often closed in February.

_____ **3.** When businessmen meet in Chile at dinners, they do not hug.

_____ **4.** When you eat a meal in Chile, you should keep your hands in your lap.

_____ **5.** Egyptians do business on Friday, Saturday, and Sunday.

_____ **6.** You should not use your right hand when you eat in Egypt.

_____ **7.** You should not add salt to your food in an Egyptian home.

STEP 2 GRAMMAR PRESENTATION

MODALS

Should, *Shouldn't*, and *Ought to*

Affirmative Statements		
Subject	***Should / Ought to***	**Base Form of Verb**
I You He She We They	**should** **ought to**	**go**.
It	**should** **ought to**	**happen**.

Negative Statements		
Subject	***Should not***	**Base Form of Verb**
I You He She We They	**should not** **shouldn't**	**go**.
It	**should not** **shouldn't**	**happen**.

Yes / No Questions			
Should	**Subject**	**Base Form of Verb**	
Should	we he they	**wear**	a suit?

Short Answers					
Affirmative			**Negative**		
Yes,	you he they	**should**.	No,	you he they	**shouldn't**.

Wh- Questions			
***Wh-* Word**	***Should***	**Subject**	**Base Form of Verb**
What	**should**	I	**do**?
When		we	**go**?

Had Better and *Had Better Not*

Affirmative Statements		
Subject	***Had Better***	**Base Form of Verb**
We You	**had better** **('d better)**	**go**.

Negative Statements		
Subject	***Had Better Not***	**Base Form of Verb**
We You	**had better not** **'d better not**	**go**.

Contractions	
I had better → **I'd better**	we had better → **we'd better**
you had better → **you'd better**	you had better → **you'd better**
he had better → **he'd better**	they had better → **they'd better**
she had better → **she'd better**	

GRAMMAR NOTES

1	Use ***should*** to **give advice** or **talk about what is right to do**. Use *should* + the base form of the verb. Use ***should not*** for the negative. Use the contraction ***shouldn't*** in speaking and informal writing.	• He should **bring** them a gift. NOT: He should ~~to bring~~ them a gift. NOT: He should ~~brings~~ them a gift. • We **should not** bring roses. • We **shouldn't** bring roses.
2	We use *should* to talk about the **present** or **future**.	• You **should** do the report **now**. • You **should** turn in the report **tomorrow**.
3	***Ought to*** means the same as *should*.	• You **ought to read** that book about Chile. It's very helpful.
4	*Ought to* is not usually used in questions or negatives. We use *should* instead. **USAGE NOTE:** To sound more polite, use *I think* or *Maybe* before saying, "*you should*" or "*you ought to*."	• Should I wear a suit? NOT: ~~Ought I to wear~~ a suit? • **I think you should** bring a small gift. • **Maybe you ought to** ask him first.
5	Use ***had better*** to **give advice**. *Had better* is stronger than *should*. It implies that something bad might happen if you don't follow the advice. Use *had better* + the base form of the verb. The negative of *had better* is ***had better not***. We often use the short form ***'d better*** in speaking and informal writing.	• You had better **call** before you go to the store. *(It may be closed.)* • He **had better send** an email message. • He **had better not** forget his passport. • We**'d better ask** the doctor.
6	***Had better*** is used to talk about the **present** or the **future**. (The *had* in *had better* does not refer to the past.)	• I**'d better** finish my report now. • She**'d better not** miss her flight tomorrow.

STEP 3 FOCUSED PRACTICE

EXERCISE 1: Discover the Grammar

Read the questions and answers about using business cards in Japan. Underline **should, had better, ought to,** *and the base form of the verb.*

1. **Q:** When should I present my business card?
   A: Right after you shake hands or bow.
2. **Q:** Should I translate my card into Japanese?
   A: Yes. It's a good idea to have English on one side and Japanese on the other.
3. **Q:** What should I do when I get my colleague's card?
   A: Read it carefully. You ought to remember the information on it.
4. **Q:** Can we start our business before we exchange business cards?
   A: You'd better not start your business before you exchange business cards.

EXERCISE 2: *Should*: Affirmative and Negative

(Grammar Notes 1–2)

Some international students are talking about customs in their countries. Complete the sentences with **should** *or* **shouldn't** *and the verb in parentheses.*

1. I was in a school cafeteria in the U.S. A guy had a cold. He blew his nose at the table. In Korea you ___shouldn't blow___ **(blow)** your nose at the table. It's very impolite.
2. In China, you ____________ **(touch)** people. Many people feel uncomfortable when others touch them. Here I notice people touch more often.
3. I think that people in North America don't like silence. Someone always speaks. I guess you ____________ **(be)** quiet.
4. In some cultures, people can clap hands to call a waiter. You ____________ never ____________ **(do)** that here. I think here you ____________ **(wait)** until the waiter looks at you. But sometimes the waiter never looks at you.
5. In North America people often say "We'll have to get together" or "I'll see you later." But they don't plan to meet me or see me later. In Poland we don't do that. In my opinion, Americans and Canadians ____________ **(say)** that. It's confusing.

EXERCISE 3: *Should*: Affirmative and Negative

(Grammar Notes 1–2)

Complete the sentences about doing business in Hungary. Use **should** *or* **shouldn't** *and a verb from the box.*

arrive	~~avoid~~	be / not	call	keep	pay	surprise / not

1. You ___should avoid___ taking a business trip to Hungary during July and August and from mid-December to mid-January. These are holiday and vacation periods.
2. You ______________ on time in all business matters: You ______________ late for appointments.
3. You ______________ always ______________ bills on time, and you ______________ the date you promise for deliveries.
4. You ______________ adults by their titles and family names unless they ask you not to.
5. It ______________ you to get an invitation to go horseback riding. Horseback riding is a popular sport in Hungary.

EXERCISE 4: *Ought to*

(Grammar Notes 3–4)

Complete the sentences with **ought to** *and the verbs from the box.*

ask	become	~~bring~~	congratulate	invite	send

1. We're going to the Chens for dinner tomorrow night. We ___ought to bring___ a gift.
2. We had a wonderful time at their home. We ______________ them a thank-you note.
3. I ______________ Mr. Chen. His son graduated from law school last week.
4. We ______________ them to our home when the Johnsons are here. I think they'd get along well.
5. Judy Chen ______________ a party planner. She's so good at giving parties.
6. I ______________ the Chens about doing business in Taiwan. I'm going there next month.

EXERCISE 5: *Had better*: Affirmative and Negative

(Grammar Notes 5–6)

Complete the sentences with **'d better** *or* **'d better not.**

1. You ___'d better not___ show the soles of your feet in Thailand or Saudi Arabia. It is a big insult.
2. In Hindu and Islamic cultures, you ____________________ eat with your left hand. It's not polite.
3. In the United States, direct eye contact is a sign of honesty, but in other countries it is a sign of disrespect. You ____________________ understand these differences when you are meeting with people from different parts of the world.
4. We ____________________ hug them. They might feel uncomfortable. It's not their custom.
5. You ____________________ find out about gift giving in their country. The wrong gift may cause misunderstanding.

EXERCISE 6: *Had better*

(Grammar Notes 5–6)

Rewrite the sentences with **had better** *or* **had better not** *based on the information.*

1. Be on time when doing business in Germany.

   You had better be on time when doing business in Germany.

2. Don't eat everything on your plate in Cambodia.

   ____

   Leave something to show your host was generous with the food.

3. In China, keep eating while your plate is full to show you like your food.

   ____

4. Do not touch a person's head or show the soles of your feet in Thailand.

   ____

   The head is the most sacred part of the body. The foot is the lowest.

5. Don't keep your hands in your pockets in Turkey. It's a sign of disrespect.

   ____

EXERCISE 7: Editing

A | *Correct the conversations. There are six mistakes. The first mistake is already corrected. Find and correct four more. Add* **should** *or* **shouldn't.**

1. **A:** What ^should I wear?

   B: You not wear jeans or shorts.

2. **A:** I think I insulted him.

   B: You apologize.

3. **A:** They were really helpful. I send them a thank-you note?

   B: That's a good idea.

4. **A:** I take my shoes off?

   B: Yes, please leave them by the door.

5. **A:** When we leave for the business reception?

   B: At 6:15. The invitation is for 6:30, but we don't want to be the first ones there.

B | *Correct five mistakes in the conversations. Add* **'d better** *or* **'d better not.** *The first mistake is already corrected. Find and correct four more.*

1. **A:** I missed the train this morning.

   B: You ^'d better leave earlier tomorrow.

2. **A:** You don't fly today. There's a bad hurricane and all flights are late.

   B: Good idea. I'll change my flight for tomorrow.

3. **A:** Can I call John Baker now?

   B: I don't think so. He's on U.S. time. You call him at noon. You won't wake him then.

4. **A:** Is it OK to pay that bill on Friday?

   B: I don't think so. You pay it today.

5. **A:** I told John about my birthday. He doesn't forget about it.

   B: John forgets everyone's birthday except his own.

STEP 4 COMMUNICATION PRACTICE

EXERCISE 8: Pronunciation

A | *Read and listen to the Pronunciation Note.*

Pronunciation Note

When we say ***shouldn't*** followed by a verb, the **/ t /** is not fully heard. ***Shouldn't say*** sounds like **/ shʊdən səɪ /**.

B | *Listen and repeat the sentences.*

1. You shouldn't call him.
2. You shouldn't send an email.
3. You shouldn't come early.
4. You shouldn't wear shorts.
5. You shouldn't bring a gift.

EXERCISE 9: Listening

A | *Listen to a conversation between Max and his friends. Then answer the questions.*

1. Where is Max going? To ______________________
2. How is he getting there? By ______________________
3. What are his questions about? ______________________

B | *Listen again. Complete the questions. Write the friends' answers.*

1. **Max:** Should I bow when ______________________?

   Answer: ______________________

2. **Max:** Should I remove ______________ when ______________?

   Answer: ______________________

3. **Max:** Should I learn ______________________?

   Answer: ______________________

EXERCISE 10: Discussion: Gift Giving

A | *PAIRS: Ask and answer the questions below. Talk about gift giving in your culture.*

1. Are gifts exchanged in business? When are gifts usually given?
2. Is the way you wrap a gift important? How and when do you present a gift? Do you open a gift right away or do you open it later?
3. Are there gifts that you shouldn't give?
4. What are the most common gifts in business?
5. How do you feel about giving gifts?
6. What kind of gifts do you like to receive?

B | *Discuss gift giving as a class.*

EXERCISE 11: Conversation: Body Language

A | *GROUPS: Body language is a way people speak without words. Use body language: Say something with your, head, hand, shoulders, arms, eyes, nose, or lips. Does your group understand you?*

B | *Talk about body language with your group.*

C | *Present the results of your discussion to the class.*

EXERCISE 12: Writing

A | *Imagine someone wants to do business in a culture you know well. Give the person advice. Use* **should, shouldn't, had better,** *or* **had better not.** *Use a topic from the box or your own idea.*

being on time	**eating habits**	**using business cards**
dressing appropriately	**tipping**	**using forms of address**

EXAMPLE: **Forms of Address in the United States**

How do you address people when you are doing business in the United States? Do you use their first names or their last names? Do you use titles? And if so, what are the correct titles?

In the United States managers of companies sometimes tell people to call them by their first names. You shouldn't think it means that you are close. It is a part of the culture. In a business relationship, you should first call a person by a title (for example: Dr., Ms., or Mr.) and their last name. Wait for that person to tell you how he or she wants to be addressed. Some people want to be on a first-name basis and others don't. There are no set rules.

B | *Check your work. Use the Editing Checklist.*

Editing Checklist

Did you . . . ?

☐ use ***should***, ***shouldn't***, ***had better***, or ***had better not*** correctly

☐ check your spelling

UNIT 30 Review

Check your answers on page UR-6.
Do you need to review anything?

A | *Circle the correct words.*

1. You **should to / should** read that book.
2. We **better / had better** call the airline.
3. I **shouldn't not / shouldn't** wear that outfit for a business meeting.
4. We **ought / ought to** buy a small gift.
5. I'd **better no / better not** call her now. She goes to bed early.

B | *Complete the sentences with* **had better** *or* **had better not.**

1. You ____________________ forget to pay that bill. You don't want to pay a late fee.
2. She ____________________ buy the gift today. The stores will be closed tomorrow.
3. We ____________________ wait for them any longer. We'll miss our flight.
4. I ____________________ go by train. The bus is too slow, and I need to be on time.

C | *Complete the sentences with* **should** *or* **shouldn't.**

1. We ________________ take him to the hospital. He seems to be in pain.
2. She ________________ work alone. She needs to get help.
3. I ________________ talk to a plumber about that problem.
4. You ________________ forget your notes. You'll need them.

D | *Correct the sentences. There are seven mistakes.*

1. Where should we meets after work?
2. We better take an umbrella tonight. It's going to rain.
3. Should I to make a reservation now for my flight? I think I outta buy it soon.
4. What I should see during my business trip to Uruguay?
5. Should we leaves Brazil tonight or tomorrow?
6. You ought bring flowers to your hostess to thank her for dinner.

UNIT 31 Requests, Desires, and Offers: *Would you, Could you, Can you. . . ?, I'd like . . .*

NEIGHBORS

STEP 1 GRAMMAR IN CONTEXT

Before You Read

A favor is something you do for someone to help him or her. Read these requests for favors. Which ones are OK to ask a neighbor? Check (✓) your opinion.

	OK	Depends	Not OK
Would you please get my mail while I'm on vacation?			
Could you help me move to a new apartment?			
Can you drive me to the airport?			
Can you lend me $500?			

Read

Jade posts a problem on a message board. Luz reads it and posts some advice. Read their posts. Do you agree with Luz?

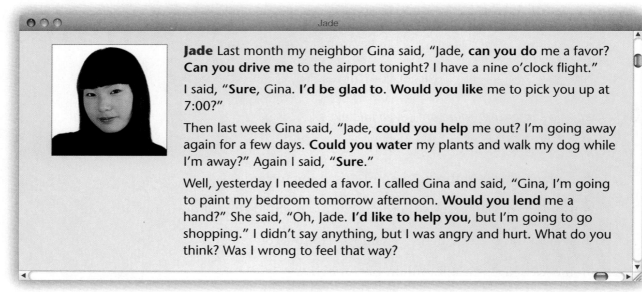

Jade

Jade Last month my neighbor Gina said, "Jade, **can you do** me a favor? **Can you drive me** to the airport tonight? I have a nine o'clock flight."

I said, "**Sure**, Gina. **I'd be glad to**. **Would you like** me to pick you up at 7:00?"

Then last week Gina said, "Jade, **could you help** me out? I'm going away again for a few days. **Could you water** my plants and walk my dog while I'm away?" Again I said, "**Sure**."

Well, yesterday I needed a favor. I called Gina and said, "Gina, I'm going to paint my bedroom tomorrow afternoon. **Would you lend** me a hand?" She said, "Oh, Jade. **I'd like to help you**, but I'm going to go shopping." I didn't say anything, but I was angry and hurt. What do you think? Was I wrong to feel that way?

Luz0426

Luz0426 No, you were right. Since Gina asks you for favors, she should do favors too. Maybe Gina is a little bit selfish. Maybe she only thinks about herself. Why don't you tell her how you feel? See what she says. Good luck!

After You Read

A | Practice *PAIRS: Now read the posts aloud. Take turns reading each paragraph.*

B | Vocabulary *Match the words and meanings.*

____	**1. lend me a hand**	**a.** leave
____	**2. post a message**	**b.** help me
____	**3. go away**	**c.** write to an online group
____	**4. be hurt**	**d.** caring only about yourself
____	**5. selfish**	**e.** feel bad

C | Comprehension *Complete the chart. Who is each sentence about? Check (✓) the correct column.*

	Gina	Jade
1. She would like a ride to the airport.		
2. She offered to pick her neighbor up at 7:00.		
3. She would like her neighbor to water her plants.		
4. She asked her neighbor to help paint her bedroom.		
5. She would like advice.		

STEP 2 GRAMMAR PRESENTATION

REQUESTS, DESIRES, AND OFFERS

Polite Requests			
Would You / Could You / Can You		**Base Form of Verb**	
Would you	(please)	**help**	me?
Could you			
Can you			

Short Answers	
Affirmative	**Negative**
Sure.	Sorry, I can't. I have to work.
Of course.	I'd like to, but I can't. I have a class.
OK.	Sorry, I'm busy now.

(continued on next page)

Desires		
Subject	***Would Like***	
I You* He She We They	**would like**	a larger apartment. to move.

Contractions
I would = **I'd** you would = **you'd** he would = **he'd** she would = **she'd** we would = **we'd** they would = **they'd**

**You* is both singular and plural.

Offers			
Would	**Subject**	***Like***	
Would	you	**like**	some blueberries? to join us?

Short Answers	
Affirmative	**Negative**
Yes, thank you. Yes, I would.	No, thanks.

GRAMMAR NOTES

1	***Would you***, ***Could you***, and ***Can you*** are some common ways to make **requests**.	**A: Would you (please)** help me carry these books? **B: Sure.**
	When we agree to a request, we say, ***Sure***. ***Of course***. ***OK***. or ***I'd be glad to***.	**A: Could you (please)** help me carry these books? **B: Of course.**
	Can you is the most common and most informal. When we don't agree to a request, we say ***sorry*** and **give a reason**.	**A: Can you (please)** help me? **B: I'd be glad to.** OR **Sorry, I can't. I have to work.**
2	***Would like*** is a polite way of saying *want*.	• The judge **would like** to see you now.
	USAGE NOTE: Use the contraction in speaking and informal writing.	• **I'd like** some advice. • We**'d like** to see you.
	Would like can be followed by **a noun** or **an infinitive**.	NOUN • I'd like **a snack**. INFINITIVE • I'd like **to get** a snack.
3	Use ***Would you like*** for offers or invitations.	• **Would you like** some help? • **Would you like** to dance?

REFERENCE NOTE

See Unit 7, page 75, for a discussion of requests.

STEP 3 FOCUSED PRACTICE

EXERCISE 1: Discover the Grammar

Write **R (Request), O (Offer),** *or* **D (Desire)** *for each sentence.*

__R__ **1.** Would you give me a ride?
_____ **2.** We'd like to see you again soon.
_____ **3.** Would you like some more lemonade?
_____ **4.** Could you lend me your car?
_____ **5.** I'd like a shorter workday.
_____ **6.** Can I see your photos?
_____ **7.** Would you like another dumpling?
_____ **8.** Would you call her for me?

EXERCISE 2: Requests, Offers, Desires, and Responses

(Grammar Notes 1–3)

Eun Young and Dae Jung are neighbors. Complete the conversation with the phrases from the box.

~~Could you please~~	I'd like to do	I'd love to	Of course	Would you like

EUN YOUNG: Dae Jung, I love to listen to your music, but sometimes I can't get to sleep. __Could you please__ (1.) stop practicing by 11:00 P.M.?

DAE JUNG: ______________ (2.) I'm sorry. Sometimes I forget the time when I practice.

EUN YOUNG: Thanks.

DAE JUNG: Listen, Eun Young, ______________ (3.) something for you. ______________ (4.) to have dinner together one day next week?

EUN YOUNG: Dinner? Sure. ______________ (5.).

EXERCISE 3: Responses to Requests and Offers

(Grammar Note 1)

Read the questions. Circle the correct letter.

1. **A:** Would you help me get up?

   B: ________________

   (a.) Sure. **b.** Yes, thanks.

2. **A:** Could you help me with these bags?

   B: ________________

   a. I could. **b.** Certainly.

3. **A:** Can you get my mail while I'm away?

   B: ________________

   a. Sorry, I'm going away too. **b.** No thanks.

4. **A:** Would you like one of these flyers?

   B: ________________

   a. Yes, I want. **b.** Thanks.

5. **A:** Can you drive me to the supermarket?

   B: ________________

   a. I could. **b.** Of course.

6. **A:** Could you do me a favor and watch my bags? I need to move my car.

   B: ________________

   a. I'm sure. **b.** Sure.

7. **A:** Would you like some of my popcorn?

   B: ________________

   a. Thanks. **b.** Sorry, I don't.

8. **A:** Could you give me some money?

   B: ________________

   a. Yes, I would. **b.** Sorry, I don't have any.

EXERCISE 4: Requests, Offers, Desires

(Grammar Notes 1–3)

Rewrite the underlined sentences. Change imperative statements to requests with **Could you please, Would you please,** *or* ***Can you please. . . ?*** *Change* **want** *to* **would like.**

ALEXA: The barbecue looks great. Anything we can do to help?

Could you please bring out the drinks?

JAVIER: Sure. ~~Bring out the drinks~~. They're in the cooler.
1.

ALEXA: OK. . . . Here they are. Where should we put them?

JAVIER: Put the lemonade on the table over there. And Roberto, put the juice over here
2. 3.

next to the buns. And there's a salad in the refrigerator. Bring it out.
4.

ALEXA: Sure. I'll get it.

JAVIER: I think the meat is ready. What do you want—chicken or hamburgers?
5.

ALEXA: Some chicken, please.

JAVIER: What about you Roberto? Do you want chicken too?
6.

ROBERTO: No, I want a burger.
7.

JAVIER: Here you go.

ALEXA: Javier, this chicken is delicious. I want the recipe.
8.

JAVIER: It's easy to make. I soak it in a honey mustard sauce. Then I grill it.

EXERCISE 5: Editing

Correct the conversations. There are five mistakes. The first mistake is already corrected. Find and correct four more.

1. **A:** Could you please move my car at 11:00?

   Sorry.

   B: ~~No, I wouldn't~~. I'll be at work at that time.

2. **A:** We like to rent this apartment. Could please you give us an application?

   B: Of course.

3. **A:** Would you like come for dinner?

   B: Yes, thank you. Would my friend come, too?

4. **A:** Would you help me with these boxes?

   B: I would.

STEP 4 COMMUNICATION PRACTICE

EXERCISE 6: Pronunciation

A | *Read and listen to the Pronunciation Note.*

Pronunciation Note

Do not pronounce the letter ***l*** in the word ***would***. *Would* is pronounced like the word *wood* / **wʊd** / . We pronounce *Would you* / **wʊdʒə** / and *Could you* / **kʊdʒə** / with the / **dʒ** / sound.

B | *Listen and repeat.*

1. Would you like some more lemonade?
2. Could you hold the door open?
3. Would you watch the burgers?
4. Could you hand me a napkin?

EXERCISE 7: Listening

A | *Listen to a telephone conversation beween neighbors. Circle the correct letter.*

Elena asks Ms. Lyons to ________________.

a. watch TV with her **b.** turn off her TV **c.** lower her TV volume

B | *Listen again and answer the questions. Circle the correct letter.*

1. How does Ms. Lyons respond?
  a. She agrees to Elena's request.
  b. She doesn't understand Elena's request.
  c. She doesn't agree to Elena's request.

2. What does Ms. Lyons think?
  a. Her neighbor isn't polite.
  b. Her TV isn't too loud.
  c. The walls in her building are thin.

3. What is Elena doing at this time?
  a. She's studying in medical school.
  b. She's working as a doctor.
  c. She's studying for a test for medical school.

4. Ms. Lyons may have a problem. What is it?
  a. She doesn't see well.
  b. She doesn't hear well.
  c. She doesn't have a kind neighbor.

EXERCISE 8: Survey

A | *GROUPS OF 4: Look at the requests in the list. Talk about these requests. Is it OK for a neighbor, a casual friend, or a close friend or relative to ask them? Is it sometimes OK? If so, when? Would you make these requests?*

Would you lend me your car?	**Could you lend me $50?**
Could you fix my computer?	**Could you walk my dog for two weeks?**
Would you take my picture?	**Could you take me to the hospital?**

EXAMPLE: **A:** Young Suk, what do you think about the first request, "Would you lend me your car?" Would you make that request?
B: Not for a neighbor, but I might ask a close relative.

B | *Take notes on your group's responses. Then discuss them with the class.*

EXERCISE 9: Making Polite Requests

PAIRS: Read the situations. Take turns making polite requests. Answer the requests.

EXAMPLE: You're in a restaurant with your neighbor. You want some napkins, which are near your neighbor.
A: Maki, can you please pass the napkins?
B: Here you go.

1. You're in a restaurant with your neighbor. The salt and pepper is in front of your friend. You would like the salt and pepper.
2. It's raining hard and you have to go out. You lost your umbrella. You ask a neighbor to lend you an umbrella.
3. You need to move your sofa. Your neighbor is at your home.
4. You want to hang a painting on the wall. You'd like your neighbor to help you.
5. Your neighbor has parties that keep you up at night. You would like the neighbor to make less noise.
6. Your neighbor borrowed a couple of books a month ago. He still has them.

EXERCISE 10: Extending Invitations

PAIRS: Take turns. Extend invitations to your partner. Your partner can accept or refuse. Use the suggestions from the box or your own ideas

EXAMPLE: **A:** Would you like to come over for dinner tonight?
B: Sure. What time? OR I'd like to, but I can't. I have too much homework.

go running	go to a concert	see a movie	study calculus together

EXERCISE 11: Role Play

PAIRS: Role-play the situations. You and your partner are neighbors.

Situations:

- Invite your neighbor to a party.
- Ask your neighbor to help you put in a new air conditioner.
- Invite your neighbor to a concert. You have an extra ticket.
- Ask your neighbor for a ride to a store.

EXAMPLE: ELENA: Hey, Pierre, I'm going to have a party tomorrow night. Would you like to come?
PIERRE: I'd love to. Is it in your apartment?
ELENA: Yes, it is. Please come at around 8:00.
PIERRE: OK. I'll be there.

EXERCISE 12: Writing

A | *Write two short email requests to neighbors. Use the situations or your own ideas. Use* **would** *or* **could.**

Situation 1

You are on vacation. You gave your neighbor a key to your home. Ask your neighbor to check your home.

Situation 2

Your neighbor has two teenage sons. They play music at all hours of the night. Ask your neighbor to ask them not to play loud music after 10:00 P.M.

Situation 3

It's winter and the landlord is not giving enough heat. Write to several neighbors and ask them to join you in writing letters of complaint to your landlord.

EXAMPLE FOR SITUATION 1: Hi John,
Boris and I are having a great time in Aruba. I read about a storm back home, and I hope all is well. Could you please check our house? We'll be back in a couple of days.
Irina

B | *Check your work. Use the Editing Checklist.*

Editing Checklist

Did you . . . ?
☐ use ***would you***, ***could you***, or ***can you*** correctly
☐ check your spelling

UNIT 31 Review

Check your answers on page UR-6.
Do you need to review anything?

A | *Circle the correct word or words.*

1. **Would you please / Would you like** another apple?
2. **Could you pass / Can you please** the salt?
3. **I'd like / I'll like** some more coffee.
4. **We'd like / We like** some more bread, please.
5. **Can you / Can you to** help me?

B | *Read each question. Circle the correct answer.*

1. Would you please help me? **(Yes, thanks. / Of course.)**
2. Could you drive me home? **(Sure. / I could.)**
3. Would you like another cupcake? **(I could. / Thanks.)**
4. Can you lend me your jacket? **(Sorry, I need it. / No, thanks.)**
5. Can you show me how the new printer works? **(I'd be glad to. / I can.)**

C | *Complete the sentences with* **I'd like, Could you please** *or* **Would you like.**

1. ________________ open the door?
2. ________________ some more coffee.
3. ________________ drive me to school?
4. ________________ some water?
5. ________________ to go to that concert.

D | *Correct the conversations. There are five mistakes.*

1. **A:** Could please you move my car at 11:00?
   B: No, I wouldn't. I'll be at work then.
2. **A:** I like to see you this weekend. Would you like to go to the park?
   B: I could.
3. **A:** Would you like have some more ice cream?
   B: No, thanks. I'm full.

UNIT 32 Necessity: *Have to, Don't have to, Must, Mustn't*

RULES AT SCHOOL

STEP 1 GRAMMAR IN CONTEXT

Before You Read

What do you have to do for your English class? Circle the letter of your answers.

a. do homework
b. wear a uniform
c. sit in the same seat for each class
d. take tests
e. answer questions in class
f. do class presentations

Read

Read about the requirements for a college history course.

PROFESSOR: Welcome to American History 102. I'm Rich Anderson. This course covers the period from the American Civil War to the present day.[1] There will be a midterm and a final exam. You **have to score** an average of 65 percent or above on both tests to pass this course. In addition there is a term paper.[2] The term paper **must be** at least 10 pages, and you **have to include** a bibliography.[3] The handout I'm passing out will explain the term paper. Now, are there any questions? . . . Yes?

STUDENT A: When is the term paper due?

PROFESSOR: You **have to hand** it **in** by the last day of class. That's December 15. It **must not be** late. You should hand in an outline by the fourth week of the term. You can email the outline. My email address is on the board and on your handout. You **don't have to give** me a hard copy of the outline, but I would like a hard copy of your paper. Any other questions? . . . Yes?

STUDENT B: Last semester, we **didn't have to buy** a textbook. Is there a textbook for this course?

PROFESSOR: Yes. The textbook is called *American History from the Civil War to Today.*

STUDENT B: Who's the author?

PROFESSOR: I am.

STUDENT B: **Do** we **have to buy** the book?

PROFESSOR: Only if you want to pass.

---

[1] ***present day:*** today (usually used when talking about history)
[2] ***term paper:*** students' most important written report of the semester
[3] ***bibliography:*** a list of the books and other sources used to write a paper

After You Read

A | Practice *PAIRS: Now read the conversation aloud.*

B | Vocabulary *Complete the sentences with the words from the box.*

average	final	midterm	pass
due	hard copy	outline	percent

1. To ________________ this course, you must hand in a paper and do a group presentation.
2. There will be two tests this semester. The ________________ will be on October 15, and the ________________ will be on December 15.
3. The ________________ of 100, 95, 99, and 90 is 96.
4. What ________________ of the students finish this program in one year?
5. Do I need to print a ________________ or is OK to send it electronically?
6. I can't meet you today. My term paper is ________________ tomorrow.
7. I wrote an ________________ of each chapter to help me study for the test.

C | Comprehension *Check (✓) what students in Professor Anderson's class* **have to do** *and* **don't have to do.**

	Students have to . . .	Students don't have to . . .
1. take a quiz every week		
2. take a midterm and final exam		
3. give an oral report		
4. hand in an outline		
5. read four books for their term paper		
6. buy the textbook		

STEP 2 GRAMMAR PRESENTATION

MODALS: *HAVE TO / DON'T HAVE TO*

Affirmative Statements			
Subject	***Have to / Has to***	**Base Form of Verb**	
I We You They	**have to**	**take**	a history class.
He She	**has to**	**take**	a history class.
It	**has to**	**be**	a three-credit class.

Negative Statements				
Subject	***Do Not / Does Not***	***Have to***	**Base Form of Verb**	
I We You They	**don't**	**have to**	**take**	a history class.
He She	**doesn't**	**have to**	**take**	a history class.
It	**doesn't**	**have to**	**be**	10 pages long.

Yes / No Questions				
Do / Does	**Subject**	***Have to***	**Base Form of Verb**	
Do	I you we they	**have to**	**study**	tonight?
Does	he she	**have to**	**study**	tonight?
Does	it	**have to**	**be**	five pages?

Short Answers					
Affirmative			**Negative**		
Yes,	you I you they	do.	No,	you I you they	don't.
Yes,	he she it	does.	No,	he she it	doesn't.

MUST AND *MUSTN'T*

Affirmative and Negative Statements			
Subject	***Must***	**Base Form of Verb**	
I You He She It We They	**must** **must not** **(mustn't)**	**arrive**	early.

Past of *Have to* and *Must*			
Subject	***Had to***	**Base Form of Verb**	
I You He She It We They	**had to**	**leave**	early.

GRAMMAR NOTES

1	Use ***have to*** and ***must*** to talk about things that are **necessary**. Both *have to* and *must* are followed by the base form of the verb. *Must* is stronger than *have to*. **USAGE NOTE:** We usually use *have to* in speaking and informal writing. **BE CAREFUL!** *Have to* is different from the verb *have*. **NOTE:** The past of *must* and *have to* is ***had to***.	• I **have to take** a test next week. • Students **must take** a three-credit history course. • I **have** a psychology class. • I **have to read** 50 pages for this class. • Last week I **had to buy** a lot of textbooks.
2	Use ***don't have to*** or ***doesn't have to*** when there is no necessity. You have a **choice**.	• I **don't have to sit** in the same seat every day. I can sit wherever I want. • He **doesn't have to wear** a suit to work. He can wear a shirt and slacks.
3	***Must not*** or the contraction ***mustn't*** means that you are **not allowed** to do something. You don't have a choice. You can't do it.	• You **must not take** scissors on a plane.
4	Do not repeat *must* or *have to* when you use two verbs or verb phrases with one subject.	• You **must take** a test and **write** a paper. • He **has to work** and **study**. NOT: He must take a test and ~~must~~ write a paper. NOT: He has to work and ~~has to~~ study.
5	**BE CAREFUL!** Do not use *to* after *must*.	• He **must write** a report. NOT: He ~~must to write~~ a report.
6	**USAGE NOTE:** We rarely use *mustn't* in conversation except when talking to small children or telling rules. We use ***can't*** instead.	• Children, you **mustn't** cross the street when the signal is red. • You can't park there. NOT: You ~~mustn't~~ park there.

EXERCISE 1: Discover the Grammar

Read about a special high school for the arts. Underline all forms of **have to, don't have to, must, mustn't,** *and the verb that follows. Circle all examples of the verb* **have.**

New York City has a special high school for music, art, dance, and drama. It's called LaGuardia High School. To be accepted, students have to pass an audition. In addition they must have good grades. The school usually has about 9,000 applicants a year. It accepts about 650 students. All prospective students, even the children of the rich and famous, must audition. They must choose to audition for acting, dance, music, or art. Here are some of the requirements for students interested in art:

1. Each student must submit a portfolio of original artwork. The artwork does not have to be a special size, but all art has to be original. Students mustn't bring in photocopies.
2. Each student must complete three drawing exercises. Students have to bring a pencil and a transcript of their last report card. Students don't have to bring drawing materials. The school has all the necessary drawing supplies for the students.

Madonna with her daughter, Lourdes. Lourdes attends LaGuardia High School.

EXERCISE 2: *Have to / Don't have to / Must*

(Grammar Notes 1–2)

A | *Read LaGuardia High School's audition requirements for dance. Complete the sentences. Use* **have to** *or* **don't have to** *and the verbs from the box.*

bring	perform
bring / not	take

Dance students ______________ (1.) two classes: a ballet dance class and a modern dance class. Students who do well in the classes return for a second audition. At the second audition, students ______________ (2.) a one-minute dance. Students ______________ (3.) their own music, but they ______________ (4.) a CD player. The school has CD players.

B | *Complete the audition requirements for music. Use* **must** *or* **don't have to** *and the verbs from the box.*

bring / not	play	sing	use

To show your musical talent, you ______________ (1.) a song or ______________ (2.) an instrument. You ______________ (3.) your own instrument if you can carry it. You ______________ (4.) a piano or a bass. The school will supply one for you.

EXERCISE 3: *Have / Have to / Had to*

(Grammar Note 1)

Complete the conversation with **have, have to,** *or* **had to.**

A: Would you like to go to the movies this evening?

B: I can't. I ___*have*___ (1.) a test tomorrow. I ______________ (2.) study this evening.

A: What do you ______________ (3.) study?

(continued on next page)

B: Grammar. I _______________ review the modals *can*, *could*, *would*, *might*, and *must*.
4.

We _______________ a test every Thursday.
5.

A: Do you _______________ memorize rules?
6.

B: No. We _______________ use the grammar to answer questions. We really
7.

_______________ understand it.
8.

A: Do you get a lot of tests?

B: Uh-huh. We _______________ a quiz after every unit. I don't mind them.
9.

A: I don't like tests. Last year I _______________ take a test every week, and I was always
10.

worried.

EXERCISE 4: *Have to / Don't have to*

(Grammar Notes 1–2)

Complete the sentences with **have to, has to, don't have to,** *or* **doesn't have to** *and the verbs from the box.*

attend	buy	hand in	listen	pass	pay	say	wear	~~work~~

1. In some classes you almost always ___have to work___ in groups.
2. In some high schools, students can wear what they like. They _______________ a uniform.
3. In many high schools students _______________ standardized tests or they can't go on to the next grade.
4. We _______________ our term paper by December 15.
5. Hugo says he _______________ all classes unless he has a doctor's note.
6. She _______________ that book. She can borrow it from the library.
7. My psychology class has many students. I _______________ to a lecture and take notes. I _______________ anything in class. I just have to pass the exams.
8. Jay goes to a college near his home, so he _______________ for room and board.

EXERCISE 5: *Have to, Must, Must not*

(Grammar Notes 1, 3)

Read the signs. Then explain the rule or warning of each. Begin with **You have to, You must,** *or* **You must not.**

1. No Smoking

You mustn't smoke on the train.
____

2. I.D. Required

____

____

3. Do Not Enter

____

____

4. Do not get hairdryer wet

____

____

5. Do not drink

____

____

6. Do not text when you drive

____

____

EXERCISE 6: Editing

Correct the sentences. There are eight mistakes. The first mistake is already corrected. Find and correct seven more.

1. We ~~has to~~ have a lot of new vocabulary words. I can't remember all of them.
2. To learn a new vocabulary word, you must hears it seven times.
3. For me to remember a word, I has to write it down.
4. Avi has a great memory. He just have to hear a word once and he remembers it.
5. Our papers are due next week. I have start working on mine today.
6. We mustn't do any homework today. Tomorrow is a holiday.
7. You mustn't to bring any notes with you to the test.
8. You must to bring a photo ID to the testing center.

STEP 4 COMMUNICATION PRACTICE

EXERCISE 7: Pronunciation

A | *Read and listen to the Pronunciation Note.*

Pronunciation Note

When ***have to*** or ***has to*** is followed by a verb, the vowel sound in ***to*** is unstressed and sounds like **/ ə /**.

EXAMPLE: **A:** Why is he selling his house?
B: He has to move.

When ***have to*** or ***has to*** is not followed by a verb, there is more stress on ***to*** and the vowel sounds more like **/ u /**.

EXAMPLE: **A:** Do you need to study tonight?
B: Yes, I have to.

B | *Listen and repeat.*

1. **A:** Do you want to go there?
   B: No, but I **have to**.
2. **A:** What does she **have to do**?
   B: She **has to write** a paper today.
3. **A:** When do we **have to pay** the tuition?
   B: We **have to pay** it before class begins.
4. **A:** Do you really **have to work** late tonight?
   B: Yes, I **have to**.

C | *PAIRS: Follow the directions. Then switch roles.*

1. **Partner A:** Tell your partner three things you have to do this week.
2. **Partner B:** Ask your partner, "Do you really have to?"

Example: **A:** This evening I have to study for our test.
B: Do you really have to?
A: Yes, I do. OR No, I don't. I could study tomorrow night.

EXERCISE 8: Listening

A | *Ali is in his second year of college. He is speaking to an advisor about graduate school. Listen to the conversation. What degree is Ali interested in getting?*

____

B | *Listen again. Write one thing you have to do to get that degree. Write one thing you don't have to do.*

1. ____
2. ____

EXERCISE 9: Discussion

Talk about regulations, management, and teaching methods in schools you know about. Use **have to, don't have to, must,** *and* **must not.**

Example: My nephew goes to P.S. 28 in Queens. It's a school for children between the ages of four and eight. Children have to be in school by 8:20. They must come on time for school. There's a school uniform, but they don't have to wear it. Children have to work in pairs and groups. They have to participate in class. They have to take a lot of standardized tests. They must not run in the halls or talk when the teacher is talking. The teachers are great, and the school is beautiful. My nephew loves his school. We're happy he goes there.

EXERCISE 10: Survey

A | *In some schools students try to copy their classmates' answers. Ask five classmates how teachers in their schools prevented cheating during tests.*

Example: **A:** We had to cover our papers.

B | *As a class, make a list of things teachers do to prevent cheating. Use* **have to** *or* **must.**

Example: Students have to sit in every other seat.
Students have to leave cell phones at the front of the class.

EXERCISE 11: Writing

A | *Write about an elementary school in the area where you grew up. Use* **have to** *and* **must.**

EXAMPLE:

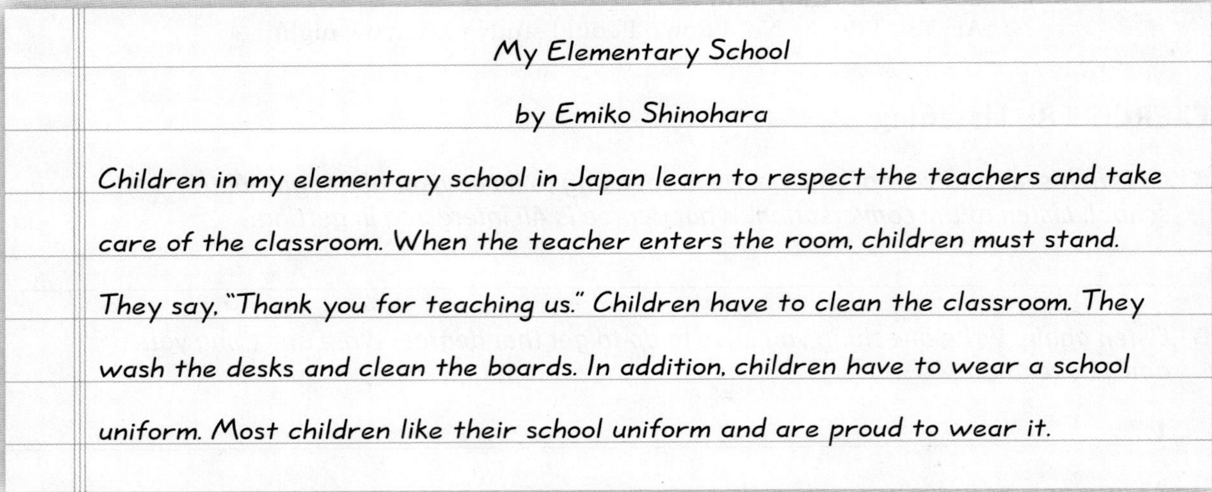

My Elementary School

by Emiko Shinohara

Children in my elementary school in Japan learn to respect the teachers and take care of the classroom. When the teacher enters the room, children must stand. They say, "Thank you for teaching us." Children have to clean the classroom. They wash the desks and clean the boards. In addition, children have to wear a school uniform. Most children like their school uniform and are proud to wear it.

B | *Check your work. Use the Editing Checklist.*

Editing Checklist

Did you . . . ?

☐ use ***have to*** and ***must*** correctly

☐ check your spelling

UNIT 32 Review

Check your answers on page UR-7.
Do you need to review anything?

A | *Circle the correct words to complete the sentences.*

1. You can wear what you want. You **mustn't / don't have to** wear a uniform.
2. It's getting late. We **have to / don't have to** leave.
3. The law says you **must / must not** drive without a license.
4. She can take the test any day this week. She **has to / doesn't have to** take it today.
5. I **have to / mustn't** hand in my term paper tomorrow. I can't go out today.

B | *Complete the sentences with the correct form of* **have, have to, don't have to,** *or* **mustn't.**

1. Children, you ________________ cross the street when the light is red.
2. She ________________ a lot of homework. She ________________ hand in a paper and study for a test.
3. The tickets are good any day this week. We ________________ use them today.
4. A doctor ________________ fill out a medical form before you can use the gym.

C | *Complete the sentences with* **have to** *and a verb from the box. Use the present or past.*

answer	bring / not	give	read	work

1. He ________________ two shifts because two co-workers were out sick.
2. We're busy. We ________________ two chapters of our history book and ________________ questions at the end of each chapter. It's due tomorrow.
3. We ________________ a presentation in front of the entire school.
4. I ________________ my own laptop. They gave me one for my presentation.

D | *Correct the paragraph. There are five mistakes.*

The test starts at 8:10. You must to be in the room at 8:00. You mustn't came late. You have to has two number two pencils and an eraser. You musts brings proper identification, such as a photo ID or a passport. You must leave your cell phone in the front of the room.

From Grammar to Writing

Expressing and Supporting an Opinion

1 | *A fact is something you know to be true; for example, a scientific fact. An opinion is what you believe. Read the sentences. Write* **F (sentences that express a fact)** *or* **O (sentences that express an opinion).**

____ **1.** I believe that Hollywood actors are not good examples for young people.

____ **2.** John was in Hollywood last summer.

____ **3.** The Himalayas are the highest mountains in the world.

____ **4.** Earth is about 93 million miles from the sun.

____ **5.** Children shouldn't watch violent movies.

2 | *Study the information about expressing and supporting an opinion.*

1	When you express your opinion, you can use expressions such as: ***In my opinion*** ***I believe*** ***I think*** ***better than*** ***It's better to . . . than to*** ***should / shouldn't***	• **In my opinion**, it's wrong to spank a child. • **I believe** tests are harmful. • **I think** tests are helpful. • Some tests are **better than** others. • **It's better to** give **than to** receive. • Parents **shouldn't** spank their children.
2	After you express your opinion, give reasons to support your opinion.	**Opinion** • In my opinion, it's wrong to spank children. **Support** • When adults use physical force, children think physical force is OK.

3 | *Read the two paragraphs about Hollywood actors. Circle the sentences that show an opinion. Underline the sentences that support the opinion.*

I believe that Hollywood actors often set a bad example for young people. Young people look up to them, but these actors show bad values. For example, many stars spend huge amounts of money on homes, cars, and clothes. When young people try to copy their lifestyle, they often buy things they can't afford. Also, most Hollywood actors do not have long-term relationships. They change boyfriends and girlfriends frequently. Finally, many Hollywood actors have cosmetic surgery and go on strict diets, all in order to be more attractive.

In my opinion, some Hollywood stars set a bad example because of their materialism, but others set a good example through their charity. For example, Angelina Jolie and George Clooney are big stars who help others. They give away a lot of their money to help the poor and the sick in different parts of the world. They also encourage others to give to good causes.

4 | *Now write a paragraph on one of the topics. Give your opinion and reasons to support your opinion.*

- Hollywood stars have a right to privacy OR Hollywood stars do not have a right to privacy
- Money can buy happiness OR Money can't buy happiness
- Children shouldn't play violent video games OR Violent video games don't harm children

5 | *Exchange papers with a partner. Did your partner follow the directions? Correct any mistakes in grammar and spelling.*

6 | *Talk to your partner. Discuss the mistakes you made. Then rewrite your own paper and make any necessary changes.*

Comparisons

UNIT	GRAMMAR FOCUS	THEME
33	The Comparative	Comparing Cities
34	Adverbs of Manner	Public Speaking
35	*Enough*, *Too* / *Very*, *As* + Adjective + *As*, *Same* / *Different*	Proms and Parties
36	The Superlative	Penguins

UNIT 33 The Comparative
COMPARING CITIES

STEP 1 GRAMMAR IN CONTEXT

Before You Read

PAIRS: Discuss. Where would you prefer to live? A big city or a small town? Why?

Read

Read the article about two U.S. cities called Portland. Which Portland would you prefer?

A TALE OF TWO PORTLANDS

Matt Groening, creator of *The Simpsons*, and Liv Tyler, the popular actress, both come from the city of Portland. However, they come from different states in the U.S.

Portland, Oregon

Portland, Maine

There are two beautiful U.S. cities named Portland. One is in Maine, and the other is in Oregon. Maine is on the East Coast of the United States, while Oregon is on the West Coast. Both Portlands have ports, but Portland, Oregon, is **farther from** the ocean. At 173 feet above sea level, it is also **higher** in elevation. Both cities are not very big, but they are **bigger than** any other city in their states. Portland, Maine, has a population of about 64,000, whereas Portland, Oregon, is much **larger**, with a population of about 540,000. Winter in Oregon is a little **milder than** winter in Maine, but they both have comfortable climates.

Liv Tyler played Arwen in three *Lord of the Rings* movies.

Both Portlands offer a nice lifestyle. Portland, Maine, is located on the coast, but the mountains are just 45 minutes away by car. So it's easy to ski in the mountains in the winter or sunbathe on the beaches in the summer. Portland, Oregon, is located on a river. It's a city of different neighborhoods with different personalities. It's much **more diverse**[1] **than** the other Portland.

Portland, Maine (founded in 1632), is a lot **older than** Portland, Oregon (founded in 1845).

[1] ***diverse:*** have people from different backgrounds

A Tale of Two Portlands

You may wonder why the two cities have the same name. There's a very good reason. Each of the founders[2] of Portland, Oregon, wanted to name his new city after his hometown. One man came from Boston, Massachusetts. The other came from Portland, Maine. They tossed a coin,[3] and the man from Portland, Maine, won.

[2] ***founder:*** someone who establishes a business, school, town, etc.
[3] ***tossed a coin:*** made a decision by throwing a coin (penny, nickel, dime, etc.) in the air and guessing the side it would fall on.

After You Read

A | Practice *PAIRS: Now read the article aloud. Take turns reading sentences.*

B | Vocabulary *Complete the sentences with the words from the box.*

coast	mild	port	ski
diverse	personality	sea level	are located

1. We drove along the ______________ and took some great photos of the ocean and the rocks.
2. The ship picked up the passengers at the ______________.
3. It was cold yesterday, but today it is ______________.
4. We like to ______________ in the mountains. We love the snow.
5. The university has a ______________ population. Students come from everywhere.
6. She has a warm ______________. That's why everyone likes her.
7. That city is high above ______________.
8. Washington, Oregon, and California ______________ on the West Coast of the United States.

C | Comprehension *Check (✓) the correct Portland.*

	Portland, Maine	Portland, Oregon
1. Which Portland has a bigger population?		
2. Which Portland is older?		
3. Which Portland has more diverse neighborhoods?		
4. Which Portland has warmer winters?		

STEP 2 GRAMMAR PRESENTATION

COMPARATIVES

Adjectives

Comparative Forms of Adjectives				
		Comparative Adjective	***Than***	
Portland, Oregon	is	**bigger** **busier**	**than**	Portland, Maine.
		more crowded		

Comparative Forms of Irregular Adjectives				
		Irregular Comparative Adjective	***Than***	
My map	is	**better** **worse**	**than**	yours.
My new office		**farther**		my old one.

Questions with *Which*

Which + Noun			
Which	**Noun**	**Verb**	**Comparative Adjective**
Which	city	is	bigger?
			more expensive?

Which		
Which	**Verb**	**Comparative Adjective**
Which	is	bigger?
		more expensive?

GRAMMAR NOTES

1 Use the **comparative form of an adjective** + ***than*** to compare two people, places, or things.

- Alaska is **bigger than** Maine.

2 To form the comparative of most **short (one-syllable) adjectives**, add ***-er*** to the adjective. Add only *-r* if the adjective ends in *e*.

long—***longer***
large—***larger***

Exceptions:

tired—***more tired***
bored—***more bored***
fun—***more fun***

- The Mississippi River is **longer** than the Hudson River.
- For me, the city is **more fun** than the suburbs.

3	To form the comparative of adjectives that end in a **consonant** + ***y***, change the ***y*** to ***i*** and add ***-er***. *busy*—***busier*** *easy*—***easier*** *heavy*—***heavier***	• These days the stores are **busier** than they were two years ago.
4	To form the comparative of most adjectives of **two** or **more syllables**, add ***more*** before the adjective. *expensive*—***more expensive*** *intelligent*—***more intelligent*** Exceptions: *quiet*—***quieter*** *simple*—***simpler***	• The train is **more expensive** than the bus. • Is life in the countryside really **simpler** and **quieter**?
5	Use ***less*** before an adjective to mean the opposite of *more*.	• A car is **more** expensive than a bicycle. • A bicycle is **less** expensive than a car.
6	The adjectives ***good***, ***bad***, and ***far*** have irregular comparative forms. *good*—***better*** *bad*—***worse*** *far*—***farther***	• My new job is **better** than my old one. • The book was bad, but the movie was **worse**. • The bus stop is **farther** than the train station.
7	Use ***much*** to make comparisons stronger.	• A two-bedroom apartment is **much** more expensive than a one-bedroom apartment. • England is **much** older than New England.
8	**USAGE NOTE:** In formal English, use the subject pronoun after *than*. In informal English, such as casual conversation between friends, you can use the object pronoun after *than*. **BE CAREFUL!** Always compare the same things. **BE CAREFUL!** Do not use two comparative forms together.	SUBJECT PRONOUN • Steve's younger **than she** is. OBJECT PRONOUN • Steve's younger **than her**. • **John's home** is larger than **William's**. OR • **John's home** is larger than **William's home**. NOT: John's home is larger than ~~William~~. NOT: John's home is ~~more~~ larger than William's.
9	Use ***which*** to ask about a comparison of **people**, **places**, or **things**.	• **Which city** is larger? • **Which** is larger, **Tokyo** or **Seoul**?

REFERENCE NOTE

See Unit 35, page 411 for a discussion of ***not as*** + **adjective** + ***as***.

STEP 3 FOCUSED PRACTICE

EXERCISE 1: Discover the Grammar

A | *Read about two cities in Canada. Underline all comparative adjectives.*

Fairmont Le Château Frontenac, Quebec City

Canada has many beautiful cities. Two of my favorites are Quebec City in eastern Canada and Vancouver in Western Canada. Vancouver is right on the Pacific coast, and it's just 7 feet above sea level. Quebec City is farther from the coast and higher than Vancouver. It overlooks the Saint Lawrence River. When I visited Quebec City, I took some great photos of the river from the famous hotel Château Frontenac.

Vancouver

Quebec City has the charm of an old historic city. It is a lot older than Vancouver. Vancouver has an old quarter too, but it's younger than Quebec City's. Vancouver, with its milder climate, is better known for its gardens and parks. Stanley Park in Vancouver is bigger than most urban parks, and people visit it all year round, but I think it's more fun to go in the spring or early summer. That's when the flowers are in bloom.

Vancouver has a larger population than Quebec City and is growing each year. These days many films are made in Vancouver because it is less expensive to make them there than in cities like Los Angeles and New York.

In Vancouver most people speak English, while 95 percent of the people in Quebec City speak French. That is because Quebec City was founded by people from France and still has a continental flavor.

All in all, both cities are great places to visit or live in.

B | *Write the base form of the ten adjectives you underlined in Part A.*

1. far
2. ______
3. ______
4. ______
5. ______
6. ______
7. ______
8. ______
9. ______
10. ______

Fortress, Quebec City

EXERCISE 2: Comparison of Adjectives

(Grammar Notes 1–9)

A | *Complete the conversations with the adjectives in parentheses. Use the comparative form. Add* **than** *when necessary.*

1. **A:** Which city is more expensive (**expensive**) to live in, Tokyo or Sydney?

   B: Tokyo is ______ (**expensive**) Sydney.

2. **A:** Which city is ______ (**hot**) in summer, Bangkok or Seoul?

   B: Bangkok summers are ______ (**hot**) summers in Seoul.

3. **A:** Which city has a ______ (**high**) elevation, Bogota or Mexico City?

   B: Bogota is ______ (**high**) Mexico City.

4. **A:** Which river is ______ (**long**), the Nile or the Amazon?

   B: The Nile is ______ (**long**) the Amazon.

5. **A:** Does New York have a ______ (**good**) subway system ______ Washington, D.C.?

   B: I don't know. The New York subway goes to more places, but the D.C. Metro is ______ (**clean**).

(continued on next page)

6. **A:** Is winter in Quebec City ______________ winter in Vancouver?
(cold)

B: Yes, it is.

7. **A:** Is New York a ______________ tourist destination
(popular)
______________ San Francisco?

B: No, they're both very popular tourist destinations.

8. **A:** Is Miami in summer ______________ in winter?
(humid)

B: Yes, it's much ______________ in summer
(humid)
______________ in winter.

9. **A:** Is Argentina ______________ from the South Pole
(far)
______________ Mexico?

B: No, Argentina is ______________ to the South Pole.
(near)

10. **A:** Was the Hudson River ______________ 10 years ago
(polluted)
______________ it is today?

B: Yes, it was. It is much ______________ today.
(clean)

11. **A:** Which highway has ______________ traffic, the West Highway
(heavy)
or the East Highway?

B: It depends on the time.

B | *Rewrite the sentences. Use* **less** *and the adjectives in parentheses. Use the comparative form.*

1. Sydney is *less expensive* to live in *than* Tokyo.
(expensive)
2. Miami is ______________ in winter ______________ in summer.
(less humid)
3. The Hudson River is ______________ today ______________ it was 10 years ago.
(less polluted)
4. Is the highway ______________ between 7:00 and 8:00 ______________ it is between 8:00 and 9:00?
(crowded)
5. Is the Eiffel Tower ______________ than the Egyptian pyramids?
(famous)

EXERCISE 3: Comparison of Adjectives

(Grammar Notes 1–2, 4, 8)

Write sentences comparing the two cities. Use the information in the chart and the words in parentheses.

	Middletown	Lakeville
number of people	100,000	50,000
average household income	$85,000	$63,000
average rent for a two-bedroom apartment	$1,300	$1,000
cost of a cup of coffee	$2.00	$1.00
percent unemployed	7	9
number of hospitals	5	1
average summer temperature	80°F	68°F

1. (average household income / high)

The average household income in Middletown is higher than the average household income in Lakeville.

2. (two-bedroom apartment / expensive)

____

____

3. (a cup of coffee / less expensive)

____

____

4. (probably / hard to find work)

____

____

5. (probably / healthcare / bad)

____

____

6. (summers / much / warm)

____

____

EXERCISE 4: Comparison of Adjectives

(Grammar Notes 1–7)

Complete the paragraph with the adjectives in parentheses. Use the comparative form.

Rodeo Drive, Los Angeles

You are choosing between two cities to live in, Los Angeles or Glendale. You aren't sure which is a ___better___ (1. good) choice. Los Angeles is a much ________________ (2. big) city than Glendale, and it has all the problems of big cities. Los Angeles is ________________ (3. polluted) than Glendale, and traffic is ________________ (4. bad). The streets of downtown Los Angeles are ________________ (5. busy) too. However, Los Angeles is much ________________ (6. exciting) than Glendale. Los Angeles has a great night life. Glendale is much ________________ (7. quiet) at night. Both cities have the same great climate. It's hard to compare housing costs. Some parts of Los Angeles are ________________ (8. more / expensive) than Glendale and other parts are ________________ (9. less / expensive). Both cities are close, so if you make a mistake, you can always move.

Bicycle trail, Glendale, California

EXERCISE 5: Editing

Correct the sentences. There are seven mistakes. The first one is already corrected. Find and correct six more.

1. Our new apartment is ^more comfortable than our old one.
2. Florida is more hotter than Maine.
3. Oregon is far north than California.
4. A motorcycle is more fast than a bicycle.
5. Traffic at 8:00 A.M. is more heavy than traffic at 10:00 A.M.
6. The climate in Portland, Oregon, is mild than the climate in Anchorage, Alaska.
7. The location of Jake's apartment is more convenient than his sister.

STEP 4 COMMUNICATION PRACTICE

EXERCISE 6: Pronunciation

A | *Read and listen to the Pronunciation Note.*

Pronunciation Note

Than is unstressed and reduced to **/ ðn /**.

EXAMPLE: Istanbul is a much larger city than Izmír.

B | *Listen and repeat each sentence.*

1. The Nile River is longer than the Amazon River.
2. The Yangtze River is shorter than the Nile.
3. Quebec City is older than Vancouver.
4. The Pacific Ocean is bigger than the Atlantic Ocean.

EXERCISE 7: Listening

A | *Listen to a conversation between two friends. The woman says, "You can thank our mayor." What is the mayor doing to the city?*

____

B | *Listen again. Circle the correct word or words to complete each sentence.*

1. The downtown area is **livelier / less lively**.
2. The seats on the bus are **more comfortable / less comfortable**.
3. It's **easier / harder** to take the bus.
4. The air is **cleaner / dirtier**.
5. It's **easier / harder** to park downtown.
6. West Park is **cleaner and safer / dirtier and more dangerous**.
7. East Park is **cleaner and safer / dirtier and more dangerous**.

EXERCISE 8: Comparing Train Systems

PAIRS: Look at the information about the London Underground and the Moscow Metro. Together write as many comparative questions as you can. Ask other pairs your questions. Answer their questions. Then compare these subways to others you know.

EXAMPLE: **A:** Is the Underground faster than the Moscow Metro?
B: No, it isn't. It's slower.

	London Underground	Moscow Metro
Year opened	1863	1935
Length of tracks	250 miles (400 kilometers)	187.2 miles (301.2 kilometers)
Number of passengers each day	4 million	6.6 million
Hours of operation	5:30 A.M. to 1:15 A.M. (Fri. & Sat. closes at 2:00 A.M.)	5:30 A.M. to 1:00 A.M.
Cost of ride in euros	4 euros for shortest distance	26 rubles = .66 euro
Speed	20.5 mph (33 km / h)	25.82 mph (41.55 km / h)

EXERCISE 9: Discussion: Making Comparisons

PAIRS: Look at the categories in the list. Tell your partner your preferences within each category. Explain why in a sentence with a comparative.

clothes **homes** **jobs** **travel** **vacation places**

EXAMPLE: **A:** Do you prefer to travel by bike or by motorcycle?
B: I prefer a motorcycle. It's faster and more exciting. What about you?
A: I prefer a bike. It's safer and better for the environment.

EXERCISE 10: Comparing Cities

Compare cities. Follow the steps.

1. Name a city you know well. (Do not name the city you are in.) Your teacher writes the names everyone suggests on the board.
2. Class: Name adjectives that describe cities, people, and climates. Your teacher writes the adjectives on the board.

EXAMPLES:

Cities	People	Climates
clean	friendly	warm
dangerous	polite	dry
exciting	relaxed	humid

3. Write questions comparing the cities on the board to the city you are in. Use the adjectives on the board or choose your own. Then with a group, ask each other questions comparing the cities.

Examples: (You are now in San Francisco.)
A: Is Paris cleaner than San Francisco?
B: I don't think so. I think San Francisco is cleaner than Paris.
C: Does Sapporo have a warmer climate than San Francisco?
D: No, it doesn't. Sapporo has a colder climate than San Francisco.

EXERCISE 11: Writing

A | *Compare two ways of travel. Use at least three comparative adjectives.*

Example: Most cities have busses and trains, but in San Francisco some people also travel by trolley, and in Venice people sometimes travel by gondola. Both the trolley and the gondola are more fun than the bus or the train. The gondola is more romantic than the trolley, but the trolley is more exciting, especially when you're traveling down one of San Francisco's steep streets.

B | *Check your work. Use the Editing Checklist.*

Editing Checklist

Did you . . . ?
☐ use comparative adjectives correctly
☐ check your spelling

UNIT 33 Review

Check your answers on page UR-7.
Do you need to review anything?

A | *Circle the correct words to complete the sentences.*

1. She is **more / much** younger than he is.
2. It is colder **then / than** it was yesterday.
3. This singing group is **more popular / popular more** than the other one.
4. The traffic is **more worse / worse** now than it was an hour ago.
5. Which city has a **high / higher** elevation, Bogota or Mexico City?
6. Which city has a **better / more good** transportation system, Quebec or Vancouver?
7. Is your car more comfortable than your **brother / brother's**?

B | *Look at the chart. Make comparisons. Use the words in parentheses.*

	New City	Sun City
Bus fare	\$2.00	\$3.00
Cup of coffee	\$1.20	\$1.50
Average home	\$200,000	\$300,000
Average income	\$65,000	\$90,000

1. ______________________________
(bus / expensive)
2. ______________________________
(cup of coffee / cheap)
3. ______________________________
(average home / less / expensive)
4. ______________________________
(average income / high)

C | *Correct the paragraph. There are nine mistakes.*

We moved to the countryside, and we're much more happier. Our home is more larger, and the air is cleaner and polluted less. It less expensive than the city too. Fruits and vegetables are more cheap. The people are friendler too. Of course, our commute is more bad; it's much more long, but we listen to Spanish tapes, and our Spanish is more good.

UNIT 34

Adverbs of Manner

PUBLIC SPEAKING

STEP 1 GRAMMAR IN CONTEXT

Before You Read

A | *PAIRS: List jobs that require speaking in front of large groups. Compare your list with other pairs' lists.*

B | *How do you feel about giving a speech in front of the following people? Check (✓) your feelings.*

How you feel when you speak in front of . . .				
	your classmates?	**your friends and relatives?**	**your bosses?**	**250 people you don't know?**
calm and confident				
nervous but confident				
nervous and not confident				
nervous and miserable				

Read

Read the blog about public speaking.

Speaking about . . .

Public Speaking by Michelle Jones

Like

Last year my boss asked me to give a presentation. It was a bit of a nightmare. I had never spoken in front of a large group before, so I was nervous. Also, I had to prepare **fast**—I had only two days to get ready. The day of the speech came. There were 40 people sitting in the room waiting for me to speak. My manager was there, and my co-workers. I wanted to run out of the room, so I spoke **quickly**, and I didn't look at anyone. Instead I read from my paper. I was afraid to tell a joke. I wanted to sound smart, so in my speech, I gave a lot of facts. I used big words and long sentences. I received polite applause, but I knew my speech was not appreciated. My friend later told me it was a good speech, but that I didn't speak **loudly** enough.

(*continued on next page*)

Speaking about . . .

The next time I gave a speech, I asked my friend for help. She offered a lot of valuable advice. She helped me to focus on three ideas and to give good examples. In my next speech I spoke **slowly** and **clearly**. I thought **carefully** about everything I wanted to say. I spoke **honestly**, and I gave personal examples. I only said things I really believed. I looked at my audience, and I smiled at the right occasions. This time the applause was long and loud. I connected with the audience, and I felt good. People gave me their time, and I gave them a speech to remember.

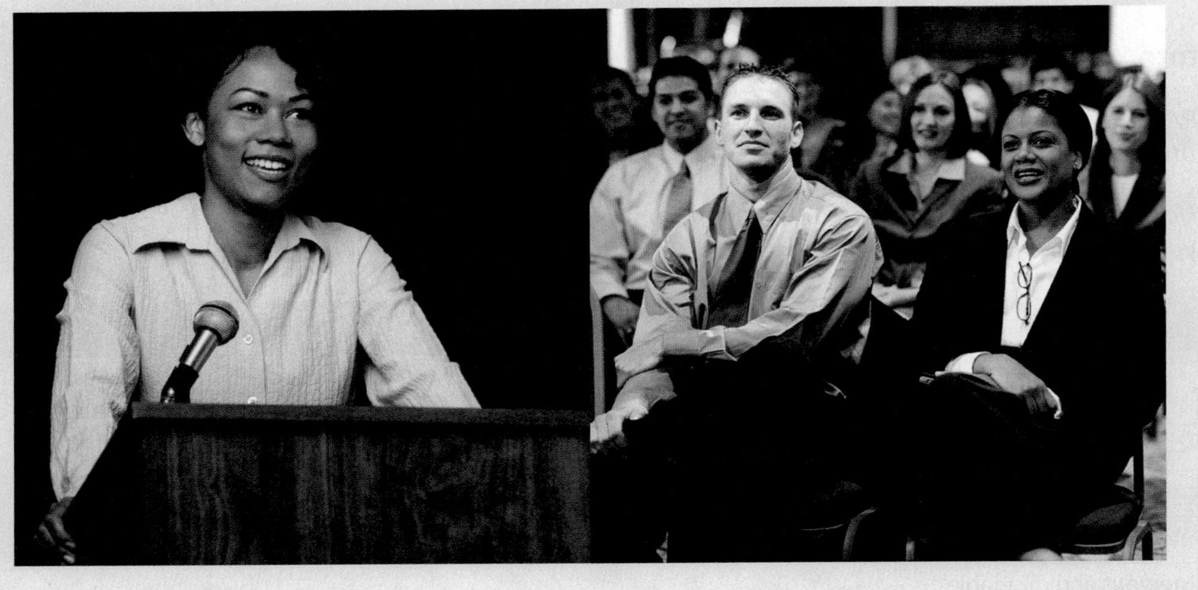

After You Read

A | Practice *PAIRS: Read the blog again aloud. Take turns reading the sentences.*

B | Vocabulary *Circle the letter of the best meaning for the words in* **blue**.

1. The **audience** was interested in every word he said.

a. people who write about a performance **b.** people who watch a performance

2. When he heard the long **applause**, he felt satisfied.

a. clapping of hands **b.** stamping of feet

3. Most of his speech was light and funny, but he spoke **seriously** at the end of his talk.

a. in a way that says something is wrong **b.** in a way that says something is important

4. He told us many **facts** about his country.

a. true things **b.** interesting things

5. We laughed at his **jokes**.

a. funny stories   b. gestures

6. The people clapped to be **polite**, but they didn't really enjoy his talk.

a. show good manners   b. show anger

7. She **appreciated** my help and thanked me many times.

a. was nervous about   b. was grateful for

C | Comprehension *Check (✓) the advice you got from the public speaking blog.*

____ 1. Speak quickly.

____ 2. Speak slowly.

____ 3. Use big words.

____ 4. Look at audience.

____ 5. Use humor.

____ 6. Give personal examples.

____ 7. Have many ideas, not just three or four.

____ 8. Speak briefly.

STEP 2 GRAMMAR PRESENTATION

ADVERBS OF MANNER

Subject	Verb	Adverb
He	**spoke**	**well**.
		badly.
		clearly.

Subject	Verb		Adverb
She	**finished**	her speech	**quickly**.

Adverb formed with Adjective + *-ly*	
Adjective	**Adverb**
bad	badly
careful	carefully
loud	loudly
quick	quickly
quiet	quietly
sarcastic	sarcastically
slow	slowly

Same Adjective and Adverb Form	
Adjective	**Adverb**
early	early
fast	fast
late	late
long	long

Irregular Adverb Form	
Adjective	**Adverb**
good	well

GRAMMAR NOTES

1	**Adverbs of manner** describe action verbs. They say **how** or the way something happens. The adverb often comes at the end of the sentence.	• She spoke **slowly**. • He walked **fast**.
2	Most adverbs of manner are formed by adding -***ly*** to an adjective. **BE CAREFUL!** Some words that end in *-ly* are adjectives, not adverbs. **EXAMPLES:** *lively, lovely, ugly, lonely, friendly* These adjectives have no adverb form.	ADJECTIVE • She's a **careful** driver. ADVERB • She drives **carefully**. ADJECTIVE • She's a **friendly** person. • It's a **lonely** job.
3	Some **adverbs** of manner have the **same form as adjectives**.	ADJECTIVE ... ADVERB • She's a **hard** worker. She works **hard**.
4	***Well*** is the adverb for the adjective *good*. *Well* is also an adjective that means "in good health." **USAGE NOTE:** In very informal speaking, when people ask, "How are you?" some people respond, "I'm good."	ADJECTIVE • She's a **good** speaker. ADVERB • She speaks **well**. ADJECTIVE • I feel **well**.
5	**Linking verbs** can connect a subject and an adjective. **Linking verbs** are followed by **adjectives**, not adverbs. Common linking verbs are *appear, be, become, feel, look, seem, smell, sound*, and *taste*.	LINKING VERB ... ADJECTIVE • The grapes **taste good**. NOT: The grapes taste ~~well~~. • She **seems sad**. • It **sounds beautiful**.

STEP 3 FOCUSED PRACTICE

EXERCISE 1: Discover the Grammar

Read the paragraph. Underline the adverbs of manner in the paragraph.

A public speaker should remember three things: to entertain, to instruct, and to inspire. Author Bob Rosner likes to say, "It's ha-ha and ah-ha." When you instruct, speak briefly and clearly. Don't speak too long. And don't speak too fast. Use humor. It helps your audience relax. And remember that great speeches inspire and move an audience. Know your audience and touch their emotions.

EXERCISE 2: Adverbs of Manner

(Grammar Notes 1–4)

Complete each sentence with the adverb form of the adjectives in parentheses.

1. He spoke ___quickly___. **(quick)**
2. Sally writes ______________. **(good)**
3. They speak Spanish ______________. **(fluent)**
4. He spoke ______________. **(clear)**
5. He drove ______________. **(fast)**
6. The audience listened ______________. **(careful)**
7. Did he drive ______________? **(dangerous)**
8. Did they sing ______________? **(bad)**
9. The movie began ______________. **(slow)**
10. It rained ______________ last night. **(hard)**

EXERCISE 3: Adverbs of Manner and Adjectives

(Grammar Notes 1–5)

Complete the conversation. Choose from the words in parentheses. Write the correct adjective or adverbs.

1. **A:** How was the debate?

   B: Good. Both sides spoke ___well___. **(good / well)**

2. **A:** How was the food at the reception after the debate?

   B: It tasted ______________. **(good / well)**

(continued on next page)

3. **A:** There were ___________________ paintings in the room.
(beautiful / beautifully)

B: The artist is from Colombia.

4. **A:** How did Roger do in his last debate?

B: Not ___________________.
(good / well)

5. **A:** Please drive ___________________.
(slow / slowly)

B: OK.

6. **A:** How was the talk?

B: The first part was very ___________________, but the second part was better.
(slow / slowly)

7. **A:** How did she sound?

B: ___________________.
(Nervous / Nervously)

EXERCISE 4: Editing

Correct the conversations. There are six mistakes. The first mistake is already corrected. Find and correct five more.

1. **A:** How did he do?

B: He did ~~good~~ well.

2. **A:** Was the food OK?

B: Everyone loved it. It really tasted well.

3. **A:** Is Harry a good driver?

B: I don't think so. He drives too slow.

4. **A:** How did they do?

B: They worked hardly and did well.

5. **A:** Did you hear him?

B: No, I didn't. He spoke too soft.

6. **A:** How did she sound?

B: A little nervously.

STEP 4 COMMUNICATION PRACTICE

EXERCISE 5: Listening

A | *Listen to some tips for giving a speech. Complete the sentences.*

You have a good ________________ and ________________. You have a couple of good ________________.

B | *Listen again and write the five tips for making a good speech better.*

1. Look directly at a few people in the audience.
2. ________________
3. ________________
4. ________________
5. ________________

EXERCISE 6: Pronunciation

A | *Read and listen to the Pronunciation Note.*

Pronunciation Note

Sometimes our manner of speaking, our intonation, gives a different meaning to a sentence.

Examples: Who's he? (questioning) Who's he? (angry)

B | *Do you know what the words in boldface mean? If not, use your dictionary. Then listen to the speakers' manner.*

angrily: I love him. He's mine, and you can't have him.

decisively: I love him. I'll love him until I die.

questioningly: Do I love him? Enough to marry him?

sadly: I love him. I miss him so much.

sarcastically: I just love him. His bark wakes me up every day at 5:00 A.M.

C | *Listen again and repeat the sentences.*

D | *PAIRS: Say, "I love him (or her)." Say it angrily, decisively, questioningly, sadly, or sarcastically. Your partner guesses your meaning.*

EXERCISE 7: Writing

A | *PAIRS: Tell about a sports event.*

B | *Write about the event. Use three adverbs of frequency.*

Example: It was the final ball game of the season for the Fogville Little League Team. Fogville was up against Lakeville, a very strong team. The score was seven to seven. The bases were loaded. Ron was up at bat. Everyone groaned loudly. Ron never played well. He was the team's worst player. But Ron hit the ball hard. He ran quickly to first base. The man on third ran home. They won. Everyone applauded loudly. It was a great game for everyone, especially Ron.

C | *Check your work. Use the Editing Checklist.*

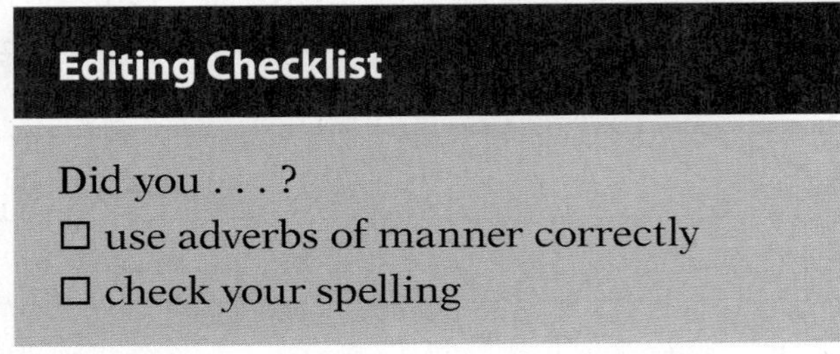

Editing Checklist

Did you . . . ?

☐ use adverbs of manner correctly

☐ check your spelling

UNIT 34 Review

Check your answers on page UR-7.
Do you need to review anything?

A | *Complete the sentences with the adjectives in parentheses. Use the adverb form.*

1. He drove ____________________.
   (quick)
2. She speaks Korean ____________________.
   (fluent)
3. Did he do ____________________ on the test?
   (good)
4. Walk ____________________ and look at the trees.
   (slow)
5. I spoke ____________________.
   (clear)

B | *Circle the correct word to complete the sentences.*

1. Both sides gave **good / well** arguments.
2. He listened very **careful / carefully**.
3. She sounded a little **nervous / nervously**.
4. He did **bad / badly** on the last test.
5. I can't understand her because she's talking too **quick / quickly**.

C | *Complete the sentences. Choose from the words in the box.*

briefly	clearly	fast	good	honestly

If you want to give a ____________________ (1.) speech, remember these things: Speak ____________________ (2.) and ____________________ (3.). Don't speak too long or swallow your words. Don't speak too ____________________ (4.). People need time to understand your ideas. Speak ____________________ (5.). Say only what you mean.

D | *Correct the conversation. There are five mistakes.*

A: I think my speech went good.

B: Did they appreciate your jokes?

A: They laughed polite, but I'm not sure they laughed sincere.

B: It's hard to be funny.

A: I hard worked, and I prepared carefully, but I was nervously.

UNIT 35

Enough, Too / Very, As + Adjective + As, Same / Different

PROMS AND PARTIES

STEP 1 GRAMMAR IN CONTEXT

Before You Read

A prom is a formal school dance. It usually takes place at the end of the senior year of high school. In the United States, proms can include dinner and dancing. Couples often come in limousines. Are there special parties or dances in your country? When are they? What are they like?

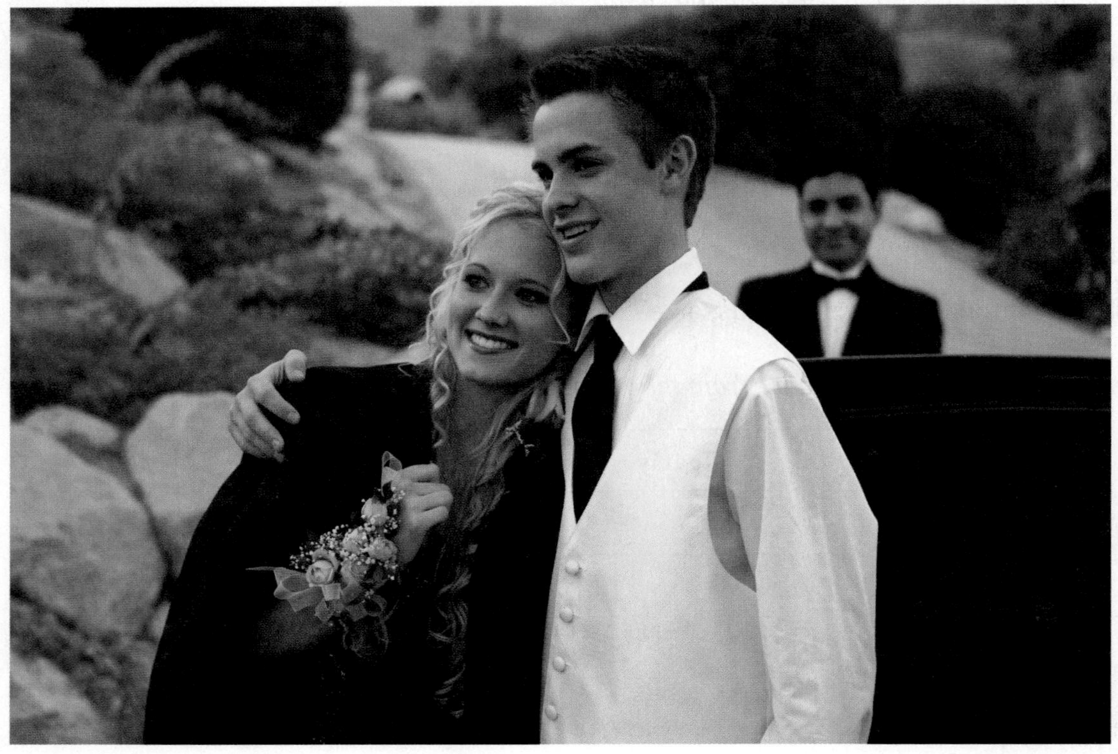

Read

Read a conversation between two high school students, Emily and Haley.

EMILY: So Haley—what did you decide? Who's your date for the prom?

HALEY: I don't have one. I'm not going.

EMILY: What do you mean? You know so many cool guys. . . . How about Mike?

HALEY: No—he's **too talkative**. When he's around, no one can get a word in edgewise.

EMILY: Oh. He *does* talk a lot. Well . . . how about David? He likes you.

Haley: David? He's **way too young** for me.

Emily: He's in **the same** grade **as** we are. What are you talking about?

Haley: No, Emily. He's a *sophomore*. He's in our Spanish class because he lived in Spain for a while. I can't go with him. People will say I'm a loser if I go with him.

Emily: Well how about Jake? He's **old enough**, and he's **very** cute.

Haley: He dresses funny.[1]

Emily: Oh, come on, Haley, Jake doesn't dress funny. You're just making excuses.

Haley: OK, OK. But Jake is **too good looking** and **too popular**. I'm not his type.

Emily: That's not true. My brother says Jake thinks you're awesome.

Haley: Really? All right. I'll tell you the real reason. I can't dance. I'm a klutz.[2] I look like an idiot on the dance floor. So . . . I'm not going to make a fool of myself.

Emily: Not a problem. Jake is sort of a klutz too. He broke his foot in art class.

Haley: What? In *art class*?

Emily: He tripped over a can of paint. So it'll be perfect. You can go with him and watch the rest of us dance. I'll talk to my brother. Then Jake will ask you. Don't say no.

---

[1] ***He dresses funny:*** (very informal) He dresses strangely, badly.

[2] ***klutz:*** a clumsy person

After You Read

A | Practice *PAIRS: Now practice the conversation aloud.*

B | Vocabulary *Circle the letter of the best meaning for the words in* **blue**.

1. "When he's around, **no one can get a word in edgewise**," means _____.
   - **a.** he never says what he means
   - **b.** he does all the talking
2. "People will say **I'm a loser**" means _____.
   - **a.** I'm unpopular
   - **b.** I get bad grades
3. "You're just **making excuses**," means _____.
   - **a.** you're sorry about something
   - **b.** you aren't telling the truth
4. "**I'm not his type**," means _____.
   - **a.** He's too old for me
   - **b.** He's different from me
5. "**I'm not going to make a fool of myself**," means _____.
   - **a.** I won't do anything that makes me look bad
   - **b.** I'm not stupid

C | Comprehension *Write* **T (True)** *or* **F (False)** *for each statement.*

_____ **1.** Mike is too young for Haley.

_____ **2.** Emily and Haley are sophomores.

_____ **3.** David likes Haley.

_____ **4.** Haley and Emily are in the same Spanish class.

_____ **5.** Haley thinks Jake likes her.

_____ **6.** Haley can't dance well.

_____ **7.** Jake hurt himself in art class.

STEP 2 GRAMMAR PRESENTATION

ENOUGH, TOO / VERY, AS + ADJECTIVE + *AS, SAME / DIFFERENT*

Adjective + *Enough*

	Adjective	*Enough*	(Infinitive)
The room was	**big**	**enough**	to hold all the students.
It wasn't	**warm**		to go without a jacket.

***Very* + Adjective**

	Very	Adjective
The prom was	**very**	**expensive.**

***Too* + Adjective**

	Too	Adjective	(Infinitive)	
His father's tuxedo was	**too**	big	(for him)	to wear.

As* + Adjective + *As

	As	Adjective	*As*	
Jake is	**as**	**tall**	**as**	his dad.
He isn't		**heavy**		his dad is.

The Same As

My first name is	**the same as**	yours.
My initials are		his.

Different From

Her dress is	**different from**	mine.
These books are		those.

The Same* + Noun (Noun Phrase) + *As

	The Same	Noun	*As*	
My eyes are	**the same**	**color**	**as**	my brother's. yours.
Max has		**last name**		James.
Jim likes		**kind of food**		I do.

GRAMMAR NOTES

1	***Enough*** means that you have the amount you need. It has a positive meaning. Use *enough* after an adjective. Use *enough* before a noun.	ADJECTIVE • He's **old enough** to drive. NOUN • There are **enough chairs**.
2	***Too*** means "more than necessary." It has a negative meaning. Use *too* before an adjective. ***Much too*** or ***way too*** makes the meaning stronger. **USAGE NOTE:** We use *way too* in informal speaking and writing.	• The coffee is **too hot**. I burned my tongue. • The suit was **much too big** for him. • The prom was **way too short**. I didn't want to go home.
3	An **infinitive** can follow **adjective** + ***enough***. An **infinitive** can follow ***too*** + **adjective**.	INFINITIVE • He's **old enough to drive**. • She's **too tired to drive**.
4	***Very*** makes the meaning of an adjective stronger. *Very* comes before an adjective. **BE CAREFUL!** *Too* has a negative meaning, but *very* doesn't.	• He's **very tall**. • He's **very young**. *(He's really young. He's 16, and the other students are 18.)* • He's **too young**. *(He's too young to do something—to drive, to work, etc.)*
5	Use ***as*** + **adjective** + ***as*** to show how two people, places, or things are alike. Use ***not as*** + **adjective** + ***as*** to show how two people, places, or things are not alike.	• Sally is **as tall as** Paula. They're the same height. • Sally is **not as tall as** Mike. Mike is taller.
6	Use ***the same as*** for things that are alike. Use ***different from*** for things that are not alike.	• His family name is **the same as** hers. *(He's Robert Lee, and she's Jennifer Lee.)* • My book is **different from** yours. *(I have a new edition.)*

STEP 3 FOCUSED PRACTICE

EXERCISE 1: Discover the Grammar

A | *Circle the adjectives in the sentences. Then underline* **too, as . . . as, enough** *and* **very.** *Draw arrows from the adjectives to the nouns they go with.*

1. Mr. Jones isn't as old as he looks.
2. The food wasn't spicy enough for him.
3. His dress shoes were too tight.
4. Her prom dress was very beautiful.
5. That tuxedo was too expensive.
6. The car wasn't big enough for all of us.

B | *Underline* **the same . . . as** *and* **different from** *in the sentences.*

1. Serena wore the same dress as Jasmin.
2. He has the same voice as his father. It's confusing when I call his home.
3. He's different from his brother. His brother loves to go to parties.
4. Adam Rusk has the same initials as Ali Rogers.

EXERCISE 2: *Enough, Too*

(Grammar Notes 1–2)

Haley is talking to her aunt about the prom. Complete their conversation with **enough** *or* **too** *and the words from the box.*

~~hot~~	ice	salty	seats	sweet

AUNT ANNE: So, Haley. How was the prom?

HALEY: I had a great time, but there were a few problems with the place. The air conditioner didn't work well, so it was ___*too hot*___ (1.) in the room.

AUNT ANNE: It was a warm night. I feel bad for the guys in those tuxedos. How was the music?

HALEY: Good, but the refreshments were so-so. The chips were ________________ (2.), and the desserts were ________________ (3.). And there wasn't ________________ (4.) for the drinks, so the drinks were warm.

Aunt Anne: That's pretty bad.

Haley: Also, there weren't ________________ (5.). All but a few of us had to stand. Since Jake hurt his foot, we were able to sit. But I'm really glad I went. Jake's a nice guy, and we have a lot in common.

Aunt Anne: I'm glad. Your mom sent me your picture. You looked very beautiful in that dress.

Haley: Thanks.

EXERCISE 3: Word Order Practice; *Enough*, *Too . . . To*

(Grammar Notes 1–3)

Write sentences with the words given.

1. to vote / She isn't / enough / old

   She isn't old enough to vote.

2. warm / that dress / to wear / It isn't / enough

   ____

3. too / This steak / is / to eat / tough / much

   ____

4. to call / him / I'm / busy / too / right now

   ____

5. weren't / the sofa / They / enough / strong / to move

   ____

6. much / restaurant / too / That / expensive / is

   ____

7. too / was / to miss / That class / important

   ____

8. before the movie / have / don't / time / enough / We / to eat

   ____

9. clear / wasn't / to read / His address / enough

   ____

EXERCISE 4: *Too* + Adjective / *The Same . . . As* (Grammar Notes 2, 6)

A | *Russ Tran, Jean Philippe, and Robert Trent are friends and co-workers. They take turns driving to work. Complete the sentences with the words from the box.*

too carelessly	too fast	too slowly

1. Russ thinks Jean drives ______________________. He thinks Jean will get a speeding ticket.
2. Jean thinks Russ and Robert drive ______________________. He complains that they drive under the speed limit.
3. Russ thinks Robert drives ______________________. He eats, drinks, and answers phone calls while driving.

B | *Look at the three licenses. Use the information from the licenses to write similarities among the people. Use* **has,** *the words in parentheses, and* **as.**

1. **(the same height)** ______________________
   Jean Philippe is the same height as
   Robert Trent.
2. **(the same color eyes)** ______________________
   ______________________.
3. **(the same initials)** ______________________
   ______________________.
4. **(the same weight)** ______________________
   ______________________.

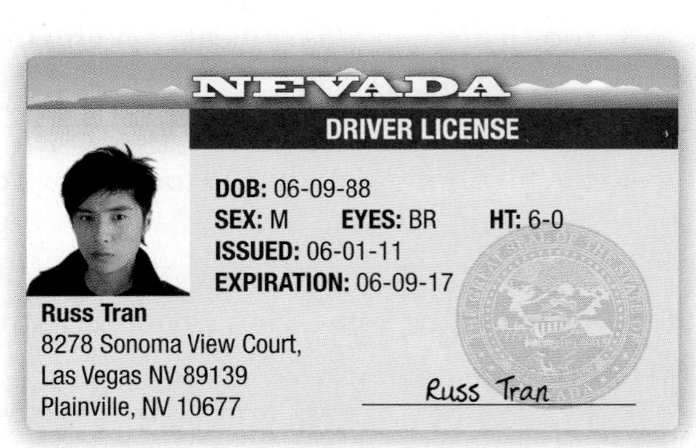

EXERCISE 5: *Too / Very*

(Grammar Notes 2–4)

Complete the sentences with **too** *or* **very.**

1. Some people think that a black dress is ___too___ dark to wear to a prom, but I think it's __________ fashionable.
2. Don't buy those shoes. They're __________ pretty, but the heels are __________ high. They will hurt your feet.
3. Jake called __________ late to order a limousine, so he picked up Haley in his car.
4. He can't reach the shelf. He's __________ short. Ask Ali. He's __________ tall.
5. Your composition is __________ well written. You did a great job.
6. I can't lift the box. It's __________ heavy. I'll ask Barry. He's __________ strong.
7. It's __________ windy outside. Put on a jacket. It's __________ cold to go outside without one.
8. It's __________ difficult to get into that school. His grades are __________ low. He probably won't get in.
9. This jacket doesn't fit. It's __________ tight in the shoulders.
10. It's __________ early to go to the party. We don't want to be the first to arrive.
11. We had a __________ good time at Joel's graduation party, but there were __________ many guests, so it was crowded.

EXERCISE 6: *As* + Adjective + *As*, *The Same* + Noun + *As*

(Grammar Note 5)

Read the conversation between Jake and Haley. Jake applied to an art school but did not get in. Complete the sentences with the phrases from the box.

~~as hard as she does~~	**the same art camp as she did**
as serious an artist as she is	**the same grades as she did**
as well as she does	

HALEY: Jake, what's wrong?

JAKE: I'm really angry. Maya got into BCA Art Institute, and I didn't. I work ___just as hard as she does___ (1.).

HALEY: And you're really talented.

JAKE: Thanks. I think I'm ______________ (2.).

HALEY: Yes, you work very hard on your drawings and paintings.

JAKE: And I hand in every project on time. I draw ______________ (3.).

HALEY: Why do you think she got into BCA Art Institute then?

JAKE: I don't know. I got ______________ (4.). We had the same art teachers. I even went to ______________ (5.). Maybe she got in because she knows someone at BCA?

HALEY: That happens sometimes.

EXERCISE 7: Editing

Correct the sentences. There are eight mistakes. The first mistake is already corrected. Find and correct seven more.

1. He doesn't have ^enough money ~~enough~~ to pay for the limousine.
2. His girlfriend isn't as nice than his old one.
3. She's very different than her sister.
4. We're very young to vote. You have to be 18 years old. We're 17.
5. She has the same dress than I do.
6. I'm as taller as my father.
7. Dan's weight is the same as his brother.
8. Is your new book bag enough big for all your books?

STEP 4 COMMUNICATION PRACTICE

EXERCISE 8: Pronunciation

A | *Read and listen to the Pronunciation Note.*

Pronunciation Note

When an adjective appears between ***as . . . as***, stress the adjective and not ***as***. ***As*** is unstressed and reduced to **/ əz /**.

Example: She's as cold as ice.

B | *Listen. Complete the sentences with the words you hear.*

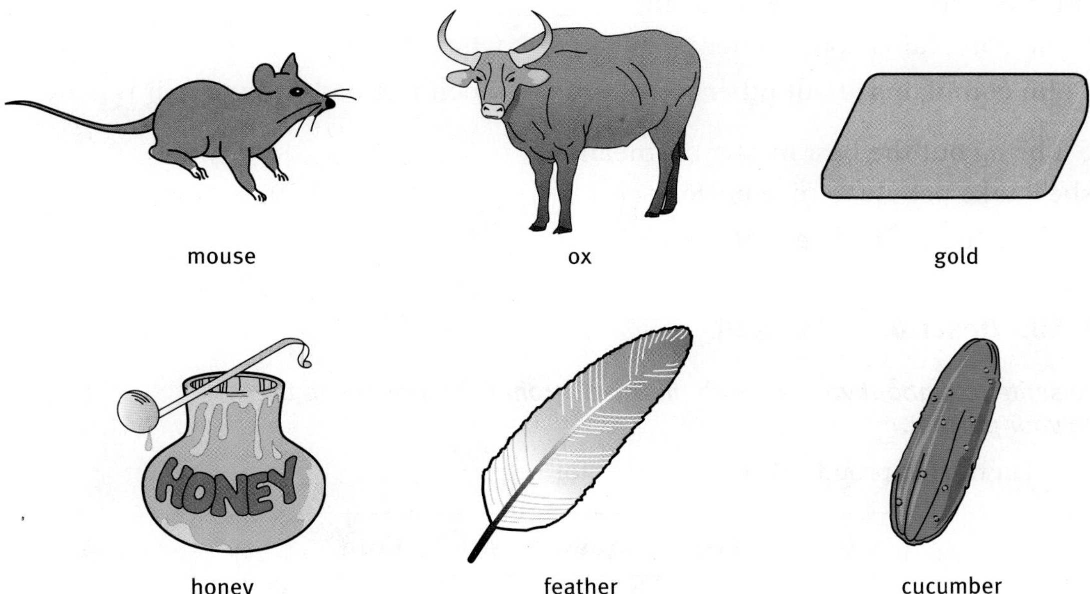

1. She's bright, but she never says a word. She just sits and smiles. She's as quiet as a ___mouse___.
2. I'm sorry I bought that chair. You have to be as strong as an ________ to lift it.
3. He never shows his feelings. He's as cool as a ________.
4. Her sister is nasty, but she's as sweet as ________.
5. She doesn't weigh much at all. She's as light as a ________.
6. I was very upset when she didn't keep her promise. I thought her word was as good as ________.

C | *Now listen and repeat each sentence. Remember not to stress the word* **as.**

EXERCISE 9: Listening

A | *Listen to the conversation. Two managers are talking about two young employees, Colin and Maria. Complete the sentence. Circle the correct letter.*

The managers _______________.

a. are planning to promote both people

b. promoted one person and didn't promote the other

B | *Listen again. Then complete the sentences. Circle the correct letter.*

1. "Maria's word is good as gold" means _______________.

a. she does what she says she will

b. she usually says nice things to others

2. "Colin is too critical of others" means _______________.

a. Colin complains about other people's work when it is bad

b. Colin complains about other people's work when it is bad *and* when it is good

3. "She'll bring out the best in others" means _______________.

a. she'll take people to nice places

b. she'll help people do a better job

EXERCISE 10: Describing Yourself

PAIRS: Write sentences about yourself with the words from the boxes. Read the sentences to your partner.

EXAMPLE: I'm not too proud to ask my friends for help.

busy	lazy	proud	shy	tired

I'm too _______________ to _______________.

I'm not too _______________ to _______________.

old	smart	strong	tall	young

I'm _______________ enough to _______________.

I'm not _______________ enough to _______________.

EXERCISE 11: Similarities

Take five minutes. Walk around your classroom. Find classmates who are like you in some way. Use the chart for suggestions. Take notes. Report to the class. The person who finds the most similarities wins.

EXAMPLES: Cecilia and I were born in the same month.
Julio and I have the same color eyes.
Ming and I like the same kind of movies.
Pierre and I have the same number of sisters.
Jasmine and I have the same lucky number.

Suggestions				
Born	**Looks**	**Likes**	**Families**	**Your Ideas**
same month same day	same color eyes same color hair same height	same kind of movies, music, sports	same number of brothers or sisters	

EXERCISE 12: Writing

A | *Write about two friends or two events. Use three of these structures:* **very, too, as . . . as, the same as,** *and* **different from.** *Underline the examples in your paragraph.*

EXAMPLE: I'm a sophomore in college. I went to two parties this year. I liked the first party. The people were very cool. There were lots of different kinds of students: musicians, artists, but also athletes. Everyone was friendly. The second party was not as good as the first party. The people were not the same—this group wasn't friendly. No one talked to me. The music was too loud.

B | *Check your work. Use the Editing Checklist.*

Editing Checklist

Did you . . . ?
☐ use ***very, too, as . . . as, the same as,*** and ***different from*** correctly
☐ check your spelling

UNIT 35 Review

Check your answers on page UR-7.
Do you need to review anything?

A | *Circle the words to complete the sentences.*

1. Is that limousine **big enough / enough big** for us to fit in it?
2. His car is the same kind **as / than** mine.
3. He's **very / too** young to get a driver's license. He can't drive legally.
4. He's not as young **from / as** he looks.
5. The new driving test is different **as / from** the old one.

B | *Complete the sentences. Use* **very, enough,** *or* **too** *and the words from the box.*

busy	good	late	short	time	warm

1. The water isn't _______________ _______________ for swimming.
2. She's taking a taxi because she's _______________ _______________.
3. I had a lot of work. I was _______________ _______________ to go to the party.
4. I don't like my hair. The hairdresser cut it _______________ _______________.
5. We don't have _______________ _______________ to go out after the prom.
6. He looks _______________ _______________ in his Dad's tuxedo.

C | *Correct the paragraph. There are nine mistakes.*

I didn't like the prom this year as much than last year. I usually like parties, but the music at the prom was much very loud. Also, my dress was same as Julia! That was a too big shock. Also, the dinner portions weren't enough large and the servers this year were very rude. Then we tried to dance, but there was no enough room and the room was too much hot. The music was also not good as last year. We had a more better time last year.

UNIT 36 The Superlative

PENGUINS

STEP 1 GRAMMAR IN CONTEXT

Before You Read

What do you know about penguins? Write **T** (**True**) *or* **F** (**False**) *for each statement.*

____ **1.** They only live in very cold climates.

____ **2.** They mostly live south of the equator.

____ **3.** They can weigh up to 90 pounds.

____ **4.** English explorers named them.

Read

Read the online article about penguins.

wild nature

WILD NATURE Animals Home | Animal Facts | Animal Photos | Animal Quizzes | Wild TV

THE PENGUIN

The penguin is one of **the easiest** birds to recognize. Penguins have black backs and white bellies.[1] They look fat. They stand upright, and they waddle.[2] Unlike other birds, most penguins can't fly, but they can swim very fast.

In 1519 Spanish explorers under Ferdinand Magellan saw penguins when they sailed around South America. They thought this type of bird was one of **the strangest** birds in the world. To them, the penguins looked like another strange bird, the Great Auk of Greenland and Iceland. The Great Auk was a large black and white bird that did not fly. The Spanish word for Great Auk is *pinguis* which means "fat." And that's how penguins got their name.

Fairy Penguin

There are 17 kinds of penguins. They all live below the equator, but they don't only live in very cold climates. Some, like the Little Blue Penguins, (sometimes called Fairy Penguins) live in warmer climates. The Little Blue Penguins are **the smallest** of all. They are 16 inches (about 41 centimeters) tall and weigh only 2.2 pounds (about 1 kilogram). They got their name because of their blue feathers. These penguins live in the warm waters off southern Australia and New Zealand.

[1] ***belly:*** stomach

[2] ***waddle:*** to walk from side to side like a duck

(continued on next page)

wild nature

The largest penguins are the Emperor Penguins. They are almost 4 feet (about 1.2 meters) tall and weigh from 70 to 90 pounds (about 32 to 41 kilograms). They live on the ice around the Antarctic continent. This is **the coldest** climate on earth.

Of the 17 different species of penguins, the Macaroni Penguins have **the biggest population**, while the Galapagos Penguins have **the smallest**. In fact, some scientists worry that the Galapagos Penguins may become extinct.

Emperor Penguin

People say penguins are **the cutest**, **the funniest**, and **the most loved** birds. They also say they're **the most formal**. Do you know why? It's because they look as if they're wearing tuxedos.[3]

[3] ***tuxedo:*** a formal suit worn at weddings or other very formal occasions

After You Read

A | Practice *PAIRS: Now read the article aloud. Take turns reading each paragraph.*

B | Vocabulary *Complete the sentences with the words from the box.*

centimeters	**extinct**	**inches**	**pounds**
explorer	**feathers**	**kilogram**	**species**

1. One centimeter is equal to .4 ________________.

2. 1 millimeter is the same as 0.1 ________________.

3. In the United States people usually measure their weight in ________________.

4. One ________________ is the same as 2.2 pounds.

5. There are 17 different ________________ of penguins.

6. Some scientists worry that oil spills and global warming may cause penguins to become ________________.

7. Most penguins' ________________ are white and black.

8. The Magellanic Penguin was named after the ________________ Ferdinand Magellan.

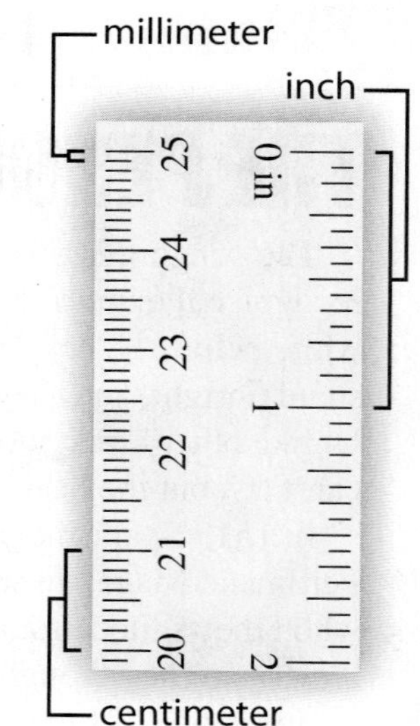

C | Comprehension *Complete the information with the words from the box.*

the Antarctic	**Galapagos Penguins**	**Little Blue Penguins**
Emperor Penguins	**Greenland and Iceland**	

1. The biggest penguins: ______________________________

2. The smallest penguins: ______________________________

3. The coldest place on earth: ______________________________

4. Home of the Great Auk: ______________________________

5. Penguin species with the smallest number: ______________________________

The puffin is descended from the Great Auk.

STEP 2 GRAMMAR PRESENTATION

SUPERLATIVE FORMS OF ADJECTIVES

Superlative Forms of Adjectives			
		Superlative Adjective	
The Emperor Penguin	is	**the biggest**	of all the penguins.
That photo		**the funniest**	of all.
That program		**the most interesting**	one on TV.

Superlative Forms of Irregular Adjectives			
		Superlative Adjective	
This	is	**the best**	photo of all.
We	had	**the worst**	weather on Saturday.
Her home	is	**the farthest**	of all.

GRAMMAR NOTES

1	Use the **superlative** form of adjectives to compare three or more people, places, or things.	• The Dead Sea is **the lowest** place on earth.
2	To form the superlative of **short (one-syllable) adjectives**, add ***the*** before the adjective and -***est*** to the adjective. *fast—**the fastest*** *long—**the longest*** If the adjective ends in ***e***, add -***st***. *large—**the largest***	• The cheetah is **the fastest** animal on earth. • Alaska is **the largest** state in the United States.
3	To form the superlative of **two-syllable adjectives that end in -*y***, add ***the*** before the adjective, then drop the -***y*** and add ***-iest*** to the adjective. *funny—**the funniest***	• The penguin is **the funniest** bird in the zoo.
4	To form the superlative of **long adjectives**, use ***the most*** before the adjective. *interesting—**the most interesting*** *dangerous—**the most dangerous***	• The bird section was **the most interesting** part of the zoo.
5	These adjectives have **irregular comparative** and **superlative** forms: **Adjective** — **Comparative Form** — **Superlative Form** *good* — *better (than)* — ***the best*** *bad* — *worse (than)* — ***the worst*** *far* — *farther (than)* — ***the farthest***	• It is **the best** time of year for bird watching. • That was **the worst** time to visit the zoo. • The Birdhouse is **the farthest** section from the entrance.
6	After the superlative, we often use a **prepositional phrase** to identify the group we are talking about.	• The giraffe is the tallest animal **in the zoo**. • The rhinoceros beetle is the strongest **of all the animals**.
7	***One of the*** often comes before a **superlative adjective**. The adjective is followed by a **plural noun**.	• It is **one of the largest animals** in the world. • It is **one of the most intelligent animals** of all. Not: It is one of the largest ~~animal~~.
8	**BE CAREFUL!** Do not use two superlative forms together.	• It's the biggest. Not: It's the **most** biggest. • It's the most important. Not: It's the most ~~importantest~~.

STEP 3 FOCUSED PRACTICE

EXERCISE 1: Discover the Grammar

A | *Underline the superlative adjective forms.*

1. Cockroaches are probably the most disliked insect in the world.
2. Cockroaches live everywhere, even in the cleanest kitchens.
3. The world's heaviest cockroach is the Australian Giant Burrowing Cockroach.
4. The best way to kill a cockroach is with boric acid.
5. The most famous cockroach was in a story by Franz Kafka. In it, a man turns into a cockroach.

B | *Write the adjectives used in the superlatives in Part A.*

1. disliked
2. __________
3. __________
4. __________
5. __________

C | *Find three more prepositional phrases that go with superlative statements in Part A.*

in the world, __________

EXERCISE 2: Superlative Form of Adjectives

(Grammar Notes 1–2, 4)

Complete the sentences with the words in parentheses. Use the superlative adjective form. Then guess the animal from the choices in the box. Write the correct letter.

a. the African elephant	**c. the hummingbird**	**e. the Macaroni Penguin**
b. ~~the blue whale~~	**d. the giraffe**	**f. the sailfish**

b 1. It is both the biggest (big) and __________ (loud) animal in the world.

____ 2. It is __________ (large) land animal.

____ 3. It is __________ (tall) animal today.

____ 4. It is __________ (small) bird. It is as small as 2.5 inches (6.2 centimeters) long and weighs only .06 ounces (1.6 grams).

____ 5. It is __________ (fast) fish. It swims up to 68 miles per hour (110 kilometers per hour).

____ 6. It is __________ (colorful) of all the penguins. It has bright yellow feathers on its head.

EXERCISE 3: Superlative Form of Adjectives

(Grammar Notes 1–4, 7)

Complete the paragraph about two deadly animals: snakes and jellyfish. Use the adjectives in parentheses and the superlative form.

Which snakes are ___*the most dangerous*___ (1. dangerous)? Which snakes are ______________ (2. deadly)? The country with ______________ (3. high) percentage of deadly snakes is Australia, but only three or four people die of snake bites in Australia each year. The country with ______________ (4. large) number of fatal snake bites is India, and ______________ (5. scary) snake in India is the king cobra.

Do you know ______________ (6. old) creature on earth? It's the jellyfish. Jellyfish were around more than 650 million years ago. They are one of ______________ (7. frightening) sea creatures. There are over 2,000 different kinds of jellyfish. Some are tiny, and others are big. ______________ (8. heavy) weigh over 450 pounds (204 kilograms), and ______________ (9. long) are 120 feet (40 meters). The ______________ (10. deadly) jellyfish are the tiny Irukandji jellyfish, which live in the waters off Australia.

EXERCISE 4: *One of the* + Superlative Adjectives

(Grammar Note 7)

Complete the conversations with **one of the** *and the words in parentheses. Use the superlative form of the adjectives and plural form of the nouns.*

1. **A:** I'm going to be in San Diego. Is the San Diego Zoo a good place to go?

   B: I think so. It's ___one of the most popular zoos___ **(popular / zoo)** in the United States.

2. **A:** I think the peacock is ______________________ **(beautiful / bird)** in the world.

   B: I agree.

3. **A:** Can an octopus open a jar?

   B: Yes, it can. It's ______________________ **(smart / animal)** of its type.

4. **A:** Are there any good nature shows on TV?

   B: Yes. ______________________ **(good / nature show)** is at 8:00 P.M. tonight on the Discovery Channel. I saw the show last month.

5. **A:** Are you laughing at that gorilla?

   B: Yes. He's ______________________ **(funny / animal)** in the zoo.

6. **A:** My son loves dinosaurs. Where can you see dinosaur bones?

   B: The Museum of Natural History in New York City has ______________________ **(good / collection)** of dinosaur bones in the world.

EXERCISE 5: Comparative and Superlative

(Grammar Notes 1–2, 4, 6)

Complete the sentences with the adjectives in parentheses. Use the comparative or superlative form.

1. African elephants are different from Asian elephants. Asian elephants have ___smaller___ **(small)** ears and ______________ **(short)** tusks than African ones. The African elephants are ______________ **(large)** and ______________ **(tall)**.

2. Bear's milk is ______________ **(rich)** of all milk from animals. It is 46 percent fat. This rich milk allows the tiny bear cub to grow very fast.

(continued on next page)

3. ________________ snake in the world is the blind snake. It reaches just slightly more
(small)
than 5 inches (13 centimeters) in length and weighs less than 0.1 ounce (less than 2 grams).

4. ________________ snakes are the anaconda and the python. They grow as long as
(large)
33 feet (about 10 meters) and can weigh up to 550 pounds (about 250 kilograms).

5. Most female snakes are ________________ than male snakes.
(large)

6. A snake's body temperature is about the same as the temperature outside. When the temperature warms up, snakes are ________________, and when it gets
(active)
________________, they are less active.
(cold)

7. Many people think the great white shark is ________________ of all sharks. Studies
(dangerous)
show that it's not true. White sharks mostly attack when they confuse humans with seals or sea lions.

EXERCISE 6: Editing

Correct the sentences. There are seven mistakes. The first mistake is already corrected. Find and correct six more.

1. The Berlin Zoological Garden is the ~~most old~~ oldest zoo in Germany. It opened in 1844.
2. It is one of the most popular zoo in the world.
3. The zoo has biggest collection of different species in the world.
4. The zoo is very crowded Sunday afternoons. That is the most bad time to visit.
5. The pandas are the most popular resident of the Berlin Zoological Garden.
6. The Birdhouse is one the most modern bird houses in Europe. There are more than 500 species of birds, many of them quite rare.
7. The most good time to visit the zoo is in the spring or the fall.

STEP 4 COMMUNICATION PRACTICE

EXERCISE 7: Pronunciation

A | *Read and listen to the Pronunciation Note.*

Pronunciation Note

Be sure to pronounce the -***est*** ending of the superlative, but do not stress the ending.

EXAMPLE: Longest

B | *Listen and repeat the sentences.*

1. The biggest is not always the strongest.
2. The loudest is not always the wisest.
3. The funniest is sometimes the saddest.
4. The quietest is sometimes the deepest.

C | *Now listen and repeat the questions.*

1. Is the biggest the best?
2. Is the youngest the fastest?
3. Is the fattest the warmest?
4. Is the slowest the heaviest?

EXERCISE 8: Listening

A | *Listen to a quiz show. Read the questions. Circle the letter of the correct answer.*

1. The first question asks, "Which animal has the longest gestation period?" A gestation period is ________________.

   a. the time the baby is carried in its mother **b.** the time the baby learns to walk

2. The second question asks, "Which animal is ________________?"

   a. the fattest **b.** the fastest

3. The third question asks, "Which animal is ________________?"

   a. the loudest **b.** the proudest

4. The last question asks, "Which animal is ________________?"

   a. the deadliest **b.** the most dangerous

B | *Listen again. Then answer the questions.*

1. What were the answers to the four questions in the quiz show? Choose from the words in the box.

ant	**cockroach**	**horse**	**mosquito**
bear	**cow**	**lion**	**peacock**
cheetah	**elephant**	**monkey**	**tiger**

Answer one: the Asian ____________________

Answer two: the ____________________

Answer three: the howler ____________________

Answer four: the ____________________

2. How much money did Marcia win? She won ____________________ dollars.

EXERCISE 9: Survey

A | *Write questions in the superlative. Use the words from the list.*

good / pet to have **interesting / animal to look at**

smart / animal you know **beautiful animal / you know**

B | *Ask four classmates the questions in Part A. Then ask each student a reason why he or she thinks so. Report results to the class.*

EXAMPLE: **A:** Florian, what's the best pet to have?
B: Fish.
A: Why? (. . .)
(Reporting to class)
A: According to Florian, fish make the best pets. They're the quietest, the most colorful, and the easiest to take care of, especially for a student who lives in an apartment.

EXERCISE 10: Discussion

PAIRS: Talk about animals or insects that are pests—for example, cockroaches, ants, mice, raccoons, squirrels, deer, or bears.

1. What's the worst pest in your area? Why?
2. What's the best way to handle this pest?

EXAMPLE: **A:** I think one of the biggest problems around here is bears.
B: Bears? I disagree. There are a lot of bears, and they are big and scary, but they rarely bother people. I think that raccoons are our worst problem. Last summer a raccoon climbed in my attic and made a home there. It was hard to get rid of her.
A: What did you do?

EXERCISE 11: Game

A | *Make a list from A to Z of as many animals as you can. On the board, write the names of all the animals.*

EXAMPLE: A = Auk
B = bear

B | *GROUPS: Students take turns. Each student asks a question using a superlative about one of the animals on the board.*

EXAMPLES: Which animal has the best memory?
Which animal is the busiest?

C | *GROUPS: Students write their answers. Compare answers.*

EXAMPLE: Ten students think that elephants have the best memory. Three students think that dolphins do.

EXERCISE 12: Writing

A | *Write about one or more animals in the zoo, in books, or in movies. Use a superlative and* **one of** *plus a superlative in your writing.*

EXAMPLE: Last August I visited the Bronx Zoo. This zoo is one of the best zoos in the world. It covers 265 acres and is home to over 6,000 animals. I enjoyed the Butterfly Zone and the World of Birds, but the most interesting part was the Congo Gorilla Forest. I saw a rain forest and a lot of gorillas. The funniest gorilla imitated one of the visitors. The people laughed a lot. I started to laugh but stopped when I realized I was the one he was imitating!

B | *Check your work. Use the Editing Checklist.*

Editing Checklist

Did you . . . ?
☐ use superlatives correctly
☐ check your spelling

UNIT 36 # Review

Check your answers on page UR-8.
Do you need to review anything?

A | *Complete the sentences with the adjectives in parentheses. Use the superlative form.*

1. Who was _______________ monkey in the cage?
   (funny)
2. What is the name of _______________ whale?
   (big)
3. What is _______________ nature show on TV?
   (good)
4. _______________ sharks are not _______________.
   (large) (dangerous)

B | *Complete the sentences with the superlative.*

1. It's 101 degrees. It's _______________ of the year.
   (hot / day)
2. She's 112 years old. She's _______________ in town.
   (old / woman)
3. The day after Thanksgiving is _______________ of the year.
   (busy / shopping day)
4. It was _______________ on TV last month.
   (interesting / show)
5. The pandas are _______________ at the zoo.
   (popular / animal)

C | *Complete the sentences with* **one of** *and the words in parentheses. Use the superlative form of the adjectives and the plural form of the nouns.*

1. The dolphin is _______________ in the world.
   (one of the / intelligent / animal)
2. The Bronx Zoo is _______________ in the world.
   (one of the / good / zoo)
3. He has _______________ in the stadium.
   (one of the / bad / seat)
4. It was _______________ of the year.
   (one of the / long / day)
5. That was _______________ in the guidebook.
   (one of the / expensive / trip)

D | *Correct the conversations. There are five mistakes.*

1. **A:** What is the most good way to get to park?

   B: The shortest route is also the complicated. I'll give you the most direct way.

2. **A:** What's the most hardest part of your job here at the zoo?

   B: Well, the nicer part is taking care of the animals. The most worst part is telling people not to feed the animals or bother them.

From Grammar to Writing

The Order of Adjectives before Nouns

1 | *Complete the sentences with the words in parentheses.*

1. I saw a ______________________________ on Main Street.
(funny / monkey / brown / little)

2. Maria wore a ______________________________.
(red / dress / beautiful / silk)

2 | *Study this information about the order of adjectives before nouns. When you use adjectives, write them in this order.*

1

1. opinion	2. size	3. shape	4. age	5. color	6. origin	7. material	8. noun
beautiful	big	square	new	red	French	silk	scarf

2

We use adjectives to describe nouns. Descriptions make writing more lively. They also help the reader form mental pictures. When **several adjectives** come before a noun, they follow a **special order**.

- I saw a **beautiful young** woman.
  NOT: I saw a ~~young beautiful~~ woman.

3

Use ***and*** to connect adjectives from the same category.

- The shirt was *cotton* **and** *polyester*.
- The blouse was *red* **and** *white*.

3 | *Complete the sentences with the words in parentheses. Use the correct order.*

1. He ate a(n) ______________________________ pear.
(brown / big / Asian)

2. His cashmere coat was not as expensive as her ______________________________
(Italian / new / leather / black)
______________ jacket.

3. They bought three ______________________________ bowls.
(silver / beautiful / Mexican)

4 | *Read the story. Then write your own story.*

Detective Work

Several years ago I was walking down the street when I saw my father's brand new shiny blue car. I expected to see my father, but to my surprise a young woman with short, curly bright red hair was behind the wheel of the car. I saw an empty taxi nearby, and I got in quickly. I said dramatically to the driver, "Follow that new blue car." And I told the driver why.

The taxi driver had a cell phone, and I told him to call the police. Soon we heard the siren of the patrol car and a loudspeaker. The police told the woman to pull over. We pulled over too. I immediately said to the woman, "That's not your car. It's my father's."

The woman smiled calmly and said, "Oh. You're Mr. Abbot's younger son. I recognize you from your picture."

Before I could say another word, the woman explained that she was my father's new assistant. My father had asked her to take his computer to the main office to get it fixed. He lent her his car. We called my father, and he confirmed her story. The police laughed, and the taxi driver laughed. I was too embarrassed to laugh. That was the beginning and the end of my career as a detective.

5 | *Exchange papers with a partner. Did your partner follow the directions? Correct any mistakes in grammar and spelling.*

6 | *Talk to your partner. Discuss the mistakes you made. Then rewrite your own paper and make any necessary changes.*

APPENDICES

1 Map of the World

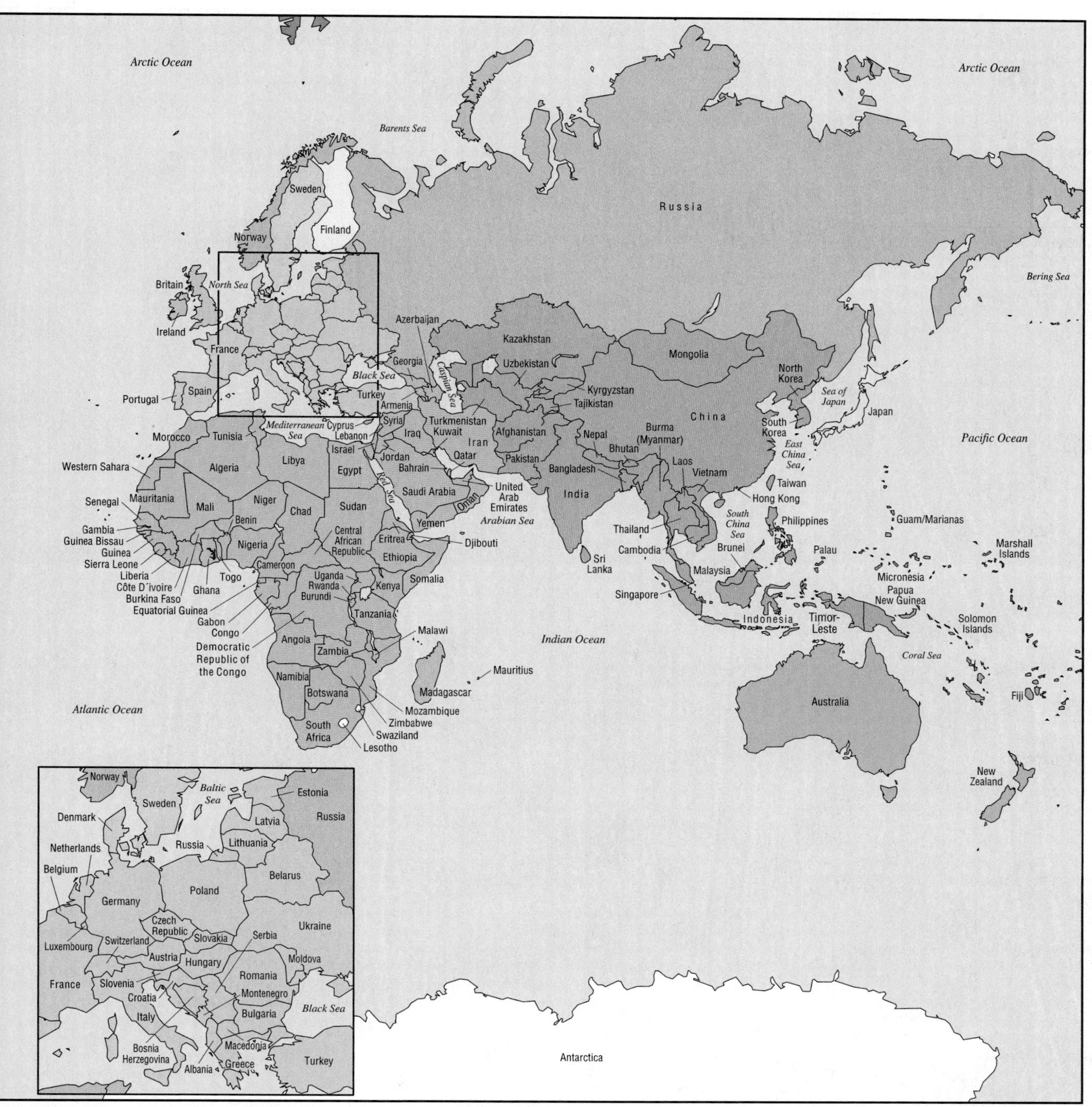

Arctic Ocean
Barents Sea
Russia
Bering Sea
Sweden
Finland
Norway
Britain
North Sea
Ireland
France
Portugal
Spain
Azerbaijan
Kazakhstan
Mongolia
Georgia
Uzbekistan
Black Sea
Caspian Sea
Kyrgyzstan
Tajikistan
North Korea
Sea of Japan
Japan
Turkey
Armenia
Turkmenistan
China
South Korea
Pacific Ocean
Morocco
Tunisia
Mediterranean Sea
Cyprus
Lebanon
Syria
Iraq
Kuwait
Afghanistan
Nepal
Bhutan
Burma (Myanmar)
East China Sea
Israel
Iran
Western Sahara
Libya
Egypt
Jordan
Qatar
Bahrain
Pakistan
Bangladesh
Laos
Vietnam
Algeria
Red Sea
Saudi Arabia
United Arab Emirates
Oman
India
Taiwan
Hong Kong
Senegal
Mauritania
Mali
Niger
Chad
Sudan
Arabian Sea
South China Sea
Philippines
Guam/Marianas
Benin
Yemen
Thailand
Gambia
Guinea Bissau
Guinea
Sierra Leone
Liberia
Côte D'ivoire
Burkina Faso
Equatorial Guinea
Nigeria
Central African Republic
Eritrea
Djibouti
Ethiopia
Cambodia
Brunei
Sri Lanka
Palau
Marshall Islands
Cameroon
Togo
Ghana
Uganda
Rwanda
Burundi
Kenya
Somalia
Malaysia
Micronesia
Singapore
Papua New Guinea
Gabon
Congo
Democratic Republic of the Congo
Tanzania
Malawi
Angola
Zambia
Indonesia
Timor-Leste
Solomon Islands
Indian Ocean
Coral Sea
Mauritius
Namibia
Botswana
Madagascar
Mozambique
Zimbabwe
Swaziland
Lesotho
South Africa
Australia
Fiji
Atlantic Ocean
New Zealand
Norway
Baltic Sea
Estonia
Sweden
Denmark
Latvia
Russia
Netherlands
Russia
Lithuania
Belgium
Belarus
Poland
Germany
Czech Republic
Ukraine
Luxembourg
Switzerland
Slovakia
Serbia
Austria
Hungary
Moldova
Romania
France
Slovenia
Montenegro
Croatia
Black Sea
Italy
Bulgaria
Bosnia Herzegovina
Macedonia
Albania
Greece
Turkey
Antarctica

2 Map of the United States and Canada

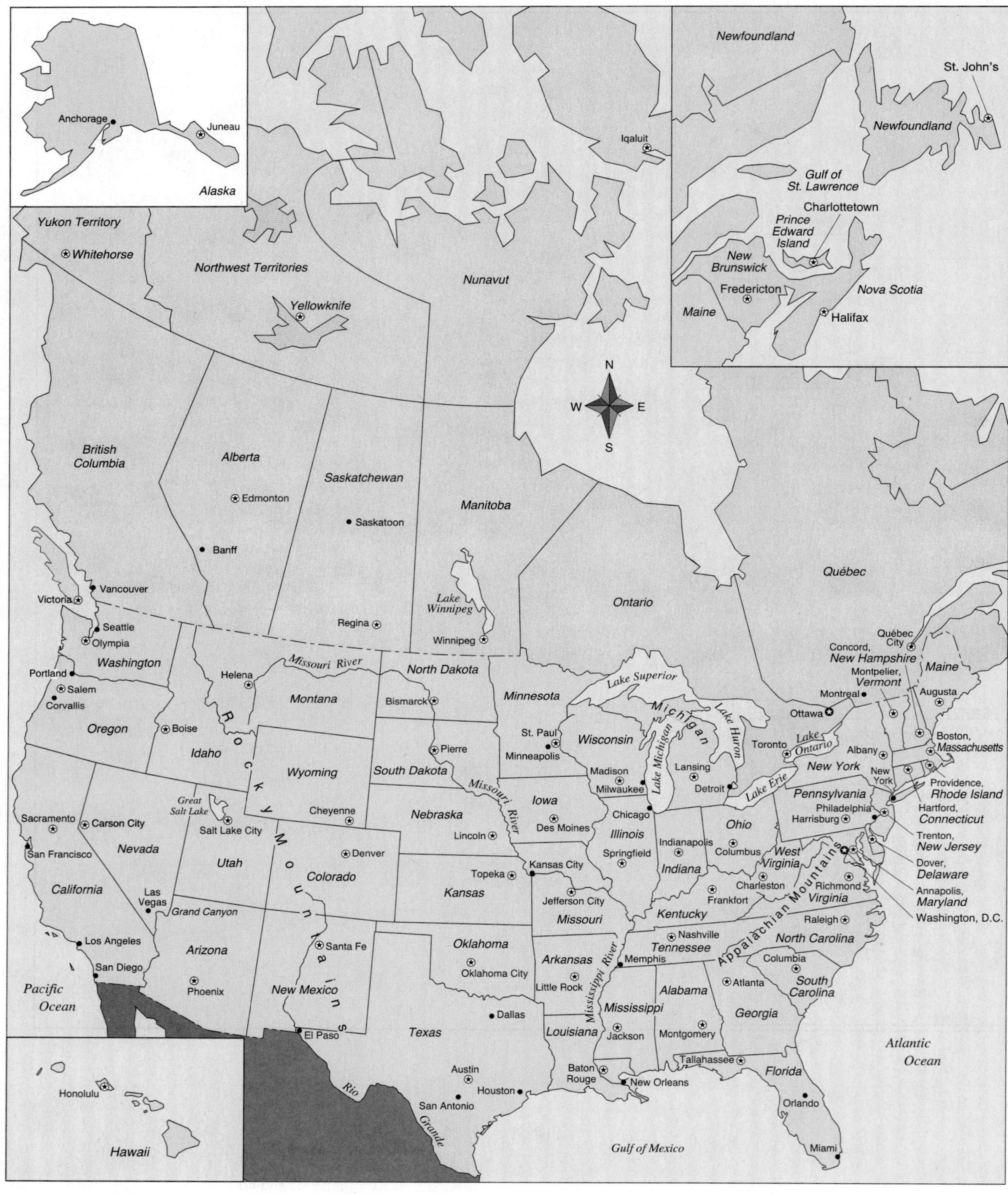

3 Numbers, Temperature, Months, Days, Seasons, Titles

Cardinal Numbers

1 = one	11 = eleven	21 = twenty-one
2 = two	12 = twelve	30 = thirty
3 = three	13 = thirteen	40 = forty
4 = four	14 = fourteen	50 = fifty
5 = five	15 = fifteen	60 = sixty
6 = six	16 = sixteen	70 = seventy
7 = seven	17 = seventeen	80 = eighty
8 = eight	18 = eighteen	90 = ninety
9 = nine	19 = nineteen	100 = one hundred
10 = ten	20 = twenty	101 = one hundred and one
		200 = two hundred
		1,000 = one thousand
		1,000,000 = one million
		10,000,000 = ten million

Examples

That building has **seventy-seven** pages.
There are **thirty** days in April.
There are **six** rows in the room.
She is **twelve** years old.
He has **four** children.

Ordinal Numbers

1st = first	11th = eleventh	21st = twenty-first
2nd = second	12th = twelfth	30th = thirtieth
3rd = third	13th = thirteenth	40th = fortieth
4th = fourth	14th = fourteenth	50th = fiftieth
5th = fifth	15th = fifteenth	60th = sixtieth
6th = sixth	16th = sixteenth	70th = seventieth
7th = seventh	17th = seventeenth	80th = eightieth
8th = eighth	18th = eighteenth	90th = ninetieth
9th = ninth	19th = nineteenth	100th = one hundredth
10th = tenth	20th = twentieth	101st = one hundred and first
		200th = two hundredth
		1,000th = one thousandth
		1,000,000th = one millionth
		10,000,000th = ten millionth

Examples

He works on the **seventy-seventh** floor.
It's April **thirtieth**.
He's in the **sixth** row.
It's her **twelfth** birthday.
Bob is his **first** child. Mary is his **second**. John is his **third**, and Sue is his **fourth**.

Temperature

We measure the temperature in degrees (°).

Changing from degrees Fahrenheit to degrees Celsius:

(°F — 32) X 5/9 = °C

Changing from degrees Celsius to degrees Fahrenheit:

(9/5 × °C) + 32 = °F

Days of the Week

Weekdays	**Weekend**
Monday	Saturday
Tuesday	Sunday
Wednesday	
Thursday	
Friday	

Months of the Year

Month	Abbreviation	Number of Days
January	Jan.	31
February	Feb.	28*
March	Mar.	31
April	Apr.	30
May	May	31
June	Jun.	30
July	Jul.	31
August	Aug.	31
September	Sept.	30
October	Oct.	31
November	Nov.	30
December	Dec.	31

*February has 29 days in a leap year, every four years.

(continued on next page)

The Seasons

NORTHERN HEMISPHERE
Spring: March 21–June 20
Summer: June 21–September 20
Autumn or Fall: September 21–December 20
Winter: December 21–March 20

SOUTHERN HEMISPHERE
Spring: September 21–December 20
Summer: December 21–March 20
Autumn or Fall: March 21–June 20
Winter: June 21–September 20

Titles

Mr. (Mister) / mɪstər /	unmarried or married man
Ms. / mɪz /	unmarried or married woman
Miss / mɪs /	unmarried woman
Mrs. / mɪsɪz /	married woman
Dr. (Doctor) / dɑktər /	doctor (medical doctor or Ph.D.)

4 Time

It's one o'clock.
(It's 1:00.)

It's five after one.
(It's 1:05.)

It's one-ten.
It's ten after one.
(It's 1:10.)

It's one-fifteen.
It's a quarter after one.
(It's 1:15.)

It's one twenty-five.
It's twenty-five after one.
(It's 1:25.)

It's one-thirty.
It's half past one.
(It's 1:30.)

It's one forty-five.
It's a quarter to two.
(It's 1:45.)

It's one-fifty.
It's ten to two.
(It's 1:50.)

TALKING ABOUT TIME

1	You can talk about time this way:	**A: What time is it?** **B:** It's one o'clock.
2	**A.M.** means before noon (the hours between midnight and noon). **P.M.** means after noon (the hours between noon and midnight). **BE CAREFUL!** When people say 12:00 A.M., they mean midnight. When people say 12:00 P.M., they mean noon.	It's 10:00 **A.M.** It's 10:00 **P.M.**
3	We often write time with numbers.	It's one o'clock. = It's **1:00.** It's two-twenty. = It's **2:20.**

5 Plural Nouns: Spelling and Pronunciation Rules

PLURAL NOUNS: SPELLING RULES

	Rule	Singular	Plural
1	Add ***-s*** to form the plural of most nouns.	student chief picture	student**s** chief**s** picture**s**
2	Add ***-es*** to form the plural of nouns that end in ***ss***, ***ch***, ***sh***, and ***x***. (This ending adds another syllable.)	class watch dish box	class**es** watch**es** dish**es** box**es**
3	Add ***-es*** to form the plural of nouns that end in ***o*** preceded by a consonant. **EXCEPTION:** Add ***-s*** to plural nouns ending in ***o*** that refer to music.	potato piano soprano	potato**es** piano**s** soprano**s**
4	Add ***-s*** to form the plural of nouns that end in ***o*** preceded by a vowel.	radio	radio**s**
5	To form the plural of words that end in a consonant + ***y***, change the ***y*** to ***i*** and add ***-es***.	dictionary fly	dictionar**ies** fl**ies**
6	To form the plural of words that end in a vowel + ***y***, add ***-s***.	boy day	boy**s** day**s**
7	To form the plural of certain nouns that end in ***f*** or ***fe***, change the ***f*** to ***v*** and add ***-es***.	half loaf knife wife	hal**ves** loa**ves** kni**ves** wi**ves**
8	Some plural nouns are **irregular**.	woman child person mother-in-law man foot tooth	women children people mothers-in-law men feet teeth
9	Some nouns **do not have a singular form**.	(eye) glasses clothes pants scissors	
10	Some plural nouns are the same as the singular noun.	Chinese fish sheep	Chinese fish sheep

PLURAL NOUNS: PRONUNCIATION RULES

1	The **final sounds** for regular plural nouns are / **s** /, / **z** /, and / **ɪz** /.	boots	boys	horses
2	The plural is pronounced / **s** / **after** the **voiceless sounds** / **p** /, / **t** /, / **k** /, / **f** /, and / **θ** /.	cups hats works	cuffs myths	
3	The plural is pronounced / **z** / **after** the **voiced sounds** / **b** /, / **d** /, / **g** /, / **v** /, / **m** /, / **n** /, / ŋ /, / **l** /, / **r** /, and / ð /.	crabs cards rugs	doves drums fans	rings girls stores
4	The plural ***s*** is pronounced / **z** / **after** all **vowel sounds**.	day toe	days toes	
5	The plural ***s*** is pronounced / **ɪz** / **after the sounds** / **s** /, / **z** /, / **ʃ** /, / **tʃ** /, and / **dʒ** /. (This adds another syllable to the word.)	races causes dishes	churches judges	

6 The Simple Present: Spelling and Pronunciation Rules

THE THIRD-PERSON SINGULAR AFFIRMATIVE: SPELLING RULES

1	Add ***-s*** to form the third-person singular of most verbs. Add ***-es*** to words that end in ***ch***, ***s***, ***sh***, ***x***, or ***z***.	Pete work**s**. I work too. Doug wear**s** sweatshirts. I wear shirts. Norma teach**es** Spanish. I teach English. Lulu wash**es** her clothes on Tuesday. Elenore and Pete wash their clothes on Sunday.
2	When a base-form verb ends in a **consonant** + ***y***, change the ***y*** to ***i*** and add ***-es***. Do not change the ***y*** when the base form ends in a **vowel** + ***y***. Add ***-s***.	I study at home. Carol stud**ies** at the library. Dan play**s** tennis. I play tennis too.
3	*Have*, *do*, and *go* have **irregular forms** for the third-person singular.	I have. He **has**. I do. She **does**. I go. It **goes**.

THE THIRD-PERSON SINGULAR AFFIRMATIVE: PRONUNCIATION RULES

1	The **final sound** for the third-person singular form of the simple present is pronounced / **s** /, / **z** /, or / **ɪz** /. The final sounds of the third-person singular are the same as the final sounds of plural nouns. See Appendix 9 on pages A-8 and A-9.	/ **s** / talk**s** · / **z** / love**s** · / **ɪz** / danc**es**
2	***Do*** and ***say*** have a change in vowel sound.	I say. / **seɪ** / He say**s**. / **sɛz** / I do. / **du** / He do**es**. / **dʌz** /

7 Possessive Nouns

1	Add ***'s*** to form the possessive of singular nouns.	Lulu***'s*** last name is Winston.
2	To form the possessive of plural nouns ending in ***s***, add only an **apostrophe (')**.	The girls**'** gym is on this floor. The boys**'** locker room is across the hall.
3	In hyphenated words (*mother-in-law, father-in-law*, etc.) and in phrases showing joint possession, only the last word is possessive in form.	My sister-in-law**'s** apartment is big. Elenore and Pete**'s** apartment is comfortable.
4	To form the possessive of plural nouns that do not end in ***s***, add ***'s***.	The men**'s** room is next to the water fountain.
5	To form the possessive of one-syllable singular nouns that end in ***s***, add ***'s***. To form the possessive of words of more than one syllable that end in ***s***, add an ***'*** or an ***'s***.	**James's** apartment is beautiful. **McCullers'** novels are interesting. OR **McCullers's** novels are interesting.
6	**BE CAREFUL!** Don't confuse possessive nouns with the contraction of the verb ***be***.	**Carol's** a student. = **Carol** ***is*** a student. **Carol's** book is open. = **Her** book is open.

8 The Present Progressive: Spelling Rules

	Rule	Base form	-ing form
1	Add ***-ing*** to the base form of the verb.	drink see eat	drink**ing** see**ing** eat**ing**
2	If a verb ends in a silent ***e***, drop the final ***e*** and add ***-ing***.	smil**e**	smil**ing**
3	If a one-syllable verb ends in a consonant, a vowel, and a consonant **(CVC)**, double the last consonant before adding ***-ing***. However, do not double the last consonant if it is a ***w***, ***x***, or ***y***.	**CVC** sit run sew mix play	 si**tting** ru**nning** se**w**ing mi**x**ing pla**y**ing
4	In words with two or more syllables that end in a consonant, a vowel, and a consonant **(CVC)**, double the last consonant only if the last syllable is stressed.	admít whísper	admi**tt**ing *(stressed)* whispe**r**ing *(not stressed)*

9 Direct and Indirect Objects

Group One

Subject	Verb	Direct Object	*To*	Indirect Object	Subject	Verb	Indirect Object	Direct Object
She	**sent**	**a gift** **it**	**to**	**us.**	She	**sent**	**us**	**a gift.**

Group Two

Subject	Verb	Direct Object	*For*	Indirect Object	Subject	Verb	Indirect Object	Direct Object
They	**found**	**a towel** **it**	**for**	**him.**	They	**found**	**him**	**a towel.**

Group Three

Subject	Verb	Direct Object	*To*	Indirect Object
He	**repeated**	**the question**	**to**	**the class.**

Group Four

Subject	Verb	Direct Object	*For*	Indirect Object
He	**fixed**	**the shelves**	**for**	**me.**

Group One Verbs (*to*)		Group Two Verbs (*for*)	Group Three Verbs (*to*)	Group Four Verbs (*for*)
email	sell	build	explain	cash
give	send	buy	prove	close
hand	show	find	repeat	fix
lend	teach	get	say	pronounce
owe	tell	make	whisper	translate
pass	throw			
read	write			

RULES FOR DIRECT AND INDIRECT OBJECTS

1 With **Group One** and **Group Two verbs**, there are **two** possible **sentence patterns** if the **direct object** is a **noun**.

	DIRECT OBJECT	*TO/FOR*	INDIRECT OBJECT	
I gave the	**money**	**to**	**him**.	=

	INDIRECT OBJECT	DIRECT OBJECT
I gave	**him**	**the money**.

	DIRECT OBJECT	*TO/FOR*	INDIRECT OBJECT	
We bought	**the book**	**for**	**him**.	=

	INDIRECT OBJECT	DIRECT OBJECT
We bought	**him**	**the book**.

If the **direct object** is a **pronoun**, it always comes **before the indirect object**.

	DIRECT OBJECT	*TO/FOR*	INDIRECT OBJECT
I gave	**it**	**to**	**him**.
Please get	**them**	**for**	**me**.

NOT: I gave ~~him it~~.
NOT: Please get ~~me them~~.

2 With **Group Three** and **Group Four verbs**, the **direct object** always comes **before the indirect object**.

	DIRECT OBJECT	*TO/FOR*	INDIRECT OBJECT
Explain	**the sentence**	**to**	**John**.
She translated	**the letter**	**for**	**us**.

NOT: Explain ~~John the sentence~~.
NOT: She translated ~~us the letter~~.

10 The Simple Past: Spelling and Pronunciation Rules

THE SIMPLE PAST: SPELLING RULES

	Rule	Verb	Simple Past
1	If the verb **ends in an *e***, add ***-d***.	arrive like	arrive**d** like**d**
2	If the verb **ends in a consonant**, add ***-ed***.	rain help	rain**ed** help**ed**
3	If a **one-syllable verb** ends in a consonant, a vowel, and a consonant **(CVC)**, double the last consonant and add ***-ed***.	**CVC** hug rub	 hu**gged** ru**bbed**
	However, do not double the last consonant if it is a ***w***, ***x***, or ***y***.	bow mix play	bo**w**ed mi**x**ed pla**y**ed
4	If a **two-syllable verb** ends in a consonant, a vowel, and a consonant **(CVC)**, double the last consonant only if the last syllable is stressed.	refer enter	refe**rr**ed *(stressed)* ente**r**ed *(not stressed)*
5	If the verb ends in a **consonant** + ***y***, change the ***y*** to ***i*** and add ***-ed***.	worry carry	worr**ied** carr**ied**
6	If the verb ends in a **vowel** + ***y***, do not change the ***y*** to ***i***. Add ***-ed***.	play annoy	play**ed** annoy**ed**
	There are **exceptions** to this rule.	pay lay say	**paid** **laid** **said**

THE SIMPLE PAST: PRONUNCIATION RULES

	Rule		Examples	
1	The **final sounds** for regular verbs in the simple past are / **t** /, / **d** /, and / **ɪd** /.	walk**ed**	plann**ed**	wait**ed**
2	The final sound is pronounced / **t** / **after** the **voiceless sounds** / **f** /, / **k** /, / **p** /, / **s** /, / **tʃ** /, and / **ʃ** /.	lau**ghed** li**cked**	si**pped** mi**ssed**	wa**tched** wi**shed**
3	The final sound is pronounced / **d** / **after** the **voiced sounds** / **b** /, / **g** /, / **dʒ** /, / **l** /, / **m** /, / **n** /, / **r** /, / **ŋ** /, / **ð** /, / **ʒ** /, / **v** /, and / **z** /.	ru**bbed** hu**gged** ju**dged** pu**lled**	hu**mmed** ba**nned** occu**rred** ba**nged**	ba**thed** massa**ged** li**ved** surpri**sed**
4	The final sound is pronounced / **d** / **after vowel sounds**.	pla**yed** sk**ied**	t**ied** sn**owed**	arg**ued**
5	The final sound is pronounced / **ɪd** / after / **t** / and / **d** /. / **ɪd** / adds a syllable.	want instruct rest attend	wan**ted** instruc**ted** res**ted** atten**ded**	

11 Base Forms and Past Forms of Common Irregular Verbs

Base Form	Past Form	Base Form	Past Form	Base Form	Past Form
become	became	give	gave	say	said
begin	began	go	went	see	saw
bite	bit	grow	grew	send	sent
blow	blew	hang	hung	shake	shook
break	broke	have	had	shoot	shot
bring	brought	hear	heard	shut	shut
build	built	hide	hid	sing	sang
buy	bought	hit	hit	sit	sat
catch	caught	hold	held	sleep	slept
choose	chose	hurt	hurt	speak	spoke
come	came	keep	kept	spend	spent
cost	cost	know	knew	stand	stood
do	did	lead	led	steal	stole
draw	drew	leave	left	swim	swam
drink	drank	lend	lent	take	took
drive	drove	lose	lost	teach	taught
eat	ate	make	made	tear	tore
fall	fell	meet	met	tell	told
feed	fed	pay	paid	think	thought
feel	felt	put	put	throw	threw
fight	fought	quit	quit	understand	understood
find	found	read*	read*	wake	woke
fly	flew	ride	rode	wear	wore
forget	forgot	ring	rang	win	won
get	got	run	ran	write	wrote

*Pronounce the base form / rid /. Pronounce the past form / rɛd /

12 Non-Count Nouns and Names of Containers

Common Non-count Nouns*

Liquids		Food		Too Small to Count		School Subjects	
milk	soda	bread	ketchup	sugar	baking powder	math	biology
coffee	water	cheese	jam	salt	cereal	history	chemistry
oil	beer	lettuce	jelly	pepper	spaghetti	geography	music
juice		broccoli	fish	cinnamon	wheat		
		ice cream	meat	rice	corn		
		butter	sour cream	sand			
		mayonnaise	soup				

City Problems	Weather	Gases	Abstract Ideas		Others	
traffic	snow	oxygen	love	advice	money	jewelry
pollution	rain	carbon dioxide	beauty	help	mail	garbage
crime	ice	nitrogen	happiness	noise	furniture	toothpaste
	fog	air	luck	time	homework	paper
					information	

*Some nouns can be either count or non-count nouns.

I'd like some **chicken**. (non-count)
There were three **chickens** in the yard. (count)

Did you eat any **cake**? (non-count)
I bought a **cake** at the bakery. (count)

Quantifiers: Containers, Measure Words, and Portions

a bottle of (milk, soda, ketchup)
a bowl of (cereal, soup, rice)
a can of (soda, beans, tuna fish)
a cup of (hot chocolate, coffee, tea)
a foot of (snow, water)
a gallon of (juice, gas, paint)
a head of (lettuce)
an inch of (snow, rain)
a loaf of (bread)

a pair of (pants, skis, gloves)
a piece of (paper, cake, pie)
a pint of (ice cream, cream)
a quart of (milk)
a roll of (film, toilet paper, paper towels)
a slice of (toast, cheese, meat)
a tablespoon of (flour, sugar, baking soda)
a teaspoon of (sugar, salt, pepper)
a tube of (toothpaste, glue)

Metric Conversion

1 liter = .26 gallons or 1.8 pints
1 gallon = 3.8 liters

1 mile = 1.6 kilometers
1 kilometer = .62 mile
1 foot = .30 meter or 30 centimeters
1 meter = 3.3 feet
1 inch = 2.54 centimeters

1 ounce = 28 grams
1 gram = .04 ounce
1 pound = .45 kilogram
1 kilogram = 2.2 pounds

13 Pronunciation Table

These are the pronunciation symbols used in this text. Listen to the pronunciation of the key words.

Vowels

Symbol	Key Word
i	beat, feed
ɪ	bit, did
eɪ	date, paid
ɛ	bet, bed
æ	bat, bad
ɑ	box, odd, father
ɔ	bought, dog
oʊ	boat, road
ʊ	book, good
u	boot, food, student
ʌ	but, mud, mother
ə	banana, among
ɚ	shirt, murder
aɪ	bite, cry, buy, eye
aʊ	about, how
ɔɪ	voice, boy
ɪr	ear, beer
ɛr	bare
ɑr	bar
ɔr	door
ʊr	tour

Consonants

Symbol	Key Word	Symbol	Key Word
p	pack, happy	ʃ	ship, machine, station, special, discussion
b	back, rubber	ʒ	measure, vision
t	tie	h	hot, who
d	die	m	men
k	came, key, quick	n	sun, know, pneumonia
g	game, guest	ŋ	sung, ringing
ʧ	church, nature, watch	w	wet, white
ʤ	judge, general, major	l	light, long
f	fan, photograph	r	right, wrong
v	van	y	yes, use, music
θ	thing, breath	t̬	butter, bottle
ð	then, breathe		
s	sip, city, psychology		
z	zip, please, goes		

GLOSSARY OF GRAMMAR TERMS

action verb A verb that describes an action. It can be used in the progressive.

- *Sachiko **is planning** a big party.*

adjective A word that describes (or modifies) a noun or pronoun.

- *That's a **great** idea.*

adverb A word that describes (or modifies) an action verb, an adverb, an adjective, or a sentence.

- *She drives **slowly**.*

adverb of frequency A word that tells the frequency of something.

- *We **usually** eat lunch at noon.*

adverb of manner A word that describes a verb. It usually answers the question *how*.

- *She speaks **clearly**.*

affirmative statement A sentence that does not use a negative verb form (*not*).

- ***I have a car***.

apostrophe A punctuation mark used to show possession and to write a short form (contraction).

- *He's in my father's car.*

base form The simple form of the verb without any ending such as *-ing*, *-ed*, or *-s*. It is the same as the infinitive without *to*.

- *Arnold will **come** at 8:00. We should **eat** then.*

***be going to* future** A verb form used to make predictions, express general facts in the future, or talk about definite plans that were made before now.

- *Mei-Ling says it**'s going to be** cold, so she**'s going to take** a coat.*

capital letter The big form of a letter of the alphabet. Sentences start with a capital letter.

- ***A**, **B**, **C**, etc.*

comma Punctuation used to separate single things in a list or parts of a sentence.

- *We went to a restaurant**,** and we ate chicken**,** potatoes**,** and broccoli.*

common noun A noun for a person, place, or thing. It is not capitalized.

- *The **man** got a **book** at the **library**.*

comparative form An adjective or adverb ending in *-er* or following *more*. It is used in comparing two things.

- *My sister is **older** and **more intelligent** than my brother.*
- *But he studies **harder** and **more carefully**.*

consonant The letters *b, c, d, f, g, h, j, k, l, m, n, p, q, r, s, t, v, w, x, y, z*.

contraction A short form of two words. An apostrophe (') replaces the missing letter.

- ***It is** late and **I am** tired. I **should not** stay up so late.*
- ***It's** late and **I'm** tired. I **shouldn't** stay up so late.*

count noun A noun you can count. It usually has a singular and a plural form.

- *In the **park**, there was a **man** with two **children** and a **dog**.*

definite article *The*; It makes a noun specific.

- *We saw a movie. **The** movie starred Sean Penn.*

demonstrative adjective An adjective used to identify the noun that follows.

- ***This** man is resting, but **those** men are busy.*

demonstrative pronoun A pronoun used in place of a demonstrative adjective and the noun that follows.

- ***This** is our classroom, and **these** are my students.*

direct object A noun or pronoun used to receive the action of a verb.

- *She sold a **car**. He bought **it**.*

exclamation point A punctuation mark (!) used at the end of a statement. It shows strong emotion.

- *Help**!** Call the police**!***

formal language Language we usually use in business settings, academic settings, and with people we don't know.

- ***Good morning**, **ladies** and **gentlemen**. **May** we begin?*

gerund The *-ing* form of a verb. It is used as a noun.

- ***Skiing*** *is fun, but we also enjoy* ***swimming****.*

imperative A sentence used to give an instruction, a direction, a command, or a suggestion. It uses the base form of the verb. The subject (you) is not a part of the sentence.

- ***Turn*** *right at the corner.* ***Drive*** *to the end of the street.* ***Stop!***

indefinite article *A* and *an*; used before singular, nonspecific non-count nouns.

- *Jaime brought* ***a*** *sandwich and* ***an*** *apple for lunch.*

infinitive *To* + the base form of a verb.

- ***To travel*** *is my dream. I want* ***to see*** *the world.*

informal language The language we usually use with family and friends, in email messages, and in other informal settings.

- ***Hey, Doug, what's up?***

inseparable phrasal verb A phrasal verb that cannot have an object between the verb and the particle.

- *She* ***ran into*** *John.*

irregular verb A verb that does not form the simple past by adding *-d* or *-ed*.

- *They* ***ate*** *a fancy meal last night. The boss* ***came*** *to dinner.*

modal A word that comes before the main verb. Modals can express ability, possibility, obligation, and necessity.

- *You* ***can*** *come early, but you* ***mustn't*** *be late, and you* ***should*** *wear a tie.*

negative statement A statement with a negative verb form.

- *He* ***didn't study****. He* ***wasn't*** *ready for the test.*

non-action verb A verb that does not describe an action. It can describe an emotion, a state, a sense, or a mental thought. We usually don't use non-action verbs in the progressive.

- *I* ***like*** *that actor. He* ***is*** *very famous, and I* ***believe*** *he won an Oscar.*

non-count noun A noun we usually do not count. We don't put *a*, *an*, or a number before a non-count noun.

- *All you'll need is* ***rice****,* ***water****,* ***salt****, and* ***butter****.*

noun A word that refers to a person, animal, place, thing, or idea.

- ***Paula*** *has a* ***friend*** *at the* ***library****. She gave me a* ***book*** *about* ***birds****.*

noun phrase A phrase formed by a noun and words that describe (modify) it.

- *It was* ***a dark brown leather jacket****.*

object A noun or pronoun following an action verb. It receives the action of the verb.

- *I sent* ***a letter****. He read* ***it****.*

object pronoun A pronoun following a verb or a preposition.

- *We asked* ***him*** *to show the photos to* ***them****.*

period A punctuation mark (.) used at the end of a statement.

- *I'd like you to call on Saturday***.** *We need to talk***.**

phrasal verb A two-part (or three-part) verb that combines a verb and a particle. The meaning of the parts together is often different from the meaning of the verb alone.

- *We* ***put on*** *our gloves and* ***picked up*** *our umbrellas.*

phrase A group of words that can form a grammatical unit.

- *She lost* ***a red hat****. He found it* ***under the table****.*

plural The form that means more than one.

- ***We*** *sat in* ***our chairs*** *reading* ***our books****.*

possessive An adjective, noun, or pronoun that shows possession.

- ***Her*** *book is in* ***John's*** *car.* ***Mine*** *is at the office.*

preposition A small word that goes before a noun or pronoun object. A preposition often shows time or place.

- *Maria saw it* ***on*** *the table* ***at*** *two o'clock.*

prepositional phrase A phrase that consists of a preposition followed by a noun or a noun phrase.

- *Chong-Dae saw it* ***under the black wooden table****.*

present progressive A verb form that shows an action happening now or planned for the future.

- ***I'm working*** *hard now, but* ***I'm taking*** *a vacation soon.*

pronoun A word that replaces a noun or a noun phrase. There are subject pronouns, object pronouns, possessive pronouns, and demonstrative pronouns.

- ***He** is a friend—I know **him** well. **This** is his coat; **mine** is black.*

proper noun The actual name of a person, place, or thing. A proper noun begins with a capital letter.

- ***Tom** is living in **New York**. He is studying **Russian** at **Columbia University**.*

quantifier A word or phrase that comes before a noun and expresses an amount of that noun.

- *Jeannette used **a little** sugar, **some** flour, **four** eggs, and **a liter of** milk.*

question mark A punctuation mark (?) used at the end of a question.

- *Where are you going**?** When will you be back**?***

quotation marks Punctuation marks (" . . . ") used before and after the actual words a person says.

- *I said, **"**Where are you going?**"** and **"**When will you be back?**"***

regular verb A verb that forms the simple past by adding *-d* or *-ed*.

- *We **lived** in France. My mother **visited** us there.*

sentence A group of words with a subject and a verb.

- ***We opened the window.***
- ***Did they paint the house?***

separable phrasal verb A phrasal verb that can have an object between the verb and the particle.

- *She **put on** her coat. She **put** it **on** before he **put** his coat **on**.*

simple past A verb form used to show a completed action or idea in the past.

- *The plane **landed** at 9:00. We **caught** a bus to the hotel.*

simple present A verb form used to show habitual actions or states, general facts, or conditions that are true now.

- *Kemal **loves** to ski, and it **snows** a lot in his area, so he**'s** very happy.*

singular The form that means only one.

- *I put on my **hat** and **coat** and closed the **door**.*

small letter The small form of a letter of the alphabet. We use small letters for most words except for proper nouns and the word that starts a sentence.

- ***a**, **b**, **c**, etc.*

subject The person, place, or thing that a sentence is about.

- ***The children** ate at the mall.*

subject pronoun A pronoun used to replace a subject noun.

- *Irene works hard. **She** loves her work.*

superlative form An adjective or adverb ending in *-est* or following *most*. It is used in comparing three or more things.

- *We climbed the **highest** mountain by the **most dangerous** route.*
- *She drives the **fastest** and the **most carelessly** of all the drivers.*

syllable A group of letters with one vowel sound. Words are made up of one or more syllables.

- *One syllable—**win***
- *Two syllables—**ta ble***
- *Three syllables—**im por tant***

verb A word used to describe an action, a fact, or a state.

- *He **drives** to work now. He **has** a new car, and he **is** a careful driver.*

vowel The letters *a*, *e*, *i*, *o*, or *u*, and sometimes *y*.

***wh-* question** A question that asks for information. It begins with *what*, *when*, *where*, *why*, *which*, *who*, *whose*, or *how*.

- ***What**'s your name?*
- ***Where** are you from?*
- ***How** do you feel?*

***will* future** A verb form used to make predictions, to talk about facts in the future, to make promises, to offer something, or to state a decision to do something at the time of speaking.

- *It **will** probably rain, so I**'ll take** an umbrella. I**'ll give** you my extra one.*

***yes/no* question** A question that has a *yes* or a *no* answer.

- ***Did you arrive on time?** Yes, I did.*
- ***Are you from Uruguay?** No, I'm not.*
- ***Can you swim well?** Yes, I can.*

Unit Review Answer Key

Note: In this answer key, where a short or contracted form is given, the full or long form is also correct (unless the purpose of the exercise is to practice the short or contracted forms).

UNIT 1

A **1.** are **2.** is **3.** am **4.** is **5.** are

B **1.** 'm **2.** 's **3.** 're **4.** 's **5.** 're

C **1.** He isn't (He's not) **2.** They're **3.** We aren't (We're not) **4.** She's

D My father and mother are from India, but they're in Canada now. My parents are doctors.

My father [is] a sports doctor and my mother ~~she~~ is a foot doctor. My parents and I love sports. My father ~~are~~ is a soccer fan, and my mother [is] a baseball fan. I'm a soccer fan. My father and I ~~am~~ are fans of Lionel Messi and Nuno Gomes. My sister ~~no is~~ isn't good at sports. She's not a sports fan. She loves movies.

UNIT 2

A **1.** Where's **2.** How's **3.** What's **4.** Are **5.** Is

B
1. I am
2. it isn't (it's not)
3. they aren't (they're not)
4. we are
5. you aren't (you're not)

C
1. What's today's date?
2. Where's the men's room?
3. Why is he absent? (Why's he absent?)
4. When's your first class?
5. Who's your teacher?

D
1. ~~She~~ Is she your teacher?
2. What [is] your name?
3. Where [is] your class?
4. ~~Is~~ Are Bob and Molly good friends?
5. Why [are] you late?

UNIT 3

A **1.** was **2.** was **3.** Were **4.** were **5.** Was

B **1.** c **2.** b **3.** d **4.** a

C **1.** was **2.** was **3.** Were **4.** was **5.** were **6.** wasn't **7.** was

D John ~~is~~ was at a job interview yesterday. It ~~were~~ was for a job at a bank. The questions ~~no were~~ weren't easy, but John's answers were good. He was happy. It [was] a good day for John.

UNIT 4

A **1.** a **2.** an **3.** Ø **4.** Ø **5.** Ø

B **1.** cities **2.** watches **3.** clothes **4.** fish or fishes **5.** people

C lin = Lin ali = Ali london = London thanksgiving = Thanksgiving

D Melanie Einzig is [an] artist and ~~an~~ a photographer. She was born in Minnesota, but lives in New ~~york~~ York. Einzig captures moments in time. Her ~~photograph~~ photographs are striking. They are in ~~museum~~ museums in San ~~francisco~~ Francisco, Chicago, and Princeton.

UNIT 5

A **1.** a **2.** Ø **3.** Ø **4.** an **5.** Ø

B **1.** c **2.** a **3.** b **4.** c **5.** b

C
1. I'm at the new museum.
2. It is full of interesting things to see.
3. It has unusual bowls from long ago.
4. It has beautiful carpets too.
5. The museum is a great place to visit.

D The Grand Canyon National Park in Arizona is ~~a~~ an awesome place to visit. Almost five million people visit this ~~park unusual~~ unusual park each year. The weather is good in the late spring and summer, but it [is] crowded ~~is~~ during those months. There are seven ~~differents~~ different places to stay in the park. I like El Tovar. It is ~~a~~ an old hotel with a great view.

UNIT 6

A **1.** on **2.** under **3.** behind **4.** next to **5.** in front of

B **1.** at **2.** at **3.** at, on the

C

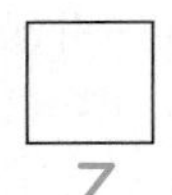

Z

D **A:** Is Jon at ~~the~~ school?

B: No. He's ~~in~~ at home.
A: Where does he live?

B: He lives ~~at~~ on Oak Street, between First and Second Avenue ~~at~~ in Lakeville.
A: Does he live in an apartment?

B: Yes. He lives ~~in~~ on the third floor.

UNIT 7

A **1.** Let's get **2.** Why don't we invite **3.** Don't buy **4.** Let's not meet **5.** Don't touch

B **1.** Wear **2.** Don't wear **3.** Bring **4.** Don't bring **5.** pay

C **1.** Let's go to the gym.
2. Let's watch a movie this afternoon.
3. Why don't we take a trip together?
4. Why don't we hang out with Pietro this weekend?

D **1.** Why ~~you~~ don't you ask Andrij for help?

2. You look really tired. ~~You~~ Why don't you take a short nap?
3. Let's ~~to~~ walk to work. Let's not drive.

4. Don't ask Boris to fix the car. ~~Asks~~ Ask Mickey.
5. I'm on a diet, so buy yogurt at the store. Don't ~~to~~ buy sour cream.

UNIT 8

A **1.** shops **2.** likes **3.** don't like **4.** go **5.** has

B **1.** don't need **2.** need **3.** play **4.** doesn't like

C **1.** is **2.** works **3.** wears **4.** don't wear **5.** are

D **1.** My son doesn't ~~has~~ have a suit.

2. He always ~~wear~~ wears jeans, T-shirts, and hoodies.

3. He ~~need~~ needs a suit for my brother's wedding.

4. Suits ~~is~~ are expensive and my son ~~don't~~ doesn't like to wear them.

5. We ~~wants~~ want to rent or borrow a suit for him.

UNIT 9

A **1.** Do **2.** Is **3.** Does **4.** Are **5.** Am

B **1.** Do / have **2.** Does / speak **3.** Does / watch **4.** Is **5.** Are

C **1.** Are the neighbors noisy?
2. Does the apartment building have an elevator?
3. Is the apartment near trains or buses?
4. Does the bedroom have two closets?
5. Is the bedroom big?

D **1. A:** Does he have a big TV in his room?

B: Yes, he ~~has~~ does.

2. A: Does she ~~needs~~ need help?

B: No, she ~~don't~~ doesn't.

3. A: ~~Do you are~~ Are you friends?

B: Yes, we ~~aren't~~ are. (OR No, we aren't.)

UNIT 10

A **1.** Why **2.** When **3.** Who **4.** How **5.** Where

B **1.** Who snores in your family?
2. What do you dream about?
3. What time does your mother get up?
4. What time do you go to bed?
5. Where does your brother sleep?

C **1.** Who meets his uncle at the diner (on Saturdays)?
2. Who does John meet at the diner (on Saturdays)?
3. Where does John meet his uncle (on Saturdays)?
4. When does John meet his uncle at the diner?

D **1.** Where do you live and who do you live with?

2. Why does he daydream in class?

3. When does she ~~gets~~ get up?

4. How do they feel about sleeping pills?

5. Who ~~does~~ do you dream about?

UNIT 11

A **1. A:** Are there **B:** there are
2. A: Are there **B:** there aren't
3. A: Is she **B:** she is

4. **A:** Are they — **B:** they aren't
5. **A:** Is there — **B:** there isn't

B 1. There's / It's
2. There are / They're
3. There's / She's

C Visit the new Shopper's Mall on Route 290. ~~There's~~ *There are* over 100 stores. ~~There~~ *There's* a movie theater, and ~~they~~ *there* are ten great places to eat. Come early. Every morning at 10:30 ~~there are~~ *there's* a free show for children. The mall is three miles from the Tappan Bridge on Route 290.

UNIT 12

A 1. Their 2. His 3. Its 4. Their 5. Her

B 1. **A:** mine — **B:** yours — **A:** your
2. **A:** Whose — **B:** Ali's
3. My / Its
4. **A:** Her / yours — **B:** Mine

C **A:** ~~Who's~~ *Whose* bag is that on the floor?

B: I think it's ~~Maria~~ *Maria's*.

A: No. Her bag is on her arm.

B: Well, it's not ~~mine bag~~ *mine* (OR *my bag*). Maybe it's ~~Rita~~ *Rita's*.

A: Rita, is that ~~bag your~~ *yours* (OR *your bag*)?

UNIT 13

A 1. couldn't understand / can understand
2. can't run / could run
3. couldn't drive / can drive

B 1. **A:** Can — **B:** can
2. **A:** Could — **B:** couldn't / can
3. **A:** Can — **B:** can

C **A:** Can you ~~to~~ get online?

B: No, I can't ~~not~~. I couldn't ~~got~~ *get* online last night either.

A: My brother is good with computers. Maybe he can ~~helps~~ *help*.

B: Great. I ~~can no~~ *can't* figure out what's wrong.

A: I ~~no can~~ *can't* reach him now, but I can ~~to~~ call him after 6 P.M.

UNIT 14

A 1. may eat 2. can't eat 3. can have 4. may not use 5. may drink

B 1. When can I return to work?
2. When can I take a shower?
3. Can I go to the gym?
4. Can I ride my bike?

C 1. You may not eat. (You may not bring food.)
2. You may not use a pencil.
3. You may not make phone calls.
4. You may bring a bottle of water.
5. You may use a black or blue pen.
6. You may use a dictionary.

D **A:** May I ~~sees~~ *see* a menu?

B: ~~Sure, you might~~ *Sure.* Here you go.

A: And can we ~~to~~ have some water?

B: I'll be right back with the water. . . . Ready?

A: Yes. I want the chicken with mushroom sauce. But may I ~~has~~ *have* the sauce on the side?

B: ~~You may not.~~ *I'm sorry.* We cook the chicken in the sauce.

A: Oh? Well, then I'll have grilled chicken with rice.

UNIT 15

A 1. 'm not getting 2. 're preparing 3. isn't playing 4. 're doing 5. 's feeling

B 1. is listening to
2. are standing and talking
3. are running
4. is driving
5. is carrying

C 1. is texting / isn't ('s not) calling
2. are working / aren't giving up
3. is swimming / 's trying

D My classmates and I ~~am~~ *are* sitting in a computer lab. One student ^*is* writing a composition. Two students are ~~check~~ *checking* their email. A teacher is ~~helps~~ *helping* a student. The other students are surfing the Internet.

UNIT 16

A 1. **A:** Are / watching — **B:** they are
2. **A:** are / doing — **B:** 'm listening
3. **A:** 's happening — **B:** is putting

B 1. Are you working?
2. Is he buying tickets online?
3. Are they watching a mystery?
4. Is she enjoying the movie?

C 1. Where are they going?
2. What music group is performing?
3. Where are they playing?
4. Why is Bob staying home?

D 1. **A:** Is ~~it's~~ *it* raining outside?

B: Yes. I hope it stops.

2. **A:** Are they playing soccer?

B: No, they ^('re) not. They're playing rugby.

3. **A:** ~~You~~ (Are you) watching a good movie?

B: It's OK.

4. **A:** What ^(are) they doing?
B: They're fixing the cabinets.

UNIT 17

A **1.** don't own **2.** doesn't like **3.** has **4.** needs **5.** want

B **1.** is using **2.** is surfing **3.** 's getting **4.** has **5.** wants

C **1.** is / doing **2.** 's trying **3.** 's **4.** don't know **5.** Does / need

D **1. A:** Where ^(are) you calling from?

B: Downtown. ~~I walk~~ (I'm walking) along Second Street.

2. A: Is she ~~play~~ (playing) tennis at West Park?

B: No, she's not. She ~~no~~ (doesn't) like those courts.

3. A: Does he ~~understands~~ (understand) Greek?

B: Yes, he does. He was in Greece for a year.

UNIT 18

A **1.** watched **2.** visited **3.** an hour ago **4.** Last night **5.** didn't land

B **1.** helped **2.** stayed **3.** didn't snow **4.** didn't ask **5.** didn't want

C **1.** canceled **2.** didn't stay **3.** didn't rain **4.** played **5.** didn't enjoy

D Hello from London. Our friends ~~did~~ invited us here for a week. We're having a great time.

Yesterday we ~~visit~~ (visited) Big Ben, and we ~~tour~~ (toured) the Royal

Palace. This morning we ~~watch~~ (watched) the Changing of the Guard. We wanted to shop this afternoon, but we didn't. The prices were high, but we ~~are~~ enjoyed looking at the store windows.

UNIT 19

A **1.** saw **2.** was / wanted **3.** tried **4.** got / didn't want

B A lucky man **found** a pot of gold. He **kept** the pot of gold in a hole in the ground of his garden. A jealous worker **stole** the gold from the man. The man **became** upset. But a neighbor laughed because the man **didn't use** the gold. He just enjoyed counting it.

C **1.** didn't stay **2.** lost **3.** ran **4.** didn't see **5.** took

D **1.** William Sidney Porter ^(was) born in North Carolina in 1862.
2. He was a famous American short story writer. He wrote under different names, but he ~~did~~ became best known as O. Henry.
3. His stories ~~were~~ had surprise endings.

4. O. Henry had many talents, but he ~~did get~~ (got) into trouble and spent time in prison.

UNIT 20

A **1.** Did they go to the theater?
2. Did she get there by bus?
3. Did you have good seats?
4. Did he understand everything?
5. Did we miss the beginning?
6. Did it have a happy ending?

B **1.** What play did you see?
2. Where did you see it?
3. How long was the show?
4. Did you enjoy the performance?
5. Who were the stars?
6. Did you go out after the show?
7. Where did you go?
8. What did you order?

C **1.** Where ~~he did~~ (did he) go last night?

2. What ~~saw he~~ (did he see)?

3. Did he ~~enjoyed~~ (enjoy) it?

4. Who ^(did) he ~~met~~ (meet)?

5. When ^(did) they go?

6. Who ~~did pay~~ (paid) for it?

UNIT 21

A **1.** was born **2.** grew up **3.** attended **4.** went **5.** started **6.** became **7.** expanded

B **1.** When did she go to college?
2. Who did they meet?
3. Where did he study?
4. How long did they live in Canada?

C **1.** Were **2.** Did **3.** Was **4.** Did **5.** Did

D Steve Paul Jobs ~~did start~~ started college in 1970, but he ~~no did~~ didn't finish it. In 1976 Jobs and his friend ~~begin~~ began to make their own computers. They worked in the Jobs' garage. That was the beginning of Apple® Computers. Their company ~~become~~ became a big success. Apple® changed the field of computers, and by the age of 30, Jobs was a multimillionaire.

UNIT 22

A 1. starting 2. to sell 3. to return 4. to become 5. flying / seeing 6. to help

B 1. to work 2. to change 3. quitting / going 4. to study 5. doing

C Carol volunteers at a hospital. She enjoys ~~to take~~ taking care of patients. Some patients refuse to do exercise, but Carol keeps ~~to push~~ pushing them. Carol intends to study physical therapy in college. She needs ~~taking~~ to take a lot of science courses. She expects to ~~went~~ go to college next fall. She hopes to get a degree in physical therapy in five years. She prefers ~~to~~ working with teenagers, but she will work with adults too.

UNIT 23

A 1. is taking 2. make 3. made 4. likes

B 1. invented 2. didn't work 3. wanted 4. became 5. started 6. use 7. are sewing

C
1. Where did you go last weekend?
2. How did you get there?
3. What did you see at the museum?
4. How was the museum?
5. Do you go there often?

D
1. Last night I ~~did watch~~ watched a movie about fish.
2. I thought the fish were beautiful, and I ~~enjoy~~ enjoyed the movie.
3. My brother is watching the movie now, but he ~~don't~~ doesn't like it.
4. He ~~is only liking~~ only likes action films.

UNIT 24

A
1. is going to build
2. 's going to cost
3. 's going to have
4. are going to be
5. isn't going to begin

B
1. are not going to increase
2. aren't going to play
3. 're going to visit
4. 's going to retire
5. 'm not going to do

C
1. **Q:** When is she going to the dentist? **A:** On Monday at 5:30.
2. **Q:** Where is she meeting Yu Chen? **A:** At Pappa Pizza.
3. **Q:** Is she meeting Yu Chen on Monday? **A:** No, she isn't.

D This city is going to change under our new mayor. ~~People's~~ People are going to ride bikes and they're ~~gonna~~ going to use public transportation. They're ~~no~~ not going to drive big cars. There are probably going to be higher tolls on bridges and more bike paths on the roads.

UNIT 25

A
1. Where will people travel in twenty years?
2. Will people fly to the moon?
3. How will they get around?
4. Will the climate change?
5. Will people look different?

B 1. won't 2. won't 3. will 4. will 5. won't

C
1. Will / be hot
2. Will / have a test
3. Will / be a storm
4. Will / rain
5. Will / work late

D I usually bring my lunch to work, but tomorrow I ~~no will~~ won't bring it because it's my birthday. My co-workers will ~~takes~~ take me out to a restaurant. We'll ~~to~~ order a few different dishes, and we'll share them. They'll ~~singing~~ sing "Happy Birthday," and they'll give me a small gift. I'm sure it will ~~is~~ be a lot of fun.

UNIT 26

A 1. go 2. buy 3. might not 4. may 5. Will

B
1. may (might) snow
2. may (might) not get
3. may (might) need
4. may (might) not see
5. may (might) stay

C 1. There may (OR There might) be a restroom in the library.
2. He may (OR might) be the director.
3. The plane might (OR may) be late.
4. They may (OR might) be cousins.
5. It might (OR may) be his coat.

D 1. He might ~~goes~~ go on vacation next week.
2. He may ~~works~~ work late tomorrow.
3. They might ~~to~~ visit him tomorrow. Are you free?
4. I might not help him. I might ~~to~~ help her instead.
5. She ~~maybe~~ may take a yoga class.

UNIT 27

A 1. a few
2. the
3. an
4. any

B 1. many
2. much
3. a little
4. a few

C 1. a
2. a
3. the
4. the
5. a
6. a

D 1. **A:** What are you looking for?
B: I need a ~~little~~ few stamps. I wrote ~~any~~ some postcards, and I want to mail them.
2. **A:** There isn't ~~some~~ much yogurt in the refrigerator. There's only half a container.
B: There ~~isn't much~~ aren't many eggs either. We need to go shopping, but we don't have ~~many~~ much time.

UNIT 28

A 1. How many
2. How much
3. How many
4. How much
5. How many

B 1. How often do you go to the movies?
2. How many close friends do you have?
3. How much time do you spend online?
4. How many people live in your home?
5. How often do you check email?

C 1. I usually bake a few times a week.
2. They never have enough food in the house.
3. Every weekend we play soccer in the park.
4. He spilled a glass of grape juice.
5. She added a little salt to the soup.

D 1. ~~Never~~ I never eat breakfast at home.
2. ~~She once in a while~~ Once in a while she bakes.
3. Do you have ~~milk enough~~ enough milk?
4. How ~~much~~ many tomatoes did they buy?
5. I rarely ~~don't~~ cook.

UNIT 29

A 1. too long
2. too much homework
3. too much milk
4. too many trucks
5. too much time

B 1. too / too little
2. too few
3. too much
4. too many

C 1. There's too little rain.
2. There are too few subways.
3. There's too little sunlight.
4. There are too few traffic lights.
5. There is too little water.

D The climate here is terrible. It gets too ~~much~~ hot in the summer and too cold in the winter. There's too ~~many~~ much snow and ice. Winters are ~~to~~ too long. There are too ~~little~~ few comfortable days with mild temperatures and blue skies. Also, there's too ~~many~~ much air pollution from all the traffic on the streets. I want to move.

UNIT 30

A 1. should
2. had better
3. shouldn't
4. ought to
5. better not

B 1. had better not
2. had better
3. had better not
4. had better

C 1. should
2. shouldn't
3. should
4. shouldn't

D 1. Where should we ~~meets~~ meet after work?
2. We'd better take an umbrella tonight. It's going to rain.
3. Should I ~~to~~ make a reservation now for my flight? I think I ~~outta~~ ought to buy it soon.
4. What ~~I should~~ should I see during my business trip to Uruguay?
5. Should we ~~leaves~~ leave Brazil tonight or tomorrow?
6. You ought to bring flowers to your hostess to thank her for dinner.

UNIT 31

A 1. Would you like
2. Could you pass
3. I'd like
4. We'd like
5. Can you

B 1. Of course.
2. Sure.
3. Thanks.
4. Sorry, I need it.
5. I'd be glad to.

C **1.** Could you please
2. I'd like
3. Could you please
4. Would you like
5. I'd like

D **1. A:** Could ~~please~~ you [please] move my car at 11:00?

B: ~~No, I wouldn't~~ [Sorry.]. I'll be at work then.

2. A: ~~I like~~ [I'd like] to see you this weekend. Would you like to go to the park?

B: ~~I could.~~ [Yes, I would.]

3. A: Would you like ~~have~~ some more ice cream?

B: No, thanks. I'm full.

UNIT 32

A **1.** don't have to **2.** have to **3.** must not **4.** doesn't have to **5.** have to

B **1.** mustn't **2.** has / has to **3.** don't have to **4.** has to

C **1.** had to work
2. have to read / answer
3. had to give OR have to give
4. didn't have to bring

D The test starts at 8:10. You must ~~to~~ be in the room at 8:00. You mustn't ~~came~~ [come] late. You have to ~~has~~ [have] two number two pencils and an eraser. You ~~musts~~ [must] ~~brings~~ [bring] proper identification, such as a photo ID or a passport. You must leave your cell phone in the front of the room.

UNIT 33

A **1.** much **2.** than **3.** more popular **4.** worse **5.** higher **6.** better **7.** brother's

B **1.** A bus ride is more expensive in Sun City than in New City.
2. A cup of coffee is cheaper in New City than in Sun City.
3. The average home is less expensive in New City than in Sun City.
4. The average income is higher in Sun City than in New City.

C We moved to the countryside, and we're much ~~more~~ happier. Our home is ~~more~~ larger, and the air is cleaner and [less] polluted ~~less~~. It [is] less expensive than the city too. Fruits and vegetables are ~~more cheap~~ [cheaper]. The people are ~~friendler~~ [friendlier]. Of course our commute is ~~more bad~~ [worse]; it's much ~~more long~~ [longer], but we listen to Spanish tapes, and our Spanish is ~~more good~~ [better].

UNIT 34

A **1.** quickly **2.** fluently **3.** well **4.** slowly **5.** clearly

B **1.** good **2.** carefully **3.** nervous **4.** badly **5.** quickly

C **1.** good **2.** briefly (clearly) **3.** clearly (briefly) **4.** fast **5.** honestly

D **A:** I think my speech went ~~good~~ [well].

B: Did they appreciate your jokes?

A: They laughed ~~polite~~ [politely], but I'm not sure they laughed ~~sincere~~ [sincerely].

B: It's hard to be funny.

A: I ~~hard worked,~~ [worked hard], and I prepared carefully, but I was ~~nervously~~ [nervous].

UNIT 35

A **1.** big enough **2.** as **3.** too **4.** as **5.** from

B **1.** warm enough **2.** very late **3.** too busy **4.** too short **5.** enough time **6.** very good

C I didn't like the prom this year as much ~~than~~ [as] last year. I usually like parties, but the music at the prom was much ~~very~~ [too] loud. Also, my dress was the same as ~~Julia~~ [Julia's]! That was a ~~too~~ [very] big shock. Also, the dinner portions weren't ~~enough large~~ [large enough] and the servers this year were very rude. Then we tried to dance, but there was ~~no~~ [not] enough room and the room was ~~too much~~ [much too] hot. The music was also not [as] good as last year. We had a ~~more~~ better time last year.

UNIT 36

A **1.** the funniest
2. the biggest
3. the best
4. The largest / the most dangerous

B **1.** the hottest day
2. the oldest woman
3. the busiest shopping day
4. the most interesting show
5. the most popular animals

C **1.** one of the most intelligent animals
2. one of the best zoos
3. one of the worst seats
4. one of the longest days
5. one of the most expensive trips

D **1. A:** What is the ~~most good~~ *best* way to get to the park?

B: The shortest route is also the *most* complicated. I'll give you the most direct way.

2. A: What's the ~~most~~ hardest part of your job here at the zoo?

B: Well, the ~~nicer~~ *nicest* part is taking care of the animals. The ~~most~~ worst part is telling people not to feed the animals or bother them.

Credits

PHOTO CREDITS:

All photos are used under license from Shutterstock.com except for the following:

Page 1 (right) Stephane Reix/For Picture/Corbis; **p. 2** (left) Jeff Kravitz/Getty Images, (right) AP Images/Peter Kramer; **p. 6** (bottom) AF archive/Alamy; **p. 9** (bottom right) Stephane Reix/For Picture/Corbis; **p. 13** iStockphoto.com; **p. 40** (left) Reuters/Corbis, (right) Henri Cartier-Bresson/Magnum Photos; **p. 41** Henri Cartier-Bresson/Magnum Photos; **p. 43** Ron Chapple/Getty Images; **p. 44** Henri Cartier-Bresson/Magnum Photos; **p. 46** Henri Cartier-Bresson/Magnum Photos; **p. 54** www.Gamirasu.com; **p. 55** (bottom) Dreamstime.com; **p. 60** (bottom left) Bigstock.com; **p. 71** (left) Anthony Redpath/Corbis; **p. 72** Photolibrary.com; **p. 81** Anthony Redpath/Corbis; **p. 84** Ocean/Corbis; **p. 113** (right) Jeffrey Mayer/Getty Images; **p. 116** James Marshall/Corbis; **p. 143** Bigstock.com; **p. 165** (right) MGM/Photofest; **p. 166** (left) Henrik Sorensen/Getty Images, (right) Photos.com; **p. 169** Photos.com; **p. 170** Hill Street Studios/Getty Images; **p. 172** Gary Conner/PhotoEdit; **p. 174** (bottom middle) Bigstock.com; **p. 175** MGM/Photofest; **p. 179** AF archive/Alamy; **p. 197** (left) AF archive/Alamy, (right) iStockphoto.com; **p. 203** Philip James Corwin/Corbis; **p. 206** Bigstock.com; **p. 207** Nik Wheeler/Corbis; **p. 213** (left) AF archive/Alamy; **p. 219** (top) AF archive/Alamy; **p. 220** iStockphoto.com; **p. 226** Hulton-Deutsch Collection/Corbis; **p. 234** (background) Fotolia.com, (inset) MIXA/Getty Images; **p. 238** iStockphoto.com; **p. 239** Kim Kulish/Corbis; **p. 258** Bettmann/Corbis; **p. 294** Jeff Greenberg/PhotoEdit; **p. 328** (pint) Bigstock.com, (containter) Bigstock.com; **p. 329** iStockphoto.com; **p. 347** (left) MGM/Photofest, (right) George Napolitano/Getty Images; **p. 348** Reuters/Corbis; **p. 349** Ocean/Corbis; **p. 355** Bigstock.com; **p. 357** (top) Fahad Shadeed/Reuters/Corbis; **p. 360** Nigel Riches/Image Source Ltd./www.imagesource.com; **p. 374** George Napolitano/Getty Images; **p. 375** MGM/Photofest; **p. 385** (left) Robert Wagenhoffer/Corbis; **p. 386** (bottom) Lisa O'Connor/ZUMA/Corbis; **p. 390** (top) Robert Wagenhoffer/Corbis, (bottom) Rudy Sulgan/Corbis; **p. 394** (top) SERDAR/Alamy; **p. 400** (left) Hill Street Studios/Getty Images, (right) Stewart Cohen/Getty Images; **p. 408** Ocean/Corbis; **p. 414** (top) Nigel Riches/Image Source Ltd./www.imagesource.com; **p. 426** Dreamstime.com

ILLUSTRATION CREDITS:

Steve Attoe: pp. 193, 290; **ElectraGraphics, Inc.:** pp. 25, 26, 29, 69, 99 (keys, iPhone, iPad), 105, 182, 328; **Jock MacRae:** pp. 198–199; **Paul McCusker:** p. 99 (lipstick, comb, watch, sunglasses, driver's license, photo); **Suzanne Mogensen:** p. 63; **Tom Newsom:** p. 370; **Dusan Petricic:** pp. 10, 126 ; **Steve Schulman:** p. 377; **Dave Sullivan:** p. 93; **Gary Torrisi:** pp. 18, 64, 65, 76, 102, 131, 185, 192

INDEX

This index is for the full and split editions. All entries are in the full book. Entries for Volume A of the split edition are in black. Entries for Volume B are in red.